Solutions Manual

Financial Accounting
An Introduction to Concepts, Methods, and Uses
ELEVENTH EDITION

Clyde P. Stickney

Dartmouth College

Roman L. Weil

University of Chicago

THOMSON

SOUTH-WESTERN

Australia · Canada · Mexico · Singapore · Spain · United Kingdom · United States

THOMSON

SOUTH-WESTERN

Solutions Manual to Accompany Financial Accounting: An Introduction to Concepts, Methods and Uses, 11edition
Clyde P. Stickney and Roman L. Weil

'VP/Editorial Director:
Jack W. Calhoun

Publisher:
Rob Dewey

Acquisitions Editor:
Julie Lindsay Moulton

Developmental Editor:
Carol Bennett

Marketing Manager:
Keith Chassé

Production Editor:
Amy A. Simms

Manager of Technology, Editorial:
Vicky True

Technology Project Editor:
Robin Browning

Manufacturing Coordinator:
Doug Wilke

Printer:
Globus
Minster, OH

Art Director:
Chris Miller

Cover Designer:
Patti Hudepohl

For more information about our products, contact us at:

Thomson Learning Academic Resource Center

1-800-423-0563

Thomson Higher Education
5191 Natorp Boulevard
Mason, OH 45040
USA

Asia (including India)
Thomson Learning
5 Shenton Way
#01-01 UIC Building
Singapore 068808

Australia/New Zealand
Thomson Learning Australia
102 Dodds Street
Southbank, Victoria 3006
Australia

Canada
Thomson Nelson
1120 Birchmount Road
Toronto, Ontario
M1K 5G4
Canada

Latin America
Thomson Learning
Seneca, 53
Colonia Polanco
11560 Mexico
D.F.Mexico

UK/Europe/Middle East/Africa
Thomson Learning
High Holborn House
50/51 Bedford Row
London WC1R 4LR
United Kingdom

Spain (including Portugal)
Thomson Paraninfo
Calle Magallanes, 25
28015 Madrid, Spain

PREFACE

This book presents answers and solutions for the questions, short exercises, exercises, problems and cases contained in each chapter of the textbook *Financial Accounting: An Introduction to Concepts, Methods and Uses* Eleventh Edition. We do not attempt to give all possible ways to work a problem, showing the multiple paths to the correct solution. We do not even try to give the most commonly chosen one, even if we know what that is, which is rare. Our students often ask the equivalent of, "Why can't I work the problem this way?" or "Is it OK to work the problem this other way?" In a word, yes. You can work most problems in several different ways. If you get the right final answer, then do not worry if you reached it via a path different from the one we show. [In some cases we worked out those solutions 30 years ago, when we thought differently from the way we do now.]

If you have any suggestions as to how this book might be improved in subsequent editions, please feel free to bring them to our attention.

C.P.S.

R.L.W.

CONTENTS

CHAPTER 12: SHAREHOLDERS' EQUITY: CAPITAL CONTRIBUTIONS,
DISTRIBUTIONS, AND EARNINGS

APPENDIX: COMPOUND INTEREST: CONCEPTS AND APPLICATIONS

CHAPTER 1

INTRODUCTION TO BUSINESS ACTIVITIES AND
OVERVIEW OF FINANCIAL STATEMENTS
AND THE REPORTING PROCESS

Questions, Short Exercises, Exercises, Problems, and Cases: Answers and Solutions

1.1   The first question at the end of each chapter requires the student to review the important concepts or terms discussed in the chapter. In addition to the definitions or descriptions in the chapter, a glossary appears at the end of the book.

1.2   *Setting Goals and Strategies*: A charitable organization would not pursue profit or increasing wealth as goals. Instead, it would direct its efforts at providing some type of service to particular constituencies.

     Financing: Charitable organizations generally obtain the majority of their financing from contributions, although they may engage in borrowing in some situations. Charitable organizations do not issue common stock or other forms of owners' equity. Because they do not operate for a profit, charitable organizations do not have retained earnings.

     Investing: Charitable organizations may acquire supplies, buildings, equipment and other assets to carry out their charitable activities.

     Operations: A charitable organization might prepare a financial statement each period that compares contributions received with operating expenses. Although such a financial statement might resemble an income statement, the organization would probably not label the difference between contributions received and operating expenses as net income or net loss.

1.3   A balance sheet reports the assets, liabilities, and shareholders' equity of a firm at a moment in time (similar to a snapshot), whereas the income statement and statement of cash flows report amounts for a period of time (similar to a motion picture).

1.4   Revenues measure the increase in net assets (assets minus liabilities) and expenses measure the decrease in net assets from selling goods and providing services. An asset such as inventory generally appears on the balance sheet at acquisition cost while it is held. Thus, the asset valuation remains the same and the firm recognizes no revenue. When the firm sells the inventory, the inventory item leaves the firm and cash or a receivable from a customer comes in. If more assets flow in than flow out, total assets increase and the firm recognizes income (revenue minus expense).

1.5   As Chapter 3 makes clear, firms do not necessarily recognize revenues when they receive cash or recognize expenses when they disburse cash. Thus, net income will not necessarily equal cash flow from operations each period. Furthermore, firms disburse cash to acquire property, plant and equipment, repay debt, and pay dividends. Thus, net income and cash flows usually differ. A profitable firm will likely borrow funds in order to remain in business, but eventually operations must generate cash to repay the borrowing.

1.6   No. The unqualified opinion of the CPA indicates that the presentation is a fair reflection of the financial position and operating results of the firm. Because the accountant bases this opinion on an audit of only a portion of the transactions occurring during the year, the CPA does not vouch for the absolute accuracy of every item in the financial statements. The unqualified opinion has evolved to mean, however, that the firm has made sufficient disclosures in the statements so they are not misleading. This interpretation of the unqualified opinion suggests that the statements are free of gross misrepresentations. In court suits against the independent accountants, where courts have found gross misrepresentation to exist, the principal issue is whether the CPA had reasonable grounds (based on audit tests) to believe that the statements were fairly presented at the time the accountant issued the unqualified opinion.

1.7   A wide range of individuals and entities (creditors, investors, security analysts, governmental agencies) use financial accounting reports for a broad range of purposes. If each firm selected whatever format and content of financial reports it deemed best, the resulting reporting process would probably be incomprehensible to many users. Accounting reports generated for internal management purposes, on the other hand, satisfy the information needs of a more limited set of users. Standardization is, therefore, not as necessary.

1.8   **Advantages**

    1. Government authorities can enforce their pronouncements by law.

    2. Firms need maintain only one set of accounting records that serves the needs of both financial and tax reporting.

1.8 continued.

3. Greater uniformity in accounting methods across firms likely results because firms either use the methods prescribed for tax purposes or, where there is a choice of several alternative methods for a particular item, use the method that minimizes the present value of tax payments.

Disadvantages

1. The objectives in setting accounting methods for tax purposes (raising tax revenues) may differ from the objectives for financial reporting (measuring financial position and results of operations).

2. Individuals in the government responsible for setting accounting methods may not have the necessary technical expertise or financial statement user perspective.

3. Political lobbying could dominate the standard-setting process.

1.9 The accounting method would be uniform but the resulting information in the financial statements may not provide uniform measures of financial position or results of operations. If the economic characteristics of firms' activities differ, then different accounting methods may be needed to reflect these differences.

1.10 Accounting standards set in the public sector (that is, by a government agency) become subject to political pressures inherent in a democratic system. Accounting standards set in the private sector become subject to political pressures of various preparer and user groups. Because accounting standards set in the private sector have no enforcement power on their own, private-sector standard-setting bodies must respond to these political pressures by gaining acceptance for their standards.

1.11 We would disagree. Within capital market settings, someone must analyze and interpret financial accounting reports if market prices are to incorporate information from those reports. The principal message of efficient market research is that digestion of such information occurs very quickly. In addition, there are many users and uses of financial accounting reports outside of a capital market setting (lending, antitrust regulation, competitor analysis).

1.12 (Harley-Davidson Company; balance sheet relations.) (Amounts in Millions)

Current Assets	+	Noncurrent Assets	=	Current Liabilities	+	Noncurrent Liabilities	+	Share-holders' Equity
$2,067	+	$1,794	=	$990	+	?	+	$2,233

Noncurrent liabilities total $638 million.

1.13   (Mattel; balance sheet relations.) (Amounts in Millions)

Current Assets		Noncurrent Assets		Current Liabilities		Noncurrent Liabilities		Shareholders' Equity
?	+	$2,071	=	$1,649	+	$832	+	$1,979

Current assets total $2,389 million.

1.14   (Reebok; retained earnings relations.) (Amounts in Millions)

Retained Earnings at End of Year 11		Net Income for Year 12		Dividends Declared for Year 12		Retained Earnings at End of Year 12
$411	+	$52	–	?	=	$446

Dividends declared during Year 12 totaled $17 million.

1.15   (Ruby Tuesday; retained earnings relations.) (Amounts in Millions)

Retained Earnings at End of Year 11		Net Income for Year 12		Dividends Declared for Year 12		Retained Earnings at End of Year 12
?	+	$58	–	$3	=	$326

Retained earnings at the end of Year 11 totaled $271 million.

1.16   (Yahoo, Inc.; cash flow relations.) (Amounts in Millions)

Cash at End of Year 11		Cash Flow from Operations		Cash Flow from Investing		Cash Flow from Financing		Cash at End of Year 12
$373	+	$303	+	($346)	+	($19)	=	?

Cash at the end of Year 12 totaled $311 million.

1.17   (Nike; cash flow relations.) (Amounts in Millions)

Cash at End of Year 11		Cash Flow from Operations		Cash Flow from Investing		Cash Flow from Financing		Cash at End of Year 12
$575.5	+	$917.4	+	?	+	($643.3)	=	$634.0

The net cash outflow for investing for Year 12 totaled $215.6 million.

1.18   (Preparing a personal balance sheet.)

There is no distinction between contributed capital and retained earnings, because an individual does not issue common stock. The excess of assets over liabilities is called an individual's *net worth*. The methods used in valuing an individual's assets and liabilities are critical variables in determining net worth. Possibilities include acquisition cost, current replacement cost, current selling price, and others.

1.19   (Classifying financial statement accounts.)

a.   NA.

b.   NI (revenue).

c.   CC.

d.   X.

e.   NA.

f.   CA.

g.   X (a footnote to the balance sheet would probably disclose the lawsuit).

h.   NI (expense).

i.   CA.

j.   CL.

k.   X (not recognized as a gain until the firm sells the land).

l.   RE.

m.   CL.

n.   NL.

1.20   (Lowe's; balance sheet relations.)

a.   The **given** (boldface) and missing items appear below (amounts in millions).

	Year 9	Year 10	Year 11	Year 12
Current Assets	**$ 2,586**	**$ 3,710**	**$ 4,175**	**$ 4,920**[b]
Noncurrent Assets	**3,759**	**5,302**	**7,201**	8,816
Total Assets	$ 6,345	$ 9,012	$11,376	$13,736
Current Liabilities	**$ 1,765**	**$ 2,386**	$ 2,929[a]	**$ 3,017**
Noncurrent Liabilities	**1,444**	**1,931**	**2,952**	**4,045**
Shareholders' Equity	**3,136**	**4,695**	**5,495**	**6,674**
Total Liabilities and Shareholders' Equity	$ 6,345	$ 9,012	$11,376	$13,736

[a]$2,929 = $4,175 − $1,246.
[b]$4,920 = $3,017 + $1,903.

b.   Noncurrent assets increased as a proportion of total assets, suggesting major new investments in property, plant, and equipment or the acquisition of a firm with heavy investments in property, plant and equipment.

c.   The proportion of current liabilities and shareholders' equity decreased while the proportion of noncurrent liabilities increased. Lowe's likely used long-term debt to finance the acquisition of property, plant and equipment.

1.21   (PepsiCo; balance sheet relations.)

a.   The **given** (boldface) and missing items appear below (amounts in millions).

	Year 8	Year 9	Year 10	Year 11
Current Assets	**$ 4,362**	**$ 4,173**	**$ 4,604**	**$ 5,853**
Noncurrent Assets	**18,298**	**13,378**	**13,735**	**15,842**
Total Assets	$ 22,660	$ 17,551	$18,339	$21,695
Current Liabilities	**$ 7,914**	**$ 3,788**	**$ 3,935**	**$ 4,998**
Noncurrent Liabilities	**8,345**	**6,882**	**7,155**	**8,023**
Shareholders' Equity	**6,401**	**6,881**	**7,249**	**8,674**
Total Liabilities and Shareholders' Equity	$ 22,660	$ 17,551	$18,339	$21,695

b.   Noncurrent assets decreased as a percentage of total assets, suggesting either that PepsiCo sold property, plant and equipment or did not increase these assets at the same pace as the growth in operations. PepsiCo may have also acquired other firms that had lower proportions of noncurrent assets than PepsiCo.

1.21 continued.

    c. Total liabilities, particularly current liabilities, decreased and shareholders' equity increased as a percentage of total financing, suggesting the use of either new issues of common stock or the retention of earnings to finance the growth in operations.

1.22   (Johnson & Johnson; balance sheet relations.)

    a. The **given** (boldface) and missing items appear below (amounts in millions).

	Year 8	Year 9	Year 10	Year 11
Current Assets	$ **11,132**	$ 13,200[a]	**$15,450**	$ **18,473**
Noncurrent Assets	15,079	15,963	**15,871**	16,015
Total Assets	$ 26,211	$ 29,163	$31,321	$ 34,488
Current Liabilities	$ **8,162**	$ **7,454**	$ **7,140**	$ 8,044[c]
Noncurrent Liabilities	**4,459**	5,496	**5,373**	2,211
Contributed Capital	34	**458**	501	**1,727**
Retained Earnings	**13,556**	**15,755**	18,307[b]	22,506[d]
Total Liabilities and Shareholders' Equity	$ **26,211**	$ 29,163	$31,321	$ **34,488**

[a]$7,454 + $5,746 = $13,200.
[b]$15,755 + $4,276 − $1,724 = $18,307.
[c]$18,473 − $10,429 = $8,044.
[d]$18,307 + $6,246 − $2,047 = $22,506.

    b. The proportion of total assets comprising noncurrent assets decreased between Year 8 and Year 11. The dollar amount of noncurrent assets remained relatively steady, suggesting that Johnson & Johnson replaced property, plant and equipment in approximately the same amount as depreciation each year.

    c. Noncurrent liabilities declined and shareholders' equity increased as proportions of total financing over the four-year period. Johnson & Johnson reduced the dollar amount of its long-term liabilities in Year 11. Its net income increased each year in an amount larger than dividends, resulting in an increase in retained earnings.

1.23   (Intel; balance sheet relations.)

a.   The **given** (boldface) and missing items appear below (amounts in millions).

	Year 9	Year 10	Year 11	Year 12
Current Assets	$ 17,819	$ 21,150	$17,633	$18,928
Noncurrent Assets	26,030	26,795	26,762	25,296
Total Assets	$ 43,849	$ 47,945	$44,395	$44,224
Current Liabilities	$ 7,099	$ 8,650	$ 6,570	$ 6,595
Noncurrent Liabilities	4,095	1,973	1,995	2,161
Contributed Capital	7,306	8,389	8,655	7,578
Retained Earnings	25,349	28,933	27,175[a]	27,890[b]
Total Liabilities and Shareholders' Equity	$ 43,849	$ 47,945	$44,395	$44,224
Current Assets/Current Liabilities	2.510	2.445	2.684	2.870

[a] $28,933 - $1,220 - $538 = $27,175.
[b] $27,175 + $1,248 - $533 = $27,890.

b.   Current assets varied between 40 percent and 44 percent of total assets and noncurrent assets varied between 56 percent and 60 percent of total assets. There are no obvious explanations for these variations (other than the fact the sales of semiconductors tend to follow cyclical patterns over time, a fact not provided in the problem information). The proportion of noncurrent liabilities declined between Year 9 and Year 10 as Intel likely repaid long-term debt. Intel replaced a portion of this financing with additional issues of common stock. The proportion of financing comprising current and noncurrent liabilities decreased and the proportion comprising shareholders' equity increased between Year 10 and Year 12. Total shareholders' equity declined during this period due to operating at a net loss in Year 11 and repurchasing common stock in Year 12. Total liabilities, however, declined more than shareholders' equity, resulting in an increasing percentage of financing coming from shareholders.

1.24   (Hewlett-Packard Corporation; retained earnings relations.)

a. The **given** (boldface) and missing items appear below (amounts in millions).

	Year 9	**Year 10**	**Year 11**	**Year 12**
Retained Earnings, Beginning of Year	$16,909	$18,285	$14,097	$13,693
Net Income	2,026	3,697	217	(919)
Dividends Declared and Paid	(650)	(7,885)	(621)	(801)
Retained Earnings, End of Year	$18,285	$14,097	$13,693	$11,973

b. The sales of Hewlett-Packard Corporation are cyclical. The economy was apparently in an upturn between Year 9 and Year 10 and then declined sharply in Year 11 and Year 12.

c. Hewlett-Packard Corporation must have declared a special dividend in Year 10. (The dividend primarily involves the spin-off of Agilent Technologies to shareholders.) Hewlett-Packard Corporation increased its dividend between Year 11 and Year 12, despite operating at a loss, a somewhat unusual move.

1.25   (Ford Motor Company; retained earnings relations.)

a. The changes in retained earnings appear below. **Given** amounts appear in boldface (amounts in millions).

	Year 9	**Year 10**	**Year 11**	**Year 12**
Retained Earnings, January 1	$ 12,221	$17,168	$17,884	$ 10,502
Net Income	7,237	3,467	(5,453)*	(1,100)*
Dividends	(2,290)	(2,751)	(1,929)	(743)
Retained Earnings, December 31	$ 17,168	$17,884	$10,502	$ 8,659

*Net loss.

b. Sales of automobiles tend to vary with the overall level of economic activity. The economy was in the up part of the cycle in Year 9 and then declined in Year 10 and still further in Year 11. The economy seemed to make a partial recovery in Year 12 but not sufficiently to result in positive net income.

1.25 continued.

c. Ford Motor Company increased its dividends between Year 9 and Year 10, despite a decrease in net income, a somewhat unusual move. When net losses developed in Year 11 and Year 12, Ford Motor Company decreased its dividends. Firms are reluctant to eliminate dividends entirely in a year of poor operating performance.

1.26 (Target Corporation; relating net income to balance sheet changes.)

a.

(Amount in Millions)	Year 12	Year 13
Retained Earnings, Beginning of Year	$ 5,542	$ 6,687
Plus Net Income (Plug)	1,348	1,638
Less Dividends Declared and Paid	(203)	(218)
Retained Earnings, End of Year	$ 6,687	$ 8,107

b.

$$\text{Net Income} = \text{Increase in Assets} - \text{Increase in Liabilities} - \text{Increase in Contributed Capital} + \text{Dividends}$$

Year 12
$$\$1,348 = \$4,664 - \$3,323 - \$196 + \$203$$

Year 13
$$\$1,638 = \$4,449 - \$2,866 - \$163 + \$218$$

1.27 (Dell Computer; income statement relations.)

a. The **given** (boldface) and missing items appear below (amounts in millions).

	Year 10	Year 11	Year 12
Sales	$ 31,888	$ 31,168	$ 35,404
Cost of Goods Sold	(25,445)	(25,661)	(29,055)
Selling and Administrative Expenses	(3,193)	(2,784)	(3,050)
Research and Development Expenses	(482)	(452)	(455)
Income Tax Expense	(830)	(636)	(846)
Net Income	$ 1,938	$ 1,635	$ 1,998

b. The common size income statement appears below:

	Year 10	Year 11	Year 12
Sales	100.0%	100.0%	100.0%
Cost of Goods Sold	(79.8)	(82.3)	(82.1)
Selling and Administrative Expenses	(10.0)	(8.9)	(8.6)
Research and Development Expenses	(1.5)	(1.5)	(1.3)
Income Tax Expense	(2.6)	(2.0)	(2.4)
Net Income	6.1%	5.3%	5.6%

1.27 b. continued.

Sales declined between Year 10 and Year 11. Dell likely reduced selling prices in an effort to stimulate sales, resulting in an increase in the cost of goods sold to sales percentage. The selling and administrative expense to sales percentage declined, probably the result of cost cutting. Note that the dollar amount of this expense declined between Year 10 and Year 11. Sales increased significantly between Year 11 and Year 12 but the selling and administrative expenses and the research and development expenses did not increase as much, so that these expense percentages declined. Note that the cost of goods sold to sales percentage remained relatively flat between Year 11 and Year 12, suggesting a somewhat more attractive pricing environment in Year 12 than in Year 11.

1.28   (Pfizer; income statement relations.)

a.   The **given** (boldface) and missing items appear below (amounts in millions).

	Year 10	Year 11	Year 12
Sales	$ 26,045	$29,024	$ 32,373
Cost of Goods Sold	(3,755)	(3,823)	(4,045)
Selling and Administrative Expenses	(9,566)	(9,717)	(10,846)
Research and Development Expense	(4,374)	(4,776)	(5,176)
Income Tax Expense	(3,074)	(2,720)	(2,830)
Net Income	$ 5,276	$ 7,988	$ 9,476

b.   The common size income statement appears below.

	Year 10	Year 11	Year 12
Sales	100.0%	100.0%	100.0%
Cost of Goods Sold	(14.4)	(13.2)	(12.5)
Selling and Administrative Expenses	(36.7)	(33.5)	(33.5)
Research and Development Expense	(16.8)	(16.4)	(16.0)
Income Tax Expense	(11.8)	(9.4)	(8.7)
Net Income	20.3%	27.5%	29.3%

Pfizer experienced an increasing net income to sales percentage during the three-year period. One possible explanation for the declining expense percentages is that Pfizer spread relatively fixed expenses over a larger sales base. The introduction of new drugs for which Pfizer has significant pricing power may explain the increased sales. A cost control program may also explain the declining expense percentages. Pfizer's income tax expense to sales percentage declined while its profit margin before taxes increased, suggesting a lower income tax rate.

1.29 (Amazon.com; statement of cash flows relations.)

a.

AMAZON.COM
Statement of Cash Flows
(Amounts in Thousands)

	Year 10	Year 11	Year 12
Operations:			
Revenues Providing Cash	$2,753,398	$ 3,143,165	$ 3,892,988
Expenses Using Cash	(2,883,840)	(3,262,947)	(3,718,697)
Cash Flow from Operations	$ (130,442)	$ (119,782)	$ 174,291
Investing:			
Acquisition of Property and Equipment	$ (134,758)	$ (50,321)	$ (39,163)
Sale (Purchase) of Marketable Securities (net)	361,269	(196,775)	(82,521)
Acquisition of Investments in Other Companies	(62,533)	$ (6,198)	$ 0
Cash Flow from Investing	$ 163,978	$ (253,294)	$ (121,684)
Financing:			
Increase in Long-term Debt ..	$ 681,499	$ 10,000	$ 0
Increase in Common Stock ...	44,697	116,456	121,689
Decrease in Long-term Debt .	(33,049)	(19,575)	(14,795)
Other Financing Activities.....	(37,557)	(15,958)	38,471
Cash Flow from Financing..........	$ 655,590	$ 90,923	$ 145,365
Change in Cash...........................	$ 689,126	$ (282,153)	$ 197,972
Cash, Beginning of Year	133,309	822,435	540,282
Cash, End of Year........................	$ 822,435	$ 540,282	$ 738,254

b. Cash flow from operations was negative during Year 10 and Year 11 as a result of an apparently rapid growth in revenues. The need to finance inventories likely reduced operating cash flows. Cash flow from operations turned positive in Year 12, despite another apparent rapid increase in revenues. Perhaps the firm experienced better control of its inventories or delayed paying its suppliers. Expenditures on property, plant, and equipment were largest in Year 10 during the firm's high growth phase and then declined in Year 11 and Year 12 as the firm used its available capacity. Amazon.com sold marketable securities and issued long-term debt and common stock during Year 10 to make up the negative cash flow from operations and the amounts needed to acquire property, plant and equipment. It financed the negative cash flow from operations in Year 11 and the cash needed for acquisitions of property, plant, and equipment by issuing common stock and reducing the balance in its cash account. The positive cash flow from operations in Year 12 was more than sufficient to finance the reduced level of expenditures on property, plant, and equipment. The firm used the excess cash flow from operations over capital expenditures plus the proceeds from issuing common stock to purchase marketable securities and to increase the balance in its cash account.

1.30 (AMR Corporation; statement of cash flows relations.)

a.
AMR CORPORATION
Statement of Cash Flows
(Amounts in Millions)

	Year 10	Year 11	Year 12
Operations:			
Revenues Increasing Cash	$19,536	$19,083	$17,233
Expenses Decreasing Cash	(16,394)	(18,541)	(18,344)
Cash Flow from Operations	$ 3,142	$ 542	$ (1,111)
Investing:			
Sale of Property, Plant and Equipment	$ 332	$ 401	$ 220
Acquisition of Property, Plant and Equipment	(3,678)	(3,640)	(1,881)
Other Investing Transactions	71	(1,501)	268
Cash Flow from Investing	$ (3,275)	$ (4,740)	$ (1,393)
Financing:			
Proceeds of Long-term Borrowing	$ 836	$ 5,096	$ 3,190
Issue of Common Stock	67	37	3
Repayments of Long-term Debt	(766)	(922)	(687)
Cash Flow from Financing	$ 137	$ 4,211	$ 2,506
Change in Cash	$ 4	$ 13	$ 2
Cash, Beginning of Year	85	89	102
Cash, End of Year	$ 89	$ 102	$ 104

b. AMR Corporation's cash flow from operations steadily declined over the three-year period. Cash expenditures for expenses increased between Year 10 and Year 11, while cash received from revenues decreased between Year 11 and Year 12. Cash flow from operations was not sufficient to finance acquisitions of property, plant, and equipment in any year. AMR Corporation relied primarily on long-term debt to finance its cash needs.

1.31 (Relations between financial statements.)

a. $630 + $3,290 − $2,780 = a; a = $1,140.

b. $1,240 + b − $8,290 = $1,410; b = $8,460.

c. $89,000 − c + $17,600 = $102,150; c = $4,450.

d. $76,200 + $14,200 − d = $83,300; d = $7,100.

1.32   (eBay; preparing a balance sheet and income statement.)   (Amounts in Thousands)

a.

eBAY
Income Statement
For the Year Ended December 31, Year 12

Revenues:	
Net Operating Revenues...	$1,214,100
Interest and Other Revenues..	96,352
Total Revenues...	$1,310,452
Less Expenses:	
Cost of Net Operating Revenues....................................	$ 213,876
Product Development Expenses......................................	104,636
Selling Expenses	349,650
Administrative Expenses..	171,785
Other Operating Expenses	28,969
Interest Expense	1,492
Income Taxes	145,946
Total Expenses	1,016,354
Net Income...	$ 294,098

b.

eBAY
Comparative Balance Sheet

	Dec 31, Year 11	Dec. 31, Year 12
Assets		
Current Assets:		
Cash	$ 723,419	$1,199,003
Accounts Receivable.......................................	101,703	131,453
Other Current Assets......................................	58,683	138,002
Total Current Assets....................................	$ 883,805	$1,468,458
Noncurrent Assets:		
Investments in Securities...............................	$ 416,612	$ 604,871
Property, Plant and Equipment—Net of		
Depreciation	142,349	218,028
Goodwill and Other Intangibles......................	198,639	1,735,489
Other Noncurrent Assets	37,124	97,598
Total Noncurrent Assets..............................	$ 794,724	$2,655,986
Total Assets	$1,678,529	$4,124,444

1.32 b. continued.

Liabilities and Shareholders' Equity

Current Liabilities:

Accounts Payable to Suppliers...................... $	33,235	$ 47,424
Other Current Liabilities...............................	146,904	338,800
Total Current Liabilities .... $	180,139	$ 386,224
Long-Term Debt	12,008	13,798
Other Noncurrent Liabilities..........................	57,244	167,949
Total Liabilities................................... $	249,391	$ 567,971

Shareholders' Equity:

Common Stock.. $1,275,517	$3,108,754
Retained Earnings....................................	153,621	447,719
Total Shareholders' Equity...................... $1,429,138	$3,556,473
Total Liabilities and Shareholders'		
Equity... $1,678,529	$4,124,444

c.
Retained Earnings, December 31, Year 11	$ 153,621
Plus Net Income for Year Ending December 31, Year 12	294,098
Subtract Dividends for Year Ending December 31, Year 12 ..	0
Retained Earnings, December 31, Year 12	$ 447,719

1.33   (The GAP; preparing a balance sheet and an income statement.) (Amounts in Thousands)

a.
THE GAP
Balance Sheet

Assets	Jan. 31, Year 9	Jan. 31, Year 10
Cash..	$ 565,253	$ 450,352
Merchandise Inventory...................................	1,056,444	1,462,045
Other Current Assets.....................................	250,127	285,393
Total Current Assets.................................	$1,871,824	$2,197,790
Property, Plant and Equipment (Net)..........	1,876,370	2,715,315
Other Noncurrent Assets.............................	215,725	275,651
Total Assets..	$3,963,919	$5,188,756

1.33 a. continued.

Liabilities and Shareholders' Equity

Accounts Payable	$ 684,130	$ 805,945
Notes Payable to Banks	90,690	168,961
Other Current Liabilities	778,283	777,973
Total Current Liabilities	$1,553,103	$1,752,879
Long-Term Debt	496,455	784,925
Other Noncurrent Liabilities	340,682	417,907
Total Liabilities	$2,390,240	$2,955,711
Common Stock	$ 354,719	$ 135,034
Retained Earnings	1,218,960	2,098,011
Total Shareholders' Equity	$1,573,679	$2,233,045
Total Liabilities and Shareholders' Equity	$3,963,919	$5,188,756

b.

THE GAP
Income Statement

For the Year Ended:	Jan. 31, Year 10
Sales	$ 11,635,398
Cost of Goods Sold	(6,775,262)
Selling Expenses	(2,239,437)
Administrative Expenses	(803,995)
Interest Expense	(31,755)
Income Taxes	(657,884)
Net Income	$ 1,127,065

c.

Retained Earnings, January 31, Year 9	$ 1,218,960
Plus Net Income for Year 10	1,127,065
Less Dividends Declared during Year 10 (Plug)	(248,014)
Retained Earnings, January 31, Year 10	$ 2,098,011

d. The Gap increased its inventories and property, plant and equipment significantly during Year 10, most likely the result of opening new stores. It financed the growth with an increase in accounts payable, short-term bank borrowing, and long-term debt. It also repurchased shares of its common stock. Despite the reduction in common stock, total shareholders' equity increased due to the retention of earnings.

1.34 (Southwest Airlines; preparing a balance sheet and an income statement.)

a.
SOUTHWEST AIRLINES
Balance Sheet
(Amounts in Thousands)

	Dec. 31, Year 8	Dec. 31, Year 9
Assets		
Cash	$ 378,511	$ 418,819
Accounts Receivable	88,799	73,448
Inventories	50,035	65,152
Other Current Assets	56,810	73,586
Total Current Assets	$ 574,155	$ 631,005
Property, Plant and Equipment (Net)	4,137,610	5,008,166
Other Noncurrent Assets	4,231	12,942
Total Assets	$4,715,996	$5,652,113
Liabilities and Shareholders' Equity		
Accounts Payable	$ 157,415	$ 156,755
Current Maturities of Long-Term Debt	11,996	7,873
Other Current Liabilities	681,242	795,838
Total Current Liabilities	$ 850,653	$ 960,466
Long-Term Debt	623,309	871,717
Other Noncurrent Liabilities	844,116	984,142
Total Liabilities	$2,318,078	$2,816,325
Common Stock	$ 352,943	$ 449,934
Retained Earnings	2,044,975	2,385,854
Total Shareholders' Equity	$2,397,918	$2,835,788
Total Liabilities and Shareholders' Equity	$4,715,996	$5,652,113

b.
SOUTHWEST AIRLINES
Income Statement
(Amounts in Thousands)

For the Year Ended:	Dec. 31, Year 9
Sales	$4,735,587
Interest Revenue	14,918
Total Revenues	$4,750,505
Salaries and Benefits Expense	(1,455,237)
Fuel Expense	(492,415)
Maintenance Expense	(367,606)
Other Operating Expenses	(1,638,753)
Interest Expense	(22,883)
Income Tax Expense	(299,233)
Net Income	$ 474,378

1.34 continued.

 c.
Retained Earnings, December 31, Year 8	$ 2,044,975
Plus Net Income for Year 9	474,378
Less Dividends Declared during Year 9 (Plug)	(133,499)
Retained Earnings, December 31, Year 9	$ 2,385,854

 d. Southwest Airlines made substantial investments in property, plant and equipment during Year 9. It financed these expenditures with additional long-term debt, additional common stock, and the retention of earnings.

1.35 (ABC Company; relation between net income and cash flows.)

 a.

Month	Cash Balance at Beginning of Month	+	Cash Receipts from Customers	−	Cash Disbursements for Production Costs	=	Cash Balance at End of the Month
January	$ 875		$ 1,000		$ 750		$ 1,125
February	1,125		1,000		1,500		625
March	625		1,500		1,875		250
April	250		2,000		2,250		0

 b. The cash flow problem arises because of a lag between cash expenditures incurred in producing goods and cash collections from customers once the firm sells those goods. For example, cash expenditures during February ($1,500) are for goods produced during February and sold during March. Cash is not collected from customers on these sales, however, until April ($2,000). A growing firm must generally produce more units than it sells during a period if it is to have sufficient quantities of inventory on hand for future sales. The cash needed for this higher level of production may well exceed the cash received from the prior period's sales. Thus, a cash shortage develops.

  The difference between the selling price of goods sold and the cost of those goods equals net income for the period. As long as selling prices exceed the cost of the goods, a positive net income results. As the number of units sold increases, net income increases. A firm does not necessarily recognize revenues and expenses in the same period as the related cash receipts and expenditures. Thus, cash decreases, even though net income increases.

 c. The income statement and statement of cash flows provide information about the profitability and liquidity, respectively, of a firm during a period. The fact that net income and cash flows can move in opposite directions highlights the need for information from both statements. A firm without sufficient cash will not survive, even if it operates profit-

1.35 c. continued.

ably. The balance sheet indicates a firm's asset and equity position at a moment in time. The deteriorating cash position is evident from the listing of assets at the beginning of each month. Examining the cash receipts and disbursements during each month, however, identifies the reasons for the deterioration.

d. Strategies for dealing with the cash flow problem center around (a) reducing the lag between cash outflows to produce widgets and cash inflows from their sale, and (b) increasing the margin between selling prices and production costs.

To reduce the lag on collection of accounts receivable, ABC might:

(1) Provide to customers an incentive to pay faster than 30 days, such as offering a discount if customers pay more quickly or charge interest if customers delay payment.

(2) Use the accounts receivable as a basis for external financing, such as borrowing from a bank and using the receivables as collateral or selling (factoring) the receivables for immediate cash.

(3) Sell only for cash, although competition may preclude this alternative.

To delay the payment for widgets, ABC might:

(1) Delay paying its suppliers (increases accounts payable) or borrow from a bank using the inventory as collateral (increases bank loan payable).

(2) Reduce the holding period for inventories by instituting a just-in-time inventory system. This alternative requires ordering raw materials only when needed in production and manufacturing widgets only to customer orders. Demand appears to be sufficiently predictable so that opportunities for a just-in-time inventory system seem attractive.

To increase the margin between selling price and manufacturing cost, ABC might:

(1) Negotiate a lower purchase price with suppliers of raw materials.

(2) Substitute more efficient manufacturing equipment for work now done by employees.

(3) Increase selling prices.

1.35 d. continued.

The cash flow problem is short-term because it will neutralize itself by June. This neutralization occurs because the growth rate in sales is declining (500 additional units sold on top of an ever-increasing sales base). Thus, the firm needs a short-term solution to the cash flow problem. If the growth rate were steady or increasing, ABC might consider obtaining a more permanent source of cash, such as issuing long-term debt or common stock.

1.36   (Balance sheet and income statement relations.)

a.   Bushels of wheat are the most convenient in this case with the given information. This question emphasizes the need for a common measuring unit.

b.
IVAN AND IGOR
Comparative Balance Sheets
(Amounts in Bushels of Wheat)

	IVAN		IGOR	
Assets	Beginning of Period	End of Period	Beginning of Period	End of Period
Wheat	20	223	10	105
Fertilizer.....................	2	--	1	--
Ox.............................	40	36	40	36
Plow..........................	--	--	--	2
Land	100	100	50	50
Total Assets...........	162	359	101	193
Liabilities and Owner's Equity				
Accounts Payable	--	3	--	--
Owner's Equity...........	162	356	101	193
Total Liabilities and Owner's Equity..................	162	359	101	193

Questions will likely arise as to the accounting entity. One view is that there are two accounting entities (Ivan and Igor) to whom the Red Bearded Baron has entrusted assets and required a periodic reporting on stewardship. The "owner" in owner's equity in this case is the Red Bearded Baron. Another view is that the Red Bearded Baron is the accounting entity, in which case financial statements that combine the financial statements for Ivan and Igor are appropriate. Identifying the accounting entity depends on the intended use of the financial statements. For purposes of evaluating the performance of Ivan and Igor, the accounting entities are separate—Ivan and Igor. To assess the change in wealth of the Red Bearded Baron during the period, the combined financial statements reflect the accounting entity.

1.36 continued.

c.

IVAN AND IGOR
Comparative Income Statement
(Amounts in Bushels of Wheat)

	IVAN	IGOR
Revenues	243	138
Expenses:		
Seed	20	10
Fertilizer	2	1
Depreciation on Ox	4	4
Plow	3	1
Total Expenses	29	16
Net Income	214	122

Chapter 1 does not expose students to the concept of depreciation. Most students, however, grasp the need to record some amount of expense for the ox and the plow.

d. (Amounts in Bushels of Wheat)

	IVAN	IGOR
Owner's Equity, Beginning of Period	162	101
Plus Net Income	214	122
Less Distributions to Owner	(20)	(30)
Owner's Equity, End of Period	356	193

e. We cannot simply compare the amounts of net income for Ivan and Igor because the Red Bearded Baron entrusted them with different amounts of resources. We must relate the net income amounts to some base. Several possibilities include:

	IVAN	IGOR
Net Income/Average Total Assets	82.2%	83.0%
Net Income/Beginning Total Assets	132.1%	120.8%
Net Income/Average Noncurrent Assets	155.1%	137.1%
Net Income/Beginning Noncurrent Assets	152.9%	135.6%
Net Income/Average Owner's Equity	82.6%	82.0%
Net Income/Beginning Owner's Equity	132.1%	120.8%
Net Income (in bushels)/Acre	10.70	12.20

This question has no definitive answer. Its purpose is to get students to think about performance measurement. The instructor may or may not wish to devote class time at this point discussing which base is more appropriate.

1.37   (Ethical issues in financial reporting.)

a.   Year 9: $7,712/$87,548 = 8.8%; Year 10: $8,093/$88,396 = 9.2%.

b.   Year 9: $11,757/$87,548 = 13.4%; Year 10: $11,534/$88,396 = 13.0%.

c.   Year 9: $4,045/$11,757 = 34.4%; Year 10: $3,441/$11,534 = 29.8%.

d.   The improved profitability clearly relates to an improved income tax position. The ratio of income before income taxes to revenues computed in Part b. indicates that profitability before taxes decreased between Year 9 and Year 10.

e.   One approach to directing the discussion of ethical issues in this scenario is first to ask if this firm's actions complied with laws and regulations. The problem states that the improved tax position results from shifting of operations to lower tax rate countries, an action not obviously contrary to established laws. GAAP require firms to report the effect of the shift in the income tax note, which the firm did. Thus, there does not seem to be an issue of illegal behavior. The second question is whether the firm adequately disclosed the reason for the improved profitability. The problem states that to understand the reason for the improved tax position the user would "need" to consult the income tax note. This wording suggests that the firm did not disclose the reason for the improved profitability in its Management Discussion and Analysis of Operations or elsewhere in its annual report, perhaps hoping that users of the financial statements overlook the reasons for the improved profitability. A related question concerns whether disclosure in the income tax note is sufficient if the average investor cannot understand these disclosures. Thus, if one defines ethical behavior in terms of the adequacy of disclosure, then ethical questions arise. A contrary view is that investors should not invest in firms if they do not have the knowledge and skills to evaluate information provided about their investment. This view would argue that the firm acted ethically and the average investor is at fault for not gaining the necessary knowledge. A third level for the discussion is to ask students to assume that the firm described the reason for the improved profitability in its Management Discussion and Analysis of Operations, which in turn refers the user to the income tax note to learn more about the improved income tax position. Has the firm now acted ethically? Layering the discussion in this way helps students to sharpen their thinking about ethical issues and to identify the critical ethical turning points.

CHAPTER 2

BALANCE SHEET: PRESENTING THE INVESTMENTS
AND FINANCING OF A FIRM

Questions, Short Exercises, Exercises, Problems, and Cases: Answers and Solutions

2.1   See the text or the glossary at the end of the book.

2.2   Based on the conservatively reported earnings, a shareholder might sell shares of stock based on the assessment that the firm is not performing well.   If the economic or "true" earnings of the firm are larger, the shareholder's assessment would result in a poor decision.   Alternatively, shareholders might dismiss the management of a firm because they feel the firm is not performing well. It should be emphasized here that the principal objective of accounting reports as currently prepared is to present *fairly* the results of operations and the financial condition of the firm.   When doubt exists as to the treatment of a particular item or transaction, accountants tend to select the procedure resulting in the more conservative measurement of earnings.

2.3   The justification relates to the need for a reasonably high degree of reliability in the preparation of the financial statements.   When there is an exchange between a firm and some other entity, there is market evidence of the economic effects of the transaction. The independent auditor verifies these economic effects by referring to contracts, cancelled checks and other documents underlying the transaction.   If accounting recognized events without such a market exchange (for example, the increase in market value of a firm's assets), increased subjectivity would enter into the preparation of the financial statements.

2.4   The justification relates to the uncertainty as to the ultimate economic effects of the contracts. One party or the other may pull out of the contract. The accountant may not know the benefits and costs of the contract at the time of signing.   Until one party or the other begins to perform under the contract, accounting gives no recognition.   Accountants often disclose significant contracts of this nature in the notes to the financial statements.

2.5   Accountants record assets at acquisition cost.   Cash discounts reduce acquisition cost and, therefore, the amount recorded for merchandise or equipment.

2.6   a.   The contract between the investors and the construction company as well as cancelled checks provide evidence as to the acquisition cost.

b.   Adjusted acquisition cost differs from the amount in Part *a.* by the portion of acquisition cost applicable to the services of the asset consumed during the first five years. There are several generally accepted methods of computing this amount (discussed in Chapter 8). A review of the accounting records for the office building should indicate how the firm calculated this amount.

c.   There are at least two possibilities for ascertaining current replacement cost. One alternative is to consult a construction company to determine the cost of constructing a similar office building (that is, with respect to location, materials, size). The accountant would then adjust the current cost of constructing a new building downward to reflect the used condition of the five-year old office building. The current replacement cost amount could be reduced by 12.5 percent (= 5/40) if the asset's service potential decreases evenly with age. The actual economic decline in the value of the building during the first five years is likely to differ from 12.5 percent and, therefore, some other rate is probably appropriate. A second alternative for ascertaining current replacement cost is to consult a real estate dealer to determine the cost of acquiring a used office building providing services similar to the building that the investors own. The accountant might encounter difficulties in locating such a similar building.

d.   The accountant might consult a local real estate dealer to ascertain the current market price, net of transactions cost, at which the investors might sell the building. There is always the question as to whether an interested buyer could be found at the quoted price. The accountant might also use any recent offers to purchase the building received by the investors.

e.   The accountant measures the present value of the future net cash flows using estimated rental receipts and operating expenses (excluding depreciation) for the building's remaining 35-year life. These cash flows are then discounted to the present using an appropriate rate of interest.

2.7   a.   Liability—Receivable from Supplier or Prepaid Merchandise Orders.

b.   Liability—Investment in Bonds.

c.   Asset—Interest Payable.

d.   Asset—Insurance Premiums Received in Advance.

e.   Liability—Prepaid Rent.

2.8   (San Francisco Giants; asset and liability recognition and valuation.)

Accounting does not normally recognize mutually unexecuted contracts as assets or liabilities. This contract is partially executed to the extent that the San Francisco Giants provided an automobile at the time of signing. Because the ball club will receive the services of Barry Bonds beginning next year, it recognizes an asset, Advances on Contracts, of $250,000 on its balance sheet at the time of signing.

2.9   (Citigroup; asset recognition and valuation.)

Although the tuition support clearly benefits future periods, the benefits to Citigroup are too difficult to measure reliably to justify recognition of an asset. Citigroup would treat the $10 million as an expense.

2.10   (Delta Air Lines; liability recognition and valuation.)

Delta Air Lines likely built into the price of the tickets sold during the current year an amount equal to, or exceeding, the cost of providing the free flights. Delta Air Lines should recognize a liability of $25 million for the estimated cost of providing these future services. As Chapter 3 discusses, the firm must also recognize an expense of $25 million to match against revenues in measuring net income.

2.11   (Pizza Hut; asset valuation.)

The acquisition cost of the van includes the purchase price of $14,500 and the cost of painting the van of $1,200, for a total of $15,700. The license fee and insurance are annual operating expenses and are not part of the acquisition cost of the van. Pizza Hut should include the license fee and insurance in Prepayments on the balance sheet.

2.12   (Target Stores; dual effects on balance sheet equation.)   (Amounts in Millions)

Transaction	Assets	=	Liabilities	+	Shareholders' Equity
(1)	+$25.0		+$25.0		
(2)	−$ 1.5		−$ 1.5		
(3)	−$23.5		−$23.5		

2.13   (Leonard Corporation; journal entry for acquisition.) (Amounts in Millions)

Inventory (Asset Increase)	20	
Land, Buildings, and Equipment (Asset Increase)	40	
Goodwill and Other Intangibles (Asset Increase)	35	
Cash (Asset Decrease)		10
Liabilities (Liability Increase)		25
Common Stock (Shareholders' Equity Increase)		60

2.14   (IBM Corporation; asset recognition and valuation.)

    a. Investment in Bond (noncurrent asset), $8,000,000. IBM should record the bond at acquisition cost, not the amount it will receive at maturity.

    b. Prepaid Rent (current asset), $600,000.

    c. Option to Purchase Land (noncurrent asset), $1,000,000.

    d. Accounting does not recognize the employment contract, a mutually unexecuted contract, as an asset.

    e. Patent (noncurrent asset), $8,500,000.

    f. The patent would not appear on IBM's balance sheet as an asset. GAAP require firms to treat research and development expenditures as an expense each period. Thus, GAAP view the patent as having zero acquisition cost.

    g. IBM does not recognize an asset for the inventory until it receives the inventory.

2.15   (Delta Air Lines; asset recognition and valuation.)

    a. The placing of an order does not give rise to an asset.

    b. Deposit on Aircraft (noncurrent asset), $5 million.

    c. Landing Rights (noncurrent asset), $4 million.

    d. Equipment (noncurrent asset), $10 million.

    e. Accounting does not recognize the employment contract, a mutually unexecuted contract, as an asset.

    f. Equipment (noncurrent asset), $60 million. The book value of the aircraft on the seller's books is not relevant to Delta Air Lines' recording of the purchase.

    g. Prepaid Advertising, $2 million. The firm will not realize any benefits of this advertising until it begins service to the Bahamas next month. Accountants would not recognize prepayments for advertising as an asset because of the difficulty of measuring any future benefits with reasonable precision.

    h. Investment in Bond (noncurrent asset), $4 million. Delta Air Lines should record the purchase of the bond at its acquisition cost, not the amount ultimately received at maturity.

2.16   (McDonalds; asset recognition and valuation.)

    a.   Accounting does not recognize as assets, under generally accepted accounting principles, expenditures firms make internally to develop new products. Too much uncertainty exists as to the existence and valuation of future benefits to justify recognition of an asset.

    b.   Contractual Rights to Food Products (or similar creative account title, a noncurrent asset), $3,900,000. In contrast to Part a., the exchange between buyer and seller of presumably a commercially feasible product permits the identification and valuation of future benefits to justify recognition of an asset. A thin line appears to distinguish the situations in Part a. and Part b.

    c.   Purchase Options on Land (noncurrent asset), $2,800,000.

    d.   Accounting does not recognize an asset because of the difficulty of identifying and measuring any future benefits from these advertising expenditures.

    e.   Investment in Securities (noncurrent asset), $20,000,000. The market value of the shares of McDonalds given in exchange is probably a more reliable indicator of value than independent appraisals.

    f.   Land (noncurrent asset), $5,266,000 (= $5,000,000 + $80,000 + $6,000 + $180,000). Acquisition cost includes all expenditures made to prepare an asset for its intended use.

2.17   (Office Depot; asset recognition and valuation.)

    a.   Prepaid Rent (current asset), $125,000; Security Deposit (noncurrent asset), $130,000.

    b.   Leasehold Improvements (noncurrent asset), $36,500 (= $10,000 + $6,500 + $20,000). These expenditures prepare the rented facility for its intended use as a retail store.

    c.   Equipment or Fixtures (noncurrent asset), $31,400 [= .98 x $30,000) + $1,200 + $800]. The latter two expenditures prepare the display counters for their intended use.

    d.   Accounting does not recognize an asset for the future services of employees.

    e.   Accounting does not recognize any portion of expenditures on advertising as assets because any future benefits of the advertising are too uncertain.

2.17 continued.

    f.   Merchandise Inventory (current asset) $145,600 [= (.98 x $120,000) + $40,000 – $12,000]. One might argue that Office Depot should reduce the acquisition cost of the $28,000 (= $40,000 – $12,000) of merchandise that it has not yet paid for by the 2 percent discount. It is possible, however, that cash discounts are not available on this merchandise. If Office Depot takes advantage of any discounts when it pays for this merchandise, it will reduce the acquisition cost at that time.

2.18   (Liability recognition and valuation.)

    a.   This arrangement is mutually unexecuted and therefore does not give rise to a liability under GAAP.

    b.   Advances from Customers (current liability), $72.

    c.   Advances from Customers (noncurrent liability), $2 million.

    d.   Common stock does not meet the definition of a liability because the firm need not repay the funds in a particular amount at a particular time.

    e.   Notes payable (current liability), $100,000.

    f.   This arrangement is mutually unexecuted and therefore does not give rise to a liability under GAAP.

    g.   This arrangement is still mutually unexecuted and therefore does not give rise to a liability.

2.19   (Kansas City Royals, Inc.; liability recognition and valuation.)

    a.   Accounting normally does not recognize a liability for mutually unexecuted contracts. When the player renders services, a liability arises.

    b.   Advances from Customers (current liability), $2,700,000.

    c.   Bonds Payable (noncurrent liability), $8,400,000.

    d.   Utilities Payable (current liability), $3,400.

2.19 continued.

e. The treatment of this item depends on the probability of having to make a cash payment in the future, whose amount and timing of payment the firm can estimate with reasonable accuracy. Most firms do not recognize unsettled lawsuits as liabilities because it is not clear (1) that the firm has received benefits in the past, and (2) that the lawsuit will require a future cash payment.

f. The firm does not recognize a liability for the uniforms until the supplier makes delivery. The $10,000 deposit appears as a Deposit on Uniforms, an asset, on the firm's balance sheet and an Advance from Customers, a liability, on the balance sheet of the supplier.

2.20   (Liability recognition and valuation.)

a. Bonds Payable (noncurrent liability), $10,000,000.

b. Accounting normally does not recognize a liability for unexecuted contracts. The $2,000,000 deposit appears as an asset, Deposit on Building, on the college's balance sheet and as a liability, Advance from Customers (noncurrent liability), on the balance sheet of the construction company.

c. Advances from Customers, $1,800,000. The college classifies $450,000 as a current liability and $1,350,000 as a noncurrent liability.

d. Accounts Payable (current liability), $170,000.

e. Compensation Payable (current liability), $280,000; Payroll Taxes Payable $16,800 (.06 x $280,000).

f. The college does not recognize a liability for the grant. Although it receives the benefits of the funds, it incurs no obligation to repay the amount of the grant in the future.

2.21   (Chicago Symphony Orchestra; liability recognition and valuation.)

a. Advances from Customers (current liability), $340,000.

b. Chicago Symphony Orchestra does not recognize a liability because it has not yet received benefits obligating it to pay.

c. Accounts Payable (current liability), $85,000.

d. Chicago Symphony Orchestra would not normally recognize a liability for an unsettled lawsuit unless payment is probable and the entity can estimate the amount and timing of payment with reasonable accuracy. Because the suit has not yet come to trial, it is unclear whether any liability exists.

2.21 continued.

       e. Chicago Symphony Orchestra would not recognize a liability for this mutually unexecuted contract.

       f. The issue of common stock increases shareholders' equity, not a liability.

       g. Loan Payable (current liability), $40,000. Chicago Symphony Orchestra records the loan at the amount received, not the amount ultimately repaid, which includes interest.

2.22   (Balance sheet classification.)

a.	2	f.	2	k.	1
b.	3	g.	1	l.	1 (if purchased from another firm)
c.	1	h.	2		4 (if created by the firm)
d.	4	i.	4	m.	4
e.	1	j.	2	n.	3

2.23   (Balance sheet classification.)

a.	3		h.	2
b.	1		i.	1
c.	4		j.	2
d.	1		k.	2
e.	3		l.	1
f.	1		m.	2
g.	1 (if purchased from another firm)		n.	3
	4 (if created by the firm)			

2.24   (Dual effects of transactions on balance sheet equation and journal entries.)

a.

Transaction Number		Assets	=	Liabilities	+	Shareholders' Equity
(1)		+$60,000				+ $60,000
	Subtotal	$60,000	=			$60,000
(2)		+ 29,200		+ $29,200		
	Subtotal	$89,200	=	$29,200	+	$60,000
(3)		+ 32,700				
		− 5,000		+ 27,700		
	Subtotal	$116,900	=	$56,900	+	$60,000
(4)		+ 4,500				
		− 4,500				
	Subtotal	$116,900	=	$56,900	+	$60,000
(5)				− 27,700		+ 27,700
	Subtotal	$116,900	=	$29,200	+	$87,700
(6)		− 29,200		− 29,200		
	Total	$87,700	=	-0-	+	$87,700

2.24 continued.

b. (1) Cash (Asset Increase).. 60,000
      Common Stock (Shareholders' Equity
        Increase)...   50,000
      Additional Paid-in Capital (Shareholders'
        Equity Increase)   10,000
    Issue 5,000 shares of $10 par value common
    stock at $60,000.

(2) Merchandise Inventory (Asset Increase)........... 29,200
      Accounts Payable (Liability Increase)   29,200
    Purchase $29,200 of inventory on account.

(3) Equipment (Asset Increase) 32,700
      Cash (Asset Decrease)...................................   5,000
      Installment Contract Payable (Liability In-
        crease)...   27,700
    Acquires equipment costing $32,700 with
    $5,000 in cash and a commitment to pay the
    remainder over three years.

(4) Prepaid Rent (or Advance to Landlord) (Asset
      Increase) 4,500
      Cash (Asset Decrease).................................   4,500
    Pays $4,500 rent in advance.

(5) Installment Contract Payable (Liability De-
      crease) 27,700
      Common Stock (Shareholders' Equity
        Increase)   20,000
      Additional Paid-in Capital (Shareholders'
        Equity Increase)...................................   7,700
    Issues 2,000 shares of $10-par value common
    stock to repay installment contract. The
    shares have a market value of $13.85 (=
    $27,700/2,000).

(6) Accounts Payable (Liability Decrease).............. 29,200
      Cash (Asset Decrease)....................................   29,200
    Pays the supplier to transaction (2).

2.25   (Dual effects of transactions on balance sheet equation and journal entries.)

a.

Transaction Number		Assets	=	Liabilities	+	Shareholders' Equity
(1)		+ $144,000				+ $144,000
	Subtotal	$144,000	=			$144,000
		− 110,000				
(2)		+ 950,000				+ 840,000
	Subtotal	$984,000	=			+ $984,000
(3)		− 6,000				
		+ 6,000				
	Subtotal	$ 984,000	=		+	$984,000
(4)		+ 150,000		+ $150,000		
	Subtotal	$1,134,000	=	$150,000	+	$984,000
(5)		− 147,000				
		− 3,000		− 150,000		
	Subtotal	$ 984,000	=	-0-	+	$984,000
(6)		+ 1,300		+ 1,300		
	Total	$ 985,300	=	$1,300	+	$984,000

b. (1) Cash (Asset Increase)....................................... 144,000
          Common Stock (Shareholders' Equity
            Increase)..   12,000
          Additional Paid-in Capital (Shareholders'
            Equity Increase)   132,000
        Issue 12,000 shares of $1-par value common
        stock for $12 per share.

   (2) Land (Asset Increase) 50,000
        Building (Asset Increase)................................... 900,000
          Cash (Asset Decrease)..   110,000
          Common Stock (Shareholders' Equity
            Increase)...   70,000
          Additional Paid-in Capital (Shareholders'
            Equity Increase)   770,000
        Gives $110,000 in cash and 70,000 shares of
        $1-par value common stock valued at
        $840,000 for land costing $50,000 and a build-
        ing costing $900,000.

   (3) Prepaid Insurance (or Advances to Supplier)
            (Asset Increase) 6,000
          Cash (Asset Decrease)...............................   6,000
        Pays $6,000 in advance to insurance com-
        pany for coverage beginning next month.

2.25 continued.

(4) Merchandise Inventory (Asset Increase)........... 150,000
        Accounts Payable (Liability Increase) 150,000
    Purchases merchandise costing $150,000 on
    account.

(5) Accounts Payable (Liability Decrease).............. 150,000
        Cash (Asset Decrease)................................... 147,000
        Merchandise Inventory (Asset Decrease)...... 3,000
    Pays suppliers of merchandise the amount
    due less a discount of $3,000 for prompt pay-
    ment.

(6) Cash (Asset Increase)... 1,300
        Advance from Customer (Liability
        Increase)... 1,300
    Receives a cash advance from a customer for
    merchandise the firm will deliver next month.

2.26 (Kirkland Corporation; journal entries for various transactions.)

(1) Inventories (Asset Increase).................................. 30,000
    Land (Asset Increase)... 15,000
    Buildings (Asset Increase).................................... 125,000
    Equipment (Asset Increase) 60,000
    Goodwill (Asset Increase)...................................... 20,000
        Common Stock (Shareholders' Equity
        Increase) 100,000
        Additional Paid-in Capital (Shareholders'
        Equity Increase).. 150,000

(2) Advance to Supplier (Asset Increase)................... 5,000
        Cash (Asset Decrease)................................ 5,000

(3) Merchandise Inventories (Asset Increase) 36,000
        Advance to Supplier (Asset Decrease) 5,000
        Accounts Payable (Liability Increase) 31,000

(4) Accounts Payable (Liability Decrease).................. 3,500
        Merchandise Inventories (Asset Decrease)....... 3,500

(5) Accounts Payable ($31,000 − $3,500) (Liability
    Decrease) 27,500
        Cash {[.98($36,000 − $3,500)] − $5,000}
        (Asset Decrease) 26,850
        Merchandise Inventories [.02($36,000 −
        $3,500)] (Asset Decrease).......................... 650

2.26 continued.

(6)   Cash (Asset Increase)..   800

         Advance from Customers (Liability Increase)..   800

(7)   Automobile (Asset Increase)....................................   18,000

         Cash (Asset Decrease)..   2,000

         Note Payable (Liability Increase)......................   16,000

(8)   Prepaid Insurance (Asset Increase).......................   24,000

         Cash (Asset Decrease)..   24,000

2.27   (Winkle Grocery Store; journal entries for various transactions.)

(1)   Cash (Asset Increase)...   30,000

         Common Stock (Shareholders' Equity Increase)...   30,000

(2)   Cash (Asset Increase)...   5,000

         Notes Payable (Liability Increase).........................   5,000

(3)   Prepaid Rent (Asset Increase)...................................   12,000

         Cash (Asset Decrease)..   12,000

(4)   Equipment (Asset Increase)   8,000

         Cash (Asset Decrease)..   8,000

(5)   Merchandise Inventory (Asset Increase)...................   25,000

         Cash (Asset Decrease)..   12,000

         Accounts Payable (Liability Increase)   13,000

(6)   Cash (Asset Increase)..   4,000

         Advances from Customers (Liability Increase).....   4,000

(7)   Prepaid Insurance (Asset Increase)............................   1,200

         Cash (Asset Decrease)..   1,200

(8)   Prepaid Advertising (Asset Increase).........................   600

         Cash (Asset Decrease)..   600

(9)   The placing of an order does not give rise to a journal entry because it represents a mutually unexecuted contract.

2.28   (Wendy's International, Inc.; journal entries for various transactions.)

(1)   The firm does not make an entry for the supplies until it receives them.

(2)   Supplies Inventory (Asset Increase)...................   1,600,000

         Accounts Payable (Liability Increase)   1,600,000

2.28 continued.

    (3) Accounts Payable (Liability Decrease)............... 40,000
          Supplies Inventory (Asset Decrease) 40,000

    (4) Accounts Payable (Liability Decrease)............... 1,400,000
          Cash (.98 x $1,400,000) (Asset Decrease) 1,372,000
          Supplies Inventory (Asset Decrease) 28,000

    (5) Accounts Payable (Liability Decrease)............... 160,000
          Cash (Asset Decrease)..................................... 160,000

    Note: Some students treat the lost discounts of $3,200 (= .02 x $160,000) as an expense and reduce Supplies Inventory accordingly. We allow this answer as well.

    (6) Deposit on Equipment (Asset Increase)............. 200,000
          Cash (Asset Decrease)..................................... 200,000

    (7) Equipment (Asset Increase) 900,000
          Deposit on Equipment (Asset Decrease)........ 200,000
          Cash (Asset Decrease)..................................... 700,000

    (8) Equipment (Asset Increase) 27,000
          Cash (Asset Decrease)..................................... 27,000

    (9) Receivable from Supplier (Asset Increase)........ 22,000
          Equipment (Asset Decrease)........................... 22,000

   (10) Cash (Asset Increase).. 22,000
          Receivable from Supplier (Asset Decrease).. 22,000

2.29 (Moulton Corporation; preparation of transactions spreadsheet and balance sheet.)
a. Transactions spreadsheet.

Balance Sheet Accounts	Balance: Beginning of Period	Transactions, By Number and Description							Balance: End of Period
		Issue Common Stock for Cash	Acquire Land and Building for Cash	Acquire Inventory on Account	Pay for Inventory Purchases	Prepay Insurance	Borrow from Bank	Acquire Equip. and Issue Note	
		1	2	3	4	5	6	7	
ASSETS									
Current Assets:									
Cash		800,000	-500,000		-245,000	-12,000	300,000		343,000
Inventory				280,000	-5,000				275,000
Prepaid Insurance						12,000			12,000
Total Current Assets	-								630,000
Noncurrent Assets:									
Land			50,000						50,000
Building			450,000						450,000
Equipment								80,000	80,000
Total Noncurrent Assets	-								580,000
Total Assets	-								1,210,000
LIABILITIES AND SHAREHOLDERS' EQUITY									
Current Liabilities:									
Accounts Payable				280,000	-250,000				30,000
Note Payable								80,000	80,000
Total Current Liabilities	-								110,000
Noncurrent Liabilities:									
Loan Payable							300,000		300,000
Total Noncurrent Liabilities	-								300,000
Total Liabilities	-								410,000
Shareholders' Equity:									
Common Stock		800,000							800,000
Total Shareholders' Equity	-								800,000
Total Liabilities and Shareholders' Equity	-								1,210,000
Imbalance, if Any	-	-	-	-	-	-	-	-	-
Income Statement Accounts									

2.29 continued.

b.

MOULTON CORPORATION
Balance Sheet
December 31

Assets

Current Assets:

Cash	$	343,000
Merchandise Inventories		275,000
Prepaid Insurance		12,000
Total Current Assets	$	630,000

Noncurrent Assets:

Land	$	50,000
Building		450,000
Equipment		80,000
Total Noncurrent Assets	$	580,000
Total Assets	$	1,210,000

Liabilities and Shareholders' Equity

Current Liabilities:

Accounts Payable	$	30,000
Note Payable		80,000
Total Current Liabilities	$	110,000

Noncurrent Liabilities:

Loan Payable	$	300,000
Total Liabilities	$	410,000

Shareholders' Equity:

Common Stock	$	800,000
Retained Earnings		0
Total Shareholders' Equity	$	800,000
Total Liabilities and Shareholders' Equity	$	1,210,000

2.30 (Regaldo Department Stores; preparation of transactions spreadsheet and balance sheet.)
a. Transactions spreadsheet.

Balance Sheet Accounts	Balance: Beginning of Period	Transactions, By Number and Description								Balance: End of Period
		1 Issue Common Stock for Cash	2 Purchase Patent for Cash	3 Order Merchandise	4 Prepay Rent	5 Receive Merchan. Pur. On Account	6 Return Defective Merchan.	7 Pay for Merchan. Purch. On Account	8 Prepay Insurance	
		1	2	3	4	5	6	7	8	
ASSETS										
Current Assets:										
Cash		500,000	-24,000		-60,000			-156,800	-12,000	247,200
Merchandise Inventory						200,000	-8,000	-3,200		188,800
Prepaid Rent					60,000					60,000
Prepaid Insurance	-								12,000	12,000
Total Current Assets										508,000
Noncurrent Assets:										
Patent			24,000							24,000
Total Noncurrent Assets	-									24,000
Total Assets	-									532,000
LIABILITIES AND SHARE-HOLDERS' EQUITY										
Current Liabilities:										
Accounts Payable	-					200,000	-8,000	-160,000		32,000
Total Current Liabilities	-									32,000
Noncurrent Liabilities:										
Total Noncurrent Liabilities	-									-
Total Liabilities	-									32,000
Shareholders' Equity:										
Common Stock	-	500,000								500,000
Total Shareholders' Equity	-									500,000
Total Liabilities and Shareholders' Equity	-									500,000
Imbalance, if Any	-	-	-		-	-	-	-	-	-
Income Statement Accounts										

2.30 continued.

b.

REGALDO DEPARTMENT STORES
Balance Sheet
January 31, Year 8

Assets

Current Assets:
Cash	Ps247,200
Merchandise Inventories	188,800
Prepaid Rent	60,000
Prepaid Insurance	12,000
Total Current Assets	Ps508,000
Patent	24,000
Total Assets	Ps532,000

Liabilities and Shareholders' Equity

Current Liabilities:
Accounts Payable	Ps 32,000
Total Current Liabilities	Ps 32,000

Shareholders' Equity:
Common Stock	Ps500,000
Retained Earnings	0
Total Shareholders' Equity	Ps500,000
Total Liabilities and Shareholders' Equity	Ps532,000

2.31 (Patterson Corporation; preparation of transactions spreadsheet and balance sheet.)
a. Transactions spreadsheet.

Transactions, By Number and Description

Balance Sheet Accounts	Balance: Beginning of Period	1 Issue Common Stock for Cash	2 Issue Common Stock for Fixed Assets	3 Issue Common Stock for Patent	4 Acquire Mer. Inv. On Account	5 Acquire Equip. for Cash	6 Pays Freight on Equip. Purchased	7 Returns Defective Mer. Inv.	8 Prepays Rent on Autos	9 Pays for Purchases on Account	10 Obtains Insurance Coverage	11 Receives Advance from Customer	12 Acquires Warehouse for Cash and Note	13 Returns Defective Mer. Inv.	14 Purchases Common Stock for Cash	Balance: End of Period
ASSETS																
Current Assets:																
Cash		210,000				-5,400	-350		-1,400	-58,200		4,500	-7,000		-95,000	47,150
Marketable Securities															95,000	95,000
Receivable from Supplier														1,455		1,455
Merchandise Inventories					75,000			-800		-1,800				-1,455		70,945
Prepaid Rent									1,400							1,400
Total Current Assets	-															215,950
Noncurrent Assets:																
Land			80,000													80,000
Building			220,000										60,000			280,000
Equipment			92,000			5,400	350									97,750
Patent				28,000												28,000
Total Noncurrent Assets	-															485,750
Total Assets	-															701,700
LIABILITIES AND SHAREHOLDERS' EQUITY																
Current Liabilities:																
Accounts Payable					75,000			-800		-60,000						14,200
Advance from Customer												4,500				4,500
Total Current Liabilities	-															18,700
Noncurrent Liabilities:																
Mortgage Payable													53,000			53,000
Total Noncurrent Liabilities	-															53,000
Total Liabilities	-															71,700
Shareholders' Equity:																
Common Stock		150,000	280,000	20,000												450,000
Additional Paid-in Capital		60,000	112,000	8,000												180,000
Total Shareholders' Equity	-															630,000
Total Liabilities and Shareholders' Equity	-															701,700
Imbalance, If Any	-	-	-	-	-	-	-	-	-	-	-	-	-	-	-	-
Income Statement Accounts																

2.31 continued.

b.

PATTERSON CORPORATION
Balance Sheet
January 31, Year 13

Assets

Current Assets:

Cash	$ 47,150	
Marketable Securities	95,000	
Receivable from Supplier	1,455	
Merchandise Inventory	70,945	
Prepaid Rent	1,400	
Total Current Assets		$ 215,950

Property, Plant, and Equipment (at Acquisition Cost):

Land	$ 80,000	
Buildings	280,000	
Equipment	97,750	
Total Property, Plant, and Equipment		457,750

Intangibles:

Patent		28,000
Total Assets		$ 701,700

Liabilities and Shareholders' Equity

Current Liabilities:

Accounts Payable	$ 14,200	
Advances from Customers	4,500	
Total Current Liabilities		$ 18,700

Long-Term Debt:

Mortgage Payable		53,000
Total Liabilities		$ 71,700

Shareholders' Equity:

Common Stock—$10 Par Value	$ 450,000	
Additional Paid-in Capital	180,000	
Total Shareholders' Equity		630,000
Total Liabilities and Shareholders' Equity		$ 701,700

Solutions

2.32 (Whitley Products Corporation; preparation of transactions spreadsheet and balance sheet.)

a. Transactions spreadsheet.

Transactions, By Number and Description

Balance Sheet Accounts	Balance: Beginning of Period	1 Issue Common Stock for Cash	2 Acq. Land and Bldg. for Cash and Note	3 Acquire Equip. for Cash	4 Pay to Transport Equip.	5 Pay to Install Equip.	6 Prepay Insurance	7 Receive Advance from Customer	8 Orders Raw Materials	9 Receives Shipment Notice for Raw Mat.	10 Receives Raw Materials	11 Returns Damaged Raw Materials	12 Pays Raw Materials Supplier	Balance: End of Period
ASSETS														
Current Assets:														
Cash		375,000	-50,000	-125,000	-2,800	-3,200	-12,000	1,500					-50,960	132,540
Raw Materials Inventory											60,000	-8,000	-1,040	50,960
Prepaid Insurance							12,000							12,000
Total Current Assets	-													195,500
Noncurrent Assets:														
Land			25,000											25,000
Building			275,000											275,000
Equipment				125,000	2,800	3,200								131,000
Total Noncurrent Assets	-													431,000
Total Assets	-													626,500
LIABILITIES AND SHAREHOLDERS' EQUITY														
Current Liabilities:														
Accounts Payable	-										60,000	-8,000	-52,000	-
Advance from Customer	-							1,500						1,500
Total Current Liabilities	-													1,500
Noncurrent Liabilities:														
Note Payable			250,000											250,000
Total Noncurrent Liabilities	-													250,000
Total Liabilities	-													251,500
Shareholders' Equity:														
Common Stock		250,000												250,000
Additional Paid-in Capital		125,000												125,000
Total Shareholders' Equity	-													375,000
Total Liabilities and Shareholders' Equity	-													626,500
Imbalance, If Any	-	-	-	-	-	-	-	-	-	-	-	-	-	-
Income Statement Accounts														

2.32 continued.

b.

WHITLEY PRODUCTS CORPORATION
Balance Sheet
April 30

Assets

Current Assets:		
Cash	$ 132,540	
Merchandise Inventory	50,960	
Prepaid Insurance	12,000	
Total Current Assets		$ 195,500
Property, Plant, and Equipment:		
Land	$ 25,000	
Buildings	275,000	
Equipment	131,000	
Total Property, Plant, and Equipment		431,000
Total Assets		$ 626,500

Liabilities and Shareholders' Equity

Current Liabilities:		
Advances from Customers	$ 1,500	
Total Current Liabilities		$ 1,500
Noncurrent Liabilities:		
Note Payable	$ 250,000	
Total Noncurrent Liabilities		250,000
Total Liabilities		$ 251,500
Shareholders' Equity:		
Common Stock—$10 Par Value	$ 250,000	
Additional Paid-in Capital	125,000	
Total Shareholders' Equity		375,000
Total Liabilities and Shareholders' Equity		$ 626,500

2.33   (Effect of recording errors on balance sheet equation.)

Transaction Number	Assets	=	Liabilities	+	Shareholders' Equity
(1)	No		No		No
(2)	O/S $ 9,000		O/S $ 9,000		No
(3)	U/S $16,000		U/S $16,000		No
(4)	No		No		No
(5)	U/S $ 1,500		U/S $ 1,500		No
(6)	U/S $12,000		No		U/S $12,000
(7)	No		No		No

2.34   (Effect of recording errors on balance sheet equation.)

Transaction Number	Assets	=	Liabilities	+	Shareholders' Equity
(1)	U/S $ 8,000		U/S $ 8,000		No
(2)	O/S $ 3,000		O/S $ 3,000		No
(3)	U/S $ 800		U/S $ 800		No
(4)	O/S $ 1,000		O/S $ 1,000		No
(5)	U/S $ 2,500		No		U/S $2,500
(6)	O/S $ 4,900[a]		No		No
	U/S $ 4,900[a]				

[a]The response "No" is also acceptable here.

2.35   (Marks and Spencer; balance sheet format, terminology, and accounting methods.)

a.
MARKS AND SPENCER, PLC
Balance Sheet
(In Millions of Pounds)

	March 30 Year 4	Year 5
Assets		
Current Assets:		
Cash	£ 266	£ 293
Marketable Securities	28	29
Accounts Receivable	192	212
Inventories	374	351
Prepayments	134	142
Total Current Assets	£ 994	£ 1,027
Property, Plant and Equipment:		
Land and Buildings	£ 1,636[a]	£ 1,733[b]
Equipment	375	419
Total Property, Plant and Equipment	£ 2,011	£ 2,152
Other Noncurrent Assets	£ 212	£ 264
Total Assets	£ 3,217	£ 3,443

2.35 a. continued.

Liabilities and Shareholders' Equity

Current Liabilities:		
Accounts Payable...	£ 187	£ 168
Bank Loans..	100	107
Other Current Liabilities.................................	638	622
Total Current Liabilities	£ 925	£ 897
Noncurrent Liabilities:		
Bonds Payable...	£ 565	£ 550
Other Noncurrent Liabilities...........................	4	19
Total Noncurrent Liabilities........................	£ 569	£ 569
Total Liabilities...	£ 1,494	£ 1,466
Shareholders' Equity:		
Common Stock...	£ 675	£ 680
Additional Paid-in Capital	50	69
Retained Earnings..	998	1,228
Total Shareholders' Equity.........................	£ 1,723	£ 1,977
Total Liabilities and Shareholders' Equity...	£ 3,217	£ 3,443

[a]£2,094 − £458 = £1,636.

[b]£2,193 − £460 = £1,733.

b. A close relation exists between the amount of current assets and current liabilities and between noncurrent assets and noncurrent liabilities plus shareholders' equity.

2.36 (United Breweries Group; balance sheet format, terminology, and accounting methods.)

a. **UNITED BREWERIES GROUP**
Balance Sheet
(In Millions of Kronor)

	September 30	
	Year 8	**Year 9**
Assets		
Current Assets:		
Cash	Kr 810	Kr 1,224
Marketable Securities	3,018	3,460
Accounts Receivable..	1,413	1,444
Inventories..	1,290	1,393
Prepayments...	317	285
Total Current Assets....................................	Kr 6,848	Kr 7,806
Investments in Securities	422	573
Property, Plant and Equipment[a].......................	3,518	3,545
Total Assets	Kr 10,788	Kr 11,924

2.36 a. continued.

Liabilities and Shareholders' Equity

Current Liabilities:

Accounts Payable................................	Kr	913	Kr	902
Bank Debt..		619		986
Other Current Liabilities....................		2,157		2,240
Total Current Liabilities	Kr	3,689	Kr	4,128
Bonds Payable		1,805		1,723
Other Noncurrent Liabilities................		1,149		1,425
Total Liabilities.........................	Kr	6,643	Kr	7,276
Shareholders' Equity:				
Common Stock..................................	Kr	976	Kr	976
Retained Earnings.............................		3,169		3,672
Total Shareholders' Equity..........	Kr	4,145	Kr	4,648
Total Liabilities and Shareholders' Equity...	Kr	10,788	Kr	11,924

aThe amounts for this account reflect historical costs instead of current market values as follows:

	As Reported By Company	−	Revalu- ation Reserve	=	As Restated
Property, Plant and Equipment:					
September 30, Year 8..................	Kr3,934	−	Kr416	=	Kr3,518
September 30, Year 9..................	Kr4,106	−	Kr561	=	Kr3,545

b. Current assets significantly exceed current liabilities, primarily because of the high proportion of current assets that comprises cash and marketable securities. United Breweries has apparently generated substantial cash flow from operations which it has not reinvested in operating assets.

2.37 (Outback Steakhouse, Inc.; interpreting balance sheet changes.)

a. The principal assets of a restaurant are land, buildings, and equipment. These assets comprise two-thirds of the assets of Outback Steakhouse. Accounts receivable represent a small percentage of total assets because this restaurant either sells for cash or customers use third-party credit cards. Inventories likewise comprise a small percentage of total assets because of the need to turn over food products quickly. The firm used long-term financing to finance its investments in property, plant, and equipment. The surprising observation is that Outback Steakhouse used primarily shareholders' equity financing instead of long-term debt financing. Long-term debt financing is usually less costly as a source of funds. It appears that the firm obtained most of the funds needed for the acquisition of property, plant, and equipment from

2.37 a. continued.

the retention of assets generated by earnings instead of issuing common stock.

b. The common-size percentage for cash increased significantly between Year 11 and Year 12 and the common-size percentage for other assets decreased significantly. One possible explanation is that the firm sold off other assets (perhaps investments in securities) for cash. The common-

percentage for retained earnings increased. Perhaps the firm was very profitable during Year 12 and retained a higher proportion of earnings, instead of paying a larger dividend. The firm may also have bought back some of its common stock with the assets generated by earnings.

c. The percentages in the common-size balance sheet are not independent of each other. A decrease in the dollar amount of property, plant, and equipment may result in an increasing, decreasing, or stable proportion for this balance sheet item, depending on the changes in other assets.

2.38   (Pacific Gas and Electric Company; interpreting balance sheet changes.)

a. The largest asset is property, plant, and equipment, which represents the generating and distribution capacity of the utility. Long-term financing dominates the financing side of the balance sheet, with the largest proportion coming from long-term debt. The historically predictable cash flows of utilities from their regulated monopoly status permit them to take on a large portion of long-term debt financing.

b. Pacific Gas and Electric operated at a net loss during Year 10 as evidenced by the change from a positive to a negative balance in retained earnings. The decreased percentages for property, plant, and equipment and for other noncurrent assets suggest that the firm wrote down these assets during the year, leading to the net loss. The mix of financing in the capital structure changed from shareholders' equity to liabilities and from noncurrent liabilities to current liabilities. The firm likely took on additional short-term financing to pay off long-term debt.

2.39   (Relating market value to book value of shareholders' equity.)

a. (1) **Coke**—One important asset missing from the balance sheet of Coke is the value of its brand names. Coke follows generally accepted accounting principles (GAAP) in expensing the cost of developing and maintaining its brand names each year (for example, product development, quality control, advertising). The future benefits of these expenditures are too difficult to identify and measure with sufficient precision to justify recognizing an asset. Coke also reports its property, plant and equipment at acquisition cost (adjusted downward for depreciation) instead of current market

2-25

2.39 a. continued.

values. Acquisition cost valuations are more objective and easier to audit than current market valuations.

(2) **Bristol**—Bristol engages in research and development to discover new drugs. GAAP require firms to expense research and development expenditures immediately. The future benefits of these expenditures are too uncertain to justify recognizing an asset. Thus, the value of patents and technologies developed by Bristol, as well as the value of the research scientists employed by Bristol, do not appear on its balance sheet.

(3) **Bankers Trust**—The market-to-book value ratio for Bankers is 1.0. Most of the assets and liabilities of Bankers are monetary items and turn over frequently. Thus, the market values and book values closely conform.

(4) **International Paper (IP)**—IP reports its forest lands on the balance sheet at acquisition cost. IP likely acquired the land many years ago. The acquisition cost of the land is considerably less than its current market value. Also, IP follows general industry practice and expenses the annual cost of maintaining its forest lands. Thus, the value of forest lands increases each year as trees grow. The market incorporates this value increase into its price of the common stock of IP even though GAAP do not reflect the value increase on the balance sheet. The value increase is too difficult to measure objectively to justify substituting market values for acquisition cost.

(5) **Disney**—Disney depreciates the cost of film inventory over its expected useful life. Fortunately for Disney and other film production companies, the value of old films has increased in recent years with the growth of cable networks. Thus, the market value of some of Disney's films exceeds their book values. The market-to-book value ratio reflects this under valuation. Also, Disney reports its property, plant and equipment at acquisition cost (adjusted downward for depreciation) instead of current market values. The land underlying its theme parks has likely increased in value since the date of acquisition, but the accounting records do not reflect the value increase under GAAP.

b. (1) **Coke**—Coke's current assets are less than its current liabilities. This relation indicates short-term liquidity risk. The high market-to-book value ratio suggests that the market value (selling price) of its inventory exceeds the book value, so current assets probably equal or exceed current liabilities at market value. Shareholders' equity represents a higher proportion of long-term financing than long-term debt. One explanation for the relatively low proportion of long-term

2.39 b. continued.

debt is that Coke is very profitable (suggested by the high market-to-book value ratio) and therefore generates most of its needed cash from operations. Further support for the internal generation of cash is the high proportion of retained earnings and significant treasury stock purchases. Another explanation for the relatively low proportion of long-term debt relates to the investments in its bottlers. Chapter 11 discusses the accounting for intercorporate investments. Because Coke owns less than 50 percent of the outstanding common stock of these bottlers, it does not consolidate them. Thus, the assets and the financing of the bottlers are "off balance sheet." These bottlers may carry significantly more long-term debt than Coke.

(2) **Bristol**—The interesting insight from studying Bristol's capital structure is the relatively small proportion of long-term debt. The products of Bristol are subject to technological obsolescence. Competitors could develop technologically superior drugs that would replace those of Bristol in the market. Given this product risk, Bristol probably does not want to add the financial risk that fixed interest and principal payments on debt create.

(3) **Bankers Trust**—Bankers relies heavily on short-term sources for financing, principally deposits and short-term borrowing. Customers can withdraw their funds on no, or very short, notice. Thus, Bankers must maintain a relatively liquid balance sheet. Most of its assets are in cash, short-term marketable securities, and loans. The loans are less liquid than cash and marketable securities but tend to have predictable cash flows. Note that shareholders' equity makes up approximately 5 percent of liabilities plus shareholders' equities. Such a low percentage is common for commercial banks. Banks carry high proportions of liabilities because of the high liquidity of their assets.

(4) **International Paper (IP)**—IP carries a high proportion of noncurrent assets and matches this with a high proportion of long-term financing. IP uses approximately equal proportions of long-term liabilities and shareholders' equity to finance its noncurrent assets. The sales of paper products vary with movements through economic cycles. During recessionary periods, demand slackens and firms reduce prices in order to utilize capital-intensive manufacturing facilities. Paper companies do not want too much debt in their capital structures that could force them into bankruptcy during these times. On the other hand, when the economy is booming, the profits and cash flows of paper companies increase significantly. Firms spread the cost of their capital-intensive plants over larger volumes of output. In these cases, shareholders benefit from debt in the capital structure (a phenome-

2.39 b. continued.

non known as *financial leverage*, discussed in Chapter 5). Thus, the approximately equal proportions of long-term debt and shareholders' equity reflect these opposing considerations.

(5) **Disney**—Disney reports a significant excess of current assets over current liabilities. Interpreting this excess involves two opposing considerations. Some of Disney's films continue to generate revenues and cash flows, even though the films carry a zero book value on Disney's books. On the other hand, Disney accumulates the cost of films in process in the inventory account without knowing whether or not the films will be a commercial success. Disney uses a higher proportion of shareholders' equity than long-term debt in its long-term financing structure. Its property, plant and equipment can serve as collateral for long-term borrowing. Its predictable revenue and cash flows from theme parks also argues for a high proportion of long-term debt relative to shareholders' equity. Perhaps Disney did not want to use up its borrowing capacity in case it had the opportunity to make an acquisition (such as Capital Cities/ABC) and needed to borrow to finance the transaction.

2.40   (Relating market value to book value of shareholders' equity.)

a. (1) **Pfizer**—Pharmaceutical firms make ongoing expenditures on research and development (R&D) to develop new products. Some of these expenditures result in profitable new products, while other expenditures do not provide any future benefit. The difficulty encountered in trying to identify whether or not a particular R&D expenditure results in a future benefit has led accounting standard setters to require the immediate expensing of R&D costs in the year incurred. Thus, the valuable patents for pharmaceutical products and the value of potential products in the research pipeline do not appear on the balance sheet of Pfizer. The market does place a value on these technologies in deciding on an appropriate market price for the firm's stock.

Students might suggest approaches that technology firms could follow to measure the value of their technology resources. One approach might be to study the past success record of discovering new technologies For example, if 20 percent of expenditures in the past resulted in valuable technologies, the firm might report 20 percent of the expenditures on R&D each period as an asset. If these new technologies provided benefits for, say, seven years on average, then the firm would amortize the amount recognized as an asset over seven years. An alternative approach would be to use the prices paid recently when acquiring firms purchase target firms that have similar technologies. Each of these approaches involves

2.40 a. continued.

a degree of subjectivity that has led standard setters to require the immediate expensing of R&D expenditures in the year incurred.

(2) **Nestle**—The products of Nestle carry a high degree of brand recognition, which leads loyal customers to purchase Nestle products on a regular basis and new customers to try its products. The value of the Nestle name and its other brand names is created through advertising, quality control, and new product introductions. Nestle follows GAAP in expensing these expenditures each year. Thus, the value of the brand name does not appear on the balance sheet as an asset. If the brand name did appear on the balance sheet, assets and shareholders' equity would be larger and the market-to-book value ratio would be closer to 1.0.

One might ask how Nestle might value its brand names if it were permitted to recognize these valuable resources as assets. One approach might be to determine the profit margin (that is, net income divided by sales) that Nestle realizes on sales of its products relative to the profit margin of competitors. Nestle would then multiply the excess profit margin times the number of units expected to be sold in future years to measure its excess profitability. It would then discount the future excess earnings to a present value. An alternative approach is to identify the prices paid recently by firms acquiring other branded consumer products companies to ascertain the approximate price paid for identifiable assets and the portion paid for brand names. Each of these approaches involves a degree of subjectivity and opens the door for firms to cast their balance sheets in the most favorable light possible. Accounting standard setters in most countries recognize this potential source of bias and require firms to expense brand development costs in the year expenditures are made.

(3) **Promodes**—Promodes is the largest grocery store chain in France and likely has some brand name recognition that does not appear on its balance sheet. In addition, the stores of Promodes are valued at acquisition cost adjusted downward for depreciation to date. The land and perhaps the store buildings probably have market values that exceed their book values. Standard setters in most countries require firms to account for land and buildings using acquisition costs instead of current market values because of the subjectivity in the latter valuations. This real estate is probably easier to value than brand names and technological know how because of active real estate markets. Thus, the market-to-book value ratio probably reflects brand recognition and undervalued fixed assets.

2.40 a. continued.

(4) **Deutsche Bank**—Most of the assets of a commercial bank are reported on the balance sheet at current market values. Marketable securities are revalued to market value at each balance sheet date. Loans receivable are stated net of estimated uncollectibles and should therefore reflect cash-equivalent values. Deposits and short-term borrowing on the liability side of the balance sheet appear at current cash-equivalent values. Thus, the market-to-book value ratio should be approximately 1.0. The ratio of 1.7 for Deutsche Bank suggests the presence of intangibles that do not appear on the balance sheet. Possibilities include the size and dominant influence of Deutsche Bank in the German economy, technologically sophisticated information systems, and superior work force. The financial consulting capabilities of its investment banking employees are a valuable resource that does not appear on the balance sheet as an asset.

(5) **British Airways**—The aircraft and ground facilities of British Airways appear at acquisition cost net of depreciation to date. The market values of these fixed assets likely exceed their book values. In addition, British Airways has landing and gateway rights that appear on the balance sheet only to the extent that the firm has paid amounts up front. In most cases, British Airways pays fees periodically as it uses these facilities. Thus, no asset appears on the balance sheet.

(6) **New Oji Paper Co.**—The balance sheet of New Oji Paper Co. includes a high proportion of intercorporate investments in securities and property, plant, and equipment. GAAP in Japan report these assets at acquisition cost, with plant and equipment adjusted downward for depreciation to date. The market value of land probably exceeds its book value. The market values of securities in Japan have decreased significantly in recent years but may still exceed their book values if the investments were made many years ago. Note that the market-to-book value ratio does not exceed 1.0 by as much as the consumer products and pharmaceutical companies with brand recognition.

b. (1) **Pfizer**—One question related to Pfizer is why it would use such a small percentage of long-term debt financing. Pharmaceutical firms face product obsolescence and legal liability risks. They tend not to add financial risk from having a high proportion of long-term debt on the balance sheet. Although this exercise does not provide the needed information, Pfizer is very profitable and generates sufficient cash flow from operations that it does not need much external financing.

2.40 b. continued.

A second question related to Pfizer is the large percentage for other noncurrent liabilities on the balance sheet. This amount includes its healthcare benefit obligation to employees and deferred income taxes. Students generally have not studied these two items sufficiently to generate much discussion.

A third question related to Pfizer is its high proportion of treasury stock. Economic theory would suggest that if the market fairly values a firm prior to a stock buyback, then the market price of the stock should not change. The economic value of the firm should decrease by the amount of cash paid out. The number of shares of common stock outstanding should decline proportionally and the stock price should remain the same. However, the effect of stock buybacks generally is to increase the market price of the stock. One possible explanation for the market price increase is that the market views the buyback as a positive signal by management about the firm's future prospects. Management knows about the firm's future plans and might feel that the market is underpricing the firm, given these future plans. The buyback signals this positive information and the market price increases.

(2) **Nestle**—Nestle, like Pfizer, has highly predictable cash flows from its brand name products and generates sufficient cash flows in the long term to reduce the need for long-term debt financing. Nestle, however, extends credit to customers and must carry inventory for some period of time before sale. It uses suppliers and short-term borrowing to finance this working capital.

(3) **Promodes**—The majority of the assets of Promodes is short-term receivables and inventories. The majority of its financing is likewise short-term. Thus, firms attempt to match the term structure of their financing to the term structure of their assets.

(4) **Deutsche Bank**—Deutsche Bank obtains the vast majority of its funds from depositors and short-term borrowing. Such a high proportion of short-term financing might appear risky. However, a large portion of its assets is in highly liquid cash and short-term investments. A large portion is also in loans to businesses and consumers. Although loans are generally not as liquid as cash and investments, they do have predictable cash flows. The large number of borrowers also diversifies the risk of Deutsche Bank on these loans. The low level of risk on the asset side of the balance sheet and the stability of the deposit base means that banks need only a small proportion of shareholders' equity.

2.40 b. continued.

(5) **British Airways**—The majority of the assets of British Airways is in flight and ground support equipment. British Airways matches these long-term assets with long-term financing, either in the form of long-term debt or shareholders' equity. The heavier use of debt financing stems from its lower cost and the availability of the equipment to serve as collateral for the borrowing. Lenders generally prefer that firms have more current assets than current liabilities. The excess current liabilities of British Airways stem from advance sales of airline tickets (appears in Other Current Liabilities). British Airways will satisfy this liability by providing transportation services rather than paying cash. Thus, the net current liability position is not of particular concern.

(6) **New Oji Paper Co.**—The balance sheet of Oji portrays some relationships that are typical of Japanese companies. First, note the high proportion of investments in securities. Many Japanese companies are part of corporate groups (called "Kieretsus"). The investments in firms in the corporate groups tend to represent 20 percent to 30 percent of these other companies and appear as intercorporate investments on the balance sheet. Secondly, note the relatively high proportion of short-term bank borrowing. Most corporate groups have a commercial bank as a member. This commercial bank is not likely to force a member of the group into bankruptcy if it is unable to repay a loan at maturity. The bank will more likely simply extend the term of the loan. Short-term borrowing is usually less costly than long-term borrowing and helps explain the high proportion of short-term borrowing on the balance sheet.

2.41   (Identifying industries using common-size balance sheet percentages).

Firm (1) has a high percentage of receivables among its assets and substantial borrowing in its capital structure. This mix of assets and financing is typical of the finance company, Household International. We ask students why the capital markets allow a finance company to have such a high proportion of borrowing in its capital structure. The answer is threefold: (1) finance companies have contractual rights to receive cash flows in the future from borrowers; the cash flow tends to be highly predictable, (2) finance companies lend to many different individuals, which diversifies their risk, and (3) borrowers often pledge collateral to back up the loan, which provides the finance companies with an alternative for collecting cash if borrowers default on their loans. The relative mix of current liabilities and long-term debt suggests that loans with maturities longer than one year exceed loans maturing within the next year, since companies attempt to match the maturities of their debt with the maturities of their assets.

2.41 continued.

Firms (2) and (3) have a high proportion of their assets in property, plant, and equipment. Commonwealth Edison and Newmont Mining are both capital intensive. These firms differ primarily with respect to their financing. Firm (2) has a higher proportion of long-term debt and Firm (3) has a higher proportion of financing from shareholders' equity. Commonwealth Edison has essentially a monopoly position in its market area and is subject to regulation with respect to rates charged. The reasonably assured cash flows permit it to take on more debt than Newmont Mining. Newmont Mining faces uncertainties with respect to the amount of gold and other minerals that it will discover and the price it will obtain for gold and minerals sold. Its high proportion of fixed costs in its cost structure means that its earnings can vary significantly as revenues increase and decrease over time. This larger business risk for Newmont Mining suggest that it should take on less long-term debt than Commonwealth Edison. Thus, Firm (2) is Commonwealth Edison and Firm (3) is Newmont Mining.

This leaves Hewlett Packard and May Department Stores and Firms (4) and (5). Firms (4) and (5) both have substantial receivables and inventories, which we would expect for both firms. Firm (4) has a lower proportion of property, plant, and equipment than Firm (5). Hewlett-Packard outsources the manufacturing of components and then assembles the components in its factories. The outsourcing reduces somewhat its need for fixed assets. May Department Stores, on the other hand, has fixed assets from its retail stores. This suggests that Firm (4) is Hewlett-Packard and Firm (5) is May Department Stores. The financing provides additional evidence for this pairing. Technological change reduces the product life cycles of computers and printers. Long-term lenders are reluctant to lend when substantial uncertainty exists about the long-term sales potential of a firm's products. The land and buildings of department stores serve as collateral for borrowing and permit a higher level of long-term debt in the capital structure. Firm (4) has a lower proportion of long-term debt than Firm (5), consistent with Firm (4) being Hewlett-Packard and Firm (5) being May Department Stores.

2.42 (Unilever plc; ethical issues in asset revaluations.)

a. £39,689/£43,318 = 91.6%.

b. £39,689/(£43,318 − £9,240 + £10,529) = 89.0%.

c. Revaluing the property, plant and equipment permits Unilever's total liabilities to total asset ratio to fall the 90 percent threshold in its borrowing agreements. A legal question is whether the lending agreements specify which method of valuating fixed assets the lenders will use in measuring this ratio. If the lending agreements are silent as to the accounting for property, plant and equipment and Unilever chooses to switch its accounting method this year from one acceptable

2.42 c. continued.

method to another acceptable method, then Unilever would not appear to violate any law. The ethical issue would then come down to whether Unilever disclosed the change in accounting method or tried to hide it. The firm has previously disclosed in notes to the financial statements the amount for property, plant and equipment based on both acquisition cost and current replacement cost. Thus, lenders should know roughly the amount by which current replacement cost amounts exceed acquisition cost amounts, even if the firm does not clearly state the amounts of the difference this year. The difference in the two valuations would appear to materially affect total shareholders' equity, but largely because shareholders' equity is relatively small to begin with. It is unlikely that the borrowers' assessments of bankruptcy would change significantly with either valuation method. A related ethical issue is whether disclosure of the change in the notes is adequate or whether some more prominent reporting is appropriate.

CHAPTER 3

INCOME STATEMENT: REPORTING THE RESULTS OF OPERATING ACTIVITIES

Questions, Short Exercises, Exercises, Problems, and Cases: Answers and Solutions

3.1   See the text or the glossary at the end of the book.

3.2   Net income equals cash inflows minus cash outflows from operating, investing, and non-owner (that is, debt servicing) financing activities. If the period were long enough, then sales of goods and services (revenue under the accrual basis) and cash receipts from customers (revenue under the cash basis) would both occur in the same long-enough time period. Revenues would therefore not differ between the cash and accrual basis. Likewise, costs incurred to generated revenues (expenses under the accrual basis) and cash expenditures for goods and services consumed (expenses under the cash basis) would both occur in the same period. Expenses would also not differ between the cash and accrual basis. With the same amounts of revenues and expenses, net income on an accrual basis would equal net income on a cash basis.

3.3   The amount of revenue recognized equals the amount of cash the firm expects to collect from customers. The firm does not necessarily recognize the revenue, however, at the time it receives the cash. It typically recognizes revenue at the time of sale even though it has not yet collected cash from customers. Likewise, the amount of expense recognized equals the cash disbursement made for equipment, materials, labor, and so forth. However, the firm recognizes the expense when it consumes the services of these factor inputs, not when it makes the cash expenditure.

3.4   Revenues measure the inflow of net assets from operating activities and expenses measure the outflow of net assets consumed in the process of generating revenues. Thus, recognizing revenues and expenses always involves a simultaneous entry in an asset and/or liability account. Likewise, adjusting entries almost always involve an entry in at least one income statement and one balance sheet account.

3.5   Cost is the economic sacrifice made to acquire goods or services. When the good or service acquired has measurable future benefits to a firm, the cost is an unexpired cost, or an asset. When the firm consumes the good or service, the cost is an expired cost, or expense.

3.6   Accrual accounting attempts to relate inputs with outputs to obtain a measure of the economic value added by a firm's operating activities. Accrual accounting recognizes expenses in the same period as related revenues. Costs not closely related to particular revenues become expenses in the period when the firm consumes the services of assets in operations. Thus, expenses either match with particular revenues or with a particular accounting period.

3.7   Current accounting practice takes the viewpoint of shareholders by reporting the amount of net income available to shareholders after subtracting from revenues all expenses incurred in generating the revenue by claimants (for example, employees, lenders, governments) other than shareholders. Critics point out that funds provided by shareholders have a cost just as much as funds provided by lenders and accounting should subtract this cost as well in measuring net income.

3.8   Contra accounts provide disaggregated information concerning the net amount of an asset, liability, or shareholders' equity item. For example, the account, Property, Plant and Equipment net of Accumulated Depreciation, does not indicate separately the acquisition cost of fixed assets and the portion of that acquisition cost written off as depreciation since acquisition. If the firm used a contra account, it would have such information. The alternative to using contra accounts is to debit or credit directly the principal account involved (for example, Property, Plant and Equipment). This alternative procedure, however, does not permit computation of disaggregated information about the net balance in the account. Note that the use of contra accounts does not affect the total of assets, liabilities, shareholders' equity, revenues, or expenses, but only the balances in various accounts that comprise the totals for these items.

3.9   (Microsoft Corporation; analyzing changes in accounts receivable.) (Amounts in Millions)

Accounts Receivable, Beginning of Year 13	$ 5,129
Plus Sales on Account during Year 13	32,120
Less Cash Collections during Year 13	(?)
Accounts Receivable, End of Year 13	$ 5,196

Cash collections during Year 13 total $32,053 million.

3.10   (General Electric Company; analyzing changes in inventory.) (Amounts in Millions)

Inventory, Beginning of Year 12	$ 8,565
Plus Purchases or Production of Inventory during Year 12	?
Less Cost of Goods Sold for Year 12	(63,072)
Inventory, End of Year 12	$ 9,247

Purchases or production of inventory during Year 12 total $63,754 million.

3.11   (Ann Taylor Stores; analyzing changes in inventory and accounts payable.) (Amounts in Millions)

Inventory, Beginning of Year 13	$ 180.1
Plus Purchases of Inventory during Year 13	?
Less Cost of Goods Sold for Year 13	(633.5)
Inventory, End of Year 13	$ 185.5

Purchases during Year 13 total $638.9 million.

Accounts Payable, Beginning of Year 13	$ 52.0
Plus Purchases of Inventory on Account during Year 13 from above	638.9
Less Cash Payments to Suppliers during Year 13	(?)
Accounts Payable, End of Year 13	$ 57.1

Cash payments to suppliers during Year 13 total $633.8 million.

3.12   (AMR; analyzing changes in salaries payable.) (Amounts in Millions)

Salaries Payable, Beginning of Year 12	$ 721
Plus Salary Expense for Year 12	8,392
Less Cash Payments to Employees during Year 12	(?)
Salaries Payable, End of Year 12	$ 705

Cash payments to employees during Year 12 total $8,408 million.

3.13   (Johnson & Johnson; analyzing changes in retained earnings.) (Amounts in Millions)

Retained Earnings, Beginning of Year 12	$ 23,066
Plus Net Income for Year 12	?
Less Dividends Declared and Paid during Year 12	(3,092)
Retained Earnings, End of Year 12	$ 26,571

Net income for Year 12 totals $6,597 million.

3.14   (Gillette; computing interest expense.) (Amounts in Millions)

Interest expense for Year 12 is $3.75 million (= $250 x .06 x 3/12).

3.15   (Radio Shack; computing income tax expenses and income taxes paid.) (Amounts in Millions)

Income Taxes Payable, Beginning of Year 13	$ 78.1
Plus Income Tax Expense for Year 13 (.38 x $424.9)	161.5
Less Income Taxes Paid during Year 13	(?)
Income Taxes Payable, End of Year 13	$ 60.1

Income taxes paid during Year 13 total $179.5 million.

3.16   (Journal entry for prepaid rent.)

Prepaid Rent (Asset Increase).. 300
    Retained Earnings (Rent Expense) (Shareholders'
    Equity Increase)..   300

The required balance in the Prepaid Rent account on December 31, Year 12, is $1,500, which equals one-twelfth of the $18,000 payment for the period February 1, Year 12, through January 31, Year 13. The Prepaid Rent account had a balance of $1,200 on January 1, Year 12, and the firm made no entry affecting this account during Year 12. Thus, the entry above increases the balance from $1,200 to $1,500. The entry made on February 1, Year 12, decreased retained earnings (rent expense) by $18,000. Rent expense for Year 12 should be $17,700 [= $1,200 + (11/12 x $18,000)]. The entry above reduces the expenses (that is, increases retained earnings) from $18,000 to $17,700.

3.17   (Journal entry to correct recording error.)

Entry Made:
Retained Earnings (Equipment Expense) (Share-
    holders' Equity Decrease)... 20,000
    Cash (Asset Decrease)   20,000

Correct Entries:
Equipment (Asset Increase)... 20,000
    Cash (Asset Decrease)...   20,000

Retained Earnings (Depreciation Expense) (Share-
    holders' Equity Decrease) ($20,000/5)........................ 4,000
    Accumulated Depreciation (Asset Decrease)........   4,000

Correcting Entry:
Equipment (Asset Increase)... 20,000
Retained Earnings (Depreciation Expense) (Share-
    holders' Equity Decrease)... 4,000
    Retained Earnings (Equipment Expense) (Share-
    holders' Equity Increase).....................................   20,000
    Accumulated Depreciation (Asset Decrease).......   4,000

3.18   (Neiman Marcus; revenue recognition.)

	February	March	April
a.	--	--	$ 800
b.	--	$ 2,160	--
c.	$39,200	--	--
d.	--	$ 59,400	--
e.	--	$ 9,000	$ 9,000
f.	--	$ 9,000	$ 9,000

3.19   (Revenue recognition.)

a. No. (One might argue that receipt of the order and completion of manufacturing are sufficient to justify recognition of revenue. However, the purchaser may reject the T-shirts when received. Furthermore, the concert may not take place and the purchaser would fail to pay for the T-shirts.   Thus, sufficient uncertainties remain to justify delaying revenue recognition until at least the time of delivery.)

b. Yes (the firm has provided the services).

c. No (the baseball games will not take place until next year).

d. Yes (on an accrual basis, accounting recognizes interest as time passes).

e. No (accrual accounting usually recognizes revenue when a firm sells goods or services).

f. Yes (the agency has provided the services).

3.20   (Sun Microsystems; expense recognition.)

	June	July	August
a.	--	$ 15,000	$ 15,000
b.	$ 4,560	--	--
c.	--	$ 5,800	$ 6,300
d.	$ 600	$ 600	$ 600
e.	--	--	--
f.	--	--	$ 4,500
g.	$ 6,600	--	--

3.21   (Kroger Stores; expense recognition.)

    a. None (this is a September expense).

    b. $200 (= $12,000/60).

    c. $2,000 (= $24,000/12).

    d. $12,300 (= $2,900 + $12,900 − $3,500).

    e. $1,200 (the repair does not extend the life beyond that originally expected).

    f. None (the firm will include the deposit in the acquisition cost of the land).

    g. $10,000 (the firm includes the remaining $10,000 in prepaid rent).

3.22   (Corner Grocery Stores; journal entries for notes receivable and notes payable.)

    a. **Year 12**
       Dec. 1

Cash (Asset Increase)	100,000	
Notes Payable (Liability Increase)		100,000

       Dec. 31

Retained Earnings (Interest Expense) (Shareholders' Equity Decrease)	500	
Interest Payable (Liability Increase)		500

       $100,000 X .06 X 30/360.

       Year 13
       March 1

Note Payable (Liability Decrease)	100,000	
Interest Payable (Liability Decrease)	500	
Retained Earnings (Interest Expense) (Shareholders' Equity Decrease)	1,000	
Cash (Asset Decrease)		101,500

    b. **Year 12**
       Dec. 1

Notes Receivable (Asset Increase)	100,000	
Cash (Asset Decrease)		100,000

       Dec. 31

Interest Receivable (Asset Increase)	500	
Retained Earnings (Interest Revenue) (Shareholders' Equity Increase)		500

3.22 b. continued.

Year 13
March 1

Cash (Asset Increase)...	101,500	
Note Receivable (Asset Decrease).......................		100,000
Interest Receivable (Asset Decrease).................		500
Retained Earnings (Interest Revenue) (Share-holders' Equity Increase)...................................		1,000

3.23 (Dollar General; journal entries for inventories.) (Amounts in Millions)

Merchandise Inventories (Asset Increase)......................	4,368	
Accounts Payable (Liability Increase)........................		4,368

Retained Earnings (Cost of Goods Sold) (Shareholders' Equity Decrease)......................................	4,376	
Merchandise Inventories (Asset Decrease).............		4,376

$4,376 = $1,131 + $4,368 − $1,123.

Accounts Payable (Liability Decrease).........................	4,349	
Cash (Asset Decrease)..		4,349

$4,349 = $322 + $4,368 − $341.

3.24 (Eason Corporation; journal entries for insurance.)

September 1, Year 12

Prepaid Insurance (Asset Increase)..............................	3,600	
Cash (Asset Decrease)..		3,600

December 31, Year 12

Retained Earnings (Insurance Expense) (Share-holders' Equity Decrease).................................	1,200	
Prepaid Insurance (Asset Decrease).......................		1,200

September 1, Year 13

Prepaid Insurance (Asset Increase)..............................	4,800	
Cash (Asset Decrease)..		4,800

December 31, Year 13

Retained Earnings (Insurance Expense) (Share-holders' Equity Decrease).................................	4,000	
Prepaid Insurance (Asset Decrease).......................		4,000

$4,000 = ($3,600 \times 8/12) + ($4,800 \times 4/12).

3.25   (Effect of errors on financial statements.)

	Assets	Liabilities	Shareholders' Equity
a.	U/S $ 6,000	NO	U/S $ 6,000
b.	NO	U/S $ 1,200	O/S $ 1,200
c.	U/S $ 4,600	NO	U/S $ 4,600
d.	O/S $ 250	NO	O/S $ 250
e.	NO	U/S $ 1,500	O/S $ 1,500
f.	NO	O/S $11,600	U/S $11,600

3.26   (Forgetful Corporation; effect of recording errors on financial statements.)

Note: The actual and correct entries appear below to show the effect and amount of the errors, but are not required.

a. **Actual Entry:**

Cash (Asset Increase)...	1,400	
Retained Earnings (Sales Revenue) (Share-holders' Equity Increase)....................................		1,400

Correct Entry:

Cash (Asset Increase)...	1,400	
Advance from Customer (Liability Increase)......		1,400

Liabilities understated by $1,400 and shareholders' equity overstated by $1,400.

b. **Actual Entry:**

Retained Earnings (Cost of Goods Sold) (Share-holders' Equity Decrease)..	5,000	
Cash (Asset Decrease)...		5,000

Correct Entries:

Machine (Asset Increase)..	5,000	
Cash (Asset Decrease)..		5,000
Retained Earnings (Depreciation Expense) (Shareholders' Equity Decrease)..........................	500	
Accumulated Depreciation (Asset Decrease)..		500

Assets understated by $4,500 and shareholders' equity understated by $4,500.

c. **Actual Entry:**
None for accrued interest.

3.26 c. continued.

Correct Entry:

Interest Receivable (Asset Increase) ($2,000 x
.12 x 60/360).. 40

   Retained Earnings (Interest Revenue)
    (Shareholders' Equity Increase)..................... 40

Assets understated by $40 and shareholders' equity understated by $40.

d. The entry is correct as recorded.

e. **Actual Entry:**

None for declared dividend.

Correct Entry:

Retained Earnings (Dividend Declared) (Share-
holders' Equity Decrease)..................................... 1,500

   Dividend Payable (Liability Increase) 1,500

Liabilities understated by $1,500 and shareholders' equity overstated by $1,500.

f. **Actual Entries:**

Machinery (Asset Increase)..................................... 50,000

   Accounts Payable (Liability Increase)................ 50,000

Accounts Payable (Liability Decrease).................... 50,000

   Cash (Asset Decrease)... 49,000

   Retained Earnings (Miscellaneous Revenue)
    (Shareholders' Equity Increase) 1,000

Retained Earnings (Maintenance Expense)
(Shareholders' Equity Decrease).......................... 4,000

   Cash (Asset Decrease).. 4,000

Correct Entries:

Machinery (Asset Increase)..................................... 50,000

   Accounts Payable (Liability Increase)................ 50,000

Accounts Payable (Liability Decrease).................... 50,000

   Cash (Asset Decrease)... 49,000

   Machinery (Asset Decrease) 1,000

Machinery (Asset Increase)..................................... 4,000

   Cash (Asset Decrease).. 4,000

Assets understated by $3,000 and shareholders' equity understated by $3,000.

3.27   (Ailawadi Corporation; cash versus accrual basis of accounting.)

a. and b.

	a. Accrual Basis	b. Cash Basis
Sales Revenue	$ 69,500[a]	$ 61,200[b]
Less Expenses:		
Cost of Merchandise Sold	$ 43,200[c]	--
Payments on Merchandise Purchased	--	$ 44,800
Depreciation Expense	1,000[d]	--
Payments on Equipment Purchased	--	36,000
Utilities Expense	1,010[e]	750
Salaries Expense	4,760[f]	3,500
Rent Expense	3,000	6,000
Insurance Expense	100	1,200
Interest Expense	200[g]	--
Total Expenses	$(53,270)	$ (92,250)
Net Income (Loss)	$ 16,230	$ (31,050)

[a]$69,500 = $60,000 + $9,500.

[b]$61,200 = $60,000 + $1,200.

[c]$43,200 = $44,800 + $3,900 − $5,500.

[d]$1,000 = ($36,000/3)/12.

[e]$1,010 = $750 + $260.

[f]$4,760 = $3,500 + $1,260.

[g]$200 = (.06 x $40,000) x 30/360.

c.   The accrual basis of accounting provides superior measures of operating performance because it matches revenues generated from selling activities during January with the costs incurred in generating that revenue. Note that the capital contribution and bank loan do not give rise to revenue under either basis of accounting because they represent financing, not operating, activities.

3.28   (McKindly Consultants, Inc.; cash versus accrual basis of accounting.)

a. and b.

	a. Accrual Basis	b. Cash Basis
Consulting Revenue	$135,000	$109,000
Less Expenses:		
Rental Expense	$ 7,500	$ 7,500
Depreciation Expense	2,000[a]	--
Payments on Equipment Purchased	--	24,000
Utilities Expense	4,040[b]	3,460
Salaries Expense	109,800[c]	98,500
Supplies Expense	3,630[d]	2,790
Interest Expense	2,000[e]	--
Total Expenses	$128,970	$136,250
Net Income (Loss)	$ 6,030	$ (27,250)

[a]$2,000 = ($24,000/5) \times 5/12.$
[b]$4,040 = $3,460 + $580.
[c]$109,800 = $98,500 + $11,300.
[d]$3,630 = $2,790 + $840.
[e]$2,000 = ($60,000 \times .08) \times 5/12.$

c.   See the answer for Problem 3.27, Part c. above.

3.29   (Hansen Retail Store; preparing income statement and balance sheet using accrual basis.)

a.   **HANSEN RETAIL STORE**
                              Income Statement
                    For the Year Ended December 31, Year 8

Sales ($52,900 + $116,100)	$ 169,000
Cost of Goods Sold ($125,000 − $15,400)	(109,600)
Salary Expense ($34,200 + $2,400)	(36,600)
Utility Expense ($2,600 + $180)	(2,780)
Depreciation Expense ($60,000/30)	(2,000)
Interest Expense (.10 × $40,000)	(4,000)
Net Income before Income Taxes	$ 14,020
Income Taxes at 40 Percent	(5,608)
Net Income	$ 8,412

3.29 continued.

b.

HANSEN RETAIL STORE
Balance Sheet
December 31, Year 8

Assets

Cash ($50,000 + $40,000 – $60,000 – $97,400 + $52,900 + $54,800 – $34,200 – $2,600)	$ 3,500
Accounts Receivable ($116,100 – $54,800)	61,300
Inventories	15,400
Total Current Assets	$ 80,200
Building ($60,000 – $2,000)	58,000
Total Assets	$ 138,200

Liabilities and Shareholders' Equity

Accounts Payable ($125,000 – $97,400)	$ 27,600
Salaries Payable	2,400
Utilities Payable	180
Income Taxes Payable	5,608
Interest Payable	4,000
Loan Payable	40,000
Total Current Liabilities	$ 79,788
Common Stock	$ 50,000
Retained Earnings	8,412
Total Shareholders' Equity	$ 58,412
Total Liabilities and Shareholders' Equity	$ 138,200

3.30 (Miscellaneous transactions and adjusting entries.)

a. (1)

Accounts Payable (Liability Decrease)	6,000	
Notes Payable (Liability Increase)		6,000

(2)

Retained Earnings (Interest Expense) (Shareholders' Equity Decrease)	50	
Interest Payable (Liability Increase)		50

[$6,000 x .10 x (30/360)] = $50.

b. (1)

Cash (Asset Increase)	18,000	
Advances from Customers (Liability Increase)		18,000

(2)

Advances from Customers (Liability Decrease)	3,000	
Retained Earnings (Insurance Revenue) (Shareholders' Equity Increase)		3,000

($18,000 x 4/24) = $3,000.

3.30 continued.

   c. (1) Equipment (Asset Increase) 40,000
                 Cash (Asset Decrease) 40,000

       (2) Retained Earnings (Depreciation Expense)
            (Shareholders' Equity Decrease)................. 2,250
                 Accumulated Depreciation (Asset De-
                    crease).. 2,250
            [.25($40,000 − $4,000)/4].

   d. (1) Automobile (Asset Increase)........................... 24,000
                 Cash (Asset Decrease) 24,000

       (2) Retained Earnings (Depreciation Expense)
            (Shareholders' Equity Decrease)................. 3,500
                 Accumulated Depreciation (Asset De-
                    crease).. 3,500
            .5 × [($24,000 − $3,000)/3] = $3,500.

   e. (1) Prepaid Rent (Asset Increase)........................ 12,000
                 Cash (Asset Decrease) 12,000

       (2) Retained Earnings (Rent Expense) (Share-
            holders' Equity Decrease)............................ 4,000
                 Prepaid Rent (Asset Decrease)................. 4,000

   f. (1) Office Supplies Inventory (Asset Increase).... 7,000
                 Accounts Payable (Liability Increase)........ 7,000

       (2) Accounts Payable (Liability Decrease)............ 5,000
                 Cash (Asset Decrease) 5,000

       (3) Retained Earnings (Office Supplies Expense)
            (Shareholders' Equity Decrease)................. 5,500
                 Office Supplies Inventory (Asset De-
                    crease).. 5,500
            ($7,000 − $1,500) = $5,500.

3.31   (Miscellaneous transactions and adjusting entries.)

   a. (1) Cash (Asset Increase)...................................... 48,000
                 Rental Fees Received in Advance (Liabil-
                   ity Increase)... 48,000

       (2) Rental Fees Received in Advance (Liability
            Decrease)... 12,000
                 Retained Earnings (Rent Revenue)
                   (Shareholders' Equity Increase).......... 12,000

3.31 continued.

b. (1) Notes Receivable (Asset Increase).................. 10,000

Accounts Receivable (Asset Decrease)....... 10,000

(2) Interest Receivable (Asset Increase).............. 50

Retained Earnings (Interest Revenue)
(Shareholders' Equity Increase) 50

$10,000 x .06 x 30/360 = $50.

c. (1) Prepaid Insurance (Asset Increase)................. 6,600

Cash (Asset Decrease) 6,600

(2) Retained Earnings (Insurance Expense)
(Shareholders' Equity Decrease)................. 3,250

Prepaid Insurance (Asset Decrease)....... 3,250

$500 + ($6,600 x 10/24) = $3,250.

Alternate entries for Part c. are:

(1) Retained Earnings (Insurance Expense)
(Shareholders' Equity Decrease)................. 500

Prepaid Insurance ($6,600 – $500) (Asset
Increase)... 6,100

Cash (Asset Decrease).............................. 6,600

(2) Retained Earnings (Insurance Expense)
(Shareholders' Equity Decrease)................. 2,750

Prepaid Insurance (Asset Decrease)....... 2,750

$6,600 x 10/24 = $2,750.

d. (1) Retained Earnings (Repair Expense) (Shareholders' Equity Decrease)............................ 14,900

Cash (Asset Decrease)............................... 14,900

(2) Retained Earnings (Repair Expense) (Shareholders' Equity Decrease)............................ 200

Repair Parts Inventory (Asset De-
crease)... 200

e. (1) Equipment (Asset Increase) 200,000

Cash (Asset Decrease) 200,000

(2) Retained Earnings (Depreciation Expense)
(Shareholders' Equity Decrease)................. 9,000

Accumulated Depreciation (Asset De-
crease)... 9,000

($200,000 – $20,000) x .5/10.

3.31 continued.

    f. (1) Retained Earnings (Property Tax Expense)
                 (Shareholders' Equity Decrease).................. 12,000
                     Cash (Asset Decrease)............................   12,000

       (2) No adjusting entry required because the full amount paid is an expense for Year 3.

3.32   (Moulton Corporation; spreadsheet analysis of transactions and preparation of income statement and balance sheet.)

    a. See following page for the transactions spreadsheet.

    b.

MOULTON CORPORATIION
Income Statement
For Year 13

Sales Revenue..	$ 2,000,000
Expenses:	
Cost of Goods Sold...	$ 1,200,000
Selling and Administrative Expenses	625,000
Insurance...	12,000
Depreciation..	34,000
Interest ($2,400 + $24,000)......................................	26,400
Total Expenses..	$ 1,897,400
Net Income before Income Taxes	$ 102,600
Income Tax Expense at 40 Percent................................	(41,040)
Net Income	$ 61,560

3.32 (Moulton Corporation; spreadsheet analysis of transactions and preparation of income statement and balance sheet.)

a. Transactions spreadsheet.

Balance Sheet Accounts	Balance: Beginning of Period	Transactions, By Number and Description											Balance: End of Period
		Acquire Inventory on Account	Sell Inventory on Account	Recog. COGS	Collect Accts. Rec.	Pay Accts. Pay.	Pay S&A Expenses	Repay Note Payable	Recog. Int. on Bank Loan	Recog. Insur. Expired	Recog. Depre.	Recog. Inc. Tax Exp.	
		1	2	3	4	5	6	7	8	9	10	11	
ASSETS													
Current Assets:													
Cash	343,000				1,400,000	-950,000	-625,000	-82,400					85,600
Accounts Receivable			2,000,000		-1,400,000								600,000
Inventory	275,000	1,100,000		-1,200,000									175,000
Prepaid Insurance	12,000									-12,000			0
Total Current Assets	630,000												860,600
Noncurrent Assets:													
Land	50,000												50,000
Building	450,000												450,000
Equipment	80,000												80,000
Accumulated Depreciation											-34,000		(34,000)
Total Noncurrent Assets	580,000												546,000
Total Assets	1,210,000												1,406,600
LIABILITIES AND SHARE-HOLDERS' EQUITY													
Current Liabilities:													
Accounts Payable	30,000	1,100,000				-950,000							180,000
Note Payable	80,000							-80,000					-
Interest Payable									24,000				24,000
Income Tax Payable												41,040	41,040
Total Current Liabilities	110,000												245,040
Noncurrent Liabilities:													
Loan Payable	300,000												300,000
Total Noncurrent Liabilities	300,000												300,000
Total Liabilities	410,000												545,040
Shareholders' Equity:													
Common Stock	800,000												800,000
Retained Earnings			2,000,000	-1,200,000			-625,000	-2,400	-24,000	-12,000	-34,000	-41,040	61,560
Total Shareholders' Equity	800,000												861,560
Total Liabilities and Shareholders' Equity	1,210,000												1,406,600
Imbalance, if Any	-	-	-	-	-	-	-	-	-	-	-	-	-
Income Statement Accounts			Sales Rev.	COGS			S&A Exp.	Int. Exp.	Int. Exp.	Insur. Exp.	Depre. Exp.	Inc Tax Exp.	

3.32 continued.

c.

MOULTON CORPORATION
Comparative Balance Sheet

	December 31, Year 12	December 31, Year 13
Assets		
Cash	$ 343,000	$ 85,600
Accounts Receivable	0	600,000
Inventories	275,000	175,000
Prepaid Insurance	12,000	0
Total Current Assets	$ 630,000	$ 860,600
Land (at Cost)	$ 50,000	$ 50,000
Building	450,000	450,000
Equipment	80,000	$ 80,000
Less Accumulated Depreciation	0	(34,000)
Land, Building, and Equipment (Net)	$ 580,000	$ 546,000
Total Assets	$1,210,000	$1,406,600
Liabilities and Shareholders' Equity		
Accounts Payable	$ 30,000	$ 180,000
Notes Payable	80,000	0
Interest Payable	0	24,000
Income Tax Payable	0	41,040
Total Current Liabilities	$ 110,000	$ 245,040
Loan Payable	300,000	300,000
Total Liabilities	$ 410,000	$ 545,040
Common Stock	$ 800,000	$ 800,000
Retained Earnings	0	61,560
Total Shareholders' Equity	$ 800,000	$ 861,560
Total Liabilities and Shareholders' Equity	$1,210,000	$1,406,600

3.33 (Regaldo Department Stores; spreadsheet analysis of transactions and preparation of income statement and balance sheet.)

a. Transactions spreadsheet.

Transactions, By Number and Description

Balance Sheet Accounts	Balance: Beginning of Period	1 Purchase Equip. with Loan	2 Acquire Merchan. On Acct.	3a Sell Mer. For Cash & on Acct.	3b Recog. COGS	4 Paid Compen. To Emp.	5 Paid Utilities	6 Collects Accts. Rec.	7a Pay Accts. Pay. With Discount	7b Pay Accts. Pay. W/O Discount	8 Recog. Unpaid Comp. Exp.	9 Recog. Unpaid Util. Exp.	10 Recog. Depre. Exp.	11 Recog. Rent Exp.	12 Recog. Insur. Exp.	13 Recog. Patent Amort.	14 Recog. Int. Exp.	15 Recog. Inc. Tax Exp.	Balance: End of Period
ASSETS																			
Current Assets:																			
Cash	247,200			62,900		-32,400	-2,700	84,600	-205,800	-29,000									124,800
Accounts Receivable				194,600				-84,600											110,000
Merchandise Inventories	188,800		217,900		-162,400				-4,200										240,100
Prepaid Rent	60,000													-30,000					30,000
Prepaid Insurance	12,000														-1,000				11,000
Total Current Assets	508,000																		515,900
Noncurrent Assets:																			
Equipment		90,000																	90,000
Accumulated Depreciation													-1,500						(1,500)
Patent	24,000															-400			23,600
Total Noncurrent Assets	24,000																		112,100
Total Assets	532,000																		628,000
LIABILITIES AND SHARE-HOLDERS' EQUITY																			
Current Liabilities:																			
Accounts Payable	32,000		217,900						-210,000	-29,000									10,900
Note Payable		90,000																	90,000
Compensation Payable											6,700								6,700
Utilities Payable												800							800
Interest Payable																	900		900
Income Tax Payable																		5,610	5,610
Total Current Liabilities	32,000																		114,910
Noncurrent Liabilities:																			
Total Noncurrent Liabilities																			-
Total Liabilities	32,000																		114,910
Shareholders' Equity:																			
Common Stock	500,000																		500,000
Retained Earnings				257,500	-162,400	-32,400	-2,700				-6,700	-800	-1,500	-30,000	-1,000	-400	-900	-5,610	13,090
Total Shareholders' Equity	500,000																		513,090
Total Liabilities and Shareholders' Equity	532,000																		628,000
Imbalance, if Any	-																		-
Income Statement Accounts				Sales Rev.	COGS	Comp. Exp.	Utility Exp.				Comp. Exp.	Utility Exp.	Depre. Exp.	Rent Exp.	Insur. Exp.	Amort. Exp.	Int. Exp.	Income Tax Exp.	

3.33 continued.

b.

REGALDO DEPARTMENT STORES
Income Statement
For the Month of February Year 8

Sales Revenue	Ps257,500
Expenses:	
Cost of Goods Sold	Ps162,400
Compensation (Ps32,400 + Ps6,700)	39,100
Utilities (Ps2,700 + Ps800)	3,500
Depreciation	1,500
Rent	30,000
Insurance	1,000
Patent Amortization	400
Interest	900
Total Expenses	Ps238,800
Net Income before Income Taxes	Ps 18,700
Income Tax Expense at 30 Percent	(5,610)
Net Income	Ps 13,090

3.33 continued.

c.

REGALDO DEPARTMENT STORES
Comparative Balance Sheet

	January 31, Year 8	February 28, Year 8
Assets		
Cash	Ps 247,200	Ps 124,800
Accounts Receivable	0	110,000
Inventories	188,800	240,100
Prepaid Rent	60,000	30,000
Prepaid Insurance	12,000	11,000
Total Current Assets	Ps 508,000	Ps 515,900
Equipment (at Cost)	Ps 0	Ps 90,000
Less Accumulated Depreciation	0	(1,500)
Equipment (Net)	Ps 0	Ps 88,500
Patent	24,000	23,600
Total Noncurrent Assets	Ps 24,000	Ps 112,100
Total Assets	Ps 532,000	Ps 628,000

Liabilities and Shareholders' Equity

	January 31, Year 8	February 28, Year 8
Accounts Payable	Ps 32,000	Ps 10,900
Notes Payable	0	90,000
Compensation Payable	0	6,700
Utilities Payable	0	800
Interest Payable	0	900
Income Tax Payable	0	5,610
Total Liabilities	Ps 32,000	Ps 114,910
Common Stock	Ps 500,000	Ps 500,000
Retained Earnings	0	13,090
Total Shareholders' Equity	Ps 500,000	Ps 513,090
Total Liabilities and Shareholders' Equity	Ps 532,000	Ps 628,000

a. Transactions spreadsheet.

Balance Sheet Accounts	Balance: Beginning of Period	1 Pays Insur. Premium	2 Acquire Mer. Inv. On Acct	3 Sell Mer. Inv. On Acct	4 Recog. COGS	5 Pays S&A Exp.	6 Collect Cash from Cust.	7 Pays Sup. For Pur. On Acct	8 Recog. Rent Exp.	9 Recog. Depre. Exp.	10 Recog. Patent Amort.	11 Recog. Insur. Exp.	12 Recog. Int. Exp.	13 Recog. Inc. Tax Exp.	Balance: End of Period
ASSETS															
Current Assets:															
Cash	47,150	-2,400				-235,000	1,206,000	-710,000							305,750
Marketable Securities	95,000														95,000
Accounts Receivable				1,495,500			-1,206,000								289,500
Receivable from Supplier	1,455		-1,455												-
Merchandise Inventories	70,945		1,050,000		-950,000										170,945
Prepaid Rent	1,400								-1,400						-
Prepaid Insurance		2,400										-100			2,300
Total Current Assets	215,950														863,495
Noncurrent Assets:															
Land	80,000														80,000
Building	280,000														280,000
Equipment	97,750														97,750
Accumulated Depreciation										-2,500					(2,500)
Patent	28,000										-450				27,550
Total Noncurrent Assets	485,750														482,800
Total Assets	701,700														1,346,295
LIABILITIES AND SHAREHOLDERS' EQUITY															
Current Liabilities:															
Accounts Payable	14,200		1,048,545	-4,500				-710,000							352,745
Advance from Customer	4,500			-4,500											-
Interest Payable													265		265
Income Tax Payable														124,114	124,114
Total Current Liabilities	18,700														477,124
Noncurrent Liabilities:															
Mortgage Payable	53,000														53,000
Total Noncurrent Liabilities	53,000														53,000
Total Liabilities	71,700														530,124
Shareholders' Equity:															
Common Stock	450,000														450,000
Additional Paid-in Capital	180,000														180,000
Retained Earnings [Insert Rows as Needed]				1,500,000	-950,000	-235,000			-1,400	-2,500	-450	-100	-265	-124,114	186,171
Total Shareholders' Equity	630,000														816,171
Total Liabilities and Shareholders' Equity	701,700														1,346,295
Imbalance, If Any	-	-	-	-	-	-	-	-					-	-	-
Income Statement Accounts				Sales Rev.	COGS	S&A Exp.			Rent Exp.	Depre Exp.	Amort. Exp.	Insur. Exp.	Int. Exp.	Inc. Tax Exp.	

Transactions, By Number and Description

3.34 continued.

b.

PATTERSON CORPORATIION
Income Statement
For the Month of February, Year 13

Sales Revenue	$ 1,500,000
Expenses:	
Cost of Goods Sold	$ 950,000
Selling and Administrative Expenses	235,000
Rent	1,400
Depreciation	2,500
Amortization	450
Insurance	100
Interest	265
Total Expenses	$ 1,189,715
Net Income before Income Taxes	$ 310,285
Income Tax Expense at 40 Percent	(124,114)
Net Income	$ 186,171

3.34 continued.

c.

PATTERSON CORPORATION
Comparative Balance Sheet

	January 31, Year 13	February 28, Year 13
Assets		
Cash	$ 47,150	$ 305,750
Marketable Securities	95,000	95,000
Accounts Receivable	0	289,500
Receivable from Supplier	1,455	0
Merchandise Inventories	70,945	170,945
Prepaid Rent	1,400	0
Prepaid Insurance	0	2,300
Total Current Assets	$ 215,950	$ 863,495
Land (at Cost)	$ 80,000	$ 80,000
Building (at Cost)	280,000	280,000
Equipment (at Cost)	97,750	$ 97,750
Less Accumulated Depreciation	0	(2,500)
Land, Building, and Equipment (Net)	$ 457,750	$ 455,250
Patent (Net)	28,000	27,550
Total Noncurrent Assets	$ 485,750	$ 482,800
Total Assets	$ 701,700	$1,346,295

Liabilities and Shareholders' Equity

	January 31, Year 13	February 28, Year 13
Accounts Payable	$ 14,200	$ 352,745
Advance from Customers	4,500	0
Interest Payable	0	265
Income Tax Payable	0	124,114
Total Current Liabilities	$ 18,700	$ 477,124
Mortgage Payable	53,000	53,000
Total Liabilities	$ 71,700	$ 530,124
Common Stock	$ 450,000	$ 450,000
Additional Paid-In Capital	180,000	180,000
Retained Earnings	0	186,171
Total Shareholders' Equity	$ 630,000	$ 816,171
Total Liabilities and Shareholders' Equity	$ 701,700	$1,346,295

3.35 (Zealock Bookstore; spreadsheet analysis of transactions and preparation of income statement and balance sheet.)

a. Transactions spreadsheet.

Transactions, By Number and Description

Balance Sheet Accounts	Balance: Beginning of Period	1 Issue Common Stock for Cash	2 Obtain Bank Loan for Cash	3 Pay Rent in Advance	4 Acquire Book-shelves for Cash	5 Acquire Computers for Cash	6 Make Deposit with Supplier	7 Pur. Books on Acct.	8a Sell Books for Cash and on Acct.	8b Recog. COGS	9 Return Unsold Books	10 Collect Cash from Credit Sales	11 Pay Compensation to Emp.	12 Pay Sup. For Pur. On Acct.	13 Receive Adv. From Cust.	14 Recog. Int Exp.	15 Recog. Rent Exp.	16 Recog. Depre. On Book-shelves	17 Recog. Depre. On Comp.	18 Recog. Inc. Tax Exp.	Balance: End of Period
ASSETS																					
Current Assets:																					
Cash		25,000	30,000	-20,000	-4,000	-10,000	-8,000		24,600			142,400	-16,700	-139,800	850						24,350
Accounts Receivable									148,200			-142,400									5,800
Merchandise Inventories								160,000		-140,000	-14,600										5,400
Prepaid Rent				20,000													-10,000				10,000
Deposit with Suppliers							8,000														8,000
Total Current Assets																					53,550
Noncurrent Assets:																					
Equipment					4,000	10,000															14,000
Accumulated Depreciation																		-400	-1,500		(1,900)
Total Noncurrent Assets																					12,100
Total Assets																					65,650
LIABILITIES AND SHAREHOLDERS' EQUITY																					
Current Liabilities:																					
Accounts Payable								160,000			-14,600			-139,800							5,600
Note Payable			30,000																		30,000
Advances from Customers															850						850
Interest Payable																900					900
Income Tax Payable																				1,320	1,320
Total Current Liabilities																					38,670
Noncurrent Liabilities:																					
Total Noncurrent Liabilities																					-
Total Liabilities																					38,670
Shareholders' Equity:																					
Common Stock		25,000																			25,000
Retained Earnings																					1,980
Total Shareholders' Equity																					26,980
Total Liabilities and Shareholders' Equity																					65,650
Imbalance, if Any	-	-	-	-	-	-	-	-	-	-	-	-	-	-	-	-	-	-	-	-	-
Income Statement Accounts									172,800 Sales Rev.	-140,000 COGS			-16,700 Comp. Exp.			-900 Int. Exp.	-10,000 Rent Exp.	-400 Depre. Exp.	-1,500 Depre. Exp.	-1,320 Inc. Tax Exp.	

3.35 continued.

b.

ZEALOCK BOOKSTORE
Income Statement
For the Six Months Ending December 31, Year 10

Sales Revenue	$ 172,800
Less Expenses:	
Cost of Goods Sold	$ 140,000
Compensation Expense	16,700
Interest Expense	900
Rent Expense	10,000
Depreciation Expense	1,900
Income Tax Expense	1,320
Total Expenses	$ 170,820
Net Income	$ 1,980

c.

ZEALOCK BOOKSTORE
Balance Sheet
December 31, Year 10

Assets

Current Assets:	
Cash	$ 24,350
Accounts Receivable	5,800
Merchandise Inventories	5,400
Prepaid Rent	10,000
Deposit with Suppliers	8,000
Total Current Assets	$ 53,550
Equipment	$ 14,000
Less Accumulated Depreciation	(1,900)
Equipment (Net)	$ 12,100
Total Assets	$ 65,650

3.35 c. continued.

Liabilities and Shareholders' Equity

Current Liabilities:	
Accounts Payable	$ 5,600
Note Payable	30,000
Advances from Customers	850
Interest Payable	900
Income Tax Payable	1,320
Total Current Liabilities	$ 38,670
Shareholders' Equity:	
Common Stock	$ 25,000
Retained Earnings	1,980
Total Shareholders' Equity	$ 26,980
Total Liabilities and Shareholders' Equity	$ 65,650

d. Net income was positive, which is unusual for a new business in its first year. The profit margin, however, is only 1.1 percent (= $1,980/$172,800). This small margin does not leave much room for unexpected events. Current Assets exceed Current Liabilities by a comfortable margin. The firm sells its inventory quickly and collects its accounts receivable soon after sale. It must also pay its suppliers quickly.

3.36 (Zealock Bookstore; spreadsheet analysis of transactions and preparation of comparative income statements and balance sheets)

a. Transactions spreadsheet.

Transactions, By Number and Description

Balance Sheet Accounts	Balance: Beginning of Period	1 Pay Yr. 10 Inc. Tax	2 Repay Bank Loan with Int.	3 Obtain Bank Loan	4 Rec. Refund of Sec. Dep.	5 Pay Annual Rent	6 Pur. Books on Acct.	7a Sells Books for Cash and on Acct.	7b Recog. COGS	8 Return Unsold Books	9 Collect Cash from Credit Sales	10 Pay Emp. Compen.	11 Pay Sup.	12 Dec. and Pay Div.	13 Rec. Int. Exp.	14 Recog. Rent Exp.	15 Recog. Depre. On Book-shelves	16 Recog. Depre. On Comp.	17 Recog. Inc. Tax Exp.	Balance: End of Period
ASSETS																				
Current Assets:																				
Cash	24,350	-1,320	-31,800	75,000	8,000	-20,000		24,900			320,600	-29,400	-281,100	-4,000						85,230
Accounts Receivable	5,800							327,950			-320,600									13,150
Merchandise Inventories	5,400						310,000		-286,400	-22,700										6,300
Prepaid Rent	10,000					20,000										-20,000				10,000
Deposit with Suppliers	8,000				-8,000															
Total Current Assets	53,550																			114,680
Noncurrent Assets:																				
Equipment	14,000																			14,000
Accumulated Depreciation	-1,900																-800	-3,000		(5,700)
Total Noncurrent Assets	12,100																			8,300
Total Assets	65,650																			122,980
LIABILITIES AND SHARE-HOLDERS' EQUITY																				
Current Liabilities:																				
Accounts Payable	5,600						310,000			-22,700			-281,100							11,800
Note Payable	30,000		-30,000	75,000																75,000
Advances from Customers	850							-850												-
Interest Payable	900		-900												3,000					3,000
Income Tax Payable	1,320	-1,320																	4,080	4,080
Total Current Liabilities	38,670																			93,880
Noncurrent Liabilities:																				
Total Noncurrent Liabilities	-																			-
Total Liabilities	38,670																			93,880
Shareholders' Equity:																				
Common Stock	25,000																			25,000
Retained Earnings	1,980							353,700	-286,400			-29,400		-4,000	-3,000	-20,000	-800	-3,000	-4,080	4,100
Total Shareholders' Equity	26,980																			29,100
Total Liabilities and Shareholders' Equity	65,650																			122,980
Imbalance, If Any	-	-	-	-	-	-	-	-	-	-	-	-	-	-	-	-	-	-	-	-
Income Statement Accounts		Int. Exp.	Int. Exp.					Sales Rev.	COGS			Comp. Exp.			Int. Exp.	Rent Exp.	Depre. Exp.	Depre. Exp.	Inc. Tax Exp.	

3-27

Solutions

3.36 continued.

b.

ZEALOCK BOOKSTORE
Comparative Income Statement
For Year 10 and Year 11

	Year 10	Year 11
Sales Revenue	$172,800	$353,700
Less Expenses:		
Cost of Goods Sold	$140,000	$286,400
Compensation Expense	16,700	29,400
Interest Expense	900	3,900
Rent Expense	10,000	20,000
Depreciation Expense	1,900	3,800
Income Tax Expense	1,320	4,080
Total Expenses	$170,820	$347,580
Net Income	$ 1,980	$ 6,120

c.

ZEALOCK BOOKSTORE
Comparative Balance Sheet
December 31, Year 10 and Year 11

	Year 10	Year 11
Assets		
Current Assets:		
Cash	$ 24,350	$ 85,230
Accounts Receivable	5,800	13,150
Merchandise Inventories	5,400	6,300
Prepaid Rent	10,000	10,000
Deposit with Suppliers	8,000	--
Total Current Assets	$ 53,550	$114,680
Noncurrent Assets:		
Equipment	$ 14,000	$ 14,000
Less Accumulated Depreciation	(1,900)	(5,700)
Equipment (Net)	$ 12,100	$ 8,300
Total Assets	$ 65,650	$122,980

3.36 c. continued.

Liabilities and Shareholders' Equity

Current Liabilities:		
Accounts Payable	$ 5,600	$ 11,800
Note Payable	30,000	75,000
Advances from Customers	850	--
Interest Payable	900	3,000
Income Tax Payable	1,320	4,080
Total Current Liabilities	$ 38,670	$ 93,880
Shareholders' Equity:		
Common Stock	$ 25,000	$ 25,000
Retained Earnings	1,980	4,100
Total Shareholders' Equity	$ 26,980	$ 29,100
Total Liabilities and Shareholders' Equity	$ 65,650	$ 122,980

d. Schedule 1 of this solution presents selected financial ratios for Zealock Bookstore. The profit margin percentage increased slightly. The principal driver was a decrease in the compensation expense to sales percentage. The bookstore must have employees operating the store regardless of the number of books sold. Sales more than doubled between the six-month period in Year 10 and the 12-month period in Year 11. Compensation did not increase proportionally, suggesting the benefits of spreading relatively fixed costs over a larger sales base. The interest expense to revenues percentage increased because of the larger amount of debt and larger interest rate. The income tax expense to sales percentage increased because of higher pre-tax profitability. The income tax rate was 40 percent in both years.

The current ratio declined, although it is still at a healthy level. The proportion of liabilities in the capital structure increased significantly. It appears that Zealock Bookstore may have taken on more short-term borrowing than it needed. Inventories did not increase as fast as sales. Thus, the firm collected cash more quickly in Year 11 than in Year 10 and may not have needed as much financing as it obtained.

3.36 d. continued.

SCHEDULE 1
Financial Ratios for Zealock Bookstore

	Year 10	Year 11
Sales	100.0%	100.0%
Cost of Goods Sold	(81.0)	(81.0)
Compensation Expense	(9.7)	(8.3)
Interest Expense	(.5)	(1.1)
Rent Expense	(5.8)	(5.7)
Depreciation Expense	(1.1)	(1.1)
Income Tax Expense	(.8)	(1.1)
Net Income	1.1%	1.7%
Current Assets/Current Liabilities	1.4	1.2
Liabilities/(Liabilities + Shareholders' Equity)	58.9%	76.3%

3.37 (Prima Company; working backwards to balance sheet at beginning of the period.) Transactions spreadsheet.

Balance Sheet Accounts	Balance: Beginning of Period	Recog. Sales Rev. (1)	Acct. Rec. Collected (2)	Recog. Pur. Of Merchn. (3)	Recog. COGS (4)	Recog. Cash Pay. To Supp. (5)	Recog. Depre. Exp. (6)	Recog. Tax Exp. (7)	Recog. Tax Paid (8)	Recog. Prepay. Made (9)	Recog. Oper. Exp. (10)	Recog. Int. Exp. (11)	Recog. Int. Paid (12)	Recog. Div. Dec. and Paid (13)	Record Mkt. Sec. Pur. (14)	Balance: End of Period
ASSETS																
Current Assets:																
Cash	11,700	47,000	150,000			-128,000			-7,500	-49,000			-1,200	-5,000	-8,000	10,000
Marketable Securities	12,000														8,000	20,000
Accounts Receivable	22,000	153,000	-150,000													25,000
Merchandise Inventory	33,000			127,000	-130,000											30,000
Prepayments for Miscellaneous Ser.	1,700									49,000	-47,700					3,000
Total Current Assets	80,400															88,000
Noncurrent Assets:																
Land, Building, & Equip.	40,000															40,000
Accumulated Depreciation	-12,000						-4,000									(16,000)
Total Noncurrent Assets	28,000															24,000
Total Assets	108,400															112,000
LIABILITIES AND SHAREHOLDERS' EQUITY																
Current Liabilities:																
Accounts Payable	26,000			127,000		-128,000										25,000
Interest Payable	300											1,200	-1,200			300
Taxes Payable	3,500							8,000	-7,500							4,000
Total Current Liabilities	29,800															29,300
Noncurrent Liabilities:																
Note Payable	20,000															20,000
Total Noncurrent Liabilities	20,000															20,000
Total Liabilities	49,800															49,300
Shareholders' Equity:																
Common Stock	50,000															50,000
Retained Earnings	8,600	200,000			-130,000		-4,000	-8,000			-47,700	-1,200		-5,000		12,700
Total Shareholders' Equity	58,600															62,700
Total Liabilities and Shareholders' Equity	108,400															112,000
Imbalance, If Any	-	-	-	-	-	-	-	-	-	-	-	-	-	-	-	-
Income Statement Accounts		Sales Rev.			COGS		Depre. Exp.	Tax Exp.			Ot. Op. Exp.	Int. Exp.				

Transactions, By Number and Description

3-31

Solutions

3.37 continued.

PRIMA COMPANY
Balance Sheet
As of January 1, Year 2

Assets

Cash...		$ 11,700
Marketable Securities....................................		12,000
Accounts Receivable.......................................		22,000
Merchandise Inventory...................................		33,000
Prepayments		1,700
Total Current Assets.................................		$ 80,400
Land, Buildings, and Equipment	$ 40,000	
Less Accumulated Depreciation.........................	(12,000)	28,000
Total Assets...		$ 108,400

Liabilities and Shareholders' Equity

Accounts Payable.......................................	$ 26,000
Interest Payable	300
Taxes Payable	3,500
Total Current Liabilities...........................	$ 29,800
Notes Payable (6 Percent)...........................	20,000
Total Liabilities	$ 49,800
Capital Stock..	$ 50,000
Retained Earnings	8,600
Total Shareholders' Equity	$ 58,600
Total Liabilities and Shareholders' Equity.....	$ 108,400

3.38 (The Secunda Company; working backwards to cash receipts and disbursements.) Transactions spreadsheet.

Balance Sheet Accounts	Balance: Beginning of Period	(1) Recog. Sales on Acct.	(2) Cash Collect. From Cus.	(3) Recog. COGS	(4) Pur. Of Mer. On Acct.	(5) Cash Pay. For Merchn.	(6) Recog. Int. Exp.	(7) Int. Paid	(8) Recog. Depre. Exp.	(8) Recog. Of Oper. Exp.	(9) Cash Paid for Prepay.	(10) Recog. Mort. Paid	(11) Recog. Div. Dec. & Paid	(12) Check on Ending Bal. Sheet Amts.	Balance: End of Period
ASSETS															
Current Assets:															
Cash	20,000		85,000			-55,000		-2,000			-26,000	-3,000	-10,000	9,000	9,000
Accounts Receivable	36,000	100,000	-85,000											51,000	51,000
Merchandise Inventory	45,000			-50,000	65,000									60,000	60,000
Prepayments	2,000									-27,000	26,000			1,000	1,000
Total Current Assets	103,000													121,000	121,000
Noncurrent Assets:															
Land, Buildings, & Equip.	40,000													40,000	40,000
Accumulated Depreciation	-16,000								-2,000					-18,000	(18,000)
Total Noncurrent Assets	24,000													22,000	22,000
Total Assets	127,000													143,000	143,000
LIABILITIES AND SHARE-HOLDERS' EQUITY															
Current Liabilities:															
Interest Payable	1,000						3,000	-2,000						2,000	2,000
Accounts Payable	30,000				65,000	-55,000								40,000	40,000
Total Current Liabilities	31,000													42,000	42,000
Noncurrent Liabilities:															
Mortgage Payable	20,000											-3,000		17,000	17,000
Total Noncurrent Liabilities	20,000													17,000	17,000
Total Liabilities	51,000													59,000	59,000
Shareholders' Equity:															
Common Stock	50,000													50,000	50,000
Retained Earnings	26,000	100,000		-50,000			-3,000		-2,000	-27,000			-10,000	34,000	34,000
Total Shareholders' Equity	76,000													84,000	84,000
Total Liabilities and Shareholders' Equity	127,000													143,000	143,000
Imbalance, if Any	-	-	-	-	-	-	-	-	-	-	-	-	-	-	-
Income Statement Accounts		Sales Rev.		COGS			Int. Exp.		Ot. Oper. Exp.	Ot. Oper. Exp.					

3-33

3.38 continued.

SECUNDA COMPANY
Cash Receipts and Disbursements Schedule

Receipts:		
Collections from Customers...........................		$85,000
Disbursements:		
Suppliers of Merchandise and Other Services..	$81,000	
Mortgage..	3,000	
Dividends	10,000	
Interest...	2,000	
Total Disbursements.............................		96,000
Decrease in Cash		$11,000
Cash Balance, January 1...................................		20,000
Cash Balance, December 31		$ 9,000

3.39 (Tertia Company; working backwards to income statements.) Transactions spreadsheet.

Transactions, By Number and Description

Balance Sheet Accounts	Balance: Beginning of Period	1 Collect. From Credit Cust.	2 Recog. Sales Rev.	3 Collect. Of Interest	Recog. Int. Rev.	4 Pay. To Sup. Of Merchn.	5 Pur. Of Merchn.	6 Recog. COGS	7 Repay. Of Mort.	8 Pay. Of Int.	9 Pay. For Misc. Ser.	10 Acq. Of Misc. Ser.	11 Pay. For Prop. Taxes	12 Recog. Prop. Tax Exp.	13 Dec. and Pay. Div.	14 Recog. Depre. Exp.	15 Check on Ending Bal. Sheet Amts.	Balance: End of Period
ASSETS																		
Current Assets:																		
Cash	40,000	144,000	63,000	1,000		-114,000			-5,000	-500	-57,500		-1,200		-2,000		67,800	67,800
Accounts & Notes Rec.	36,000	-144,000	149,000														41,000	41,000
Merchandise Inventory	55,000						121,000	-126,500									49,500	49,500
Interest Receivable	1,000			-1,000	700												700	700
Prepaid Misc. Services	4,000										1,200						5,200	5,200
Total Current Assets	136,000																164,200	164,200
Noncurrent Assets:																		
Bldg., Mach., & Equipment	47,000																47,000	47,000
Accumulated Depreciation	(10,000)															-2,000	(12,000)	(12,000)
Total Noncurrent Assets	37,000																35,000	35,000
Total Assets	173,000																199,200	199,200
LIABILITIES AND SHAREHOLDERS' EQUITY																		
Current Liabilities:																		
Accounts Pay. (miscellaneous ser.)	2,000										-56,300	56,800					2,500	2,500
Accounts Pay. (mer. pur.)	34,000					-114,000	121,000										41,000	41,000
Property Taxes Payable	1,000												-1,200	1,700			1,500	1,500
Total Current Liabilities	37,000																45,000	45,000
Noncurrent Liabilities:																		
Mortgage Payable	35,000								-5,000								30,000	30,000
Total Noncurrent Liabilities	35,000																30,000	30,000
Total Liabilities	72,000																75,000	75,000
Shareholders' Equity:																		
Common Stock	25,000																25,000	25,000
Retained Earnings	76,000		212,000		700			-126,500		-500		-56,800		-1,700	-2,000	-2,000	99,200	99,200
Total Shareholders' Equity	101,000																	124,200
Total Liabilities and Shareholders' Equity	173,000																	199,200
Imbalance, if Any	-	-	-	-	-	-	-	-	-	-	-	-	-	-	-	-	-	-
Income Statement Accounts			Sales Rev.	Int. Rev.				COGS		Int. Exp.		Mis. Ser. Exp.		Prop. Tax Exp.		Depre. Exp.		

3-35

3.39 continued.

TERTIA COMPANY
Statement of Income and Retained Earnings

Revenues:		
Sales..	$ 212,000	
Interest Revenue...	700	
Total Revenues..		$ 212,700
Expenses:		
Cost of Goods Sold	$ 126,500	
Property Tax Expense....................................	1,700	
Depreciation Expense.....................................	2,000	
Interest Expense	500	
Miscellaneous Expenses.................................	56,800	
Total Expenses...		187,500
Net Income..		$ 25,200
Less Dividends..		(2,000)
Increase in Retained Earnings......................		$ 23,200
Retained Earnings, Beginning of Year		76,000
Retained Earnings, End of Year.............................		$ 99,200

3.40 (Portobello Co.; reconstructing the income statement and balance sheet.) Transactions spreadsheet.

Balance Sheet Accounts	Balance: Beginning of Period	1 Recog. Insur. Exp.	2a Pay Yr. 9 Dividend	2b Dec. and Pay. Yr. 10 Div.	3 Rec. Repay. Of Note & Int.	4a Issue Common Stock for Merch.	4b Pay Merch. Suppliers	4c Pur. Of Merch. On Acct.	4d Recog. COGS	5a Acquire Del. Trucks	5b Recog. Int. Exp. On Note Pay.	5c Recog. Dep. Exp. On Del. Equip.	6 Recog. Dep. Exp. On Comp. System	7a Cash Col. From Cust.	7b Record Sales from Cus. Adv.	7c Recog. Sales on Acct.	8a Cash Paid to Emp.	8b Recog. Unpaid Sal. Exp.	9a Cash Paid for Taxes	9b Recog. Unpaid Taxes	10 Recog. Unpaid Consult. Ser. Exp.	Balance: End of Period
ASSETS																						
Current Assets:																						
Cash	18,600		-1,800	-3,000	10,900		-115,000				-3,000			210,000			-85,000		-27,000			4,700
Accounts Receivable	33,000													-208,600		226,600						51,000
Notes Receivable	10,000				-10,000																	-
Interest Receivable	600				-600																	-
Merchandise Inventory	22,000					11,000		95,000	-88,000													40,000
Prepaid Insurance	4,500	-3,000																				1,500
Advances to Employees																	4,000					4,000
Prepaid Property Taxes																			3,000			3,000
Total Current Assets	88,700																					104,200
Noncurrent Assets:																						
Computer System	78,000																					78,000
Delivery Trucks										60,000												60,000
Accum. Depre.: Comp. Sys.	-26,000												-13,000									(39,000)
Accum. Depre.: Del. Trucks												-4,500										(4,500)
Total Noncurrent Assets	52,000																					94,500
Total Assets	140,700																					198,700
LIABILITIES AND SHAREHOLDERS' EQUITY																						
Current Liabilities:																						
Accounts Payable	36,000						-115,000	95,000														16,000
Dividend Payable	1,800		-1,800	3,000																		3,000
Salaries Payable	6,500																-6,500	1,300				1,300
Taxes Payable	10,000																		-10,000	4,000		4,000
Advances from Customers	600													1,400	-600							1,400
Interest Payable											2,000											2,000
Consulting Services Pay.																					4,800	4,800
Total Current Liabilities	54,900																					32,500
Noncurrent Liabilities:																						
Note Payable										60,000												60,000
Total Noncurrent Liabilities	-																					60,000
Total Liabilities	54,900																					92,500
Shareholders' Equity:																						
Common Stock	40,000					11,000																51,000
Retained Earnings	45,800	-3,000		-6,000	300				-88,000		-5,000	-4,500	-13,000		600	226,600	-74,500	-1,300	-14,000	-4,000	-4,800	55,200
Total Shareholders' Equity	85,800																					106,200
Total Liabilities and Shareholders' Equity	140,700																					198,700
Imbalance, if Any	-	-	-	-	-	-	-	-	-	-	-	-	-	-	-	-	-	-	-	-	-	-
Income Statement Accounts		Insur. Exp.			Int. Rev.				COGS		Int. Exp.	Depre. Exp.	Depre. Exp.		Sales Rev.	Sales Rev.	Sal. Exp.	Sal. Exp.	Tax Exp.	Tax Exp.	Consul. Exp.	

3.40 continued.

PORTOBELLO CO.
Income Statement
For the Year Ended December 31, Year 10

Revenues:

Sales..	$ 227,200
Interest..	300
Total Revenues...	$ 227,500

Expenses:

Cost of Goods Sold	$ 88,000
Depreciation...	17,500
Salaries...	75,800
Taxes..	18,000
Insurance	3,000
Consulting	4,800
Interest...	5,000
Total Expenses	$ 212,100
Net Income	$ 15,400

3.40 continued.

PORTOBELLO CO.
Balance Sheet
December 31, Year 10

Assets

Current Assets:
Cash		$ 4,700
Accounts Receivable		51,000
Merchandise Inventories		40,000
Prepaid Insurance		1,500
Advances to Employees		4,000
Prepaid Property Taxes		3,000
Total Current Assets		$ 104,200

Noncurrent Assets:
Computer System—at Cost	$ 78,000	
Less Accumulated Depreciation	(39,000)	$ 39,000
Delivery Trucks	$ 60,000	
Less Accumulated Depreciation	(4,500)	55,500
Total Noncurrent Assets		$ 94,500
Total Assets		$ 198,700

Liabilities and Shareholders' Equity

Current Liabilities:
Accounts Payable		$ 16,000
Interest Payable		2,000
Dividend Payable		3,000
Salaries Payable		1,300
Taxes Payable		4,000
Consulting Fee Payable		4,800
Advances from Customers		1,400
Total Current Liabilities		$ 32,500
Note Payable		60,000
Total Liabilities		$ 92,500

Shareholders' Equity:
Common Stock		$ 51,000
Retained Earnings		55,200
Total Shareholders' Equity		$ 106,200
Total Liabilities and Shareholders' Equity		$ 198,700

3.41 (Computer Needs, Inc.; reconstructing the income statement and balance sheet.)

a. Transactions spreadsheet.

Transactions, By Number and Description

Balance Sheet Accounts	Balance: Beginning of Period	1 Cash Col. From Cust.	2 Recog. Sales on Acct.	3 Pay. To Mer. Sup.	4 Recog. Merch. Pur. On Acct.	5 Recog. COGS	6 Pay Emp. & Prov. Of S&A Serv.	7 Pay Income Taxes	8 Recog. Depre. Exp.	9 Pay Prin. & Int. on Mort.	10 Acq. Equip.	11 Recog. Inc. Tax Exp.	Balance: End of Period
ASSETS													
Current Assets:													
Cash	15,600	189,000		-164,600			-21,000	-3,388		-4,800	-6,000		4,812
Accounts Receivable	32,100	-151,500	159,700										40,300
Inventories	46,700				172,100	-158,100							60,700
Prepayments	1,500						300						1,800
Total Current Assets	95,900												107,612
Noncurrent Assets:													
Prop., Plant, & Equipment	59,700										6,000		65,700
Accumulated Depreciation	-2,800								-3,300				(6,100)
Total Noncurrent Assets	56,900												59,600
Total Assets	152,800												167,212
LIABILITIES AND SHAREHOLDERS' EQUITY													
Current Liabilities:													
Acct. Pay.—Merchan.	37,800			-164,600	172,100								45,300
Income Tax Payable	3,388							-3,388				3,584	3,584
Other Current Liabilities	2,900						-1,700						1,200
Total Current Liabilities	44,088												50,084
Noncurrent Liabilities:													
Mortgage Payable	50,000									-800			49,200
Total Noncurrent Liabilities	50,000												49,200
Total Liabilities	94,088												99,284
Shareholders' Equity:													
Common Stock	50,000												50,000
Retained Earnings	8,712	37,500	159,700			-158,100	-19,000		-3,300	-4,000		-3,584	17,928
Total Shareholders' Equity	58,712												67,928
Total Liabilities and Shareholders' Equity	152,800												167,212
Imbalance, if Any	-	-	-	-	-	-	-	-	-	-	-	-	-
Income Statement Accounts		Sal. Rev.	Sal. Rev.			COGS	S&A Exp.		Depre. Exp.	Int. Exp.		Inc. Tax Exp.	

3.41 a. continued.

COMPUTER NEEDS, INC.
Income Statement
For the Years Ended December 31

	Year 8		Year 9	
	Amounts	**Percentages**	**Amounts**	**Percentages**
Sales	$152,700	100.0%	$197,200	100.0%
Cost of Goods Sold..............	(116,400)	(76.2)	(158,100)	(80.2)
Selling and Administra-				
tion Expenses	(17,400)	(11.4)	(19,000)	(9.6)
Depreciation........................	(2,800)	(1.9)	(3,300)	(1.7)
Interest	(4,000)	(2.6)	(4,000)	(2.0)
Income Taxes......................	(3,388)	(2.2)	(3,584)	(1.8)
Net Income.........................	$ 8,712	5.7%	$ 9,216	4.7%

3.41 a. continued.

COMPUTER NEEDS, INC.
Balance Sheet
December 31

	Year 8 Amounts	Year 8 Percentages	Year 9 Amounts	Year 9 Percentages
Assets				
Cash..	$ 15,600	10.2%	$ 4,812	2.9%
Accounts Receivable...........	32,100	21.0	40,300	24.1
Inventories	46,700	30.6	60,700	36.3
Prepayments	1,500	1.0	1,800	1.1
Total Current Assets.....	$ 95,900	62.8%	$107,612	64.4%
Property, Plant and Equipment:				
At Cost...........................	$ 59,700	39.0%	$ 65,700	39.3%
Less Accumulated Depreciation...............	(2,800)	(1.8)	(6,100)	(3.7)
Net....................................	$ 56,900	37.2%	$ 59,600	35.6%
Total Assets.....................	$152,800	100.0%	$167,212	100.0%
Liabilities and Shareholders' Equity				
Accounts Payable— Merchandise.....................	$ 37,800	24.8%	$ 45,300	27.1%
Income Tax Payable...........	3,388	2.2	3,584	2.2
Other Current Liabilities...	2,900	1.9	1,200	.7
Total Current Liabilities	$ 44,088	28.9%	$ 50,084	30.0%
Mortgage Payable...............	50,000	32.7	49,200	29.4
Total Liabilities	$ 94,088	61.6%	$ 99,284	59.4%
Common Stock.....................	$ 50,000	32.7%	$ 50,000	29.9%
Retained Earnings	8,712	5.7	17,928	10.7
Total Shareholders' Equity.............................	$ 58,712	38.4%	$ 67,928	40.6%
Total Liabilities and Shareholders' Equity...	$152,800	100.0%	$167,212	100.0%

3.41 continued.

b. Although sales increased between Year 8 and Year 9, net income as a percentage of sales declined from 5.7% to 4.7%. The decline occurs primarily as a result of an increase in the cost of goods sold to sales percentage. The increased percentage might suggest (1) increased competition, which forced Computer Needs, Inc. to lower its prices, (2) increased cost of merchandise, which Computer Needs, Inc. could not or chose not to pass on to customers, or (3) a shift in product mix to lower margin products. The percentage is also affected by the estimates made for the December 31, Year 9 balances in Accounts Receivable, Inventories, and Accounts Payable. The following summarizes the effects of an overstatement (O/S), understatement (U/S), or no effect (NO) of each of these three accounts, assuming the other two accounts are correctly stated, on the cost of goods sold to sales percentage.

December 31, Year 9 Balance Is:	Effect on Cost of Goods Sold to Sales Percentage		
	Numerator	Denominator	Net Effect
Accounts Receivable Overstated....	NO	O/S	U/S
Accounts Receivable Understated.	NO	U/S	O/S
Inventories Overstated......................	U/S	NO	U/S
Inventories Understated..................	O/S	NO	O/S
Accounts Payable Overstated.........	O/S	NO	O/S
Accounts Payable Understated......	U/S	NO	U/S

Of course, there could be compounding or offsetting errors in each of these three accounts.

The selling and administrative expense to sales percentage declined. Compensation of employees is largely a fixed cost, so the increased sales should permit Computer Needs, Inc. to spread this cost over the larger sales base. The estimate of Accounts Receivable and Other Current Liabilities on December 31, Year 9 also can affect this percentage.

The reduced expense percentage for depreciation reflects the spreading of this fixed cost over a larger sales base. Although depreciation expense increased between Year 8 and Year 9, sales increased by a higher percentage.

The reduced expense percentage for interest likewise results from spreading this fixed cost over a larger sales base. Note that interest expense was the same amount in Year 8 and Year 9. Given that the amount of the loan outstanding decreased, the interest rate on the loan must have increased.

The decreased income tax percentage results from a lower income before taxes to sales percentage. The income tax rate was 28 percent in both years.

3.41 b. continued.

	Year 8		Year 9	
	Amounts	**Percentages**	**Amounts**	**Percentages**
Income before Taxes	$ 12,100	100.0%	$ 12,800	100.0%
Income Tax Expense..........	(3,388)	(28.0)	(3,584)	(28.0)
Net Income..........................	$ 8,712	72.0%	$ 9,216	72.0%

The balance sheet shows a significant decline in cash and a buildup of accounts receivable, inventories, and accounts payable. It is possible that each of these accounts is overstated. The decline in cash, however, is consistent with the buildup of accounts receivable. The buildup of accounts payable is consistent with a buildup in inventories.

3.42   (The GAP and The Limited; interpreting common-size income statements.)

a.   The decreasing cost of goods sold to sales percentages for both firms suggest a common explanation. One possibility is that the economy was doing well and both firms were able to increase selling prices and thereby their profit margins. Another possibility is that the firms were able to purchase merchandise in larger quantities or pay more quickly to take advantage of discounts. A third possibility is that the firms implemented more effective inventory control systems, thereby reducing obsolescence and the need to reduce selling prices to move their merchandise. Another possibility is that sales grew rapidly and the firms were able to spread their relatively fixed occupancy costs over a larger sales base.

b.   The Limited relies more heavily on in-store promotions, which tend to increase its cost of goods sold to sales percentages, whereas The GAP relies more on advertising to stimulate sales, which The GAP includes in selling and administrative expenses.

c.   The increasing selling and administrative expenses to sales percentages for both firms suggest a common explanation. One possibility is that the specialty retailing industry became more competitive over this period (from new entrants and from the Internet) and the firms had to increase marketing expenses to compete. This explanation, however, is inconsistent with a more attractive pricing environment suggested in Part *a.* above. Another possibility is that both firms experienced increased administrative expenses as they introduced new store concepts and opened new stores.

d.   The explanation in Part *b.* applies here as well. The GAP includes its promotion costs in selling and administrative expenses, whereas more of those of The Limited appear in cost of goods sold.

e. The interest expense to sales percentage decreased for The GAP and increased for The Limited. One possible explanation is The GAP reduced the amount of debt outstanding or grew it at a slower pace than that of The Limited. Another possibility is that the market viewed The GAP as increasingly less risky, permitting it to borrow at lower interest rates. On the other hand, the market viewed The Limited as more risky and required it to pay a higher interest rate. These two possibilities are not independent. Perhaps The GAP was able to borrow at a lower rate because it reduced the amount of debt in its capital structure. The higher interest rate for The Limited may reflect increased risk from an increased proportion of debt in its capital structure.

f. Both firms experienced increased net income relative to sales. Both firms should therefore experience increased income tax expense relative to sales. A more meaningful way to interpret income taxes is to relate income tax expense to income before income taxes. The latter is the base on which governments impose income taxes. Consider the following:

	The GAP			The Limited		
	Year 8	Year 9	Year 10	Year 8	Year 9	Year 10
(1) Income before Income Taxes (plug)...............	12.4%	14.6%	16.3%	5.8%	6.5%	6.9%
(2) Income Tax Expense...........	(4.2)	(5.5)	(6.6)	(2.0)	(2.3)	(2.4)
(3) Net Income	8.2%	9.1%	9.7%	3.8%	4.2%	4.5%
(2)/(1).......................	33.9%	37.7%	40.5%	34.5%	35.4%	34.8%

The income tax expense to income before income taxes percentages for The GAP continually increased while those of The Limited remained relatively stable. One possible explanation is that The GAP expanded its operations into other countries and perhaps experienced higher income tax rates in those countries than it experiences in the United States.

g. The profit margins of The Limited are just slightly larger than that for Wal-Mart in Exhibit 3.8. One would expect specialty retailers to differentiate their products and services more than Wal-Mart and achieve a higher profit margin percentage. The question is: How much higher? The GAP achieves profit margins similar to those for Kellogg (branded foods) and Omnicom Group (creative marketing services). Extensive competition characterizes specialty apparel retailing, which dampens profit margins. However, new fashions and trends stimulate demand and permit higher profit margins. One might therefore expect an average profit margin for specialty retailers somewhere between

3.42 g. continued.

that of The Limited and The GAP. The Limited appears to have performed worse during this period than one might expect and The GAP performed better.

3.43   (The Coca-Cola Company and PepsiCo; interpreting common-size income statements.)

a. The creation, manufacture, and distribution of beverages involve six principal activities:

(1) Research and development to create the beverage, which generally involves developing the formula for the syrup.

(2) Promoting the beverage through advertising and other means.

(3) Manufacturing the syrup.

(4) Mixing water with the syrup to manufacture the beverage.

(5) Placing the beverage in a container.

(6) Distributing the beverage to retail and other outlets.

Coke primarily engages in the first three activities and its independent bottlers engage in the last three activities. PepsiCo engages more heavily in all six activities. The lower cost of goods sold to sales percentage for Coke might suggest that the market views the first three activities as higher value added than the last three, permitting Coke to extract a relatively high price from its bottlers for the syrup sold to them. PepsiCo's cost of goods sold to sales percentage reflects both the higher value added of the first three activities and the lower value added of the last three activities. Another possible explanation is that Coke dominates its bottlers and can extract a higher price because of the bottlers' reliance on Coke for most of their purchases.

b. The beverage industry, particularly for cola beverages, is relatively mature. The increasing selling and administrative expense to sales percentages for Coke might reflect increased advertising to gain market share or to introduce new beverages. Note that both firms experienced poor sales results in Year 10. Perhaps Coke increased advertising expenditures in Year 11 and Year 12 to stimulate sales. The decreasing percentages are consistent with not increasing advertising in light of the Year 10 sales results. Note that sales growth for PepsiCo in Year 11 and Year 12 is less than the corresponding rates for Coke, suggesting less aggressiveness on the part of PepsiCo.

3.43 continued.

c. One possibility is that both firms reduced their levels of interest-bearing debt, which reduced interest expense. Another possibility is that declining interest rates permitted both firms to borrow at lower rates.

d.

	Coca-Cola Company			PepsiCo		
	Year 10	Year 11	Year 12	Year 10	Year 11	Year 12
(1) Income before Income Taxes (plug)................	27.9%	32.3%	28.1%	17.5%	18.8%	20.3%
(2) Income Tax Expense...........	(10.0)	(9.6)	(7.8)	(5.6)	(6.4)	(6.5)
(3) Net Income	17.9%	22.7%	20.3%	11.9%	12.4%	13.8%
(2)/(1)......................	35.8%	29.7%	27.8%	32.0%	34.0%	32.0%

Coke's tax burden by this measure is less than that of PepsiCo in Year 11 and Year 12. The income tax is a tax on income before taxes and not on sales. Thus, this measure more accurately reflects the income tax burden. The larger income tax expense to sales percentages for Coke results from Coke having higher income before taxes to sales percentages.

e. The products of Coke and PepsiCo have brand recognition. Consumers willingly pay a higher price for branded products than non-branded products. One might argue that little intrinsic difference exists between the products of these two companies, so that competition between them should lower the profit margins, as occurs for AK Steel and Wal-Mart. The two companies dominate the nonalcoholic beverage market however. An unwritten understanding not to compete too heavily on low prices permits both firms to realize relatively large profit margins. The greater competition among branded food companies and advertising companies might explain their lower profits relative to Coke and PepsiCo. The profit margins of Coke and PepsiCo are lower than Pfizer's, because consumers view pharmaceutical products as necessities and insurance companies bear some of the cost.

3.44 (Nokia; interpreting common-size income statements.)

The improved profit margin results primarily from decreases in the cost of goods sold to sales percentage and in the selling and administrative expense to sales percentage. One possible explanation for these decreased percentages is that either Nokia's market dominance or the rapid growth in industry sales gave it pricing flexibility and Nokia was able to price its products favorably relative to its costs. Another possibility is that the rapid sales growth permitted Nokia to spread fixed manufacturing, selling, and administrative expenses over a much larger sales base. The decreasing interest expense to sales percentage also favorably affected the profit mar-

3.44 continued.

gin. Nokia may have reduced the amount of debt in its capital structure or replaced debt with a higher interest rate with debt carrying a lower interest rate. It is also possible that Nokia grew its debt but at a less rapid pace than the growth in sales, permitting the interest expense to sales percentage to decline.

Offsetting these favorable effects on the profit margin percentage is a reduction in the other revenues percentage. We have no information to interpret this change. The income tax expense to sales percentage increased, the result in part of an increase in net income before income taxes. The average income tax rate also increased, as the following analysis shows.

	Year 7	Year 8	Year 9
(1) Income before Income Taxes (plug)	15.7%	18.3%	18.9%
(2) Income Tax Expense	(4.0)	(5.7)	(6.1)
(3) Net Income	11.7%	12.6%	12.8%
(2)/(1)	25.5%	31.1%	32.3%

3.45 (McDonalds; interpreting common-size income statements.)

The principal reason for the declining profit margin is an increase in the cost of goods sold to sales percentage. Increased competition in the fast food segment of the restaurant industry led McDonalds either to reduce selling prices or not increase selling prices in line with increases in operating expenses. Offsetting the increasing cost of goods sold to sales percentage is a decline in income tax expense as a percentage of income before taxes, as the following analysis shows:

	Year 10	Year 11	Year 12
(1) Income before Income Taxes (plug)	21.8%	20.3%	16.7%
(2) Income Tax Expense	(7.1)	(6.4)	(5.0)
(3) Net Income	14.7%	13.9%	11.7%
(2)/(1)	32.6%	31.5%	29.9%

3.46   (Identifying industries using common-size income statement percentages.)

Exhibit 3.27 indicates that two firms have relatively low profit margins, two firms have medium profit margins, and two firms have relatively large profit margins. Low barriers to entry, extensive competition, and commodity products characterize firms with low profit margins. The likely candidates for Firms (1) and (2) are Kelly Services and Kroger Stores. The office services offered by Kelly Services are clerical in nature and not particularly unique. Kelly Services serves essentially as an intermediary between the employee and the customer, offering relatively little value added. Grocery products are commodities, with little, if any, differentiation between grocery stores. Firms (1) and (2) differ primarily with respect to depreciation and interest expense. Grocery stores require retail and warehouse space. Kelly Services should require relatively little space, since its employees work on the customers' premises. Thus, Firm (1) is Kroger Stores and Firm (2) is Kelly Services.

Firms with the highest profit margin should operate in industries with high barriers to entry, relatively little competition, and differentiated products. Electric utilities have operated until recently as regulated utilities and require extensive amounts of capital to build capital-intensive plants. Regulation and capital serve as barriers to entry. Gillette offers brand name products. The brand names serve as an entry barrier. Customers also perceive its products to be differentiated. Thus, Firm (5) and Firm (6) are likely to be Commonwealth Edison and Gillette in some order. Firm (5) has considerably more depreciation and interest expense than Firm (6) and Firm (6) has considerably more selling and administrative expenses than Firm (5). Thus, Firm (5) is Commonwealth Edison and Firm (6) is Gillette.

This leaves Hewlett-Packard and Delta Airlines with medium profit margins. Hewlett-Packard offers products that are somewhat differentiated and with some brand name appeal. However, competition in the computer industry and rapid technological change drive down profit margins. Delta Airlines offers a commodity product, but the need for capital to acquire airplanes serves as a barrier to entry. Thus, these two firms have some characteristics of firms with relatively low profit margins and some characteristics of firms with relatively high profit margins. Firm (3) appears to have considerably more debt in its capital structure than Firm (4). The short product life cycles in the computer industry tend to drive down their use of debt. The aircraft of Delta Airlines can serve as collateral for borrowing. Thus, one would expect Delta Airlines to have a higher amount of borrowing. This clue suggests that Firm (3) is Delta Airlines and Firm (4) is Hewlett-Packard.

3.47   (Preparing adjusting entries.)

a. The Prepaid Rent account on the year-end balance sheet should represent eight months of prepayments. The rent per month is $2,000 (= $24,000/12), so the balance required in the Prepaid Rent account is $16,000 (= 8 x $2,000). Rent Expense for Year 2 is $8,000 (= 4 x $2,000 = $24,000 − $16,000).

3.47 a. continued.

Prepaid Rent (Asset Increase)................................... 16,000
   Retained Earnings (Rent Expense) (Share-
      holders' Equity Increase)...................................   16,000
To increase the balance in the Prepaid Rent ac-
count, reducing the amount in the Rent Expense
account.

b. The Prepaid Rent account on the balance sheet for the end of Year 3 should represent eight months of prepayments. The rent per month is $2,500 (= $30,000/12), so the required balance in the Prepaid Rent account is $20,000 (= 8 x $2,500). The balance in that account is already $16,000, so the adjusting entry must increase it by $4,000 (= $20,000 – $16,000).

Prepaid Rent (Asset Increase)................................... 4,000
   Retained Earnings (Rent Expense) (Share-
      holders' Equity Increase)...................................   4,000
To increase the balance in the Prepaid Rent ac-
count, reducing the amount in the Rent Expense
account.

The Rent Expense account will have a balance at the end of Year 3 before closing entries of $26,000 (= $30,000 – $4,000). This amount comprises $16,000 (= $2,000 x 8) for rent from January through August and $10,000 (= $2,500 x 4) for rent from September through December.

c. The Prepaid Rent account on the balance sheet at the end of Year 4 should represent two months of prepayments. The rent per month is $3,000 (= $18,000/6), so the required balance in the Prepaid Rent account is $6,000 (= 2 x $3,000). The balance in that account is $20,000, so the adjusting entry must reduce it by $14,000 (= $20,000 – $6,000).

Retained Earnings (Rent Expense) (Shareholders'
   Equity Decrease)... 14,000
     Prepaid Rent (Asset Decrease)...........................   14,000
To reduce the balance in the Prepaid Rent ac-
count, increasing the amount in the Rent Expense account.

The Rent Expense account will have a balance at the end of Year 4 before closing entries of $32,000 (= $18,000 + $14,000). This amount comprises $20,000 (= $2,500 x 8) for rent from January through August and $12,000 (= $3,000 x 4) for rent from September through December.

3.47 continued.

d. The Wages Payable account should have a credit balance of $4,000 at the end of April, but it has a balance of $5,000 carried over from the end of March. The adjusting entry must reduce the balance by $1,000, which requires a debit to the Wages Payable account.

Wages Payable (Liability Decrease)........................ 1,000
   Retained Earnings (Wage Expense) (Share-
      holders' Equity Increase)................................... 1,000
To reduce the balance in the Wages Payable account, reducing the amount in the Wage Expense account.

Wage Expense is $29,000 (= $30,000 – $1,000).

e. The Prepaid Insurance account balance of $3,000 represents four months of coverage. Thus, the cost of insurance is $750 (= $3,000/4) per month. The adjusting entry for a single month is as follows:

Retained Earnings (Insurance Expense) (Share-
   holders' Equity Decrease)..................................... 750
      Prepaid Insurance (Asset Decrease)................. 750
To recognize cost of one month's insurance cost as expense of the month.

f. The Advances from Tenants account has a balance of $25,000 carried over from the start of the year. At the end of Year 3, it should have a balance of $30,000. Thus, the adjusting entry must increase the balance by $5,000, which requires a credit to the liability account.

Retained Earnings (Rent Revenue) (Share-
   holders' Equity Decrease)..................................... 5,000
      Advance from Tenants (Liability Increase)...... 5,000
To increase the balance in the Advances from Tenants account, reducing the amount in Rent Revenue.

Rent Revenue for Year 3 is $245,000 (= $250,000 – $5,000).

g. The Depreciation Expense for the year should be $2,000 (= $10,000/5). The balance in the Accumulated Depreciation account should also be $2,000; thus, the firm must credit Retained Earnings (Depreciation Expense) by $8,000 (= $10,000 – $2,000). The adjusting entry not only reduces recorded depreciation for the period but also sets up the asset account and its accumulated depreciation contra account.

3.47 g. continued.

  Equipment (Asset Increase) 10,000

   Accumulated Depreciation (Asset Decrease)   2,000

   Retained Earnings (Depreciation Expense)

   (Shareholders' Equity Increase)   8,000

  To reduce the recorded amount in Retained Earn-

  ings (Depreciation Expense) from $10,000 to

  $2,000, setting up the asset and its contra ac-

  count.

3.48 (Ethical issues in accounting choices.)

Each of these firms received an unqualified opinion from their independent auditor, suggesting that they applied generally accepted accounting principles properly. Each firm disclosed sufficient information about their application of accounting principles for the user to ascertain that UAL applied its accounting principles in more income-enhancing ways than AMR and Delta. Thus, the remaining question is whether UAL's aggressiveness relative to AMR and Delta creates an ethical concern. Using an average life of 21.1 years, the average life for Delta, results in depreciation expense of $1,082.3 (= $22,835.5/21.1). The longer depreciable life decreases depreciation by approximately $112.3 million (= $1,082.3 − $970.0), a 10.4 percent reduction (= $112.3/$1,082). This reduction appears material, given the importance of depreciable assets to airlines. The differences in the estimated uncollectible accounts percentages seem even more material. However, most customers prepay for their airline tickets, so accounts receivable do not represent a significant proportion of total assets.

CHAPTER 4

STATEMENT OF CASH FLOWS:
REPORTING THE EFFECTS OF OPERATING,
INVESTING, AND FINANCING ACTIVITIES
ON CASH FLOWS

Questions, Short Exercises, Exercises, Problems, and Cases: Answers and Solutions

4.1   See the text or the glossary at the end of the book.

4.2   One can criticize a single income statement using a cash basis of accounting from two standpoints: (1) it provides a poor measure of operating performance each period because of the inaccurate matching of revenues and expenses (see discussion in Chapter 3), and (2) it excludes important investing (acquisitions and sales of long-lived assets) activities and financing (issuance or redemption of bonds or capital stock) activities of a firm that affect cash flow.

4.3   Accrual accounting attempts to provide a measure of operating performance that relates inputs to output without regard to when a firm receives or disburses cash. Accrual accounting also attempts to portray the resources of a firm and the claims on those resources without regard to whether the firm holds the resource in the form of cash. Although accrual accounting may satisfy user's needs for information about operating performance and financial position, it does not provide sufficient information about the cash flow effects of a firm's operating, investing, and financing activities. The latter is the objective of the statement of cash flows.

4.4   The statement of cash flows reports changes in the investing and financing activities of a firm. Significant changes in property, plant, and equipment affect the maturity structure of assets on the balance sheet. Significant changes in long-term debt or capital stock affect both the maturity structure of equities as well as the mix of debt versus shareholder financing.

4.5   The indirect method reconciles net income, the primary measure of a firm's profitability, with cash flow from operations. Some argue that the relation between net income and cash flow from operations is less evident when a firm reports using the direct method. More likely, the frequent use of the indirect method prior to the issuance of FASB *Statement No. 95*

4.5 continued.

probably explains its continuing popularity. Why might accountants have preferred the indirect method before FASB *Statement No. 95*? We have heard the following, but cannot vouch for this from first-hand experience: The direct method's format resembles the income statement. Where the income statement has a line for revenues, the direct method has a line for cash collections from customers. Where the income statement has a line for cost of goods sold, the direct method might have a line for payments to suppliers of income. Where the income statement has a line for income tax expense, the direct method has a line for income tax payments. The old-timers thought the resemblance of the two statements, the income statement and the direct method, but lack of identity, would cause confusion. They were likely right, but we think its confusion is less than the confusion resulting from the indirect method.

4.6   The classification in the statement of cash flows parallels that in the income statement, where interest on debt is an expense but payments on the principal amount of the debt are not an expense but a reduction in a liability. This is, in our opinion, a feeble explanation. The overarching rule seems to be that 'if it's in the income statement, it's operating.' We think that repayment of principal on borrowings and interest on borrowings are both financing transactions, but we are in the minority.

4.7   The classification in the statement of cash flows parallels that in the income statement, where interest on debt is an expense but dividends are a distribution of earnings, not an expense. This is, in our opinion, a feeble explanation. The overarching rule seems to be that 'if it's in the income statement, it's operating.' We think that dividends on shares and interest on borrowings are both financing transactions, but we are in the minority.

4.8   Firms generally use accounts payable directly in financing purchases of inventory and other operating costs. Firms might use short-term bank financing indirectly in financing accounts receivable, inventories, or operating costs or use it to finance acquisitions of noncurrent assets or reductions in long-term financing. Thus, the link between short-term bank financing and operations is less direct and may not even relate to operating activities. To achieve consistency in classification, the FASB stipulates that changes in short-term bank loans are financing activities. This is not compelling. We suspect the opposite treatment could be justified.

4.9   This is an investing and financing transaction whose disclosure helps the statement user understand why property, plant and equipment and long-term debt changed during the period. Because the transaction does not affect cash directly, however, firms must distinguish it from investing and financing transactions that do affect cash flow. The rules used to allow the firm to report this single transaction as though it were two—the issue

4.9 continued.

of debt for cash and the use of cash to acquire the property—and the appearance of both of these two in the so-called funds statement, the predecessor Statement of Changes in Financial Position.

4.10   Both are correct, but the writer's point is not expressed clearly. Depreciation expense is a charge to operations, but does not require cash. If revenues precisely equal total expenses, there will be a retention of net funds in the business equal to the amount of the depreciation. As long as replacement of the depreciating assets is not necessary, it is possible to finance considerable expansion without resorting to borrowing or the issuance of additional stock.

The "reader" is correct in saying that depreciation in itself is not a source of cash and that the total cash available would not have increased by adding larger amounts to the depreciation accounts. The source of cash is sales to customers.

When one considers income tax effects, however, depreciation expenses do save cash because taxable income and, hence, income tax expense using cash are lower than they would be in the absence of depreciation charges.

4.11   The firm must have increased substantially its investment in accounts receivable or inventories or decreased substantially its current liabilities.

4.12   The firm might be capital intensive and, therefore, subtracted substantial amounts of depreciation expense in computing net income. This depreciation expense is added back to net income in computing cash flow from operations. In addition, the firm might have decreased significantly its investment in accounts receivable or inventories or increased its current liabilities.

4.13   Direct Method: The accountant classifies the entire cash proceeds from the equipment sale as an investing activity. Indirect Method: As above, the entire cash proceeds appear as an investing activity. Because the calculation of cash flow from operations starts with net income (which includes the gain on sale of equipment), the accountant must subtract the gain to avoid counting cash flow equal to the gain twice, once as an operating activity and once as an investing activity.

4.14   (Microsoft; derive sales revenue from data in the statement of cash flows and balance sheet.) (Amounts in Millions)

Cash Collections for Year 14		$ 33,551
Accounts Receivable, End of Year	$ 5,334	
Accounts Receivable, Beginning of Year	5,196	
Add: Increase in Receivables		138
Sales for Year 14		$ 33,689

4.15 (General Electric; derive cost of goods sold from data in the statement of cash flows.) (Amounts in Millions)

Cash Payments for Inventories for Year 13..................................	$ 64,713
Subtract: Increase in Inventories for Year 13.............................	(1,753)
Cost of Goods Sold for Year 13..	$ 62,960

4.16 (Ann Taylor Stores; derive cost of goods sold from data in the statement of cash flows.) (Amounts in Millions)

Cash Payments for Inventories for Year 13..................................	$ 646.9
Add: Increase in Accounts Payable for Inventories....................	5.9
Subtract: Increase in Inventories for Year 13.............................	(5.7)
Cost of Goods Sold for Year 13..	$ 647.1

4.17 (AMR; derive wages and salaries expense from data in the statement of cash flows.) (Amounts in Millions)

Cash Payments for Wages and Salaries for Year 13....................	$ 8,853
Subtract: Decrease in Wages and Salaries Payable during Year 13..	(21)
Wages and Salaries Expense for Year 13.....................................	$ 8,832

4.18 (Johnson & Johnson; derive cash disbursements for dividends.) (Amounts in Millions)

Net Income for Year 13..		$ 5,030
Retained Earnings, End of Year...............................	$ 28,132	
Retained Earnings, Beginning of Year.....................	(26,571)	
Subtract: Increase in Retained Earnings................		(1,561)
Dividends Declared for Year 13..............................		$ 3,469
Subtract: Increase in Dividends Payable for Year 13 ..		(233)
Cash Paid for Dividends in Year 13 (Financing Activity)		$ 3,236

Refer to Exhibit 4.12. Line 10 increases by $3,236.

4.19 (Gillette; effect of borrowing and interest on statement of cash flows.) (Amounts in Millions)

Cash (Asset Increase)...	250.00	
Bonds Payable (Liability Increase)........................		250.00

October 1 bond issue. Refer to Exhibit 4.12. Line 11 increases by 250. Line 8 increases by 250.

Retained Earnings (Interest Expense) (Shareholders' Equity Decrease)...	3.75	
Interest Payable (Liability Increase) (.06/12) x $250.00 x 3 months.		3.75

Refer to Exhibit 4.12. Line 3 decreases by 3.75. Line 4 increases by 3.75.

4.20 (Radio Shack; effect of income taxes on statement of cash flows.) (Amounts in Millions)

Retained Earnings (Income Tax Expense) (Shareholders' Equity Decrease)	161.5	
Income Taxes Payable (Liability Decrease)	18.0	
Cash (Asset Decrease)		179.5

18.0 = 78.1 – 60.1. Refer to Exhibit 4.12. Line 2 increases by 179.5. Line 3 decreases by 161.5. Line 5 increases by 18.0. Line 11 decreases by 179.5.

4.21 (Effect of rent transactions on statement of cash flows.)

Retained Earnings (Rent Expense) (Shareholders' Equity Decrease)	1,200	
Prepaid Rent (Advances to Landlord) (Asset Decrease)		1,200

January rent expense.

Prepaid Rent (Advances to Landlord) (Asset Increase)	18,000	
Cash (Asset Decrease)		18,000

Payment on February 1.

Retained Earnings (Rent Expense) (Shareholders' Equity Decrease)	16,500	
Prepaid Rent (Advances to Landlord) (Asset Decrease)		16,500

Rent expense for February through December; $18,000/12 per month = $1,500. 11 x $1,500 = $16,500.

All of these combine as:

Retained Earnings (Rent Expense) (Shareholders' Equity Decrease)	17,700	
Prepaid Rent (Advances to Landlord) (Asset Increase)	300	
Cash (Asset Decrease)		18,000

All transactions of the year. Refer to Exhibit 4.12. Line 2 increases by 18,000. Line 3 decreases by 17,700. Line 5 increases by 300.

4.22 (Information Technologies; calculating components of cash flow from operations.) (Amounts in Thousands)

Sales for Year 2	$ 14,508
Add: Decrease in Receivables	782
Cash Collections from Customers for Year 2	$ 15,290

4.23   (Information Technologies; calculating components of cash flow from operations.) (Amounts in Thousands)

Cost of Goods Sold for Year 2	$ 11,596
Subtract: Increase in Accounts Payable for Inventories	(90)
Subtract: Decrease in Inventories for Year 2	(66)
Cash Payments for Inventories for Year 2	$ 11,440

4.24   (Information Technologies; calculating components of cash flow from operations.) (Amounts in Thousands)

Other Expenses, Total	$ 2,276
Subtract: Decrease in Prepayments for Other Costs	(102)
Add: Decrease in Wages and Salaries Payable during Year 2	240
Cash Payments for Wages and Salaries Payable for Year 2	$ 2,414

4.25   (American Airlines; working backwards from changes in buildings and equipment account.) (Amounts in Millions)

Buildings and Equipment (Original Cost)		Accumulated Depreciation	
Balance, 12/31/Year 3	$16,825	Balance, 12/31/Year 3	$ 4,914
Outlays in Year 4	1,314	Depreciation in Year 4	1,253
	$18,139		$ 6,167
Balance, 12/31/Year 4	17,369	Balance, 12/31/Year 4	5,465
Retirements in Year 4	$ 770	Retirements in Year 4	$ 702

Proceeds = Book Value
= $770 – $702
= $68.

4.26   (Amazon.com; calculating and interpreting cash flows.) (Amounts in Thousands)

a. **Year 4**

	Balance Sheet Changes	Operations	Investing	Financing
(Increases) Decreases in Assets				
Marketable Securities	—			
Inventories	$ (554)	$ (554)		
Prepayments	(307)	(307)		
Property, Plant and Equipment (at Cost)	(1,360)		$ (1,360)	
Accumulated Depreciation	286	286		

Increases (Decreases) in Liabilities and Share-holders' Equity

	Balance Sheet Changes	Operations	Investing	Financing
Accounts Payable—Merchandise Suppliers	2,753	2,753		
Other Current Liabilities	2,010	2,010		
Long-Term Debt	—			
Common Stock	8,201			$ 8,201
Retained Earnings	(5,777)	(5,777)		
Increase (Decrease) in Cash	$ 5,252	$ (1,589)	$ (1,360)	$ 8,201

Year 5

	Balance Sheet Changes	Operations	Investing	Financing
(Increases) Decreases in Assets				
Marketable Securities	$ (15,256)		$ (15,256)	
Inventories	(8,400)	$ (8,400)		
Prepayments	(2,977)	(2,977)		
Property, Plant and Equipment (at Cost)	(15,283)		(15,283)	
Accumulated Depreciation	4,742	4,742		
Increases (Decreases) in Liabilities and Shareholders' Equity				
Accounts Payable—Merchandise Suppliers	29,845	29,845		
Other Current Liabilities	7,603	7,603		
Long-Term Debt	78,202			$ 78,202
Common Stock	52,675			52,675
Retained Earnings	(27,590)	(27,590)		
Increase (Decrease) in Cash	$ 103,561	$ 3,223	$ (30,539)	$ 130,877

4.26 continued.

b.

AMAZON.COM
Statement of Cash Flows
For Year 4 and Year 5

	Year 4	Year 5
Operations:		
Net Income (Loss)...	$ (5,777)	$ (27,590)
Depreciation	286	4,742
(Increase) Decrease in Inventories....................	(554)	(8,400)
(Increase) Decrease in Prepayments	(307)	(2,977)
Increase (Decrease) in Accounts Payable—		
Merchandise Suppliers..................................	2,753	29,845
Increase (Decrease) in Other Current Lia-		
bilities...	2,010	7,603
Cash Flow from Operations................................	$ (1,589)	$ 3,223
Investing:		
Acquisition of Property, Plant, Equipment,		
and Marketable Securities............................	$ (1,360)	$ (30,539)
Financing:		
Increase in Long-Term Debt.............................		$ 78,202
Issue of Common Stock.....................................	$ 8,201	52,675
Cash Flow from Financing.................................	$ 8,201	$ 130,877
Increase (Decrease) in Cash	$ 5,252	$ 103,561
Cash, Beginning of Year....................................	996	6,248
Cash, End of Year..	$ 6,248	$ 109,809

c. Amazon.com operated at a net loss each year. Its cash flow from operations was not as negative as the net loss, and even turned positive in Year 5, because the firm delayed paying its creditors. Note that the increase in accounts payable to merchandise suppliers exceeds the increase in merchandise inventories each year. Cash flow from operations was not sufficient in Year 5 to finance the substantial growth in capital expenditures. Amazon.com used a mixture of long-term debt and common stock to finance these long-term assets.

4.27 (Yahoo, Inc.; calculating and interpreting cash flows.)

a. **Year 8**

(Increases) Decreases in Assets	Balance Sheet Changes	Operations	Investing	Financing
Marketable Securities........	$ (60,689)		$ (60,689)	
Accounts Receivable...........	(4,267)	$ (4,267)		
Prepayments.......................	(384)	(384)		
Property, Plant and Equipment (at Cost)......	(3,155)		(3,155)	
Accumulated Depreciation...................................	552	552		
Investment in Securities...	(10,477)		(10,477)	
Increases (Decreases) in Liabilities and Shareholders' Equity				
Accounts Payable................	1,086	1,086		
Other Current Liabilities..	6,447	6,447		
Common Stock.....................	103,796			$ 103,796
Retained Earnings..............	(4,659)	(4,659)		
Increase (Decrease) in Cash...................................	$ 28,250	$ (1,225)	$ (74,321)	$ 103,796

Year 9

(Increases) Decreases in Assets	Balance Sheet Changes	Operations	Investing	Financing
Marketable Securities........	$ 32,917		$ 32,917	
Accounts Receivable...........	(5,904)	$ (5,904)		
Prepayments.......................	(5,509)	(5,509)		
Property, Plant and Equipment (at Cost)......	(14,930)		(14,930)	
Accumulated Depreciation...................................	2,554	2,554		
Investment in Securities...	(9,053)		(9,053)	
Increases (Decreases) in Liabilities and Shareholders' Equity				
Accounts Payable................	3,605	3,605		
Other Current Liabilities..	11,598	11,598		
Common Stock.....................	36,980			$ 36,980
Retained Earnings..............	(23,267)	(23,267)		
Increase (Decrease) in Cash...................................	$ 28,991	$ (16,923)	$ 8,934	$ 36,980

4.27 continued.

b.

YAHOO, INC.
Statement of Cash Flows
For Year 8 and Year 9

	Year 8	Year 9
Operations:		
Net Income (Loss)	$ (4,659)	$ (23,267)
Depreciation	552	2,554
(Increase) Decrease in Accounts Receivable	(4,267)	(5,904)
(Increase) Decrease in Prepayments	(384)	(5,509)
Increase (Decrease) in Accounts Payable	1,086	3,605
Increase (Decrease) in Other Current Liabilities	6,447	11,598
Cash Flow from Operations	$ (1,225)	$ (16,923)
Investing:		
Acquisition of Property, Plant and Equipment	$ (3,155)	$ (14,930)
Sale of Marketable Securities	--	32,917
Acquisition of Marketable Securities	(60,689)	--
Acquisition of Investment in Securities	(10,477)	(9,053)
Cash Flow from Investing	$ (74,321)	$ 8,934
Financing:		
Issue of Common Stock	$103,796	$ 36,980
Increase (Decrease) in Cash	$ 28,250	$ 28,991
Cash, Beginning of Year	5,297	33,547
Cash, End of Year	$ 33,547	$ 62,538

c. Yahoo, Inc. operated at a loss and generated negative cash flow from operations each year. Such operating results are not unusual for a startup company. Although its expenditures on property, plant and equipment increased significantly between the two years, Yahoo, Inc. is not heavily capital intensive. The firm used common stock to finance its growth during the startup phase. The main resources of an internet service provider are its software and customer list, neither of which serves as safe collateral for borrowing. Yahoo, Inc., therefore, did not use long-term borrowing to finance itself. The firm did not need all of the cash immediately to finance operations and capital expenditures. It invested the excess cash in marketable securities and investments in securities. Yahoo, Inc. sold some of its marketable securities during Year 9 to provide cash for conducting its operations.

4.28 (Green Mountain Coffee Roasters; preparing a columnar work sheet for a statement of cash flows from changes in balance sheet accounts.) (Amounts in Thousands.)

a.

(Increases) Decreases in Assets	Balance Sheet Changes	Operations	Investing	Financing
Accounts Receivable	$(2,231)	$ (2,231)		
Inventories	59	59		
Prepayments	475	475		
Property, Plant and Equipment (at Cost)	(2,129)		$ 2,468[a]	
			(4,597)	
Accumulated Depreciation	1,038	2,968	(1,930)[a]	
Other Noncurrent Assets	(434)	(434)		
Increases (Decreases) in Liabilities and Shareholders' Equity				
Accounts Payable	1,574	1,574		
Other Current Liabilities	560	560		
Bonds Payable	2,827			$ 5,567
				(2,740)
Common Stock	(5,878)			(5,878)
Retained Earnings	4,213	4,213		
Increase (Decrease) in Cash	$ 74	$ 7,184	$ (4,059)	$ (3,051)

[a]Cash proceeds of sale are $538 thousand (= $2,468 – $1,930).

b. Cash flow from operations approximately equaled net income plus depreciation. Accounts receivable increased during the year. The firm appeared to increase accounts payable to finance the buildup in accounts receivable. Cash flow from operations was more than sufficient to finance capital expenditures. The firm used the excess cash flow and the proceeds of additional long-term borrowing to repay long-term debt and reacquire common stock.

4.29 (Nokia; calculating and interpreting cash flow from operations.) (Amounts in Millions of €)

a.

	Year 8	Year 9	Year 10	Year 11
Net Income	€ 1,032	€ 1,689	€ 2,542	€ 3,847
Depreciation Expense	465	509	665	1,009
(Inc.) Dec. in Accounts Receivable	(272)	(1,573)	(982)	(2,304)
(Inc.) Dec. in Inventories........................	(121)	(103)	(362)	(422)
(Inc.) Dec. in Prepayments.....................	77	(17)	(33)	49
Inc. (Dec.) in Accounts Payable	90	140	312	458
Inc. (Dec.) in Other Current Liabilities ..	450	1,049	867	923
Cash Flow from Operations	€ 1,721	€ 1,694	€ 3,009	€ 3,560

b. The addback for depreciation, a noncash expense, causes cash flow from operations to exceed net income each year, except Year 11. Inventories increased in line with increases in net income. Nokia increases its accounts payable to finance the increased inventories. The firm also increased other current liabilities to finance growing operations. Variations in the relation between net income and cash flow from operations result from variations in accounts receivable. Unusually large increases in accounts receivable in Year 9 and Year 11 cause cash flow from operations to approximately equal net income in Year 9 and to be less than net income in Year 11. The variations in accounts receivable might result from a conscious effort by Nokia to vary credit terms to stimulate sales. It may also reflect conditions in the economy that cause its customers to delay payments in some years.

4.30 (Omnicom Group; calculating and interpreting cash flows.)

a.
OMNICOM GROUP
Comparative Statement of Cash Flows
(Amounts in Millions)

	Year 3	Year 4	Year 5
Operations			
Net Income....................................	$ 279	$ 363	$ 499
Depreciation and Amortization....	164	196	226
(Inc.) Dec. in Accounts Receivable..	(238)	(648)	(514)
(Inc.) Dec. in Inventories...............	(35)	(13)	(98)
(Inc.) Dec. in Prepayments...........	(64)	10	(125)
Inc. (Dec.) in Accounts Payable....	330	786	277
Inc. (Dec.) in Other Current Liabilities....................................	70	278	420
Cash Flow from Operations......	$ 506	$ 972	$ 685
Investing			
Acquisition of Property, Plant and Equipment.........................	$ (115)	$ (130)	$ (150)
Acquisition of Investments in Securities...................................	(469)	(643)	(885)
Cash Flow from Investing.........	$ (584)	$ (773)	$ (1,035)
Financing			
Long-term Debt Issued..................	$ 208	$ 83	$ 599
Common Stock Issued (Reacquired)...................................	42	(252)	(187)
Dividends Paid...............................	(88)	(104)	(122)
Cash Flow from Financing........	$ 162	$ (273)	$ 290
Change in Cash...................................	$ 84	$ (74)	$ (60)

b. Interpreting cash flow from operations for a marketing services firm requires a comparison of the change in accounts receivable from clients and accounts payable to various media. Marketing services firms act as agents between these two constituents. In Year 3 and Year 4, the increase in accounts payable slightly exceeded the increase in accounts receivable, indicating that Omnicom Group used the media to finance its accounts receivable. In Year 5, however, accounts payable did not increase nearly as much as accounts receivable. It is unclear whether the media demanded earlier payment, whether the media offered incentives to pay more quickly, or some other reason. As a consequence, cash flow from operations decreased in Year 5. Cash flow from operations continually exceeds expenditures on property, plant, and equipment. This relation is not surprising, given that marketing services firms are not capital intensive. Omnicom Group invested significantly in other entities during the three years. The classification of these investments as noncurrent suggests that they were not made with temporarily excess

4.30 b. continued.

cash but as a more permanent investment. Cash flow from operations was not sufficient to finance both capital expenditures and these investments, except in Year 4. The firm relied on long-term debt to finance the difference. Given the marketing service firms are labor-intensive, one might question the use of debt instead of equity financing for these investments. In fact, Omnicom Group repurchased shares of its common stock in Year 4 and Year 5. Thus, the capital structure of the firm became more risky during the three years.

4.31   (Largay Corporation; effects of gains and losses from sales of equipment on cash flows.) (Amounts in Thousands) Note that the text does not tell students how to do this; they will need to puzzle through this on their own.

	a.	b.	c.
Operations:			
Net Income	$ 100	$ 102	$ 98
Depreciation Expense	15	15	15
Gain on Sale of Equipment	--	(2)	--
Loss on Sale of Equipment	--	--	2
Changes in Working Capital Accounts	(40)	(40)	(40)
Cash Flow from Operations	$ 75	$ 75	$ 75
Investing:			
Sale of Equipment	$ 10	$ 12	$ 8
Acquisition of Buildings and Equipment	(30)	(30)	(30)
Cash Flow from Investing	$ (20)	$ (18)	$ (22)
Financing:			
Repayment of Long-term Debt	$ (40)	$ (40)	$ (40)
Change in Cash	$ 15	$ 17	$ 13
Cash, Beginning of Year	27	27	27
Cash, End of Year	$ 42	$ 44	$ 40

The instructor should note for the students that Cash Flow from Operations remains constant. Income changes, but the gain or loss on sale of equipment is not operating.

4.32   (Effect of various transactions on statement of cash flows.)

If you use transparencies in class, it is effective to flash onto the screen the answer transparency for some problem showing a comprehensive statement of cash flows. Then you can point to the lines affected as the students attempt to answer the question. It helps them by letting them see the possibilities. We use this question for in-class discussion. We seldom assign it for actual homework. A favorite form of question for examinations is to present a schematic statement of cash flows and to ask which lines certain transactions affect and how much. When we use this problem in class, we invariably tell students that it makes a good examination question; this serves to strengthen their interest in the discussion.

4.32 continued.

    a. Retained Earnings (Amortization Expense) (Share-
          holders' Equity Decrease) 600
             Patent (Asset Decrease)...   600

      (3) Decreases by $600; reduces net income through amortization
            expense.

      (4) Increases by $600; amount of expense is added back to net income
            in deriving cash flow from operations.

    No effect on net cash flow from operations.

    b. Factory Site (Asset Increase)... 50,000
         Common Stock (Shareholders' Equity Increase)...   50,000

    The transaction does not appear in the statement of cash flows
    because it does not affect cash. The firm must disclose information
    about the transaction in a supplemental schedule or note.

    c. Inventory (Asset Increase)... 7,500
         Accounts Payable (Liability Increase)....................   7,500

      (4) Increases by $7,500; operating increase in cash from increase in
            Accounts Payable.

      (5) Increases by $7,500; operating decrease in cash for increase in
            inventory.

    The net effect of these two transactions is to leave cash from
    operations unchanged, because the amounts added and subtracted
    change in such a way as to cancel out each other.

    d. Inventory (Asset Increase)... 6,000
         Cash (Asset Decrease)   6,000

      (2) Increases by $6,000; use of cash in operations.

      (5) Increase the subtraction by $6,000; increase in Inventory account,
            subtracted.

    The net effect is to reduce cash from operations by $6,000 the cash
    expenditure for an operating asset, inventory.

4.32 continued.

   e. Retained Earnings (Fire Loss) (Shareholders'
          Equity Decrease)...   1,500
             Inventory (Asset Decrease)................................   1,500

     (1) Decreases by $1,500; net income goes down.

     (2) Increases by $1,500; additions go up because inventory, not cash, was destroyed.

   No net effect on cash flow including cash flow from operations.

   f. Cash (Asset Increase)...   1,450
          Accounts Receivable (Asset Decrease).....................   1,450

     (2) Increases by $1,450 for collection of cash from customers.

     (4) Increases by $1,450; operating increase in cash reflected by decrease in the amount of Accounts Receivable.

   (11) Increases by $1,450.

   Cash flow from operations increases by $1,450, which causes cash to increase by $1,450.

   g. Cash (Asset Increase)... 10,000
          Bonds Payable (Liability Increase)   10,000

     (8) Increases by $10,000; increase in cash from security issue.

   (11) Increases by $10,000.

   h. Cash (Asset Increase)...   4,500
          Equipment (Net of Accumulated Depreciation)
             (Asset Decrease)..   4,500

     (6) Increases by $4,500; increase in cash from sale of noncurrent asset.

   (11) Increases by $4,500.

4.33   (The GAP; preparing and interpreting the statement of cash flows using a columnar work sheet.) (Amounts in Millions)

a. **Year 6**

(Increases) Decreases in Assets	Balance Sheet Changes	Operations	Investing	Financing
Marketable Securities	$ (46)		$ (46)	
Merchandise Inventories	(96)	$ (96)		
Prepayments	(1)	(1)		
Property, Plant and Equipment (at Cost)	(372)		(372)	
Accumulated Depreciation	215	215		
Other Noncurrent Assets	(51)		(51)	
Increases (Decreases) in Liabilities and Shareholders' Equity				
Accounts Payable—Merchandise Suppliers	114	114		
Notes Payable to Banks	18			$ 18
Income Taxes Payable	26	26		
Other Current Liabilities	90	90		
Common Stock	(360)			(360)
Retained Earnings	369	453		(84)
Increase (Decrease) in Cash	$ (94)	$ 801	$ (469)	$ (426)

4.33 a. continued.

Year 7

(Increases) Decreases in Assets	Balance Sheet Changes	Operations	Investing	Financing
Marketable Securities..............	$ 46		$ 46	
Merchandise Inventories........	(154)	$ (154)		
Prepayments	(56)	(56)		
Property, Plant and Equipment (at Cost)	(466)		(466)	
Accumulated Depreciation.....	270	270		
Other Noncurrent Assets........	(15)		(15)	
Increases (Decreases) in Liabilities and Shareholders' Equity				
Accounts Payable—Merchandise Suppliers...............	134	134		
Notes Payable to Banks..........	45			$ 45
Income Taxes Payable	(7)	(7)		
Other Current Liabilities.......	123	123		
Bonds Payable	577			577
Common Stock.........................	(524)			(524)
Retained Earnings...................	455	534		(79)
Increase (Decrease) in Cash......................................	$ 428	$ 844	$ (435)	$ 19

4.33 continued.

b.

THE GAP
Statement of Cash Flows
For Year 6 and Year 7

	Year 6	Year 7
Operations:		
Net Income...	$ 453	$ 534
Depreciation	215	270
(Increase) Decrease in Merchandise Inventories...	(96)	(154)
(Increase) Decrease in Prepayments	(1)	(56)
Increase (Decrease) in Accounts Payable—		
Merchandise Suppliers..	114	134
Increase (Decrease) in Income Taxes Payable........	26	(7)
Increase (Decrease) in Other Current Liabil-		
ities..	90	123
Cash Flow from Operations.......................................	$ 801	$ 844
Investing:		
Acquisition of Property, Plant and Equipment......	$ (372)	$ (466)
Sale of Marketable Securities	--	46
Acquisition of Marketable Securities.......................	(46)	--
Acquisition of Other Noncurrent Assets.................	(51)	(15)
Cash Flow from Investing...	$ (469)	$ (435)
Financing:		
Increase in Short-Term Borrowing	$ 18	$ 45
Increase in Long-Term Borrowing	--	577
Decrease in Common Stock.......................................	(360)	(524)
Dividends	(84)	(79)
Cash Flow from Financing...	$ (426)	$ 19
Increase (Decrease) in Cash	$ (94)	$ 428
Cash, Beginning of Year...	580	486
Cash, End of Year	$ 486	$ 914

4.33 continued.

c. **Year 6**

	Income Statement Account	+	Operating Balance Sheet Changes	=	Cash Receipts	−	Cash Disburse-ments	=	Cash Flow from Operations
Sales	$ 5,284				$ 5,284				
Cost of Goods Sold	(3,285)		$ (96)				$(3,267)		
			114						
Selling and Administrative Expenses	(1,250)		(1)				(946)		
			215						
			90						
Income Tax Expense	(296)		26				(270)		
Net Income	$ 453	+	$ 348	=	$ 5,284	−	$(4,483)	=	$ 801

Year 7

	Income Statement Account	+	Operating Balance Sheet Changes	=	Cash Receipts	−	Cash Disburse-ments	=	Cash Flow from Operations
Sales	$ 6,508				$ 6,508				
Cost of Goods Sold	(4,022)		$(154)				$(4,042)		
			134						
Selling and Administrative Expenses	(1,632)		(56)				(1,295)		
			270						
			123						
Income Tax Expense	(320)		(7)				(327)		
Net Income	$ 534	+	$ 310	=	$ 6,508	−	$(5,664)	=	$ 844

d. Cash flow from operations exceeded net income each year primarily because of the addback for depreciation and the delay in paying Other Current Liabilities. Cash flow from operations was more than sufficient to finance acquisition of property, plant, and equipment. The Gap used its excess cash flow during each year to repurchase shares of its common stock. The firm increased its long-term borrowing in Year 7, thereby increasing the balance in its cash account.

4.34   (Circuit City; preparing and interpreting the statement of cash flows using a columnar work sheet.) (Amounts in Millions)

a. **Year 7**

	Balance Sheet Changes	Operations	Investing	Financing
(Increases) Decreases in Assets				
Accounts Receivable...............	$(208)	$ (208)		
Merchandise Inventories........	(69)	(69)		
Prepayments............................	8	8		
Property, Plant and Equipment (at Cost)......................	(209)		$ (209)	
Accumulated Depreciation.....	99	99		
Increases (Decreases) in Liabilities and Shareholders' Equity				
Accounts Payable—Merchandise Suppliers..............	117	117		
Notes Payable to Banks.........	(92)			$ (92)
Other Current Liabilities.......	(71)	(71)		
Bonds Payable..........................	31			31
Common Stock.........................	428			428
Retained Earnings...................	125	136		(11)
Increase (Decrease) in Cash..	$ 159	$ 12	$ (209)	$ 356

Year 8

	Balance Sheet Changes	Operations	Investing	Financing
(Increases) Decreases in Assets				
Accounts Receivable...............	$ (66)	$ (66)		
Merchandise Inventories........	(19)	(19)		
Prepayments............................	15	15		
Property, Plant and Equipment (at Cost)......................	(291)		$ (291)	
Accumulated Depreciation.....	116	116		
Increases (Decreases) in Liabilities and Shareholders' Equity				
Accounts Payable—Merchandise Suppliers..............	44	44		
Notes Payable to Banks.........	27			$ 27
Other Current Liabilities.......	(9)	(9)		
Bonds Payable..........................	(19)			(19)
Common Stock.........................	25			25
Retained Earnings...................	91	104		(13)
Increase (Decrease) in Cash..	$ (86)	$ 185	$ (291)	$ 20

4.34 continued.

b.

CIRCUIT CITY
Statement of Cash Flows
For Year 7 and Year 8

	Year 7	Year 8
Operations:		
Net Income	$ 136	$ 104
Depreciation	99	116
(Increase) Decrease in Accounts Receivable	(208)	(66)
(Increase) Decrease in Merchandise Inventories	(69)	(19)
(Increase) Decrease in Prepayments	8	15
Increase (Decrease) in Accounts Payable—		
Merchandise Suppliers	117	44
Increase (Decrease) in Other Current Liabilities	(71)	(9)
Cash Flow from Operations	$ 12	$ 185
Investing:		
Acquisition of Property, Plant and Equipment	$ (209)	$ (291)
Financing:		
Increase (Decrease) in Short-Term Borrowing	$ (92)	$ 27
Increase (Decrease) in Long-Term Borrowing	31	(19)
Increase (Decrease) in Common Stock	428	25
Dividends	(11)	(13)
Cash Flow from Financing	$ 356	$ 20
Increase (Decrease) in Cash	$ 159	$ (86)
Cash, Beginning of Year	44	203
Cash, End of Year	$ 203	$ 117

c.

	Year 7	Year 8
Sales Revenue	$ 7,664	$ 8,871
Less Increase in Accounts Receivable	(208)	(66)
Cash Collected from Customers	$ 7,456	$ 8,805

d.

	Year 7	Year 8
Cost of Goods Sold	$ (5,903)	$ (6,827)
Plus Increase in Inventories	(69)	(19)
Less Increase in Accounts Payable—Merchandise Suppliers	117	44
Cash Paid to Suppliers	$ (5,855)	$ (6,802)

e.

	Year 7	Year 8
Selling and Administrative Expenses	$ (1,511)	$ (1,849)
Plus Decrease in Prepayments	8	15
Less Decrease in Other Current Liabilities	(71)	(9)
Plus Depreciation	99	116
Cash Paid to Suppliers of Selling and Administrative Services	$ (1,475)	$ (1,727)

4.34 continued.

    f. Cash flow from operations was significantly less than net income during Year 7, primarily because of a buildup of accounts receivable from customers. Circuit City financed its acquisitions of property, plant and equipment by issuing common stock. Cash flow from operations exceeded net income during Year 8 because of the addback for depreciation and a smaller increase in accounts receivable. Cash flow from operations was not sufficient to finance capital expenditures. Circuit City used cash on hand at the beginning of the year to finance the shortfall.

4.35 (Heidi's Hide-Out; inferring cash flows from trial balance data.)

    a.

Sales Revenue from Retail Customers	$ 120,000
Less Increase in Accounts Receivable from Retail Customers ($8,900 – $8,000)	(900)
Plus Increase in Advances from Retail Customers ($10,000 – $9,000)	1,000
Cash Collected from Retail Customers	$ 120,100

    b.

Rent Expense	$ (33,000)
Less Increase in Advances to Landlords ($5,600 – $5,000)	(600)
Less Decrease in Rent Payable to Landlords ($5,300 – $6,000)	(700)
Cash Paid to Landlords	$ (34,300)

    c.

Wage Expense	$ (20,000)
Less Increase in Advances to Employees ($1,500 – $1,000)	(500)
Less Decrease in Wages Payable to Employees ($1,800 – $2,000)	(200)
Cash Paid to Employees	$ (20,700)

    d.

Cost of Retail Merchandise Sold	$ (90,000)
Plus Decrease in Inventory of Retail Merchandise ($10,000 – $11,000)	1,000
Less Increase in Advances to Suppliers of Retail Merchandise ($10,500 – $10,000)	(500)
Less Decrease in Accounts Payable to Suppliers of Retail Merchandise ($7,700 – $8,000)	(300)
Cash Paid to Suppliers of Retail Merchandise	$ (89,800)

4.36 (Digit Retail Enterprises, Inc.; inferring cash flows from balance sheet and income statement data.)

a.
Sales Revenue	$ 270,000
Less Increase in Accounts Receivable ($38,000 – $23,000)	(15,000)
Less Decrease in Advances from Customers ($6,100 – $8,500)	(2,400)
Cash Received from Customers during the Year	$ 252,600

b.
Cost of Goods Sold	$ (145,000)
Less Increase in Merchandise Inventory ($65,000 – $48,000)	(17,000)
Acquisition Cost of Merchandise Purchased during the Year	$ (162,000)

c.
Acquisition Cost of Merchandise Purchased during the Year (from Part b.)	$ (162,000)
Plus Increase in Accounts Payable—Merchandise Suppliers ($20,000 – $18,000)	2,000
Cash Paid for Acquisitions of Merchandise during the Year	$ (160,000)

d.
Salaries Expense	$ (68,000)
Plus Increase in Salaries Payable ($2,800 – $2,100)	700
Cash Paid to Salaried Employees during the Year	$ (67,300)

e.
Insurance Expense	$ (5,000)
Less Increase in Prepaid Insurance ($12,000 – $9,000)	(3,000)
Cash Paid to Insurance Companies during the Year	$ (8,000)

f.
Rent Expense	$ (12,000)
Plus Decrease in Prepaid Rent ($0 – $2,000)	2,000
Plus Increase in Rent Payable ($3,000 – $0)	3,000
Cash Paid to Landlords for Rental of Space during the Year	$ (7,000)

g.
Increase in Retained Earnings ($11,800 – $11,500)	$ 300
Less Net Income	(9,600)
Dividend Declared	$ (9,300)
Less Decrease in Dividend Payable ($2,600 – $4,200)	(1,600)
Cash Paid for Dividends during the Year	$ (10,900)

4.36 continued.

h.

Depreciation Expense	$ (20,000)
Plus Increase in Accumulated Depreciation ($35,000 – $20,000)	15,000
Accumulated Depreciation of Property, Plant and Equipment Sold	$ (5,000)
Cost of Property, Plant and Equipment Sold ($100,000 – $90,000)	10,000
Book Value of Property, Plant and Equipment Sold	$ 5,000
Plus Gain on Sale of Property, Plant and Equipment	3,200
Cash Received from Sale of Property, Plant and Equipment	$ 8,200

4.37 (Swan Corporation; preparing and interpreting a statement of cash flows using a columnar work sheet.)

a.

	Balance Sheet Changes	Operations	Investing	Financing
(Increases) Decreases in Assets				
Accounts Receivable	$(12,000)	$(12,000)		
Merchandise Inventories	(20,000)	(20,000)		
Property, Plant and Equipment	(75,000)		$(75,000)	
Accumulated Depreciation	79,000	79,000		
Increases (Decreases) in Liabilities and Shareholders' Equity				
Accounts Payable	(25,000)	(25,000)		
Income Taxes Payable	5,000	5,000		
Bonds Payable	(4,000)			$ (4,000)
Common Stock	5,000			5,000
Retained Earnings	50,000	50,000		
Increase (Decrease) in Cash	$ 3,000	$ 77,000	$(75,000)	$ 1,000

4.37 continued.

b.

SWAN CORPORATION
Statement of Cash Flows
For the Current Year

Operations:		
Net Income..	$ 50,000	
Additions:		
Depreciation Expense	79,000	
Increase in Income Taxes Payable.................	5,000	
Subtractions:		
Increase in Accounts Receivable	(12,000)	
Increase in Merchandise Inventories.............	(20,000)	
Decrease in Accounts Payable	(25,000)	
Cash Flow from Operations....................................		$ 77,000
Investing:		
Acquisition of Property, Plant, and Equip-		
ment...		(75,000)
Financing:		
Issue of Common Stock.......................................	$ 5,000	
Retirement of Bonds..	(4,000)	
Cash Flow from Financing.......................................		1,000
Net Change in Cash		$ 3,000
Cash, January 1		12,000
Cash, December 31		$ 15,000

c. Cash flow from operations was positive and sufficient to finance acquisitions of property, plant and equipment. The firm issued common stock to finance the retirement of long-term debt.

4.38 (Hale Company; preparing a statement of cash flows with disposal of long-term assets.)

a. Columnar work sheet

	Balance Sheet Changes	Cash Flow Implications		
B/S Accounts	**Total Change**	**Operating**	**Investing**	**Financing**
Accounts Receivable.............................	(13,000)	(13,000)		
Inventory...	(11,000)	(11,000)		
Land..	--	--		
Buildings and Equipment...................	(40,000)			
Sold B&E Costing $15,000 for $5,000............................ 15,000			5,000	
Purchased New Buildings and Equipment .... (55,000)			(55,000)	
Less Accumulated Depreciation	44,000			
Total Depreciation Expense. for the Year........................ 54,000		54,000		
Sold B&E with Accumu-lated Depreciation of .... (10,000)				
Accounts Payable for Inventory..	5,000	5,000		
Interest Payable.................................	(2,000)	(2,000)		
Mortgage Payable	(11,000)			(11,000)
Common Stock....................................	--			
Retained Earnings..............................	34,000	44,000		(10,000)
Increase (Decrease) in Cash..	6,000	77,000	(50,000)	(21,000)

Income Statement		Adjustments		Cash Receipts	Cash Payments	Net Cash Inflow (Outflow)
Net Income..	44,000					
Revenues............................. 1,200,000		(13,000)	(Accounts Receivable)	1,187,000		1,187,000
Cost of Goods Sold.............. (788,000)		(11,000)	(Inventory)			--
		5,000	(Accounts Payable)		(794,000)	(794,000)
Wages and Salaries .... (280,000)					(280,000)	(280,000)
Depreciation.......................... (54,000)		54,000	(No Cash Flow)			--
Interest................................. (12,000)		(2,000)	(Interest Payable)		(14,000)	(14,000)
Income Taxes....................... (22,000)					(22,000)	(22,000)
Net Income........................... 44,000						
Cash Flow from Operations.............................	77,000			1,187,000	(1,110,000)	77,000

4.38 a. continued.

HALE COMPANY
Statement of Cash Flows
For the Year

Indirect Method

Operating Activities:

Net Income	$ 44,000	
Depreciation	54,000	
Changes in Operating Accounts:		
Accounts Receivable	(13,000)	
Inventory	(11,000)	
Accounts Payable	5,000	
Interest Payable	(2,000)	
Cash from Operations		$ 77,000
Investing Activities:		
Cash Used for Acquisition	$ (55,000)	
Cash Received by Sale	5,000	
Net Cash Used for Investing		(50,000)
Financing Activities:		
Cash Used for Dividends	$ (10,000)	
Cash Used to Repay Mortgage	(11,000)	
Net Cash Used for Financing		(21,000)
Net Change in Cash for Year		$ 6,000
Cash, January 1		52,000
Cash, December 31		$ 58,000

4.38 a. continued.

Direct Method

Operating Activities:
  Sources of Cash:
    Cash Received from Customers .... $ 1,187,000
  Uses of Cash:
    Payments to Suppliers .... (794,000)
    Payments to Employees .... (280,000)
    Interest Payments .... (14,000)
    Tax Payments .... (22,000)
Cash Flow from Operations .... $ 77,000

Reconciliation of Net Income to Cash:		
Net Income	$	44,000
Depreciation		54,000
Changes in Operating Accounts:		
Accounts Receivable		(13,000)
Inventory		(11,000)
Accounts Payable		5,000
Interest Payable		(2,000)
Cash from Operations	$	77,000

Investing Activities:
  Cash Used for New Acquisition .... $ (55,000)
  Cash Received from Disposition 5,000
Net Cash Provided by (Used for) Investing ....   (50,000)
Financing Activities:
  Cash Used for Dividends .... $ (10,000)
  Cash Used to Repay Mortgage .... (11,000)
Net Cash Provided by (Used for) Financing ....   (21,000)
Net Change in Cash for Year .... $ 6,000
Cash, January 1   52,000
Cash, December 31 .... $58,000

b. Sales Revenue .... $ 1,200,000
    Less Increase in Accounts Receivable ($106,000 –
      $93,000) .... (13,000)
    Cash Collected from Customers during the Year .... $ 1,187,000

c. Cost of Goods Sold .... $ (788,000)
    Less Increase in Inventories ($162,000 – $151,000) .... (11,000)
    Plus Increase in Accounts Payable for Inventory
      ($141,000 – $136,000) 5,000
    Cash Paid to Suppliers of Inventory during the Year ...... $ (794,000)

d. Interest Expense .... $ (12,000)
    Less Decrease in Interest Payable ($8,000 – $10,000) ..... (2,000)
    Cash Paid for Interest during the Year .... $ (14,000)

4.38 continued.

e. Cash flow from operations was sufficient to finance acquisitions of equipment during the year. The firm used the excess cash flow to pay dividends and retire long-term debt.

4.39 (GTI, Inc.; preparing and interpreting a statement of cash flows using a columnar work sheet.) (Amounts in Thousands)

a. Derivation with columnar work sheet.

Year 8		Balance Sheet Changes	Cash Flow Implications		
B/S Accounts:		Total Change	Operating	Investing	Financing
Accounts Receivable.....		(168)	(168)		
Inventories......................		(632)	(632)		
Prepayments		(154)	(154)		
Property, Plant and Equipment (Net)		(792)			
Purchased New Property, Plant and Equipment (Plug).......	(1,433)			(1,433)	
Depreciation Expense for the Year..................	641		641		
Other Noncurrent Assets............................		(366)			
Purchased New Patents (Plug).............	(391)			(391)	
Amortization Expense of Patents.....................	25		25		
Accounts Payable..........		(769)	(769)		
Notes Payable to Banks...........................		220			220
Other Current Liabilities...........................		(299)	(299)		
Long-Term Debt.............		2,339			2,339
Other Non current Liabilities........................		(37)	(37)		
Preferred Stock.............		289			289
Common Stock...............		2			2
Additional Paid-in Capital..........................		7			7
Retained Earnings........		405	417		(12)
Increase (Decrease) in Cash..........................		45	(976)	(1,824)	2,845

4.39 a. continued.

Year 8	Income Statement		Adjustments	Cash Receipts	Cash Payments	Net Cash Inflow (Outflow)
Net Income	417					
Sales	22,833	(168)	(Accounts Receivable)	22,665		22,665
Cost of Goods Sold	(16,518)	(632)	(Inventory)			--
		(769)	(Accounts Payable)		(17,919)	(17,919)
Depreciation	(641)	641	(No Cash Flow)			
Amortization of Patents	(25)	25	(No Cash Flow)			
Other Selling and Administrative Expenses	(4,183)	(299)	(Other Current Liabilities)			
		(154)	(Prepayments)			
		(37)	(Other Noncurrent Liabilities)		(4,673)	(4,673)
Interest	(459)	--	(Interest Payable)		(459)	(459)
Income Taxes	(590)				(590)	(590)
Net Income	417					
Cash Flow from Operations	(976)			22,665	(23,641)	(976)

4.39 a. continued.

Year 9	Balance Sheet Changes	Cash Flow Implications		
B/S Accounts:	**Total Change**	**Operating**	**Investing**	**Financing**
Accounts Receivable.....	1,391	1,391		
Inventories.....................	872	872		
Prepayments	148	148		
Property, Plant and Equipment (Net)	571			
Purchased New Property, Plant and Equipment (Plug).......	(54)		(54)	
Depreciation Expense for the Year..................	625		625	
Other Noncurrent Assets..........................	103			
Sale of Existing Patents (Plug).............	63		63	
Amortization Expense of Patents.....................	40		40	
Accounts Payable..........	(13)	(13)		
Notes Payable to Banks...........................	2,182			2,182
Other Current Liabilities..........................	(82)	(82)		
Long-Term Debt............	(2,608)			(2,608)
Other Noncurrent Liabilities.......................	24	24		
Preferred Stock..............	--			--
Common Stock..............	1			1
Additional Paid-in Capital.........................	2			2
Retained Earnings........	(2,699)	(2,691)		(8)
Increase (Decrease) in Cash	(108)	314	9	(431)

4.39 a. continued.

Year 9	Income Statement		Adjustments	Cash Receipts	Cash Payments	Net Cash Inflow (Outflow)
Net Income	(2,691)					
Sales	11,960	1,391	(Accounts Receivable)	13,351		13,351
Cost of Goods Sold.......	(11,031)	872	(Inventory)			--
		(13)	(Accounts Payable)		(10,172)	(10,172)
Depreciation...............	(625)	625	(No Cash Flow)			
Amortization of Patents...................	(40)	40	(No Cash Flow)			
Other Selling and Administrative Expenses	(2,831)	(82)	(Other Current Liabilities)			
		148	(Prepayments)			
		24	(Other Noncurrent Liabilities)		(2,741)	(2,741)
Interest......................	(452)	--	(Interest Payable)		(452)	(452)
Income Taxes.............	328				328	328
Net Income	(2,691)					
Cash Flow from Operations	314			13,351	(13,037)	314

4.39 continued.

b.

GTI, INC.
Statement of Cash Flows
For Year 8

Direct Method
Operating Activities:
  Sources of Cash:
    Cash Received from Customers .... $ 22,665
  Uses of Cash:
    Payments to Suppliers of Inventory .... (17,919)
    Payments to Other Suppliers .... (4,673)
    Interest Payments... (459)
    Tax Payments .... (590)
Cash Flow from Operations....................................... $ (976)

Reconciliation of Net Income to Cash:		
Net Income	$	417
Depreciation..		641
Amortization of Patents		25
Changes in Operating Accounts:		
Accounts Receivable..		(168)
Inventory...		(632)
Prepayments		(154)
Accounts Payable		(769)
Other Current Liabilities		(299)
Other Noncurrent Liabilities..............................		(37)
Cash from Operations	$	(976)

Investing Activities:
  Cash for New Property, Plant and Equipment..... $ (1,433)
  Cash for New Patents .... (391)
Net Cash Provided by (Used for) Investing...............   (1,824)
Financing Activities:
  Cash Raised from Banks.................................... $ 220
  Cash Raised from Issue of Long-Term Debt.......... 2,339
  Cash Used for Dividends.................................... (12)
  Cash Raised from Preferred Stock Issue............... 289
  Cash Raised from Common Stock Issue 9
Net Cash Provided by Financing...............................   2,845
Net Change in Cash for Year .... $ 45
Cash, December 31, Year 7..   430
Cash, December 31, Year 8.. $ 475

4.39 b. continued.

GTI, INC.
Statement of Cash Flows
For Year 9

Direct Method

Operating Activities:

Sources of Cash:

Cash Received from Customers	$ 13,351	
Uses of Cash:		
Payments to Suppliers of Inventory	(10,172)	
Payments to Other Suppliers	(2,741)	
Interest Payments	(452)	
Tax Payments	328	
Cash Flow from Operations		$ 314

Reconciliation of Net Income to Cash:		
Net Income	$ (2,691)	
Depreciation	625	
Amortization of Patents	40	
Changes in Operating Accounts:		
Accounts Receivable	1,391	
Inventory	872	
Prepayments	148	
Accounts Payable	(13)	
Other Current Liabilities	(82)	
Other Noncurrent Liabilities	24	
Cash from Operations	$ 314	

Investing Activities:		
Cash for New Property, Plant and Equipment	$ (54)	
Cash Received for Disposition of Patents	63	
Net Cash Provided by (Used for) Investing		9
Financing Activities:		
Cash Raised from Banks	$ 2,182	
Cash Paid to Reduce Long-Term Debt	(2,608)	
Cash Used for Dividends	(8)	
Cash Raised from Preferred Stock Issue	--	
Cash Raised from Common Stock Issue	3	
Net Cash Provided by (Used for) Financing		(431)
Net Change in Cash for Year		$ (108)
Cash, December 31, Year 8		475
Cash, December 31, Year 9		$ 367

4.39 b. continued.

Indirect Method

GTI, INC.
Statement of Cash Flows
For Year 8 and Year 9

	Year 8	Year 9
Operations:		
Net Income (Loss)..	$ 417	$ (2,691)
Depreciation Expense..	641	625
Amortization Expense..	25	40
Inc. (Dec.) in Other Noncurrent Liabilities....	(37)	24
(Inc.) Dec. in Accounts Receivable....................	(168)	1,391
(Inc.) Dec. in Inventories	(632)	872
(Inc.) Dec. in Prepayments.............................	(154)	148
Inc. (Dec.) in Accounts Payable.........................	(769)	(13)
Inc. (Dec.) in Other Current Liabilities...........	(299)	(82)
Cash Flow from Operations....................................	$ (976)	$ 314
Investing:		
Sale of Patents...	$ --	$ 63
Acquisition of Property, Plant and Equipment..	(1,433)	(54)
Acquisition of Patents	(391)	--
Cash Flow from Investing......................................	$ (1,824)	$ 9
Financing:		
Inc. (Dec.) in Notes Payable to Banks	$ 220	$ 2,182
Inc. (Dec.) in Long-Term Debt..........................	2,339	(2,608)
Increase in Preferred Stock	289	--
Increase in Common Stock................................	9	3
Dividends Paid..	(12)	(8)
Cash Flow from Financing...................................	$ 2,845	$ (431)
Net Change in Cash	$ 45	$ (108)
Cash, Beginning of Year.......................................	430	475
Cash, End of Year..	$ 475	$ 367

c. Cash flow from operations was negative during Year 8, despite positive net income, primarily because GTI reduced accounts payable and other current liabilities. The increases in receivables, inventories, and prepayments suggest that GTI grew during Year 8 relative to Year 7. One usually finds in these cases that current operating liabilities increase as well. The reduction in these current liabilities occurred either because GTI chose to use cash to liquidate these obligations or because creditors forced the firm to repay. GTI obtained the cash needed to finance the operating cash flow shortfall and capital expenditures by increasing short- and long-term debt and issuing preferred stock.

4.39 c. continued.

GTI experienced a net loss in Year 9 but its cash flow from operations turned positive. The firm reduced receivables, inventories and prepayments with only minor reductions in current operating liabilities. The small reductions in current operating liabilities relative to the declines in current operating assets reflect either a stretching of short-term creditors or a return to a normal level of current operating liabilities after the repayment made in Year 8. GTI dramatically decreased capital expenditures in Year 9 and replaced long-term debt with short-term borrowing.

4.40   (Quinta Company; working backwards through the statement of cash flows.)

QUINTA COMPANY
Balance Sheet
January 1, Year 5
($ in 000's)

Assets

Current Assets:
Cash	$ 20	
Accounts Receivable	190	
Merchandise Inventories	280	
Total Current Assets		$ 490
Land		50
Buildings and Equipment	$ 405	
Less Accumulated Depreciation	(160)	245
Investments		140
Total Assets		$ 925

Liabilities and Shareholders' Equity

Current Liabilities:
Accounts Payable	$ 255	
Other Current Liabilities	130	
Total Current Liabilities		$ 385
Bonds Payable		60
Common Stock		140
Retained Earnings		340
Total Liabilities and Shareholders' Equity		$ 925

Shown on the following page is the Transactions Spreadsheet. Entries (1)—(13) are reconstructed from the statement of cash flows. Changes for the year are appropriately debited or credited to end-of-year balances to get beginning-of-year balances. Amounts are shown in thousands.

4.40 continued.

Transactions spreadsheet.

Transactions, By Number and Description

Balance Sheet Accounts	Balance: Beginning of Period (Derived)	Net Income for Year	Depreciation Expense	Increase in Accounts Payable	Increase in Accounts Receivable	Increase in Merchandise Inventories	Decrease in Other Current Liabilities	Sale of Investments	Sale of Buildings and Equipment	Sale of Land	Acquire New Buildings and Equipment	Issue Common Stock	Issue Bonds Payable	Dividends Paid in Cash	Balance: End of Period (Given)
		1	2	3	4	5	6	7	8	9	10	11	12	13	
ASSETS															
Current Assets:															
Cash	20	200	60	25	-30	-40	-45	40	15	10	-130	60	40	-200	25
Accounts Receivable	190				30										220
Merchandise Inventories	280					40									320
Total Current Assets	490														565
Noncurrent Assets:															
Land	50									-10					40
Building and Equipment	405								-35		130				500
Accumulated Depreciation	-160		-60						20						(200)
Investments	140							-40							100
Total Noncurrent Assets	435														440
Total Assets	925														1,005
LIABILITIES AND SHAREHOLDERS' EQUITY															
Current Liabilities:															
Accounts Payable	255			25											280
Other Current Liabilities	130						-45								85
Total Current Liabilities	385														365
Noncurrent Liabilities:															
Bonds Payable	60												40		100
Total Noncurrent Liabilities	60														100
Total Liabilities	445														465
Shareholders' Equity:															
Common Stock	140											60			200
Retained Earnings	340	200												-200	340
Total Shareholders' Equity	480														540
Total Liabilities and Shareholders' Equity	925														1,005
Imbalance, if Any	-	-	-	-	-	-	-	-	-	-	-	-	-	-	-
Income Statement Accounts	Income Summary														

4.41   (Analog for direct and indirect methods for preparing the statement of cash flows.)

   a.   **Direct Method:**

Mary's Earnings	$ 1,200
Mary's Expenditures	(650)
Mary's Contribution to Family Savings	$ 550

   b.   **Indirect Method:**

Family Savings	$ 850
Add Back John's Expenditures Not Affecting Mary's Savings	700
Subtract John's Earnings, Not Contributing to Mary's Savings	(1,000)
Mary's Contribution to Family Savings	$ 550

No one in a right mind would use the method in Part *b*. to derive Mary's savings. We use this exhibit to illustrate the difficulties in thinking about the indirect method when the direct method makes interpretation so much easier.

4.42   (NIKE, Inc.; interpreting the statement of cash flows.)

   a.   NIKE's growth in sales and net income led to increases of account receivable and inventories. NIKE, however, did not increase its accounts payable and other current operating liabilities to help finance the buildup in current assets. Thus, its cash flow from operations decreased.

   b.   NIKE increased its acquisitions of property, plant and equipment to provide the firm with operating capacity to sustain its rapid growth. NIKE also acquired investments in securities of other firms. It is not clear from the statement of cash flows whether the investments represented short-term investments of temporarily excess cash (a current asset) or long-term investments made to develop an operating relation with another firm (noncurrent asset).

   c.   NIKE used cash flow from operations during Year 7 and Year 8 to finance its investing activities. The excess cash flow after investing activities served to repay short- and long-term debt and pay dividends. Cash flow from operations during Year 9 was insufficient to finance investing activities. NIKE engaged in short-term borrowing to make up the shortfall and finance the payment of dividends.

4.42 continued.

    d. Operating cash flows should generally finance the payment of dividends. Either operating cash flows or long-term sources of capital should generally finance acquisitions of property, plant and equipment. Thus, NIKE's use of short-term borrowing seems inappropriate. One might justify such an action if NIKE (1) expected cash flow from operations during Year 10 to return to its historical levels, (2) expected cash outflows for property, plant and equipment to decrease during Year 10, or (3) took advantage of comparatively low short-term borrowing rates during Year 9 and planned to refinance this debt with long-term borrowing during Year 10.

4.43   (Boise Cascade; interpreting the statement of cash flows.)

    a. Forest products companies are capital intensive. Depreciation is therefore a substantial non-cash expense each year. The addback for depreciation converts a net loss each year into positive cash flow from operations. Note that cash flow from operations increased each year as the net loss decreased.

    b. Boise Cascade had substantial changes in its property, plant and equipment during the three years. It likely built new, more efficient production facilities and sold off older, less efficient facilities.

    c. For the three years combined, Boise Cascade reduced its long-term debt and replaced it with preferred stock. The sales of forest products are cyclical. When the economy is in a recession, as apparently occurred during the three years, the high fixed cost of capital-intensive manufacturing facilities can result in net losses. If Boise Cascade is unable to repay debt on schedule during such years, it causes expensive financial distress or even bankruptcy. Firms have more latitude with respect to dividends on preferred stock than interest on debt. Thus, a shift toward preferred stock and away from long-term debt reduces the bankruptcy risk of Boise Cascade. Note that Boise Cascade continued to pay, and even increase, dividends despite operating at a net loss. Most shareholders prefer less rather than more fluctuation in their dividends over the business cycle.

4.44   (Interpreting the statement of cash flow relations.)

American Airlines—Property, plant and equipment comprises a large proportion of the total assets of American Airlines. Depreciation expense is a major expense for the airline. The firm operated at a net loss for the year, but the addback for depreciation resulted in a positive cash flow from operations. Cash flow from operations was not sufficient to fund capital expenditures on new property, plant and equipment. American Airlines is apparently growing since its capital expenditures exceed depreciation expense for the year. The firm financed its capital expendi-

4.44 continued.

tures in part with cash flow from operations and in part with the issuance of additional long-term debt and capital stock. The net effect of the cash flow from financing is a reduction in liabilities and an increase in capital stock (actually preferred stock). Operating at a net loss increases the risk of bankruptcy. Perhaps American Airlines reduced the amount of debt in its capital structure to reduce fixed payment claims and substituted preferred stock that generally requires dividend payments only when declared by the board of directors.

American Home Products—Because of patent protection, pharmaceutical companies tend to generate relatively high profit margins and significant cash flows from operations. Although the manufacturing process for pharmaceutical products is capital intensive, cash flow from operations is usually sufficient to fund capital expenditures. American Home Products used the excess cash flow to pay dividends and repurchase capital stock. The firm also borrowed short-term funds and invested the proceeds in the acquisition of another business. Borrowing short term to finance investments in long-term assets is usually undesirable, because the firm must repay the debt before the long-term assets generate sufficient cash flow. Perhaps American Home Products needed to borrow short term to consummate the acquisition, with the expectation of refinancing the short-term debt with long-term borrowing soon after the acquisition. Alternatively, American Home Products might have anticipated a decline in long-term rates in the near future and borrowed short term until long-term rates actually declined.

Interpublic Group—An advertising agency serves as a link between clients desiring advertising time and space and various media with advertising time and space to sell. Thus, the principal asset of an advertising agency is accounts receivable from clients and the principal liability is accounts payable to various media. Interpublic Group reports an increase in accounts receivable of $66 million and an increase in accounts payable of $59 million. Thus, the firm appeared to manage its receivables/payables position well. Advertising agencies lease most of the physical facilities used in their operations. They purchase equipment for use in designing and producing advertising copy. Thus, they must make some capital expenditures. Cash flow from operations, however, is more than sufficient to finance acquisitions of equipment. Interpublic Group used the excess cash flow plus the proceeds of additional short- and long-term borrowing to pay dividends, repurchase capital stock, and increase cash on the balance sheet.

Procter & Gamble—Procter & Gamble's brand names create high profit margins and cash flows from operations. Cash flow from operations is more than adequate to finance capital expenditures. Note that capital ex-

4.44 continued.

penditures significantly exceed depreciation, suggesting that the firm is still in a growth mode. The firm used the excess cash flow to repay short- and long-term debt and to pay dividends.

Reebok—Cash flow from operations for Reebok is less than net income plus depreciation, a somewhat unusual relationship for a seasoned firm. Reebok increased its accounts receivable and inventories during the year but did not stretch its accounts payable commensurably. The financing section of the statement of cash flows suggests that Reebok might have used short-term debt to finance some of its working capital needs. Cash flow from operations was still more than sufficient to fund capital expenditures. One explanation for the sufficiency of cash flow from operations to cover capital expenditures is that Reebok is not very capital intensive. The relation between depreciation expense and net income supports this explanation. Reebok outsources virtually all of its manufacturing. Reebok used the excess cash flows from operating and investing activities to pay dividends and repurchase its capital stock.

Texas Instruments—Like American Home Products and Upjohn (discussed later), Texas Instruments invests heavily in technology to create a competitive advantage. Patents and copyrights on computer hardware, software, and other products serve as a barrier to entry by competitors and provide Texas Instruments with an attractive profit margin. Texas Instruments differs from the two pharmaceutical companies with respect to the amount of depreciation relative to net income. Despite generating less than one-half of the net income of American Home Products, Texas Instruments has more than twice the amount of depreciation expense and capital expenditures. Thus, Texas Instruments is likely more capital intensive than the other two technology-based companies. Note that the changes in individual working capital accounts are relatively large, compared to the amount of net income. These relations suggest, although do not prove, that the operations of Texas Instruments grew significantly during the year. Cash flow from operations was sufficient to fund capital expenditures and increase the balance of cash on the balance sheet. Note that Texas Instruments issued capital stock during the year and repaid long-term debt. The amounts involved, however, are small.

Limited Brands—Current assets and current liabilities dominate the balance sheets of retailers. Thus, working capital management is of particular importance. Limited Brands increased its current liabilities in line with increases in accounts receivable and inventories. Thus, cash flow from operations approximately equals net income plus depreciation. Limited Brands invested most of the cash flow from operations in additional property, plant and equipment, the acquisition of other businesses, the repayment of short-term debt, and the payment of dividends.

4.44 continued.

Upjohn—This problem includes Upjohn primarily to compare and contrast it with American Home Products, also a pharmaceutical company. Both companies generated sufficient cash flow from operations to fund capital expenditures and pay dividends. Upjohn sold a portion of its business during the year and invested the proceeds in marketable securities.

4.45 (Northrop Grumman Corporation; interpreting direct and indirect methods.)

a. We think this is hopeless. We cannot write a coherent explanation of the decline from these data alone, at least not without further analysis.

b. Some academics think that even the question is nonsense—that is, trying to explain changes in the data which themselves explain changes in cash. The statement of cash flows explains the change in the cash account from year to year. Consider that the statement of income and retained earnings explains the change in Retained Earnings from year to year. Most analysts think it sensible comparing income statements from one year to the next, to understand the causes of the change in income (which itself explains the causes of part of the changes in Retained Earnings). We think it sensible comparing statements of cash flows from one year to the next to explain the causes of the changes in cash flow from operations (which itself explains the causes of part of the changes in Cash). In this case, the decline in cash flow from operations appears to result from a decreased margin of collections from customers for sales. The focus must be on what is going on with long-term and other sales contracts. We cannot be sure what is happening, but we can see where to inquire. Focus on those contracts, not on the changes in balance sheet operating accounts.

c. The fundamental problem is that not a single number in the indirect method is itself a cash flow. So, changes in those numbers from year to year do not illuminate.

4.46 (Ethical issues in manipulating cash flows from operations.)

a. This will increase cash flow from operations, assuming that had the maintenance been done this period, the firm would have paid for it this period. This may be an unsound management practice, as improper maintenance will increase long-run costs. Most managers would likely consider this ethical, but likely unwise.

4.46 continued.

b. This will not increase cash flow from operations. It will conserve cash, but when the firm spends the cash, it appears as an investing use, not an operating use. This can be an unsound management practice.

c. There is a continuing race between clever financial managers and accounting standard setters about transactions such as this. Most simple transactions of this sort will not increase cash flow from operations, but will generate investing or financing cash flows. Chapter 11 discusses some of these complications. The Special Purpose Entities (created in 1990, but curtailed in 2003) enabled firms to treat some financing transactions as though they were operating. Many financial managers think it is a badge of honor to devise transactions that will comply with accounting rules while showing larger operating cash flows.

d. Not paying on time for items related to employment activities will, in the short run, increase cash flow from operations. Suppliers will catch on and will likely demand different payment terms, or higher prices, to compensate them for the slower payments. Many firms appear to engage in this practice without qualm. Others say: bargain hard for low price and delayed payments, but once you make a deal, pay on time.

e. Same issues as in Part *d*. above.

f. This will increase cash flow from operations in the period of sale, but will reduce it in the next period when the customers get cash refunds. This practice is fraud and will result in overstated revenue and income, as well as increased cash flow from operations. Such side agreements, often written by sales staff into so-called *side letters*, are illegal. Even ethical managers sometimes cannot detect side letters offered by sales staff to customers.

CHAPTER 5

INTRODUCTION TO FINANCIAL STATEMENT ANALYSIS

Questions, Short Exercises, Exercises, Problems, and Cases: Answers and Solutions

5.1   See the text or the glossary at the end of the book.

5.2   1. The firm may have changed its methods of accounting over time.

       2. The firm may have changed its product lines, production techniques, investment or financing strategies, or even its managerial personnel.

5.3   1. The firms may use different methods of accounting.

       2. The firms may pursue different operating, investing, or financing strategies, so that they have different technologies, production techniques, and selling strategies.

5.4   The adjustment in the numerator of rate of return on assets is for the *incremental* effect on *net* income of having versus not having interest expense. Because interest expense reduces taxable income and, therefore, income taxes otherwise payable, the tax savings from interest expense incrementally affect net income. The computation of the numerator must, therefore, incorporate this tax effect.

5.5   The first company apparently has a relatively small profit margin and must rely on turnover to generate a satisfactory rate of return. A discount department store is an example. The second company, on the other hand, has a larger profit margin and does not need as much turnover as the first company to generate a satisfactory rate of return.

5.6   Management strives to keep its inventories at a level that is neither too low so that it loses sales nor too high so that it incurs high storage costs. Thus, there is an optimal level of inventory for a particular firm in a particular period and an optimal inventory turnover ratio.

5.7   The rate of return on common shareholders' equity exceeds the rate of return on assets when the latter rate exceeds the return required by creditors and preferred shareholders (net of tax effects). In this situation, financial leverage is working to the benefit of the common shareholders. The rate of return on common shareholders' equity will be less than the return on assets when the latter rate is less than the return required by creditors and preferred shareholders. This situation generally occurs during periods of very poor earnings performance.

5.8 This statement suggests that the difference between the rate of return on assets and the aftertax cost of debt is positive but small. Increasing the amount of debt will require a higher interest rate that will eliminate this positive difference and financial leverage will work to the disadvantage of the common shareholders.

5.9 Financial leverage involves using debt capital that has a smaller aftertax cost than the return a firm can generate from investing the capital in various assets. The excess return belongs to the common shareholders. A firm cannot continually increase the amount of debt in the capital structure without limit. Increasing the debt level increases the risk to the common shareholders. These shareholders will not tolerate risk levels that they consider too high. Also, the cost of borrowing increases as a firm assumes larger proportions of debt. Sooner or later, the excess of the rate of return on assets over the aftertax cost of borrowing approaches zero or even becomes negative. Financial leverage then works to the disadvantage of the common shareholders.

5.10

	Dec. 31, Year 1	Dec. 31, Year 2
Current Assets	$ 800,000	$ 600,000
Current Liabilities	(400,000)	(240,000)
Working Capital	$ 400,000	$ 360,000
Current Ratio	2:1	2.5:1

5.11 (Cracker Barrel Old Country Store and Outback Steakhouse; calculating and disaggregating rate of return on assets.)

a. **Cracker Barrel:** $\dfrac{\$106,529 + (1 - .35)(\$8,892)}{\$1,295,077} = 8.7$ percent.

Outback: $\dfrac{\$91,273 + (1 - .35)(\$2,489)}{\$531,312} = 12.1$ percent.

b.

Rate of Return on Assets	**=**	**Profit Margin for ROA**	**x**	**Total Asset Turnover Ratio**
Cracker Barrel:				
$\dfrac{\$106,529 + (1 - .35)(\$8,892)}{\$1,295,077}$	=	$\dfrac{\$106,529 + (1 - .35)(\$8,892)}{\$2,198,182}$	x	$\dfrac{\$2,198,182}{\$1,295,077}$
8.7 percent	=	5.1 percent	x	1.70
Outback:				
$\dfrac{\$170,206 + (1 - .35)(\$1,810)}{\$1,413,810}$	=	$\dfrac{\$170,206 + (1 - .35)(\$1,810)}{\$2,724,600}$	x	$\dfrac{\$2,724,600}{\$1,413,810}$
12.1 percent	=	6.3 percent	x	1.93

5.11 continued.

    c. Outback has a higher ROA, the result of a higher profit margin for ROA and a higher total assets turnover. Outback's higher profit margin for ROA likely results from its serving primarily the dinner meal, whereas Cracker Barrel serves meals all day. The profit margins on breakfast and lunch are likely smaller than on dinner. Cracker Barrel also must hire more employees to cover the longer hours. In addition, Cracker Barrel aims at a more price-conscious customer than Outback. One might expect the profit margin on the craft items of Cracker Barrel to exceed those on meals, but the problem does not provide the necessary information to assess this possibility. The slower total assets turnover for Cracker Barrel likely relates to its carrying an inventory of craft items that turn over less rapidly than food.

5.12   (Ann Taylor Stores and Family Dollar Stores; profitability analysis for two types of retailers.)

Company A is the specialty retailer (Ann Taylor Stores) because of its higher profit margin and lower total assets turnover, relative to Company B (Family Dollar Stores).

	Rate of Return On Assets	=	Profit Margin for ROA	x	Total Assets Turnover Ratio
Company A:	$\dfrac{\$100,942 + (1 - .35)(\$6,665)}{\$1,080,200}$	=	$\dfrac{\$100,942 + (1 - .35)(\$6,665)}{\$1,587,708}$	x	$\dfrac{\$1,587,708}{\$1,080,200}$
	9.7 percent	=	6.6 percent	x	1.47
Company B:	$\dfrac{\$247,475 + (1 - .35)(\$0)}{\$1,870,157}$	=	$\dfrac{\$247,475 + (1 - .35)(\$0)}{\$4,750,171}$	x	$\dfrac{\$4,750,171}{\$1,870,157}$
	13.2 percent	=	5.2 percent	x	2.54

5.13   (Dell Computer and Sun Microsystems; analyzing accounts receivable for two companies.)

    a.   **Dell Computer**   **Sun Microsystems**

$$\frac{\$41,444}{.5(\$2,586 + \$3,635)}\qquad\qquad \frac{\$11,434}{.5(\$2,745 + \$2,381)}$$

$$= 13.3 \text{ Times per Year.}\qquad\qquad = 4.5 \text{ Times per Year.}$$

    b. $\dfrac{365}{13.3} = 27.4$ days. $\dfrac{365}{4.5} = 81.1$ days.

5.13 continued.

    c.   Dell Computer sells primarily to individuals who pay with credit cards. Dell Computer collects these accounts receivable quickly. Sun Microsystems sells to businesses. Customers may require Sun Microsystems to finance their purchases. Customers may also delay paying Sun Microsystems until their computers are set up and working properly. Sun Microsystems may also offer liberal credit terms as an inducement to businesses to purchase its computers.

5.14   (Mattel; analyzing inventories over three years.)

a.

Year	Numerator	Denominator	Inventory Turnover
11	$ 2,539	$ 488	5.20
12	2,524	413	6.11
13	2,531	388	6.52

b.

Year	Numerator	Denominator	Days Inventory Held
11	365	5.20	70.2
12	365	6.11	59.7
13	365	6.52	56.0

c.

Year	Numerator	Denominator	Cost of Goods Sold Percentage
11	$ 2,539	$ 4,688	54.2%
12	2,524	4,885	51.7%
13	2,531	4,960	51.0%

    d.   Mattel experienced an increasing inventory turnover and a decreasing cost of goods sold to sales percentage. Toys are trendy products. Mattel's products might have received rapid market acceptance, so that it was both able to move products more quickly and to achieve a higher gross margin on products sold. The faster turnover for trendy products means that Mattel would not need to mark down products in order to sell them or to incur additional storage costs.

5.15   (The Walt Disney Company; analyzing fixed asset turnover over three years.)

a.

Year	Numerator	Denominator	Fixed Asset Turnover
11	$25,172	$12,609	2.00
12	25,329	12,843	1.97
13	27,061	12,729	2.13

5.15 continued.

    b. The fixed asset turnover declined between Year 11 and Year 12, the net result of relatively flat sales between the two years but substantial capital expenditures in Year 11. Disney reduced its capital expenditures in Year 12 and Year 13, whereas sales increased significantly between these two years. The fixed asset turnover, therefore, increased.

5.16   (Exxon Mobil; calculating and disaggregating rate of return on common shareholders' equity.)

    a.

Year	Numerator	Denominator	Rate of Return on Common Shareholders' Equity
11	$ 15,003	$ 71,959	20.8%
12	11,011	73,879	14.9%
13	20,960	82,256	25.5%

    b. **Profit Margin for ROCE**

Year	Numerator	Denominator	Profit Margin for ROCE
11	$ 15,003	$ 212,785	7.1%
12	11,011	204,506	5.4%
13	20,960	246,738	8.5%

Total Asset Turnover

Year	Numerator	Denominator	Total Asset Turnover
11	$ 212,785	$ 146,087	1.46
12	204,506	147,909	1.38
13	246,738	163,461	1.51

Capital Structure Leverage Ratio

Year	Numerator	Denominator	Capital Structure Leverage Ratio
11	$ 146,087	$71,959	2.03
12	147,909	73,879	2.00
13	163,461	82,256	1.99

    c. The rate of return on common shareholders' equity declined between Year 11 and Year 12 and increased between Year 12 and Year 13. Revenues declined between Year 11 and Year 12 and likely resulted in diseconomies of scale as Exxon Mobil spread its relatively fixed operating expenses over a smaller sales volume. The diseconomies of scale resulted in a decreased profit margin for ROCE and a decreased total assets turnover. Revenues increased between Year 12 and Year 13, providing benefits of economies of scale. Both the profit margin for ROCE and total assets turnover increased. The capital structure lev-

5.16 c. continued.

erage ratio declined slightly over the three years, but was not a major factor in explaining changes in ROCE.

5.17   (Profitability analysis for two companies.)

a.

	Rate of Return on Assets	=	Profit Margin for ROA	X	Total Asset Turnover
Company A:	$\dfrac{\$268}{\$2,472}$	=	$\dfrac{\$268}{\$4,076}$	X	$\dfrac{\$4,076}{\$2,472}$
	10.8 percent	=	6.6 percent	X	1.65
Company B:	$\dfrac{\$772}{\$4,392}$	=	$\dfrac{\$772}{\$4,624}$	X	$\dfrac{\$4,624}{\$4,392}$
	17.6 percent	=	16.7 percent	X	1.05

b.

	Rate of Return on Common Shareholders' Equity	=	Profit Margin for ROCE	X	Total Assets Turnover	X	Capital Structure Leverage Ratio
Company A:	$\dfrac{\$268}{\$1,903}$	=	$\dfrac{\$268}{\$4,076}$	X	$\dfrac{\$4,076}{\$2,472}$	X	$\dfrac{\$2,472}{\$1,903}$
	14.1 percent	=	6.6 percent	X	1.65	X	1.30
Company B:	$\dfrac{\$761}{\$2,595}$	=	$\dfrac{\$761}{\$4,624}$	X	$\dfrac{\$4,624}{\$4,392}$	X	$\dfrac{\$4,392}{\$2,595}$
	29.3 percent	=	16.5 percent	X	1.05	X	1.69

c. Company A is Starbucks and Company B is Harley Davidson. Starbucks typically leases the space for its restaurants and, therefore, has few fixed assets. It sells for cash and, therefore, has few accounts receivable. It will maintain some inventory, but the need for freshness of its foods suggests a rapid turnover. Thus, we would expect Starbucks to have the fastest total assets turnover. Harley Davidson needs fixed assets to manufacture its motor cycles. The smaller profit margins for Starbucks are somewhat of a surprise. Competition from other coffee shops and supermarkets with fresh ground coffees probably dampens its profit margins. Starbucks' low capital structure leverage ratio reflects its lack of assets to use as collateral for borrowing. The manufacturing of motorcycles is essentially an assembly operation, but Harley Davidson needs facilities for the assembly operation. These assets serve as collateral for borrowing.

5.18   (Profitability analysis for two companies.)

a.

	Rate of Return on Assets	=	Profit Margin for ROA	X	Total Asset Turnover
Company A:	$\dfrac{\$5,679}{\$45,684}$	=	$\dfrac{\$5,679}{\$30,141}$	X	$\dfrac{\$30,141}{\$45,684}$
	12.4 percent	=	18.8 percent	X	.66
Company B:	$\dfrac{\$4,989}{\$166,718}$	=	$\dfrac{\$4,989}{\$67,752}$	X	$\dfrac{\$67,752}{\$166,718}$
	3.0 percent	=	7.4 percent	X	.41

b.

	Rate of Return on Common Shareholders' Equity	=	Profit Margin for ROCE	X	Total Assets Turnover	X	Capital Structure Leverage Ratio
Company A:	$\dfrac{\$5,641}{\$36,657}$	=	$\dfrac{\$5,641}{\$30,141}$	X	$\dfrac{\$30,141}{\$45,684}$	X	$\dfrac{\$45,684}{\$36,657}$
	15.4 percent	=	18.7 percent	X	.66	X	1.25
Company B:	$\dfrac{\$3,077}{\$33,041}$	=	$\dfrac{\$3,077}{\$67,752}$	X	$\dfrac{\$67,752}{\$166,718}$	X	$\dfrac{\$166,718}{\$33,041}$
	9.3 percent	=	4.5 percent	X	.41	X	5.05

c.   Company A is Intel and Company B is Verizon Communications. Both of these firms are fixed-asset intensive, so their total assets turnovers are small. Their ROAs and ROCEs differ with respect to profit margin and capital structure leverage. Semiconductors are technology-intensive products and can command high profit margins if the products are on the technology edge. Telecommunication services, on the other hand, are commodity products and are difficult to differentiate from competitors. The technological intensity of semiconductors leads to short product life cycles. Firms in this industry tend not to take on substantial debt because of the short product life cycles. Telecommunication services are somewhat less technology intensive, at least with respect to the need to create the technologies. Firms in the telecommunications industry have capital-intensive fixed assets that can serve as collateral for borrowing and a somewhat more stable revenue stream, relative to semiconductors.

5.19   (Relating profitability to financial leverage.)

a.

Case	Net Income Plus Aftertax Interest Expense[a]	Aftertax Interest Expense[b]	Net Income[c]	Rate of Return on Common Shareholders' Equity
A	$12	$6.0	$ 6	$ 6/$100 = 6%
B	$16	$6.0	$ 10	$ 10/$100 = 10%
C	$16	$7.2	$ 8.8	$ 8.8/$80 = 11%
D	$ 8	$6.0	$ 2	$ 2/$100 = 2%
E	$12	$3.0	$ 9	$ 9/$100 = 9%
F	$10	$3.0	$ 7	$ 7/$100 = 7%

[a]Numerator of the rate of return on assets. In Case A, $12 = .06 \times \$200$.

[b]After tax cost of borrowing times interest-bearing debt. In Case A, $\$6.0 = .06 \times \$100$.

[c]Net income plus after tax interest expense minus after tax interest expense. In Case A, $\$6 = \$12 - \$6$.

b.   Leverage works successfully in Cases B, C, E, and F with respect to total debt. With respect to interest-bearing debt, leverage works successfully in Cases B and C.

5.20   (Company A/Company B; interpreting changes in earnings per share.)

a.   **Company A Earnings per Share:**

Year 1................ $\dfrac{\$100,000}{100,000 \text{ Shares}} = \$1$ per Share.

Year 2................ $\dfrac{\$100,000}{100,000 \text{ Shares}} = \$1$ per Share.

Company B Earnings per Share:

Year 1................ $\dfrac{\$100,000}{100,000 \text{ Shares}} = \$1$ per Share.

Year 2................ $\dfrac{.10 \times (\$1,000,000 + \$100,000)}{100,000 \text{ Shares}} = \$1.10$ per Share.

5.20 continued.

    b.   Company A: No growth.
           Company B: 10 percent annual growth.

    c.   Company B: This result is misleading. Comparisons of growth in earnings per share are valid only if firms employ equal amounts of assets in the business. Both the rate of return on assets and on shareholders' equity are better measures of growth performance. Earnings per share results do not, in general (as in this problem), take earnings retention into account.

5.21   (NIKE; calculating and interpreting short-term liquidity ratios.)

    a. **Current Ratio**

Year End	Numerator	Denominator	Current Ratio
10	$ 3,596	$ 2,140	1.68
11	3,625	1,787	2.03
12	4,155	1,833	2.27
13	4,680	2,015	2.32

Quick Ratio

Year End	Numerator	Denominator	Quick Ratio
10	$ 1,823	$ 2,140	.85
11	1,925	1,787	1.08
12	2,380	1,833	1.30
13	2,735	2,015	1.36

    b. **Cash Flow from Operations to Current Liabilities Ratio**

Year	Numerator	Denominator	Cash Flow from Operations to Current Liabilities Ratio
11	$ 657	$ 1,963.5[a]	33.5%
12	1,082	1,810.0[b]	59.8%
13	917	1,924.0[c]	47.7%

[a].5($2,140 + $1,787) = $1,963.5.
[b].5($1,787 + $1,833) = $1,810.0.
[c].5($1,833 + $2,015) = $1,924.0.

5.21 b. continued.

Accounts Receivable Turnover Ratio

Year	Numerator	Denominator	Accounts Receivable Turnover Ratio
11	$ 9,489	$ 1,595.0[a]	5.95
12	9,893	1,712.5[b]	5.78
13	10,697	1,952.5[c]	5.48

[a].5($1,569 + $1,621) = $1,595.0.
[b].5($1,621 + $1,804) = $1,712.5.
[c].5($1,804 + $2,101) = $1,952.5.

Inventory Turnover Ratio

Year	Numerator	Denominator	Inventory Turnover Ratio
11	$ 5,785	$ 1,435.0[a]	4.03
12	6,005	1,399.0[b]	4.29
13	6,314	1,444.5[c]	4.37

[a].5($1,446 + $1,424) = $1,435.0.
[b].5($1,424 + $1,374) = $1,399.0.
[c].5($1,374 + $1,515) = $1,444.5.

Accounts Payable Turnover Ratio

Year	Numerator	Denominator	Accounts Payable Turnover Ratio
11	$ 5,763[a]	$ 488.0[d]	11.81
12	5,955[b]	468.0[e]	12.72
13	6,455[c]	538.5[f]	11.99

[a]$5,785 + $1,424 – $1,446 = $5,763.   [d].5($544 + $432) = $488.0.
[b]$6,005 + $1,374 – $1,424 = $5,955.   [e].5($432 + $504) = $468.0.
[c]$6,314 + $1,515 – $1,374 = $6,455.   [f].5($504 + $573) = $538.5.

c. The short-term liquidity risk of Nike decreased during the three-year period. The current and quick ratios increased continually. Nike increased its inventory turnover each year, providing operating cash flows. Its accounts receivable turnover decreased using operating cash flows. Although the accounts payable turnover also increased between Year 11 and Year 12, using operating cash flows, the change in the accounts payable turnover either decreased the amount of accounts payable or dampened its increase. Another important factor explaining the increased current and quick ratios is the decline in bank borrowing.

5.21 c. continued.

The cash flow from operations to current liabilities ratio is now above the 40 percent benchmark for a healthy company. Another factor affecting the improved short-term liquidity risk is the increasing profit margin, net income divided by revenues. The increasing profit margin ultimately provides more cash than if the profit margin had remained stable.

5.22   (Nokia; calculating and interpreting short-term liquidity ratios.)

a. **Current Ratio**

Year End	Numerator	Denominator	Current Ratio
2	EUR 5,431	EUR 3,091	1.76
3	7,814	4,453	1.75
4	10,792	6,372	1.69
5	13,560	8,594	1.58

Quick Ratio

Year End	Numerator	Denominator	Quick Ratio
2	EUR 3,700	EUR 3,091	1.20
3	5,697	4,453	1.28
4	7,986	6,372	1.25
5	9,835	8,594	1.14

b. **Cash Flow from Operations to Current Liabilities Ratio**

Year	Numerator	Denominator	Cash Flow from Operations to Current Liabilities Ratio
3	EUR 1,694	EUR 3,772.0[a]	44.9%
4	3,009	5,412.5[b]	55.6%
5	3,560	7,483.0[c]	47.6%

[a].5(EUR3,091 + EUR4,453) = EUR3,772.0.
[b].5(EUR4,453 + EUR6,372) = EUR5,412.5.
[c].5(EUR6,372 + EUR8,594) = EUR7,483.0.

5.22 b. continued.

Accounts Receivable Turnover Ratio

Year	Numerator	Denominator	Accounts Receivable Turnover Ratio
3	EUR13,326	EUR 2,223.0[a]	5.99
4	19,772	3,316.5[b]	5.96
5	30,376	4,710.5[c]	6.45

[a].5(EUR1,640 + EUR2,806) = EUR2,223.0.
[b].5(EUR2,806 + EUR3,827) = EUR3,316.5.
[c].5(EUR3,827 + EUR5,594) = EUR4,710.5.

Inventory Turnover Ratio

Year	Numerator	Denominator	Inventory Turnover Ratio
3	EUR 8,299	EUR 1,261.0[a]	6.58
4	12,227	1,532.0[b]	7.98
5	19,072	2,017.5[c]	9.45

[a].5(EUR1,230 + EUR1,292) = EUR1,261.0.
[b].5(EUR1,292 + EUR1,772) = EUR1,532.0.
[c].5(EUR1,772 + EUR2,263) = EUR2,017.5.

Accounts Payable Turnover Ratio

Year	Numerator	Denominator	Accounts Payable Turnover Ratio
3	EUR 8,361[a]	EUR 1,087.5[d]	7.69
4	12,707[b]	1,779.5[e]	7.14
5	19,563[c]	2,508.0[f]	7.80

[a]EUR8,299 + EUR1,292 − EUR1,230 = EUR8,361.
[b]EUR12,227 + EUR1,772 − EUR1,292 = EUR12,707.
[c]EUR19,072 + EUR2,263 − EUR1,772 = EUR19,563.
[d].5(EUR818 + EUR1,357) = EUR1,087.5.
[e].5(EUR1,357 + EUR2,202) = EUR1,779.5.
[f].5(EUR2,202 + EUR2,814) = EUR2,508.0.

c. The current and quick ratios both declined during the last four years. The decline occurs primarily because of the increase in the accounts receivable and inventory turnovers. Although the amount of accounts receivable and inventory increased, they did not increase as rapidly as the level of sales and operations. The levels of the current and quick ratios are still quite healthy. The cash flow from operations to average

5.22 c. continued.

current liabilities ratio increased in Year 4, primarily as a result of reducing the accounts payable turnover (that is, stretching accounts payable) and increasing other current liabilities. The cash flow ratio declined in Year 5 as Nokia increased its accounts payable turnover. The cash flow ratio still exceeds the 40 percent level commonly found for healthy firms. Thus, the short-term liquidity risk was healthy in all three years and did not change significantly.

5.23 (Ericsson; calculating and interpreting long-term liquidity ratios.)

a. **Long-Term Debt Ratio**

Year End	Numerator	Denominator	Long-Term Debt Ratio
1	Kr 14,407	Kr 14,407 + Kr 57,364	20.1%
2	19,667	19,667 + 70,320	21.9%
3	32,298	32,298 + 85,616	27.4%
4	35,247	35,247 + 109,217	24.4%

Debt-Equity Ratio

Year End	Numerator	Denominator	Debt-Equity Ratio
1	Kr 103,483	Kr 103,483 + Kr 57,364	64.3%
2	115,152	115,152 + 70,320	62.1%
3	148,895	148,895 + 85,616	63.5%
4	180,208	180,208 + 109,217	62.3%

b. **Cash Flow from Operations to Total Liabilities Ratio**

Year	Numerator	Denominator	Cash Flow from Operations to Total Liabilities Ratio
2	Kr 7,394	.5(Kr 103,483 + Kr 115,152)	6.8%
3	12,925	.5(Kr 115,152 + Kr 148,895)	9.8%
4	(10,848)	.5(Kr 148,895 + Kr 180,208)	(6.6)%

Interest Coverage Ratio

Year	Numerator	Denominator	Interest Coverage Ratio Earned
2	Kr 25,020	Kr 2,532	9.9
3	24,293	3,041	8.0
4	17,191	5,166	3.3

5.23 continued.

    c. The proportion of debt in the capital structure changed relatively little during the three-year period. There was a slight shift from short-term to long-term debt. The cash flow from operations to average total liabilities ratio is low, relative to the 20 percent level commonly found for healthy firms. The cash flow ratio declined sharply during Year 4. Earnings declined in Year 4 and cash flow from operations turned negative. The interest coverage ratio, while at healthy levels in Year 2 and Year 3, dropped nearer to a worrisome level in Year 4. Thus, the long-term liquidity risk appeared to increase during the three years.

5.24   (Nucor; calculating and interpreting long-term liquidity ratios.)

    a. **Long-Term Debt Ratio**

Year End	Numerator	Denominator	Long-Term Debt Ratio
10	$ 460,450	$ 460,450 + $2,432,296	15.9%
11	450,450	450,450 + 2,485,347	15.3%
12	878,550	878,550 + 2,539,644	25.7%
13	903,550	903,550 + 2,519,357	26.4%

Debt-Equity Ratio

Year End	Numerator	Denominator	Debt-Equity Ratio
10	$1,278,572	$1,278,572 + $2,432,296	34.5%
11	1,274,001	1,274,001 + 2,485,347	33.9%
12	1,841,357	1,841,357 + 2,539,644	42.0%
13	1,972,996	1,972,996 + 2,519,357	43.9%

    b. **Cash Flow from Operations to Total Liabilities Ratio**

Year	Numerator	Denominator	Cash Flow from Operations to Total Liabilities Ratio
11	$ 495,115	.5($1,278,572 + $1,274,001)	38.8%
12	497,220	.5($1,274,001 + $1,841,357)	31.9%
13	494,620	.5($1,841,357 + $1,972,996)	25.9%

Interest Coverage Ratio

Year	Numerator	Denominator	Interest Coverage Ratio Earned
11	$ 201,371	$ 22,002	9.15
12	252,971	22,918	11.04
13	94,029	27,152	3.46

5.24 continued.

    c. The long-term liquidity risk of Nucor worsened over the three-year period but is not yet at worrisome levels. The debt ratios increased. The cash flow from operations to total liabilities ratio declined with the increasing debt levels, but is still above the 20 percent benchmark for a healthy company. The drastic decline in the interest coverage ratio results from a substantial decrease in income before interest and taxes in Year 13. If the decline in profitability is temporary, Nucor should experience improved long-term liquidity risk ratios in the future.

5.25   (Effect of various transactions on financial statement ratios.)

Transaction	Rate of Return on Common Shareholders' Equity	Current Ratio	Debt-Equity Ratio
a.	No Effect	(1)	Increase
b.	Increase	Increase	Decrease
c.	No Effect	No Effect	No Effect
d.	No Effect	(2)	Decrease
e.	No Effect	Increase	No Effect
f.	Increase	Decrease	Increase
g.	Decrease	Increase	Decrease
h.	No Effect	Decrease	Increase

(1) The current ratio remains the same if it was one to one prior to the transaction, decreases if it was greater than one, and increases if it was less than one.

(2) The current ratio remains the same if it was equal to one prior to the transaction, increases if it was greater than one, and decreases if it was less than one.

5.26   (Effect of various transactions on financial statement ratios.)

Transaction	Earnings per Common Share	Working Capital	Quick Ratio
a.	Increase	Increase	Increase
b.	No Effect	Decrease	Decrease
c.	No Effect	No Effect	Decrease
d.	No Effect	Increase	Increase
e.	No Effect	No Effect	Increase
f.	Decrease	Increase	Decrease

5.27   (Target Corporation; calculating and interpreting profitability and risk ratios in a time series setting.)

a. 1.   Rate of Return on Assets $= \dfrac{\$1,841 + (1 - .35)(\$559)}{.5(\$29,527 + \$32,390)} = 7.1$ percent.

2.   Profit Margin for Rate of Return on Assets $= \dfrac{\$1,841 + (1 - .35)(\$559)}{\$46,781}) = 4.7$ percent.

3.   Total Assets Turnover $= \dfrac{\$46,781}{.5(\$29,527 + \$32,390)} = 1.5$ times.

4.   Cost of Goods Sold/Sales $= \dfrac{\$31,790}{\$46,781} = 68.0$ percent.

5.   Selling and Administrative Expense/Sales $= \dfrac{\$12,854}{\$46,781} = 27.5$ percent.

6.   Interest Expense/Sales $= \dfrac{\$559}{\$46,781} = 1.2$ percent.

7.   Income Tax Expense/Sales $= \dfrac{\$1,119}{\$46,781} = 2.4$ percent.

8.   Accounts Receivable Turnover Ratio $= \dfrac{\$46,781}{.5(\$5,565 + \$5,776)} = 8.2$ times.

9.   Inventory Turnover Ratio $= \dfrac{\$31,790}{.5(\$4,760 + \$5,343)} = 6.3$ times.

10.   Fixed Asset Turnover $= \dfrac{\$46,781}{.5(\$16,231 + \$17,967)} = 2.7$ times.

11.   Rate of Return on Common Shareholders' Equity $= \dfrac{\$1,841}{.5(\$9,443 + \$11,065)} = 18.0$ percent.

12.   Profit Margin for Return on Common Shareholders' Equity $= \dfrac{\$1,841}{\$46,781} = 3.9$ percent.

5.27 a. continued.

13. Capital Structure Leverage Ratio $= \dfrac{.5(\$29,527 + \$32,390)}{.5(\$9,443 + \$11,065)} = 3.0.$

14. Current Ratio $= \dfrac{\$12,928}{\$8,314} = 1.55.$

15. Quick Ratio $= \dfrac{\$716 + \$5,776}{\$8,314} = .78.$

16. Accounts Payable Turnover $= \dfrac{(\$31,790 + \$5,343 - \$4,760)}{.5(\$4,684 + \$5,448)} = 6.4 \text{ times.}$

17. Cash Flow from Operations to Current Liabilities Ratio $= \dfrac{\$3,160}{.5(\$7,523 + \$8,314)} = 39.9 \text{ percent.}$

18. Long-Term Debt Ratio $= \dfrac{\$11,215}{(\$11,215 + \$11,065)} = 50.3 \text{ percent.}$

19. Debt Equity Ratio $= \dfrac{\$21,325}{\$32,390} = 65.8 \text{ percent.}$

20. Cash Flow from Operations to Total Liabilities Ratio $= \dfrac{\$3,160}{.5(\$20,084 + \$21,325)} = 15.3 \text{ percent.}$

21. Interest Coverage Ratio $= \dfrac{(\$1,841 + \$1,119 + \$559)}{\$559} = 6.3 \text{ times.}$

5.27 continued.

b. **Rate of Return on Assets (ROA)**
The ROA of Target Corporation increased slightly between Year 12 and Year 13 and then decreased between Year 13 and Year 14. The improved ROA between Year 12 and Year 13 results from an increased profit margin for ROA offset by a decreased total assets turnover. The decreased ROA between Year 13 and Year 14 results from both a decreased profit margin for ROA and a decreased total assets turnover.

Profit Margin for ROA The changes in the profit margin for ROA results from the net effect of an increase in other revenues to sales, a decrease in the cost of goods sold to sales percentage, and an increase in the selling and administrative expense to sales percentage. Most of the change in the overall profit margin occurred between Year 12 and Year 13. The profit margin for ROA was relatively stable between Year 13 and Year 14.

Other Revenues/Sales Target Corporation offers its own credit cards to customers and derives interest revenues from unpaid balances. The increasing percentage for other revenues to sales coupled with the decrease in the accounts receivable turnover suggest either that a higher percentage of customers used the credit cards for their purchases or customers took longer to pay for their purchases on account.

Cost of Goods Sold/Sales The cost of goods sold to sales percentage steadily declined during the three years. Possible explanations include the following:

- Shift in sales mix from the lower margin Mervyn's and Marshall Field's stores to the higher margin Target stores.

- Improved profit margins in the Target stores segment, due perhaps to increased buying power as Target grew its number of stores.

- Improved inventory control systems, which reduced the need for inventory markdowns.

Selling and Administrative Expense to Sales The selling and administrative expense to sales percentage steadily increased during the three years. Possible explanations include the following:

- Increased administrative costs to identify possible sites for new stores and to manage the process of building and opening the new stores.

- Increased selling and administrative costs to deal with the declining profitability of the Mervyn's and Marshall Field's stores.

5.27 b. continued.

- Increased marketing costs to promote the supercenter concept and establish new stores.

- Increased marketing costs during a recession period.

Income Taxes. Income tax expense as a percentage of sales varied between 2.1 percent and 2.4 percent of sales between Year 12 and Year 14. Because income taxes are a tax on income and not sales, we obtain better insight by expressing income taxes as a percentage of income before income taxes. The average income tax rate each year is as follows:

Year 12: $\$839/(\$1,368 + \$839) = 38.0\%$
Year 13: $\$1,022/(\$1,654 + \$1,022) = 38.2\%$
Year 14: $\$1,119/(\$1,841 + \$1,119) = 37.8\%$

Thus, the average income tax rate did not change much during the three-year period.

Total Assets Turnover The total assets turnover steadily declined during the three-year period. We obtain additional insight into the change in the total assets turnover by examining turnover ratios for accounts receivable, inventories, and fixed assets.

Accounts Receivable Turnover The accounts receivable turnover steadily declined during the three-year period. Various explanations are possible:

- Customers increased the percentage of their purchases charged on credit cards of the three retail chains.

- Customers took longer to pay for purchases on account. The delayed payment period may result from recession conditions in the economy or to Target Corporation's encouragement to delay payment to permit the earnings of interest revenue on outstanding balances.

Inventory Turnover The inventory turnover increased between Year 12 and Year 13 and decreased between Year 13 and Year 14. There is no discernable pattern of change here. Factors affecting the inventory turnover include:

- Target Corporation stocks its new stores with merchandise before those new stores commence generating revenues. The pattern of growth in stores will affect the pattern of changes in the inventory turnover ratio.

5.27 b. continued.

- The rate of increase in sales of stores opened at least two full years may not increase as expected, resulting in an unanticipated buildup or workdown of inventory.

Fixed Assets Turnover The decreased fixed asset turnover results from fixed assets growing faster than sales. The growth in fixed assets relates in part to the building of new stores. New stores enter into the denominator of the fixed asset turnover when the capital investment is made, although a full year of sales does not enter the numerator of the ratio for at least a year. Growing the number of stores will, therefore, have a dampening effect on the fixed asset turnover. The decline in the fixed asset turnover may also result in the recession conditions in the U.S. economy, which kept the growth rate in sales of stores open at least two years to a rate approximately equal to the rate of inflation.

c. **Rate of Return on Common Shareholders' Equity**
The ROCE increased slightly between Year 12 and Year 13 and then decreased in Year 14. The profit margin for ROCE increased between Year 12 and Year 13, primarily for the same reasons for the increased profit margin for ROA. The total assets turnover declined during the three-year period for the reasons discussed in Part *b.* above. The capital structure leverage ratio declined. Although Target Corporation increased the dollar amount of long-term debt during the three years, its shareholders' equity increased even more because of the retention of earnings.

d. **Short-Term Liquidity Risk**
The short-term liquidity ratios do not suggest any major concerns. The increased current and quick ratios and the decreased cash flow to current liabilities ratio between Year 12 and Year 13 result from the increase in days receivable that are outstanding. As discussed above, the decline in the accounts receivable turnover ratio (increase in days receivable) may be due to recession conditions in the economy or to Target Corporation's efforts to increase interest revenues on outstanding credit card balances. Target Corporation steadily decreased its accounts payable turnover (increased the days accounts payable that are outstanding), perhaps indirectly to provide financing for the increased accounts receivable. The cash flow from operations to current liabilities ratio is near the 40 percent benchmark by Year 14. The issue going forward is whether Target Corporation will continue to emphasize its credit card operations and, if so, how it intends to finance the increasing accounts receivable.

e. **Long-Term Solvency Risk**
Target Corporation's debt ratios declined during the three-year period and its interest coverage ratio increased. These changes suggest decreased long-term liquidity risk. Its cash flow from operations to total liabilities ratio, however, is below the 20 percent benchmark. The firm does not appear to have undue long-term liquidity risk at this time.

5.28   (Target Corporation and Wal-Mart; profitability and risk analysis in a cross section setting.)

Schedules 1, 2, and 3 in this Solution's Manual summarize the financial statement ratios for Wal-Mart and Target Corporation for Year 12, Year 13, and Year 14. Note that the percentages for income taxes in Schedule 1 exclude tax savings from interest expense.

SCHEDULE 1
Cross Section ROA Profitability Analysis for Target Corporation and Wal-Mart

ROA

	Year 12	Year 13	Year 14
Target	7.4%	7.5%	7.1%
Wal-Mart	8.8%	9.3%	9.3%

	Profit Margin for ROA			Total Assets Turnover		
	Year 12	Year 13	Year 14	Year 12	Year 13	Year 14
Target	4.3%	4.8%	4.7%	1.7	1.6	1.5
Wal-Mart	3.5%	3.6%	3.8%	2.5	2.6	2.4

	Target			Wal-Mart		
	Year 12	Year 13	Year 14	Year 12	Year 13	Year 14
Sales......................	100.0%	100.0%	100.0%	100.0%	100.0%	100.0%
Other Revenues...	1.8	2.8	3.0	.9	.9	1.0
Cost of Goods Sold...................	(69.4)	(68.5)	(68.0)	(78.8)	(78.4)	(77.6)
Selling and Administrative......	(25.6)	(26.7)	(27.5)	(16.6)	(16.9)	(17.5)
Income Taxes.......	(2.6)	(2.9)	(2.8)	(2.0)	(2.0)	(2.1)
Profit Margin for ROA..................	4.3%	4.8%	4.7%	3.5%	3.6%	3.8%
Receivable Turnover..................	13.6	9.1	8.2	115.6	119.0	152.5
Inventory Turnover..................	6.2	6.4	6.3	7.8	8.1	7.7
Fixed Asset Turnover..................	2.9	2.8	2.7	4.5	4.6	4.3

5.28 continued.

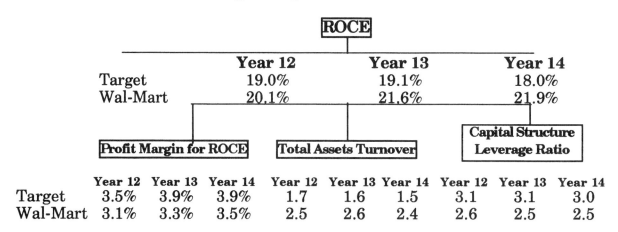

SCHEDULE 2
Cross Section ROCE Profitability Analysis for
Target Corporation and Wal-Mart

	ROCE		
	Year 12	Year 13	Year 14
Target	19.0%	19.1%	18.0%
Wal-Mart	20.1%	21.6%	21.9%

	Profit Margin for ROCE			Total Assets Turnover			Capital Structure Leverage Ratio		
	Year 12	Year 13	Year 14	Year 12	Year 13	Year 14	Year 12	Year 13	Year 14
Target	3.5%	3.9%	3.9%	1.7	1.6	1.5	3.1	3.1	3.0
Wal-Mart	3.1%	3.3%	3.5%	2.5	2.6	2.4	2.6	2.5	2.5

5.28 continued.

SCHEDULE 3
Cross Section Risk Analysis for Target Corporation and Wal-Mart

Short-Term	Target			Wal-Mart		
Liquidity	Year 12	Year 13	Year 14	Year 12	Year 13	Year 14
Current Ratio.......	1.37	1.59	1.55	1.04	.93	.92
Quick Ratio...........	.61	.84	.78	.15	.15	.17
Cash Flow from Operations/ Average Current Liabilities..........	30.1%	21.8%	39.9%	36.5%	41.8%	46.0%
Days Receivable ..	27	40	44	3	3	2
Days Inventory	58	57	58	47	45	47
Days Payable	52	55	57	32	31	33
Long-Term Liquidity						
Long-Term Debt Ratio..................	53.0%	54.1%	50.3%	40.1%	38.1%	37.0%
Debt-Equity Ratio..................	68.5%	68.0%	65.8%	60.2%	60.4%	60.4%
Cash Flow from Operations/ Average Total Liabilities..........	13.0%	8.6%	15.3%	19.7%	22.2%	25.5%
Interest Coverage Ratio..................	5.7	5.6	6.3	9.0	12.8	15.3

5.28 continued.

a. Wal-Mart consistently has a higher ROA than Target Corporation. Although Target Corporation has a higher profit margin for ROA, Wal-Mart has a significantly higher total assets turnover.

Target Corporation's advantage on profit margin for ROA results from higher other revenues (interest on credit cards) and a lower cost of goods sold to sales percentage (likely related to its trend merchandising strategy, more sales of brand name products, and sales through department stores). Target Corporation's selling and administrative expense to sales percentages, however, are much larger than Wal-Mart's. Wal-Mart's advantage here might be due to its larger size (economies of scale) and greater productivity of its sales space (see the discussion of the fixed asset turnovers).

Wal-Mart's advantage on total assets turnover results from larger accounts receivable, inventory, and fixed asset turnovers. Wal-Mart does not have its own credit card, accounting for the larger accounts receivable turnover. Wal-Mart's advantage on inventory turnover might result from more effective inventory control systems or to a larger proportion of grocery products in its sales mix. The major difference in the total assets turnover likely stems from Wal-Mart's significantly larger fixed asset turnover. Wal-Mart likely generates more sales per square foot than Target. The preceding problem indicates that Target Corporation attempts to make the shopping experience more pleasurable for customers, with wider aisles and less cluttered stores.

b. Wal-Mart consistently has a higher ROCE than Target Corporation. Wal-Mart's advantage on ROA more than offsets Target Corporation's greater use of debt in financing its assets. Target Corporation's debt-equity ratios are higher than those of Wal-Mart and Target Corporation's long-term debt ratios are significantly larger. Target Corporation apparently relies more on debt to finance its capital expenditures, whereas Wal-Mart relies more on a mixture of cash flow from operations and external borrowing. Wal-Mart's ratio of cash flow from operations to fixed assets acquired during Year 14 was 1.56 (= $16,091/$10,308), whereas the corresponding ratio for Target Corporation was 1.05 (= $3,160/$3,004).

c. The short-term liquidity risk ratios give mixed signals as to which firm has more short-term liquidity risk. The current and quick ratios of Wal-Mart are lower than the corresponding ratios for Target Corporation. The lower ratios for Wal-Mart, however, are due primarily to Wal-Mart's lack of its own credit card and the quick collection of receivables. Wal-Mart turns over its inventory more quickly than Target Corporation. Wal-Mart also pays its suppliers much more quickly than Target Corporation. Wal-Mart's cash flow from operations to current liabilities ratios are stronger than those of Target Corporation. Thus,

5.28 c. continued.

Wal-Mart appears to have less short-term liquidity risk than Target Corporation. Target Corporation, however, does not appear to have significant short-term liquidity risk.

d. Target Corporation has more long-term liquidity risk than Wal-Mart. Target Corporation has higher debt levels, lower interest coverage, and lower cash flow from operations to total liabilities ratios. However, Target Corporation does not appear to have significant long-term liquidity risk.

5.29 (Carrefour, Metro AG, and Wal-Mart; profitability and risk analysis in a cross section setting.)

a. Wal-Mart's advantage on ROA is a higher profit margin for ROA and a higher total assets turnover. Carrefour's advantage over Metro is a higher profit margin for ROA; their total assets turnovers are similar.

Profit Margin for ROA: The three firms rank order on profit margin for ROA is their rank order from lowest to highest on selling and administrative expenses to sales. Their cost of goods sold to sales percentages are virtually the same. Possible explanations for Wal-Mart's lower selling and administrative expenses to sales percentages include:

- Economies of scale. Wal-Mart is three times the size of Carrefour and four times the size of Metro. Wal-Mart spreads relatively fixed administrative expenses, such as information systems, legal, and strategic planning, over a much larger sales base.

- Selling and administrative expenses include depreciation expense. Exhibit 5.28 indicates that fixed assets per square meter are significantly lower for Wal-Mart than for Carrefour and Metro. This may be due to Wal-Mart's larger stores (fewer government approvals), lower construction costs, or less costly land. Wal-Mart also generates significantly more sales per investments in fixed assets, due either to higher sales productivity or to the lower acquisition costs discussed above.

- Selling and administrative expenses also include compensation of employees. Wal-Mart's compensation per employee is significantly less than Metro in all years and less than Carrefour in two of the three years. Exchange rate changes affect the compensation data for Wal-Mart..

Carrefour's lower selling and administrative expense to sales percentages relative to Metro likely relates to:

5.29 a. continued.

- Lower compensation cost per employee. Although Carrefour's personnel costs per employee are lower than those for Metro, its sales per employee are also lower. To assess the relation between the two measures, we can compute the ratio of personnel cost per employee to sales per employee. This ratio is personnel cost as a percentage of sales. The ratios for Carrefour are 9.5 percent (= 23,134/242,280) in Year 12, 9.4 percent (= 21,022/223,574) in Year 13, and 9.2 percent (= 19,449/210,261) in Year 14. The corresponding ratios for Metro are 11.2 percent (= 29,778/265,087) in Year 12, 10.9 percent (= 29,340/269,048) in Year 13, and 10.7 percent (= 28,979/270,019) in Year 14. The corresponding ratios for Wal-Mart are 9.8 percent (= 21,806/222,866) in Year 12, 9.5 percent (= 21,836/231,003) in Year 13, and 9.4 percent (= 17,652/188,049) in Year 14.

- More focused strategy. Metro's involvement with specialty and department stores in addition to discount and grocery stores likely adds administrative complexity.

- Metro's sales per square meter are lower than Carrefour's, indicating less sales productivity.

Total Assets Turnover: Wal-Mart's advantage on total assets turnover results primarily from a faster fixed assets turnover, as discussed above. Although Wal-Mart's sales per square meter are less than those of Carrefour, Wal-Mart's fixed assets per square meter are significantly less than Carrefour's. Although the total assets turnovers of Carrefour and Metro are similar, differences emerge in their individual asset turnovers. Carrefour has a slower accounts receivable turnover. It is not clear why this is the case. Carrefour operates in part through franchisees and likely has receivables from these entities. Its inventory turnover is the highest of the three companies. Wal-Mart is renown for its state-of-the-art inventory control systems, so Carrefour's advantage likely relates to a higher proportion of grocery products in its sales mix. Metro has the lowest inventory and fixed asset turnovers. It is surprising that its total assets turnover is approximately the same as Carrefour's. One hypothesis is that Metro has more goodwill arising from acquisitions, which increases other noncurrent assets and decreases the total assets turnover. This possibility is not the case, however, because other noncurrent assets as a percentage of total assets are similar for the three companies (data not provided in the problem).

b. The advantage from using financial leverage stems from two principal factors: (1) an excess of ROA over the after-tax cost of borrowing, and (2) the proportion of borrowing in the capital structure. Although the case does not permit calculation of the after-tax cost of borrowing, one

5.29 b. continued.

would expect that Wal-Mart would have the advantage here because of its higher ROA, followed by Carrefour, and then Metro. Carrefour and Metro have significantly more debt in their capital structures than Wal-Mart. We can assess the leveraging impact of these two factors by computing the ratio of ROCE/ROA. The ratios for the three companies are as follows:

	Year 12	Year 13	Year 14
Carrefour:			
15.6%/4.1%	3.8%		
19.3%/4.7%		4.1%	
24.4%/5.1%			4.8%
Metro:			
9.7%/2.8%	3.5%		
10.7%/2.6%		4.1%	
12.1%/2.9%			4.2%
Wal-Mart:			
20.1%/8.8%	2.3%		
21.6%/9.3%		2.3%	
21.9%/9.3%			2.4%

Thus, Carrefour appears to use financial leverage more effectively than Metro and Wal-Mart. One might question Metro's large capital structure leverage ratios in light of its weak profitability. Question c. addresses the risk levels of these firms.

c. Metro is the most risky, followed by Carrefour, and then Wal-Mart. Carrefour appears to have the most short-term liquidity risk and Metro appears to have the most long-term liquidity risk.

Short-term Liquidity Risk: Carrefour has the lowest current ratios and those ratios are significantly less than 1.0 Its cash flow from operations to current liabilities ratios are much smaller than the desired 40 percent level. It stretches its creditors longer than Metro or Wal-Mart. Its days receivable have increased and are significantly longer than Metro and Wal-Mart. Metro's short-term liquidity ratios are marginally better than Carrefour's, but not at healthy levels. Both Carrefour and Metro stretch their suppliers longer than their days receivables plus days inventory. Wal-Mart's short-term liquidity ratios are at healthy levels in general. One might question its low quick ratio. However, Wal-Mart essentially sells for cash, so has few accounts receivable.

Long-term Liquidity Risk: Metro's debt levels are the highest of the three firms and its cash flow from operations to total liabilities ratios and interest coverage ratios are the worst. These ratios would appear to be at worrisome levels, particularly when considering its weak profit-

5.29 c. continued.

ability record. Carrefour's ratios are marginally better, but not at particularly healthy levels. Its interest coverage ratio trended upward during the three-year period, an encouraging sign. None of Wal-Mart's long-term liquidity ratios suggest concerns.

5.30   (The GAP and Limited Brands; calculating and interpreting profitability and risk ratios.)

The financial statement ratios on pages 5-29, 5-30, and 5-31 form the basis for the responses to the questions raised.

a. The GAP is more profitable in Year 14, the result of a higher profit margin and higher total assets turnover. The higher profit margin results primarily from a lower cost of goods sold to sales percentage. The clothes of The GAP are more standardized than those of Limited Brands, perhaps permitting lower manufacturing costs (for example, from quantity discounts on materials, fewer machine setups, less training of employees). The GAP probably also incurs fewer inventory writedowns from obsolescence because its clothing line is less fashion oriented. The faster total asset turnover of The GAP is not due to either inventories or fixed assets, because Limited Brands has faster turnover ratios for these assets. Accounts receivable comprises such a small proportion of the total assets of Limited Brands that the differences in the accounts receivable turnover ratios exert very little influence on the total assets turnover. The difference in total assets turnover related to the proportion of Other Noncurrent Assets on the balance sheet of each company. Other Noncurrent Assets averages 2.3 percent of total assets for The GAP for the two years, whereas it averages 21.1 percent of total assets for Limited Brands. Other Noncurrent Assets likely relates to goodwill and other intangibles from corporate acquisitions. The larger rate of return on assets of The GAP carries over to the rate of return on common shareholders' equity. In addition to larger operating profitability, The GAP carries substantially more financial leverage, enhancing its profitability advantage over Limited Brands even more.

b. The current and quick ratios suggest that The GAP has somewhat more short-term liquidity risk than Limited Brands, although neither company appears overly risky in this regard. Limited Brands also pays its suppliers more quickly than The GAP. The cash flow from operations to average current liabilities ratios for The GAP and Limited Brands are similar and very large.

c. The GAP has substantially higher levels of debt than Limited Brands. However, the superior profitability of The GAP provides it with similar cash flow from operations to average total liabilities and interest coverage ratios. Neither company appears to have significant long-term liquidity risk.

5.30 continued

The GAP   **The Limited**

1. Rate of Return on Assets

$$= \frac{\$1,030 + (1-.35)(\$528)}{.5(\$14,101 + \$14,479)} = 9.6 \text{ percent.}$$

$$\frac{\$582 + (1-.35)(\$220)}{.5(\$9,506 + \$10,079)} = 7.4 \text{ percent.}$$

2. Profit Margin for Return on Assets

$$= \frac{\$1,030 + (1-.35)(\$528)}{\$15,854} = 8.7 \text{ percent.}$$

$$\frac{\$582 + (1-.35)(\$220)}{\$8,934} = 3.1 \text{ percent.}$$

3. Total Assets Turnover

$$= \frac{\$15,854}{.5(\$14,101 + \$14,479)} = 1.1 \text{ times per year.}$$

$$\frac{\$8,934}{.5(\$9,506 + \$10,079)} = .9 \text{ times per year.}$$

4. Cost of Goods Sold to Sales

$$= \frac{\$9,592}{\$15,854} = 60.5 \text{ percent.}$$

$$\frac{\$5,525}{\$8,934} = 61.8 \text{ percent.}$$

5. Selling and Administration Expenses to Sales

$$= \frac{\$4,089}{\$15,854} = 25.8 \text{ percent.}$$

$$\frac{\$2,288}{\$8,934} = 25.6 \text{ percent.}$$

6. Interest Expenses to Sales

$$= \frac{\$528}{\$15,854} = 3.3 \text{ percent.}$$

$$\frac{\$220}{\$8,934} = 2.5 \text{ percent.}$$

7. Income Tax Expenses to Sales

$$= \frac{\$653}{\$15,854} = 4.1 \text{ percent.}$$

$$\frac{\$382}{\$8,934} = 4.3 \text{ percent.}$$

8. Accounts Receivable Turnover

No Accounts Receivable

$$\frac{\$8,934}{.5(\$151 + \$110)} = 68.5 \text{ times per year.}$$

9. Inventory Turnover

$$= \frac{\$9,592}{.5(\$2,048 + \$1,704)} = 5.1 \text{ times per year.}$$

$$\frac{\$5,525}{.5(\$966 + \$943)} = 5.8 \text{ times per year.}$$

10. Fixed Asset Turnover

$$= \frac{\$15,854}{.5(\$7,976 + \$7,504)} = 2.0 \text{ times per year.}$$

$$\frac{\$8,934}{.5(\$3,752 + \$3,655)} = 2.4 \text{ times per year.}$$

5.30 continued

11. Rate of Return on Common Shareholders' Equity

$$= \frac{\$1,030}{.5(\$3,659 + \$4,783)} = 24.4 \text{ percent.} \qquad = \frac{\$582}{.5(\$4,860 + \$5,266)} = 11.5 \text{ percent.}$$

12. Profit Margin for Return on Common Shareholders' Equity

$$= \frac{\$1,030}{\$15,854} = 6.5 \text{ percent.} \qquad = \frac{\$582}{\$8,934} = 6.5 \text{ percent.}$$

13. Capital Structure Leverage Ratio

$$= \frac{.5(\$14,401 + \$14,479)}{.5(\$3,659 + \$4,783)} = 3.4. \qquad = \frac{.5(\$9,506 + \$10,079)}{.5(\$4,860 + \$5,266)} = 1.9.$$

14. Current Ratio: Beginning of Year

$$= \frac{\$5,740}{\$2,726} = 2.1. \qquad = \frac{\$3,606}{\$1,259} = 2.9.$$

End of Year

$$= \frac{\$6,689}{\$2,482} = 2.7. \qquad = \frac{\$4,433}{\$1,392} = 3.2.$$

15. Quick Ratio: Beginning of Year

$$= \frac{\$3,027 + \$362}{\$2,726} = 1.2. \qquad = \frac{\$2,262 + \$151}{\$1,259} = 1.9.$$

End of Year

$$= \frac{\$2,261 + \$2,424}{\$2,482} = 1.9. \qquad = \frac{\$3,129 + \$110}{\$1,392} = 2.3.$$

16. Cash Flow from Operations to Current Liabilities

$$= \frac{\$2,171}{.5(\$2,726 + \$2,482)} = 83.4 \text{ percent.} \qquad = \frac{\$1,062}{.5(\$1,259 + \$1,392)} = 80.1 \text{ percent.}$$

17. Accounts Payable Turnover

$$= \frac{\$9,592 + \$1,704 - \$2,048}{.5(\$1,159 + \$1,178)} = 7.9 \text{ times per year.} \qquad = \frac{\$5,525 + \$943 - \$966}{.5(\$456 + \$453)} = 12.1 \text{ times per year.}$$

18. Long-Term Debt Ratio:

   Beginning of Year

   $$= \frac{\$7,095}{(\$7,095 + \$3,659)} = 66.0 \text{ percent.}$$

   $$\frac{\$2,807}{(\$2,807 + \$4,860)} = 36.6 \text{ percent.}$$

   End of Year

   $$= \frac{\$6,633}{(\$6,633 + \$4,783)} = 58.1 \text{ percent.}$$

   $$\frac{\$2,854}{(\$2,854 + \$5,266)} = 35.1 \text{ percent.}$$

19. Debt-Equity Ratio:

   Beginning of Year

   $$= \frac{\$10,442}{\$14,101} = 74.1 \text{ percent.}$$

   $$\frac{\$4,646}{\$9,506} = 48.9 \text{ percent.}$$

   End of Year

   $$= \frac{\$9,696}{\$14,479} = 67.0 \text{ percent.}$$

   $$\frac{\$4,813}{\$10,079} = 47.8 \text{ percent.}$$

20. Cash Flow from Operations to Total Liabilities

   $$= \frac{\$2,171}{.5(\$10,442 + \$9,696)} = 21.6 \text{ percent.}$$

   $$\frac{\$1,062}{.5(\$4,646 + \$4,813)} = 22.5 \text{ percent.}$$

21. Interest Coverage Ratio

   $$= \frac{\$1,030 + \$653 + \$528}{\$528} = 4.2 \text{ times.}$$

   $$\frac{\$582 + \$382 + \$220}{\$220} = 5.4 \text{ times.}$$

5.31   (International Paper Company; interpreting profitability and risk ratios.)

a. The main reason for the decrease in the cost of goods sold to sales percentage from 80.0 percent in Year 8 to 75.4 percent in Year 9 is the increase in sales volume of 32.3 percent. This is a very capital-intensive company, with significant fixed manufacturing costs. With the greater volume, fixed costs are spread over more units, lowering the unit cost. We also may presume from the increased demand that IPC enjoyed a more favorable marketing climate, enabling price increases, a more profitable sales mix, etc. Finally, the faster inventory turnover should be noted. This typically results in lower carrying costs and obsolescence costs.

b. Two interacting factors explain the decrease in fixed asset turnover from 1.67 in Year 9 to 1.33 in Year 10. On the one hand, the rate of sales growth slows from 32.3 percent to 1.7 percent. Thus, the numerator essentially is flat. On the other hand, the denominator continues to increase, as International Paper Company expands its productive capacity. Capital expenditures' growth drops from 69.2 percent to 16.7 percent but still is substantially greater than sales growth.

c. Financial leverage was favorable in Year 10 as evidenced by the fact that the rate of return on common equity of 5.1 percent exceeded the rate of return on assets of 3.6 percent. International Paper Company earns more on its non-common capital (liabilities and preferred stock, if any) than the cost of that capital; the excess goes to the benefit of the common equity.

d. The reason for the decrease in the current ratio from 1.21 in Year 9 to 1.02 in Year 10 must be that current liabilities have grown relatively more than current assets. The evidence points toward a growth in current assets—cash continues to grow and the turnover of both receivables and inventory slows. The days accounts payable that are outstanding have increased, which increases current liabilities. Also suggestive of an increase in current liabilities is the decrease in the quick ratio.

e. The decrease in cash flow from operations to total liabilities from 16.3 percent in Year 9 to 9.9 percent in Year 10 is very substantial and is explained primarily by a significant slowing of cash flow from operations. Sales growth has declined from 32.3 percent to 1.7 percent, and the profit margin for ROA is down from 8.2 percent to 4.7 percent. Also slowing the cash flow from operations is that the turnover of both receivables and inventory has slowed, resulting in added investment of operating cash flows in these current assets.

5.32 (Marks & Spencer; interpreting profitability and risk ratios.)

a. Sales grew only 4.7 percent between Year 5 and Year 6 and then decreased in Year 7 and Year 8. Marks & Spencer probably had to mark down its merchandise in order to move it. It may also have had to write down merchandise that it could not sell.

b. Marks & Spencer likely increased advertising and other marketing expenditures in an effort to stimulate sales. It may have experienced diseconomies of scale as it spread increased administrative expenses over a declining sales base.

c. The decrease in the income tax expense percentage occurs because of decreased operating profitability. The average income tax rate (income tax expense as a percentage of income before income taxes) actually increased during the period.

Year 6: 4.5%/(10.8% + 4.5%) = 29.4%
Year 7: 2.5%/(5.3% + 2.5 %) = 32.1%
Year 8: 2.5%/(4.2% + 2.5%) = 37.3%

d. Mark & Spencer increased its capital expenditures significantly in Year 6 and Year 7, relative to Year 5, yet sales increased only slightly in Year 6 and decreased in Year 7 and Year 8.

e. Mark & Spencer increased the proportion of debt in the capital structure, particularly long-term debt. Yet, sales declined in Year 7 and Year 8, causing the interest expense to sales percentage to increase.

f. Financial leverage worked to the advantage of the common shareholders in each year because the rate of return on common shareholders' equity exceeds the rate of return on assets. Financial leverage worked less effectively each year relative to the previous year, however, as decreasing operating profitability narrowed the gap between the return on assets and the after-tax cost of borrowing.

5.33 (Detective analysis; identify company.)

There are various approaches to this exercise. One approach begins with a particular company, identifies unique financial characteristics (for example, steel companies have a high proportion of property, plant, and equipment among their assets), and then searches the common-size financial data to identify the company with that unique characteristic. Another approach begins with the common-size data, identifies unusual financial statement relationships (for example, Firm (12) has a high proportion of cash, marketable securities, and receivables among its assets), and then looks over the list of companies to identify the one most likely to have that unusual financial statement relationship. This teaching note employs both approaches.

5.33 continued.

Firm 12—The high proportions of cash, marketable securities, and receivables for Firm (12) suggest that it is Fortis, the Dutch insurance and banking company. Insurance companies receive cash from premiums each year and invest the funds in various investment vehicles until needed to pay insurance claims. They recognize premium revenue from the cash received and investment income from investments each year. They must match against this revenue an appropriate portion of the expected cost of insurance claims from policies in force during the year. Fortis includes this amount on the line labeled Operating Expenses in Exhibit 5.33. Operating revenues also includes interest revenue on loans made. One might ask: Why does Fortis have such a high proportion of financing in the form of current liabilities? This balance sheet category includes the estimated cost of claims not yet paid from insurance in force. It also includes deposits by customers to its banks. One might also ask: What types of quality of earnings issues arise for a company like Fortis? One issue relates to the measurement of insurance claims expense each period. The ultimate cost of claims will not be known with certainty until customers make claims and the firm makes settlements. Prior to that time, Fortis must estimate what that cost will be. The need to make such estimates creates the opportunity to manage earnings and lowers the quality of earnings. Another issue relates to estimated uncollectible loans. Fortis recognizes interest revenue from loans each year and must match against this revenue the cost of any loans that will not be repaid. The need to make such estimates also provides management with an opportunity to manage earnings and therefore lowers the quality of earnings.

Firms (2), (3), (5), and (9)—There are four firms with research and development (R&D) expenses, (2), (3), (5) and (9). These are likely to be Nestle, Roche Holding, Sun Microsystems, and Toyota Motor in some combination.

Roche Holding and Sun Microsystems are more technology oriented and therefore likely to have a higher percentage of R&D to sales. This suggests that they are Firms (2) and (9) in some combination. The inventories of Firm (9) turn over more slowly at 1.4 times per year (= 27.2/20) than those of Firm (2) at 16.1 times per year (= 45.2/2.8). Firm (9) is also more capital intensive than firm (2). This suggests that Firm (2) is Sun Microsystems and Firm (9) is Roche Holdings. Sun uses only 11.8 cents in fixed assets for each dollar of sales generated. These ratios are consistent with Sun's strategy of outsourcing most of its manufacturing operations. The inventory turnover of Roche is consistent with the making of fewer production runs for each pharmaceutical product to gain production efficiencies. The manufacture of pharmaceuticals is highly automated, consistent with the slower fixed asset turnover of Roche. These two firms have the highest profit margins of the twelve firms studied. Sun is a technology leader in engineering workstations and servers. Roche sells products protected by patents. These advantages permit the firms to achieve high profit margins. Roche has a very high proportion of its assets

5.33 continued.

in cash and marketable securities. It generates interest revenue from these investments, which it includes in other revenues. It is interesting to observe the relatively small cost of goods sold to sales percentage for Roche. The manufacturing cost of pharmaceutical products primarily includes the cost of the chemical raw materials, which machines combine into various drugs. Pharmaceutical firms must price their products significantly above manufacturing costs to recoup their investments in R&D. Note also that Sun has very little long-term debt in its capital structure. Computer products have short product life cycles. Lenders are reluctant to lend for a long period because of the concern for technological obsolescence. Computer companies that outsource their production also have few assets that can serve as collateral for long-term borrowing.

This leaves Firms (3) and (5) as Nestle and Toyota Motor in some combination. Firm (5) has a larger amount of receivables relative to sales than Firm (3), consistent with Toyota Motor providing financing for its customers' purchases of automobiles. Nestle will have receivables from wholesalers and distributors of its food products as well, but not to the extent of the multi-year financing of automobiles. The inventory turnover of Firm (3) is 4.5 times a year (= 44.5%/9.9%), whereas the inventory turnover of Firm (5) is 10.6 times a year (= 68%/6.4%). One might at first expect a food processor to have a much higher inventory turnover than an automobile manufacturer, suggesting that Firm (3) is Toyota Motor and Firm (5) is Nestle. Toyota Motor, however, has implemented just-in-time inventory systems, which speed its inventory turnover. Nestle tends to manufacture chocolates to meet seasonal demands, and therefore carries inventory somewhat longer than one might expect. Firm (3) has a much higher percentage of selling and administrative expense to sales than Firm (5). Both of these firms advertise their products heavily. It is difficult to know why one would have a substantially different percentage than the other. The profit margin of Firm (3) is substantially higher than that of Firm (5). The auto industry is more competitive than at least the chocolate side of the food industry. However, other food products encounter extensive competition. Firm (5) has a high proportion of intercorporate investments. Japanese companies tend to operate within groups, called *kieretsu*. The members of the group make investments in the securities of other firms within the group. This would suggest that Firm (5) is Toyota Motor. Another characteristic of Japanese companies is their heavier use of debt in their capital structures. One of the members of these Japanese corporate groups is typically a bank, which lends to group members as needed. With this more-or-less assured source of funds, Japanese firms tend to take on more debt. Although the ratios give somewhat confusing signals, Firm (3) is Nestle and Firm (5) is Toyota Motor.

5.33 continued.

Firms 10 and 11—Firms (10) and (11) are unique in that they are both very fixed-asset intensive. Electric utilities and telecommunication firms both utilize fixed assets in the delivery of their services. Firm (11) is the most fixed-asset intensive of the two firms and carries a higher proportion of long-term debt. Electric-generating plants are more fixed-asset intensive than the infrastructure needed for distribution of telecommunication services. This would suggest that Firm (10) is Deutsche Telekon and Firm (11) is Tokyo Electric Power. The telecommunication industry is going through deregulation whereas Tokyo Electric Power still has a monopoly position in Japan. Thus, the selling and administrative expense to operating revenues percentage for Deutsche Telekon is substantially higher than for Tokyo Electric Power.

Firms (6) and (8)—Two of the remaining industries are also capital intensive, but not to the extent of Deutsche Telekon and Tokyo Electric Power. These firms are Accor, a hotel group, and Arbed-Acier, a steel manufacturer. Firms (6) and (8) require the next highest fixed assets per dollar of sales after Firms (10 and (11). Thus, Firms (6) and (8) are Accor and Arbed-Acier in some combination. Firm (8) has virtually no inventories, whereas Firm (6) has substantial inventories. This suggests that Firm (6) is Arbed-Acier, the steel company, and Firm (8) is Accor, the hotel group. Accor has grown in recent years by acquiring established hotel chains. Accor allocates a portion of the purchase price to goodwill in its acquisitions, which accounts for its higher percentage for Other Assets. Steel products are commodities, whereas hotels have some brand recognition appeal. These factors may explain the higher profit margin for Firm (6) than for Firm (8).

Firm (7)—Firm (7) has an unusually high proportion of its assets in receivables and in current liabilities. Although this pattern would be typical for a commercial bank, we identified Firm (12) earlier as the financial institution. The pattern is also typical for an advertising agency, which creates and sells advertising copy for clients (for which it has a current receivable) and purchasing time and space on various media to display it (for which it has a current liability). Additional evidence that Firm (7) is Interpublic Group is the high percentage for Other Assets, representing goodwill from acquisitions. Firm (7) also has a relatively high profit margin percentage, reflective of its ability to differentiate its creative services.

Firm (1)—Firm (1) is distinguished by its high cost of goods sold to sales and small profit margin percentages. This pattern suggests commodity products with low value added. Of the remaining firms, this characterizes a grocery business. Firm (1) is Carrefour. Its combination of a rapid receivables turnover of 11.8 times per year (= 100/8.5) and rapid inventory turnover of 8.9 times per year (= 87.8/9.9) are also consistent with a grocery business. Current liabilities comprise more than half of its financing. Current assets make up a similarly high proportion of its current assets.

5.33 continued.

> **Firm (4)** — The remaining firm is Firm (4), which is Marks & Spencer the department store chain. Firm (4) has substantial receivables, consistent with having a credit card.

5.34 (Target Corporation.; preparing pro forma financial statements requires Appendix 5.1.)

> a. See attached pro forma financial statements and related financial ratios.

> b. Target Corporation needs to increase borrowing. Cash flow from operations is positive in each year. Thus, the financing need does not appear to be short term. Although Target Corporation increases long-term debt at the growth rate in property, plant and equipment, the amount invested in property, plant and equipment at the end of Year 14 of $17,967 is significantly larger than long-term debt at the end of Year 14 of $11,215. Growing long-term debt at the same growth rate as property, plant and equipment does not adequately finance the fixed assets. If we assume that long-term debt increases at 1.5 times the growth rate in property, plant and equipment, long-term debt (after reclassifications to current liabilities), grows 15 percent (= 1.5 times 10%) annually.

> c. The pro forma financial statement ratios indicate a decreasing ROCE. The projected profit margin for ROCE and total assets turnover ratios are stable. The declining ROCE results from a declining capital structure leverage ratio. Even if we grow long-term debt at 1.5 times the growth rate in property, plant and equipment (see Part b. above), the capital structure leverage ratio and ROCE decline. The reason for the declining capital structure leverage ratio is that retained earnings grows faster than borrowing. Still further increases in borrowing to stabilize the capital structure leverage ratio results in too much cash on the balance sheet. Target Corporation would then need to increase its dividends with the excess cash. Growing dividends at 20 percent annually instead of the 8-percent rate assumed will result in a cash shortage and lead to even more borrowing. To stabilize the capital structure leverage ratio, Target Corporation needs to increase borrowing and increase the growth rate in dividends.

5.34 a. continued.

The following pro forma financial statements were generated by a spreadsheet program that rounds to many decimal places. Rounding causes some of the sub-totals and totals to differ from the sum of the amounts that comprise them.

TARGET CORPORATION
PRO FORMA INCOME STATEMENT
YEAR ENDED JANUARY 31

	Year 14	Year 15	Year 16	Year 17	Year 18	Year 19
Sales Revenue........	$ 46,781	$ 50,991	$ 55,581	$ 60,583	$ 66,035	$ 71,978
Other Revenues	1,382	1,530	1,667	1,817	1,981	2,159
Total Revenues..	$ 48,163	$ 52,521	$ 57,248	$ 62,400	$ 68,016	$ 74,138
Expenses:						
Cost of Goods Sold.................	$ 31,790	$ 34,419	$ 37,517	$ 40,893	$ 44,574	$ 48,585
Selling and Administration..	12,854	14,278	15,563	16,963	18,490	20,154
Interest................	559	608	618	640	664	666
Income Taxes.....	1,119	1,222	1,349	1,484	1,630	1,798
Total Expenses.........	$ 46,322	$ 50,527	$ 55,047	$ 59,980	$ 65,357	$ 71,204
Net Income	$ 1,841	$ 1,994	$ 2,201	$ 2,421	$ 2,659	$ 2,934
Dividends	237	256	276	299	322	348
Increase in Retained Earnings..	$ 1,604	$ 1,738	$ 1,925	$ 2,122	$ 2,337	$ 2,586

Assumptions:

Growth Rate of Sales....	9.0%	
Other Revenues.............	3.0%	of sales
Cost of Goods Sold.........	67.5%	of sales
Selling and Administration Expense...............	28.0%	of sales
Interest Expense...........	5.0%	of interest bearing debt
Income Tax Rate...........	38.0%	of income before income taxes
Dividends........................	8.0%	growth rate

5.34 a. continued.

TARGET CORPORATION
PRO FORMA BALANCE SHEET
JANUARY 31

	Year 14	Year 15	Year 16	Year 17	Year 18	Year 19
Cash	$ 716	$ 657	$ 158	$ 477	$ 6	$ (639)
Accounts Receivable	5,776	6,296	6,862	7,480	8,153	8,887
Inventories	5,343	5,824	6,348	6,919	7,542	8,221
Prepayments	1,093	1,191	1,299	1,415	1,543	1,682
Total Current Assets	$ 12,928	$ 13,969	$ 14,667	$ 16,292	$ 17,244	$ 18,151
Property, Plant and Equipment	17,967	19,764	21,740	23,914	26,305	28,936
Other Assets	1,495	1,645	1,809	1,990	2,189	2,408
Total Assets	$ 32,390	$ 35,377	$ 38,216	$ 42,196	$ 45,738	$ 49,495
Accounts Payable	$ 5,448	$ 6,185	$ 6,495	$ 7,327	$ 7,739	$ 8,682
Notes Payable	0	0	0	0	0	0
Current Portion— Long Term Debt	866	857	502	752	1,323	1,451
Other Current Liabilities	2,000	2,180	2,376	2,590	2,823	3,077
Total Current Liabilities	$ 8,314	$ 9,222	$ 9,373	$ 10,669	$ 11,885	$ 13,211
Long-Term Debt	11,215	11,394	11,981	12,352	12,132	11,749
Other Noncurrent Liabilities	1,796	1,958	2,134	2,326	2,535	2,763
Total Liabilities	$ 21,325	$ 22,574	$ 23,488	$ 25,346	$ 26,552	$ 27,723
Common Stock	$ 76	$ 76	$ 76	$ 76	$ 76	$ 76
Additional Paid-in Capital	1,341	1,341	1,341	1,341	1,341	1,341
Retained Earnings	9,648	11,386	13,311	15,432	17,769	20,356
Total Shareholders' Equity	$ 11,065	$ 12,803	$ 14,728	$ 16,850	$ 19,186	$ 21,772
Total Liabilities and Shareholders' Equity	$ 32,390	$ 35,377	$ 38,216	$ 42,196	$ 45,738	$ 49,495

(See Following Page for Assumptions)

5.34 a. continued.

(Assumptions for Pro Forma Balance Sheet)

Assumptions:

Cash...............................	PLUG					
Accounts Receivable	Sales Growth Rate					
Inventory	Sales Growth Rate					
Prepayments..................	Sales Growth Rate					
Property, Plant and Equipment..................	10.0% Growth Rate					
Other Assets	10.0% Growth Rate					
Accounts Payable Turnover	6.4	6.0	6.0	6.0	6.0	6.0
Merchandise Pur- chases..........................		34,900	38,041	41,465	45,197	49,264
Average Payables		5,817	6,340	6,911	7,533	8,211
Notes Payable................	Property, Plant and Equipment Growth Rate					
Other Current Liabilities	Sales Growth Rate					
Long-Term Debt	Property, Plant and Equipment Growth Rate					
Other Noncurrent Liabilities	Sales Growth Rate					
Common Stock, APIC...........................	0.0% Growth Rate					

5.34 a. continued.

TARGET CORPORATION
PRO FORMA STATEMENT OF CASH FLOWS
FOR THE YEAR ENDED JANUARY 31

Cash Flow Statement	Year 14	Year 15	Year 16	Year 17	Year 18	Year 19
Operations:						
Net Income	$ 1,841	$ 1,994	$ 2,201	$ 2,421	$ 2,659	$ 2,934
Depreciation	1,320	1,452	1,597	1,757	1,933	2,126
Other	669	162	176	192	209	228
(Inc.)/Dec. in Accounts Receivable	(744)	(520)	(567)	(618)	(673)	(734)
(Inc.)/Dec. in Inventory	(583)	(481)	(524)	(571)	(623)	(679)
(Inc.)/Dec. in Prepayments	(255)	(98)	(107)	(117)	(127)	(139)
Inc./(Dec.) in Accounts Payable	764	737	310	832	412	944
Inc./(Dec.) in Other Current Liabilities	148	180	196	214	233	254
Cash Flow from Operations	$ 3,160	$ 3,426	$ 3,282	$ 4,109	$ 4,023	$ 4,934
Investing:						
Acquisition of Property, Plant, and Equipment	$ (2,919)	$ (3,249)	$ (3,574)	$ (3,931)	$ (4,324)	$ 4,756
Other Investing	0	(150)	(164)	(181)	(199)	(219)
Cash Flow from Investing	$ (2,919)	$ (3,398)	$ (3,738)	$ (4,112)	$ (4,523)	$ (4,975)
Financing:						
Inc./(Dec.) in Short-Term Borrowing	$ 0	$ 0	$ 0	$ 0	$ 0	$ 0
Inc./(Dec.) in Long-Term Borrowing	(72)	170	232	621	351	(255)
Inc./(Dec.) in Common Stock	0	0	0	0	0	0
Dividends	(237)	(256)	(276)	(299)	(322)	(348)
Other Financing	26	0	0	0	0	0
Cash Flow from Financing	$ (283)	$ (86)	$ (44)	$ 322	$ 28	$ 603
Change in Cash	$ (42)	$ (59)	$ (500)	$ 320	$ (471)	$ (644)
Cash, Beginning of Year	758	716	657	158	477	6
Cash, End of Year	$ 716	$ 657	$ 158	$ 477	$ 6	$ (639)
Cash Balance from Balance Sheet	716	657	158	477	6	(639)
Difference	$ 0	$ 0	$ 0	$ 0	$ 0	$ 0

(See Following Page for Assumptions)

5.34 a. continued.

(Assumptions for Pro Forma Statement of Cash Flows)

Assumptions:

Depreciation Growth Rate	Same as Property, Plant, and Equipment
Other Operating Add-backs	Change in Noncurrent Liabilities
Other Investing Cash Flows	Change in Other Noncurrent Assets
Other Financing Cash Flows	Zero

TARGET CORPORATION
PRO FORMA FINANCIAL RATIOS

	Year 14	Year 15	Year 16	Year 17	Year 18	Year 19
Rate of Return on Assets	7.10%	7.0%	7.0%	7.0%	7.0%	7.0%
Profit Margin for ROA	4.7	4.6%	4.6%	4.6%	4.6%	4.6%
Total Assets Turnover	1.5	1.5	1.5	1.5	1.5	1.5
Cost of Goods Sold/Sales	68.0%	67.5%	67.5%	67.5%	67.5%	67.5%
Selling and Administrative Expenses/Sales	27.5	28.0%	28.0%	28.0%	28.0%	28.0%
Interest Expense/Sales	1.2%	1.2%	1.1%	1.1%	1.0%	0.9%
Income Tax Expense/Sales	2.4%	2.4%	2.4%	2.4%	2.5%	2.5%
Accounts Receivable Turn-over Ratio	8.2	8.4	8.4	8.4	8.4	8.4
Inventory Turnover Ratio	6.3	6.2	6.2	6.2	6.2	6.2
Fixed Assets Turnover Ratio	2.7	2.7	2.7	2.7	2.6	2.6
Rate of Return on Common Equity	18.0%	16.7%	16.0%	15.3%	14.8%	14.3%
Profit Margin for ROCE	3.9%	3.9%	4.0%	4.0%	4.0%	4.1%
Capital Structure Leverage Ratio	3	2.8	2.7	2.5	2.4	2.3
Current Ratio	1.55	1.51	1.56	1.53	1.45	1.37
Quick Ratio	0.78	0.75	0.75	0.75	0.69	0.62
Cash Flow from Operations/Current Liabilities	39.9%	39.1%	35.3%	41.0%	35.7%	39.3%
Accounts Payable Turnover Ratio	6.4	6.0	6.0	6.0	6.0	6.0
Long-Term Debt Ratio	50.3%	47.1%	44.9%	42.3%	38.7%	35.0%
Debt-Equity Ratio	65.8%	63.8%	61.5%	60.1%	58.1%	56.0%
Cash Flow from Operations/Total Liabilities	15.3%	15.6%	14.3%	16.8%	15.5%	18.2%
Interest Coverage Ratio	6.3	6.3	6.7	7.1	7.5	8.1

5.35   (Ethical issues involving financial statement ratios.)

a. The actions of Firm A are clearly meant to deceive the bank and present a picture of the firm's short-term liquidity risk that is inaccurate. The action would likely constitute fraud in a legal sense. The intention to deceive also suggests unethical behavior.

b. There does not appear to be anything illegal about curtailing growth. The actions of Firm B are likely unwise from a business viewpoint, given the obvious growth opportunities of the firm. Also, security analysts will likely see through the action, given their understanding that growth in earnings always lags growth in retail stores. The ethical issue that arises is management's attempts to artificially increase ROA.

c. The actions of Firm C's management do not appear to constitute illegal behavior. One might question the wisdom of having so little debt to start with and the decision to sell the profitable division. It does not appear that management is attempting to deceive current shareholders by its actions. Thus, it is not clear that ethical issues arise.

CHAPTER 6

RECEIVABLES AND REVENUE RECOGNITION

Questions, Short Exercises, Exercises, Problems, and Cases: Answers and Solutions

6.1   See the text or the glossary at the end of the book.

6.2   The allowance method, because it reports bad debt expense during the period of the sale, not during the later period(s) when specific accounts become uncollectible.

6.3   The direct write-off method matches the loss from an uncollectible account with revenue of the period when a particular account becomes uncollectible. The allowance method matches the loss from an uncollectible account with revenue of the period of the sale instead of the later period when a particular account becomes uncollectible.

6.4   a.   A firm with stable sales (both volume and price) and a constant proportion of uncollectible accounts will likely report similar amounts for bad debt expense each period.

        b.   The direct write-off method should always result in larger amounts for accounts receivable-net on the balance sheet than the allowance method.

6.5   a.   This statement is valid. Most businesses ought not to set credit policies so stringent that they have no uncollectible accounts. To do so would require extremely careful screening of customers, which is costly, and the probable loss of many customers who will take their business elsewhere. So long as the revenues collected from credit sales exceed the sum of both selling costs and the cost of goods sold on credit, then the firm should not be concerned if some percentage of its accounts receivable are uncollectible.

        b.   If a business liberalizes its credit policy by granting to a group of customers, who were not previously granted this privilege, the right to buy on account, it can find that its net revenues from the new credit customers exceed the cost of goods sold to them and the selling expenses of executing the sales. The extension of credit to new customers can increase net income even though it results in more uncollectible accounts.

6.5 continued

    c.   When the net present value of the receipts from selling to new customers is larger than the net present value of the costs of putting goods into their hands.

6.6   If a firm computes the Bad Debt Expense figure at the end of the accounting period but writes off specific accounts receivable during the period as information about uncollectible accounts becomes available, then the Allowance for Uncollectibles will have a debit balance whenever the amount of accounts written off during the period exceeds the opening credit balance in the Allowance account. Firms prepare balance sheets only after making adjusting entries. Both the Bad Debt Expense and the Allowance for Uncollectibles accounts must be made current with appropriate adjusting entries before preparing the balance sheet. Because the Allowance for Uncollectibles account is an asset contra, it will always show a credit (or perhaps a zero) balance after making adjusting entries.

6.7   Manufacturing firms typically do not identify a customer or establish a firm selling price until they sell products. Thus, these firms do not satisfy the criteria for revenue recognition while production is taking place. In contrast, construction companies usually identify a customer and establish a contract price before construction begins. In addition, the production process for a manufacturing firm is usually much shorter than for a construction firm. The recognition of revenue at the time of production or at the time of sale does not result in a significantly different pattern of income for a manufacturing firm. For a construction company, the pattern of income could differ significantly.

6.8   Under the installment method, accountants recognize proportionate parts of the costs incurred as expenses each period as they recognize proportionate parts of the selling price as revenues. Under the cost-recovery-first method, costs match dollar-for-dollar with revenues until revenues equal total costs. Thus, the income patterns differ because of the *expense*-recognition pattern, not the revenue-recognition pattern.

6.9   Under both the installment method and the cash basis of accounting, accountants recognize revenue when the firm receives cash. The installment method recognizes expenses in the same period as the associated revenues. The cash basis recognizes expenses when the firm makes cash expenditures.

6.10   Application of the installment method requires a reasonably accurate estimate of the total amount of cash the firm expects to receive from customers. The cost-recovery-first method does not require such an estimate.

6.11 Accountants are more concerned with the reliability of income data than are economists. Accountants are responsible for measuring and auditing income amounts and, therefore, require reliable measures of wealth changes. Such evidence usually takes the form of market transactions.

6.12 The user of the financial statements must identify the reason for the decline in the quality of earnings. Does the measurement of revenues and expenses for a particular business require numerous estimates? Is there evidence that the firm has used the inherent flexibility in the measurement of revenues and expenses to its advantage? Is the declining quality of earnings due to unusual or nonrecurring items which the financial statement user can exclude when assessing operating profitability? In some cases, the financial statement user can adjust net income to eliminate the source of the decreasing earnings quality; in other cases, such adjustments are not possible.

6.13 (Diversified Technologies; allowance method for uncollectible accounts.)

a. $5,076 (= .04 X $126,900).

b. Accounts Receivable Gross ($126,900 – $94,300 –
$2,200) $ 30,400
Less: Allowance for Uncollectible Accounts ($5,076 –
$2,200).. (2,876)
Accounts Receivable Net... $ 27,524

6.14 (York Company; aging accounts receivable.)

Retained Earnings (Bad Debt Expense) (Share-
holders' Equity Decrease)... 9,050
Allowance for Uncollectible Accounts (Asset
Decrease)... 9,050

The Allowance account requires a balance of $25,050 = (.005 X $1,200,000) + (.01 X $255,000) + (.10 X $75,000) + (.30 X $30,000). The adjusting entry *increases* the Allowance account by $9,050 (= $25,050 – $16,000) and recognizes Bad Debt Expense for the period by the same amount.

6.15 (Seward Corporation; reconstructing events when using the allowance method.)

a. Accounts Receivable (Asset Increase)................... 240,000
Retained Earnings (Sales Revenue) (Share-
holders' Equity Increase) 240,000

b. Retained Earnings (Bad Debt Expense) (Share-
holders' Equity Decrease)..................................... 4,800
Allowance for Uncollectible Accounts (Asset
Decrease)... 4,800

6.15 continued.

    c. Allowance for Uncollectible Accounts (Asset
        Increase).. 4,400
           Accounts Receivable (Asset Decrease)........... 4,400
        $4,400 = $8,700 + $4,800 − $9,100.

    d. Cash (Asset Increase).. 231,200
          Accounts Receivable (Asset Decrease).............. 231,200
        $231,200 = $82,900 + $240,000 − $4,400 −
        $87,300.

6.16   (Pandora Company; allowance method: reconstructing journal entry from events.)

    Retained Earnings (Bad Debt Expense) (Share-
       holders' Equity Decrease).. 3,700
        Allowance for Uncollectible Accounts (Asset
          Decrease)... 3,700
    Write-off of $2,200 + Ending Balance of Allowance of
    $5,000 − Beginning Balance of $3,500 = $3,700.

6.17   (Milton Corporation; allowance method: reconstructing journal entries from events.)

    Accounts Receivable (Asset Increase)........................ 75,000,000
       Retained Earnings (Sales) (Shareholders' Equity
        Increase)... 75,000,000
    $750,000 is 1 percent of sales; sales = $750,000/.01.

    Retained Earnings (Bad Debt Expense) (Share-
       holders' Equity Decrease).. 750,000
        Allowance for Uncollectible Accounts (Asset
          Decrease)... 750,000

    Allowance for Uncollectible Accounts (Asset
       Increase).. 600,000
        Accounts Receivable (Asset Decrease)............. 600,000
    $1,400,000 + $750,000 − $1,550,000 = $600,000.

    Cash (Asset Increase).. 72,000,000
       Accounts Receivable (Asset Decrease)................ 72,000,000
    $15,200,000 + $75,000,000 − $600,000 −
    $17,600,000 = $72,000,000.

6.18   (Reconstructing events from journal entries.)

    a. Estimated bad debt expense for the period is $2,300 using the allowance method.

6.18 continued.

    b. A firm writes off specific customers' accounts totaling $450 as uncollectible under the allowance method.

    c. A firm writes off specific customers' accounts totaling $495 as uncollectible under the direct write-off method.

6.19   (Shannon Construction Company; percentage-of-completion and completed contract methods of income recognition.)

Percentage-of-Completion Method

Year	Degree of Completion		Revenue	Expense	Income
1	$1,200,000/$4,800,000 =	25.0%	$1,500,000	$1,200,000	$ 300,000
2	$3,000,000/$4,800,000 =	62.5%	3,750,000	3,000,000	750,000
3	$ 600,000/$4,800,000 =	12.5%	750,000	600,000	150,000
			$6,000,000	$4,800,000	$1,200,000

Completed Contract Method

Year	Revenue	Expense	Income
1	--	--	--
2	--	--	--
3	$6,000,000	$4,800,000	$1,200,000
	$6,000,000	$4,800,000	$1,200,000

6.20   (Cunningham Realty Partners; installment and cost-recovery-first methods of income recognition.)

Installment Method

Year	Revenue	Percentage of Selling Price	Expense	Income
1	$ 30,000	25%	$20,000	$10,000
2	30,000	25%	20,000	10,000
3	30,000	25%	20,000	10,000
4	30,000	25%	20,000	10,000
	$120,000		$80,000	$40,000

Cost-Recovery-First Method

Year	Revenue	Expense	Income
1	$ 30,000	$ 30,000	$ -0-
2	30,000	30,000	-0-
3	30,000	20,000	10,000
4	30,000	-0-	30,000
	$120,000	$ 80,000	$40,000

6.21   (Heath Company; journal entries for the allowance method.)

a. **Year 6**
Retained Earnings (Bad Debt Expense) (Share-
     holders' Equity Decrease)...................................... 10,200
          Allowance for Uncollectible Accounts (Asset
               Decrease)... 10,200
     .03 x $340,000 = $10,200.

Allowance for Uncollectible Accounts (Asset
     Increase).. 1,800
          Accounts Receivable (Asset Decrease)........... 1,800

Year 7
Retained Earnings (Bad Debt Expense) (Share-
     holders' Equity Decrease)...................................... 13,500
          Allowance for Uncollectible Accounts (Asset
               Decrease)... 13,500
     .03 x $450,000 = $13,500.

Allowance for Uncollectible Accounts (Asset
     Increase).. 8,300
          Accounts Receivable (Asset Decrease)........... 8,300

Year 8
Retained Earnings (Bad Debt Expense) (Share-
     holders' Equity Decrease)...................................... 17,400
          Allowance for Uncollectible Accounts (Asset
               Decrease)... 17,400
     .03 x $580,000 = $17,400.

Allowance for Uncollectible Accounts (Asset
     Increase).. 14,100
          Accounts Receivable (Asset Decrease)........... 14,100

b. Yes. Uncollectible accounts arising from sales of Years 6, 7 and 8 total
   $42,600, which equals 3.1 percent (= $42,600/$1,370,000) of total sales
   on account during the three year period.

6.22   (Schneider Corporation; journal entries for the allowance method.)

a. **Year 1**
Retained Earnings (Bad Debt Expense) (Share-
     holders' Equity Decrease)...................................... 15,000
          Allowance for Uncollectible Accounts (Asset
               Decrease)... 15,000
     .02 x $750,000 = $15,000.

6.22 a. continued.

<table>
<tr><td>Allowance for Uncollectible Accounts (Asset Increase)..</td><td>1,300</td><td></td></tr>
<tr><td>   Accounts Receivable (Asset Decrease)..........</td><td></td><td>1,300</td></tr>
</table>

Year 2

<table>
<tr><td>Retained Earnings (Bad Debt Expense) (Shareholders' Equity Decrease)....................................</td><td>24,000</td><td></td></tr>
<tr><td>   Allowance for Uncollectible Accounts (Asset Decrease)..</td><td></td><td>24,000</td></tr>
</table>

.02 x $1,200,000 = $24,000.

<table>
<tr><td>Allowance for Uncollectible Accounts (Asset Increase)..</td><td>11,200</td><td></td></tr>
<tr><td>   Accounts Receivable (Asset Decrease)..........</td><td></td><td>11,200</td></tr>
</table>

Year 3

<table>
<tr><td>Retained Earnings (Bad Debt Expense) (Shareholders' Equity Decrease)....................................</td><td>48,000</td><td></td></tr>
<tr><td>   Allowance for Uncollectible Accounts (Asset Decrease)..</td><td></td><td>48,000</td></tr>
</table>

.02 x $2,400,000 = $48,000.

<table>
<tr><td>Allowance for Uncollectible Accounts (Asset Increase)..</td><td>23,600</td><td></td></tr>
<tr><td>   Accounts Receivable (Asset Decrease)..........</td><td></td><td>23,600</td></tr>
</table>

b. Yes. The actual loss experience is 1.9 percent (= $82,500/$4,350,000) of sales on account for sales during Years 1 through 3.

6.23 (Logue Corporation; reconstructing events when using the allowance method.)

a.
<table>
<tr><td>Accounts Receivable (Asset Increase).....................</td><td>450,000</td><td></td></tr>
<tr><td>   Retained Earnings (Sales Revenue) (Shareholders' Equity Increase) ....</td><td></td><td>450,000</td></tr>
</table>

b.
<table>
<tr><td>Allowance for Uncollectible Accounts (Asset Increase)..</td><td>21,100</td><td></td></tr>
<tr><td>   Accounts Receivable (Asset Decrease)..........</td><td></td><td>21,100</td></tr>
</table>

$21,100 = $18,200 + $2,900.

c.
<table>
<tr><td>Cash (Asset Increase)..</td><td>422,100</td><td></td></tr>
<tr><td>   Accounts Receivable (Asset Decrease) ....</td><td></td><td>422,100</td></tr>
</table>

$422,100 = $115,900 + $450,000 − $21,100 − $122,700.

6.23 continued.

    d. Retained Earnings (Bad Debt Expense) (Share-
        holders' Equity Decrease)...................................... 27,000
           Allowance for Uncollectible Accounts (Asset
             Decrease)... 27,000
        $27,000 = .06 X $450,000.

6.24   (Dove Company; aging accounts receivable.)

Retained Earnings (Bad Debt Expense) (Share-
    holders' Equity Decrease).. 3,700
      Allowance for Uncollectible Accounts (Asset
        Decrease)... 3,700
To adopt auditor's suggestion that total allowance
now be $20,900 [(= .005 X $400,000) + (.01 X $90,000)
+ (.10 X $40,000) + (.70 X $20,000)]. $20,900 −
$17,200 = $3,700.

6.25   (Home and Office Depot; effects of transactions involving suppliers and customers on cash flows.)

    a. $127,450 = $130,000 − ($8,600 − $8,000) + ($750 − $700) − $2,000
             = $130,000 − $600 + $50 − $2,000

    b. $85,100 = $85,000 − ($7,500 − $7,000) + ($10,400 − $10,000) +
               ($11,200 − $11,000)
             = $85,000 − $500 + $400 + $200

6.26   (Revenue recognition for various types of businesses.)

We have found this question to be an excellent one for class discussion because it forces the student to think about both revenue *and* expense timing and measurement questions. It also generates active student interest. We have found it helpful to begin consideration of each item by drawing a time line similar to that in Figure 6.1 and appropriately labeling it. Some of the items are relatively obvious while others require more discussion.

    a. Time of sale.

    b. Probably as work progresses using the percentage-of-completion method. Students normally assume the sale is to the United States Government. We ask them if it would make any difference if the sale was to a relatively weak government in Africa or South America. This question gets at the issue of whether the amount of cash the firm will receive is subject to reasonably accurate estimation.

    c. Probably as the firm collects cash using the installment method.

6.26 continued.

d. At the time of sale.

e. At the time the firm picks citrus products and delivers them to customers. We ask students if their response would change if the citrus firm had a five-year contract at a set price to supply a particular quantity of citrus products to a citrus processor. The issue here is whether, given uncertainties about future weather conditions, the citrus grower will be able to make delivery on the contract.

f. AICPA *Statement of Position 79-4* stipulates that the firm should not recognize revenue until it meets all of the following conditions:

1. The firm knows the sales price.

2. The firm knows the cost of the film or can reasonably estimate the loss.

3. The firm is reasonably assured as to the collectibility of the selling price.

4. A licensee has accepted the film in accordance with the license agreement.

5. The film is available (that is, the licensee can exercise the right to use the film and all conflicting licenses have expired).

Revenue recognition from the sale of rights to the television network is appropriate as soon as the firm meets these conditions even though the license period is three years. The firm cannot recognize revenues from the sale of subsequent rights to others until the three-year licensing period has expired. An important question in this example is when to recognize the production costs as an expense. Should the firm recognize all of the costs as an expense on the initial sale to the television network? Or, should it treat some portion of the costs as an asset, matched against future sales of license rights? Most accountants would probably match all of the costs against revenue from the television network license agreement, unless the firm has signed other license agreements for periods beginning after the initial three-year period at the same time as the television license agreement.

g. At the time of sale of each house to a specific buyer.

h. At the time of sale to a specific buyer at a set price. This will vary, depending on who owns the whiskey during the aging process. We pose the following situation: Suppose a particular whiskey producer has an on-going supplier relationship with a whiskey distributor. The quantity purchased by the distributor and the price set depend on supply and de-

6-9

6.26 h. continued.

mand conditions at the time aged whiskey is brought to the market. The supplier always purchases some minimum quantity. When should the firm recognize revenue? This question gets at the issue of measuring revenue in a reasonably reliable manner. You may also want to discuss the following other wrinkle. Suppose the whiskey producer doubles capacity. The firm cannot sell any of the whiskey produced from this new capacity for six years. What should the firm do with the costs of this new capacity?

i. As time passes and the firm lets borrowers use funds.

j. The alternatives here are (1) as customers make reservations, (2) as customers make some formal commitments to confirm their reservations, or (3) as the agency receives cash from commissions. The second alternative is probably best. However, past experience may provide sufficient evidence as to the proportion of reservations that customers ultimately confirm to justify earlier recognition.

k. At the completion of the printing activity.

l. The issue here is whether to recognize revenue when the firm sells stamps to food stores or when customers turn in the stamps for redemption. One might argue for revenue recognition at the time of sale of the stamps, since the seller must have some estimate of the redemption rate in setting the price for the sale of the stamps.

m. At the time the wholesaler delivers food products to stores.

n. The issue here is whether to recognize revenue while the livestock is growing. A grower of timber faces a similar issue. For the reasons Part *h*. above discusses, it is probably best to await the time of delivery to a specific customer at an agreed upon price.

o. Probably during each period in a manner similar to the percentage-of-completion method. In practice firms use several methods.

6.27 (Income recognition for various businesses.)

a. Company A is selling software and access to data and other software. Recognizing all of the revenue at the time of initial delivery of the software appears premature because ongoing access to data and other software is a significant part of the product. If the firm can reasonably disaggregate the initial selling price into the portion applicable to the software and the portion applicable to the later services, then it could recognize the software sales as revenues at the time of delivery and then recognize the remaining selling price over the two-year period as customers use the web-accessed services. If not, then recognizing the revenue ratably over the two-year period seems more appropriate.

6.27 continued.

b. The issue in this case for Company B is the ability of the SAPs to pay for the software. Their ability to pay depends on the number of customers they sign up and the collection of cash from these customers. Recognizing revenue using either the installment or the cost-recovery-first methods seems most appropriate in this case.

c. The issue with Company C is whether it satisfies the "substantial performance" criterion at the beginning of the two-year period (collectibility of cash is not an issue). Most accountants would argue that Company C should recognize the revenue ratably over the two-year period. It will likely add new software to the web site during the two-year period which initial subscribers will be able to access. Recognizing all of the revenue at the beginning of the two-year contract would theoretically require Company C to estimate the cost of developing the new software and match it against any revenue initially recognized.

d. Assuming that Company D can collect the up-front fee with a high degree of certainty, it should be able to recognize this fee at the time of initial listing. It should recognize the transaction fee no earlier than the time of the transaction. The timing of its recognition depends on the predictability of buyers backing out on the purchase. If the probability of buyers backing out is either low or highly predictable, then recognizing the transaction fee at the time of the transaction is appropriate. Otherwise, delaying the recognition of the transaction fee until the transaction is completed is appropriate.

e. Company E should recognize only the fee as revenue, not the selling price of the product as revenue and the cost of the good as cost of goods sold. Company E bears none of the risk of purchasing and holding the product in this case. Although it might desire to inflate its revenues to obtain a higher pricing multiple from the market for its common stock, GAAP would not permit this.

f. Company F assumes more product risk in this case than in Part e. and could probably justify recognizing revenue for the specified minimum number of units each month and expense for the cost of those units.

g. The issue for Company G is its ability to estimate at the time of the initial sale of the computer the cost of any rebates that will have to be paid to the Internet service provider after the time of the sale. If this amount is highly predictable, then Company G can justify recognizing the full selling price as revenue at the time of sale and the initial 10 percent cost of the rebate and any additional later cost of reallocated rebates as an expense. The difficulty here is that linked computer/Internet sales are a new arrangement and Company G may have difficulty estimating the cost of reallocated rebates. The $400 re-

6.27 g. continued.

bate appears to be a substantial amount relative to the selling price of the personal computer so the issue is not trivial. The arrangement seems to be more to stimulate sales of the Internet service provider than those of Company G, given the .90/.10 cost-sharing percentages. If predictability of the reallocated rebate cost is highly uncertain, than recognizing the selling price minus $360 (= .9 X $400) as revenue at the time of sale of the computer and the remaining $360 ratably over the three-year period seems appropriate. Actual costs of any reallocated rebates would be recognized as incurred each year.

h. Most accountants would likely argue that Company H should recognize one-twelfth of the annual fee each month, as time passes and the contract provisions are satisfied. Company H might argue that the likelihood of not meeting the minimums is very low because it could simply instruct its employees to call up the site a sufficient number of times each month to meet the minimum. Following this line of reasoning, Company H might argue for up-front recognition of the full year's fee.

i. The issue for Company I is the ability to measure the cash-equivalent value of the common stock. Company I would need to obtain sufficient information from Upstart Company to value the common stock received in order to justify recognizing revenue at the time of providing the advertising services.

j. This is a classic barter transaction. To justify recognizing revenue from advertising space sold and expense for advertising space purchased, these companies would need to demonstrate the price that they would charge for a cash sale of the advertising space to other customers. Note that this transaction has zero effect on earnings, because the amount of expense for space purchased equals the amount of revenue for space sold.

6.28   (American Express; analyzing changes in accounts receivable.)

a.

	Year 5	Year 6	Year 7
(1) Sales on Account			
Accounts Receivable			
(Asset Increase)........	19,132	21,278	23,675
Retained Earnings			
(Sales Revenue)			
(Shareholders'			
Equity			
Increase)...............	19,132	21,278	23,675

6.28 a. continued.

	Year 5	Year 6	Year 7
(2) Provision for Estimated Uncollectible Accounts			
Retained Earnings (Bad Debt Expense) (Shareholders' Equity Decrease).......	2,187	2,212	2,439
Allowance for Uncollectible Accounts) (Asset Decrease).............	2,187	2,212	2,439
(3) Write Off of Actual Bad Debts			
Allowance for Uncollectible Accounts (Asset Increase)........	2,195[a]	2,064[b]	2,270[c]
Accounts Receivable (Asset Decrease).............	2,195	2,064	2,270

[a] $1,419 + $2,187 − $1,411 = $2,195.
[b] $1,411 + $2,212 − $1,559 = $2,064.
[c] $1,559 + $2,439 − $1,728 = $2,270.

	Year 5	Year 6	Year 7
(4) Collection of Cash from Customers			
Cash (Asset Increase).....................	15,550[d]	12,295[e]	14,654[f]
Accounts Receivable (Asset Decrease).............	15,550	12,295	14,654

[d] $41,883 + $19,132 − $2,187 − $43,278 = $15,550.
[e] $43,278 + $21,278 − $2,212 − $50,049 = $12,295.
[f] $50,049 + $23,675 − $2,439 − $56,631 = $14,654.

6.28 continued.

b.

	Year 5	Year 6	Year 7

(1) Accounts Receivable Turnover
    Year 5: $19,132/.5($41,883 + $43,278)... **.45**
    Year 6: $21,278/.5($43,278 + $50,049)... **.46**
    Year 7: $23,675/.5($50,049 + $56,631)... **.44**

(2) Bad Debt Expense/Revenues
    Year 5: $2,187/$19,132 .... **11.4%**
    Year 6: $2,212/$21,278 .... **10.4%**
    Year 7: $2,439/$23,675 .... **10.3%**

(3) Allowance for Uncollectible Accounts/
    Gross Accounts Receivable at End of Year
    Year 5: $1,411/($43,278 + $1,411) **3.2%**
    Year 6: $1,559/($50,049 + $1,559) **3.0%**
    Year 7: $1,728/($56,631 + $1,728) **3.0%**

(4) Accounts Written Off/Average Gross
    Accounts Receivable
    Year 5: $2,195/.5($41,883 + $1,419 +
               $43,278 + $1,411) **5.0%**
    Year 6: $2,064/.5($43,278 + $1,411 +
               $50,049 + $1,559) **4.3%**
    Year 7: $2,270/.5($50,049 + $1,559 +
               $56,631 + $1,728) **4.1%**

c. The accounts receivable turnover was relatively steady during the three-year period. Write-offs as a percentage of average gross accounts receivable declined, suggesting fewer bad debts. Because of the improved collection experience, American Express reduced its provision for uncollectible accounts as a percentage of revenues and the balance in the allowance account as a percentage of gross accounts receivable.

6.29 (May Department Stores; analyzing changes in accounts receivable.)

a.

(Amounts in Millions)	Year 9	Year 10	Year 11	Year 12
Allowance for Uncollectable Accounts, Beginning of Year	$ 47	$ 61	$ 66	$ 84
Plus Bad Debt Expense	57	64	82	96
Less Accounts Written Off (Plug)	(43)	(59)	(64)	(81)
Allowance for Uncollectable Accounts, End of Year	$ 61	$ 66	$ 84	$ 99

6.29 continued.

b.

	Year 9	Year 10	Year11	Year 12
Accounts Receivable, Gross at Beginning of Year	$ 1,592	$ 2,099	$ 2,223	$ 2,456
Plus Sales on Account[a]	5,181	6,137	6,713	7,293
Less Accounts Written Off	(43)	(59)	(64)	(81)
Less Cash Collections from Credit Customers (Plug)	(4,631)	(5,954)	(6,416)	(7,061)
Accounts Receivable, Gross at End of Year	$ 2,099	$ 2,223	$ 2,456	$ 2,607

[a]Total Sales x (Credit Sales ÷ Total Sales Percentage).

c. Total Sales/Average Accounts Receivable, Net:

	Year 9	Year 10	Year11	Year 12
$8,330/.5($1,545 + $2,038)	4.65			
$9,456/.5($2,038 + $2,157)		4.51		
$10,035/.5($2,157 + $2,372)			4.43	
$10,615/.5($2,372 + $2,508)				4.35

d. Credit Sales/Average Accounts Receivable, Net:

	Year 9	Year 10	Year11	Year 12
$5,181/.5($1,545 + $2,038)	2.89			
$6,137/.5($2,038 + $2,157)		2.93		
$6,713/.5($2,157 + $2,372)			2.96	
$7,293/.5($2,372 + $2,508)				2.99

e. The accounts receivable turnover ratio based on total sales decreases because of the increasing proportion of credit sales in total sales. The increasing accounts receivable turnover ratio based on credit sales results from actions that cause customers to pay more quickly. Examples include increased finance charges on unpaid balances, reduced repayment period on credit sales, and more stringent controls on the granting of credit.

6.30   (Sears; analyzing changes in accounts receivable.)

a.

	Year 7	Year 8	Year 9
(1) Sales on Account			
Accounts Receivable (Asset Increase)	39,953	39,484	40,937
Retained Earnings (Sales Revenue) (Shareholders' Equity Increase)	39,953	39,484	40,937

6.30 a. continued.

	Year 7	Year 8	Year 9
(2) Bad Debt Expense			
Retained Earnings (Bad Debt Expense) (Shareholders' Equity Decrease).....................	1,287	871	884
Allowance for Uncollectible Accounts (Asset Decrease)..............	1,287	871	884
(3) Write Off of Actual Uncollectible Accounts			
Allowance for Uncollectible Accounts (Asset Increase)........	1,426[a]	1,085[b]	958[c]
Accounts Receivable (Asset Decrease)..............	1,426	1,085	958

[a]$1,113 + $1,287 − $974 = $1,426.
[b]$974 + $871 − $760 = $1,085.
[c]$760 + $884 − $686 = $958.

	Year 7	Year 8	Year 9
(4) Collection of Cash from Customers			
Cash (Asset Increase).....................	40,537[d]	38,552[e]	40,769[f]
Accounts Receivable (Asset Decrease)..............	40,537	38,552	40,769

[d]$19,843 + $39,953 − $1,287 − $17,972 = $40,537.
[e]$17,972 + $39,484 − $871 − $18,033 = $38,552.
[f]$18,033 + $40,937 − $884 − $17,317 = $40,769.

b.

	Year 7	Year 8	Year 9
(1) Accounts Receivable Turnover			
Year 7: $39,953/.5($19,843 + $17,972)...	2.11		
Year 8: $39,484/.5($17,972 + $18,033)...		2.19	
Year 9: $40,937/.5($18,033 + $17,317)...			2.32

6.30 b. continued.

	Year 7	Year 8	Year 9
(2) Bad Debt Expense/Revenues			
Year 7: $1,287/$39,953	3.2%		
Year 8: $871/$39,484		2.2%	
Year 9: $884/$40,937			2.2%

(3) Allowance for Uncollectible Accounts/
Gross Accounts Receivable at End of Year

	Year 7	Year 8	Year 9
Year 7: $974/($17,972 + $974)	5.1%		
Year 8: $760/($18,033 + $760)		4.0%	
Year 9: $686/($17,317 + $686)			3.8%

(4) Accounts Written Off/Average Gross
Accounts Receivable

	Year 7	Year 8	Year 9
Year 7: $1,426/.5($19,843 + $1,113 + $17,972 + $974)	7.1%		
Year 8: $1,085/.5($17,972 + $974 + $18,033 + $760)		5.8%	
Year 9: $958/.5($18,033 + $760 + $17,317 + $686)			5.2%

c. The accounts receivable turnover increased during the three-year period, indicating that Sears collected its accounts receivable more quickly. Its write-offs of uncollectible accounts as a percentage of average gross accounts receivable declined during the three-year period, suggesting improved credit experience. Consistent with this improved credit experience is a decline in the provision for uncollectible accounts as a percentage of revenues and the balance in the Allowance for Uncollectible Accounts account as a percentage of gross accounts receivable.

6.31 (Pins Company; reconstructing transactions affecting accounts receivable and uncollectible accounts.)

a. $192,000 Dr. = $700,000 − $500,000 − $8,000.

b. $6,000 Cr. = (.02 X $700,000) − $8,000.

c. $21,000 = $10,000 + $11,000.

d. $16,000 = $6,000 + $10,000.

e. $676,000 = $192,000 + $800,000 − $16,000 − $300,000.

f. $289,000 = $300,000 − $11,000.

6.32 (Effect of errors involving accounts receivable on financial statement ratios.)

		Rate of Return on Assets	Accounts Receivable Turnover Ratio	Debt Equity Ratio
a.	Retained Earnings (Bad Debt Expense) (Shareholders' Equity Decrease)............ X			
	Allowance for Uncollectible Accounts (Asset Decrease)............	$\dfrac{O/S}{O/S} = O/S$	$\dfrac{NO}{O/S} = U/S$	$\dfrac{NO}{O/S} = U/S$
b.	Allowance for Uncollectible Accounts (Asset Increase)............ X			
	Accounts Receivable (Asset Decrease)............	$\dfrac{NO}{NO} = NO$	$\dfrac{NO}{NO} = NO$	$\dfrac{NO}{NO} = NO$
c.	Advances from Customers (Liability Decrease)............ X			
	Accounts Receivable (Asset Decrease)............	$\dfrac{NO}{O/S} = U/S$	$\dfrac{NO}{O/S} = U/S$	$\dfrac{O/S}{O/S} = O/S$
d.	Retained Earnings (Sales Revenue) (Shareholders' Equity Decrease)............ X			
	Accounts Receivable (Asset Decrease)............	$\dfrac{O/S}{O/S} = O/S$	$\dfrac{O/S}{O/S} = O/S$	$\dfrac{NO}{O/S} = U/S$
	Inventory (Asset Increase)............ X			
	Retained Earnings (Cost of Goods Sold) (Shareholders' Equity Increase)............			
e.	Retained Earnings (Sales Returns) (Shareholders' Equity Decrease)............ X			
	Accounts Receivable (Asset Decrease)............	$\dfrac{O/S}{O/S} = O/S$	$\dfrac{O/S}{O/S} = O/S$	$\dfrac{NO}{O/S} = U/S$
	Inventory (Asset Increase)............ X			
	Retained Earnings (Cost of Goods Sold) (Shareholders' Equity Increase)............			

Note: This problem asks only for the net effect of each error on the three financial ratios. The journal entries and the numerator and denominator effects appear to show the reason for the net effect.

6.33 (General Electric Company; income recognition for nuclear generator manufacturer.)

a.1. Percentage-of-Completion Method

Year	Incremental Percentage Complete	Revenue Recognized	Expenses Recognized	Income
2	42/120 (.35)	$ 70,000,000	$ 42,000,000	$ 28,000,000
3	54/120 (.45)	90,000,000	54,000,000	36,000,000
4	24/120 (.20)	40,000,000	24,000,000	16,000,000
Total.....	120/120 (1.00)	$200,000,000	$120,000,000	$ 80,000,000

2. Completed Contract Method

Year	Revenue Recognized	Expenses Recognized	Income
2	-0-	-0-	-0-
3	-0-	-0-	-0-
4	$200,000,000	$120,000,000	$80,000,000
Total....	$200,000,000	$120,000,000	$80,000,000

3. Installment Method

Year	Cash Collected (= Revenue)	Fraction of Cash Collected	Expenses (= Fraction x Total Cost)	Income
2	$ 20,000,000	1/10	$ 12,000,000	$ 8,000,000
3	100,000,000	5/10	60,000,000	40,000,000
4	80,000,000	4/10	48,000,000	32,000,000
Total......	$ 200,000,000	1.00	$120,000,000	$ 80,000,000

4. Cost-Recovery-First Method

Year	Cash Collected (= Revenue)	Expenses Recognized	Income
2	$ 20,000,000	$ 20,000,000	-0-
3	100,000,000	100,000,000	-0-
4	80,000,000	-0-	$80,000,000
Total.....	$200,000,000	$120,000,000	$80,000,000

b. The percentage-of-completion method probably provides a better measure of performance over the life of the contract because each period receives a portion of the net income from the contract. General Electric's original estimates of the cost of the contract were correct. Also, the periodic payments from Consolidated Edison suggest that General Electric will probably collect cash in the amount of the contract price.

6.34   (Flanikin Construction Company; income recognition for a contractor.)

a.1. Percentage-of-Completion Method

Year	Incremental Percentage Complete		Revenue Recognized	Expenses Recognized	Income
1	12/120	(.10)	$ 18,000,000	$ 12,000,000	$ 6,000,000
2	36/120	(.30)	54,000,000	36,000,000	18,000,000
3	48/120	(.40)	72,000,000	48,000,000	24,000,000
4	24/120	(.20)	36,000,000	24,000,000	12,000,000
Total.......	120/120	(1.00)	$180,000,000	$120,000,000	$ 60,000,000

2. Completed Contract Method

Year	Revenue Recognized	Expenses Recognized	Income
1	-0-	-0-	-0-
2	-0-	-0-	-0-
3	-0-	-0-	-0-
4	$180,000,000	$120,000,000	$60,000,000
Total....	$180,000,000	$120,000,000	$60,000,000

3. Installment Method

Year	Cash Collected (= Revenue)	Percentage of Cash Collected	Expenses (= Percentage x Total Cost)	Income
1	$ 36,000,000	.20	$ 24,000,000	$ 12,000,000
2	45,000,000	.25	30,000,000	15,000,000
3	45,000,000	.25	30,000,000	15,000,000
4	54,000,000	.30	36,000,000	18,000,000
Total.....	$180,000,000	1.00	$120,000,000	$ 60,000,000

4. Cost-Recovery-First Method

Year	Cash Collected (= Revenue)	Expense Recognized	Income
1	$ 36,000,000	$ 36,000,000	-0-
2	45,000,000	45,000,000	-0-
3	45,000,000	39,000,000	$ 6,000,000
4	54,000,000	-0-	54,000,000
Total.....	$180,000,000	$120,000,000	$ 60,000,000

b. The percentage-of-completion method probably gives the best measure of Flanikin's performance each year under the contract. The original estimates of costs on the contract turned out to be correct. Also, the periodic cash collections suggest that the firm will probably collect cash in the amount of the contract price.

6.35   (J. C. Spangle; point-of-sale versus installment method of income recognition.)

a.

	Year 8	Year 9
Sales...	$200,000	$300,000
Expenses:		
Cost of Goods Sold*....................................	$120,000	$186,000
All Other Expenses....................................	32,000	44,000
Total Expenses.....................................	$152,000	$230,000
Net Income..	$ 48,000	$ 70,000
*Beginning Inventory...............................	$ 0	$ 60,000
Purchases..	180,000	240,000
Goods Available....................................	$180,000	$300,000
Ending Inventory.................................	(60,000)	(114,000)
Cost of Goods Sold...............................	$120,000	$186,000

Cost of Goods Sold/Sales:
   Year 8--$120,000/$200,000 = 60 percent.
   Year 9--$186,000/$300,000 = 62 percent.

b.

	Year 8	Year 9
Collections from Customers............................	$ 90,000	$ 230,000
Expenses:..		
Merchandise Cost of Collections*...............	$ 54,000	$ 140,400
All Other Expenses.....................................	32,000	44,000
Total Expenses.....................................	$ 86,000	$ 184,400
Net Income..	$ 4,000	$ 45,600

*Calculation:	Year 8	Year 9
Merchandise Cost of Collections:		
Of Goods Sold:		
In Year 8, 60 percent of $90,000........	$ 54,000	
In Year 9, 60 percent of $110,000......		$ 66,000
Of Goods Sold in Year 9:		
62 percent of $120,000.........................		74,400
	$ 54,000	$ 140,400

An Alternative Presentation Would Be:	Year 8	Year 9
Realized Gross Margin............................	$ 36,000	$ 89,600
All Other Expenses	32,000	44,000
Net Income	$ 4,000	$ 45,600

6.36   (Pickin Chicken; revenue recognition for a franchise.)

a. Year	Pickin Chicken, Inc.	Country Delight, Inc.
2	$ 400,000 (= $50,000 X 8)	$ 160,000 (= $20,000 X 8)
3	250,000 (= $50,000 X 5)	148,000 (= $20,000 X 5 + $6,000 X 8)
4	0	78,000 (= $6,000 X 13)
5	0	78,000 (= $6,000 X 13)
6	0	78,000 (= $6,000 X 13)
7	0	78,000 (= $6,000 X 13)
8	0	30,000 (= $6,000 X 5)
Total..	$ 650,000	$ 650,000

b. The issue here is whether sufficient uncertainty exists regarding the amount the firm will ultimately collect to justify postponing revenue recognition until the time of collection. The casualty rate among franchisees has been very high and has led some accountants to argue that the installment method is the appropriate basis for revenue recognition.

6.37   (Income recognition for various types of businesses.)

a. **Amgen**—The principal income recognition issue for Amgen is the significant lag between the incurrence of research and development expenditures and the realization of sales from any resulting products. Biotechnology firms are a relatively new industry and therefore have few commercially feasible products. Thus, research and development expenditures will likely represent a significant percentage of revenues, as is the case for Amgen. More established technology firms, such as pharmaceuticals, have established products as well as products in the pipeline and therefore research and development expenditures represent both a smaller and a more stable percentage of revenues. GAAP require biotechnology firms to expense research and development expenditures in the year incurred.

Brown Forman—The principal revenue recognition issue for Brown Forman is whether it should recognize the increase in value of hard liquors while they are aging (that is, revalue the liquors to market value each year) or wait until the liquors are sold at the end of the aging process. Most accountants would argue that the market values of aging liquors are too uncertain prior to sale to justify periodic revaluations and revenue recognition. Brown Forman should include in the cost of the liquor inventory not only the initial production costs but also the cost incurred during the aging process. In this way, the firm can match total incurred costs with revenues generated at the time of sale.

6.37 a. continued.

Deere—Deere faces issues of revenue recognition with respect to both the sale of farm equipment to dealers and the provision of financing services. The concern with respect to the sale of farm equipment to dealers is the right of dealers to return any unsold equipment. If dealers have no right of return, then recognition of revenue at the time of sale is appropriate. If dealers can return any equipment discovered to be faulty prior to sale and the amount of such returns is reasonably predictable, then Deere can reduce the amount of revenue recognized each year for estimated returns. If dealers can return any unsold equipment, then delaying recognition of revenue until the dealer sells the equipment is appropriate. Deere should match the cost of manufacturing the equipment against the sales revenue. Deere reports research and development expense in its income statement. Given the farm equipment industry, one wonders about what proportions of these expenditures Deere makes to enhance existing products versus to develop new products. Although contrary to GAAP, one can make the case that Deere should capitalize and amortize expenditures on new products.

Deere should accrue revenue from financing (interest) and insurance (premiums) services over time. To achieve matching, Deere should capitalize and amortize any initial administrative costs to check customer credit quality and prepare legal documents.

Fluor—The appropriate timing of revenue recognition for Fluor depends on the basis for pricing its services. If the fee is fixed for any particular construction project, then Fluor should recognize the fee in relation to the degree of completion of the construction project. If the fee is a percentage of total construction costs incurred on the project, then Fluor should recognize revenue in relation to costs incurred. If the fee is a percentage of the costs incurred by Fluor (salaries of their employees working on the project), then it should recognize revenue in relation to the incurrence of these costs. It seems clear that the percentage-of-completion method of revenue recognition is more appropriate than the completed contract method.

Golden West—Golden West should recognize interest revenue from home mortgage loans as time passes. It should provide for estimated uncollectible accounts each year. The uncollectible amount should reflect the resale value of homes repossessed. The more difficult question relates to recognition of revenue from points. One possibility is to recognize the full amount in the initial year of the loan. The rationale for such a procedure is that the points cover administrative costs of setting up the loan. Both the points and the administrative costs would be recognized in full in the initial year of the loan. An alternative view is that the points effectively reduce the amount lent by the savings and loan company and increase its yield beyond the stated interest rate. This view suggests that Golden West amortize

6.37 a. continued.

the points over the term of the loan and match against this revenue amortization of the initial administrative costs to set up the loan. Golden West should recognize interest expense on deposits as time passes. There is no direct relation between interest expense on deposits and interest revenue from loans so Golden West matches interest expense to the period it is incurred.

Merrill Lynch—The principal income recognition issue for Merrill Lynch is whether it should report financial instruments held as assets and liabilities at their acquisition cost or their current market value. These assets and liabilities generally have easily measured market values. They are typically held for short periods of time (days or weeks). Thus, one can argue that use of current market values is appropriate. However, we are still left with the question as to whether the unrealized gain or loss should flow through to the income statement immediately or wait until realization at the time of sale. The argument for immediate recognition is that Merrill Lynch takes short-term financing and investing positions for short-term returns. Its income statement should reflect its operating performance during this period. The case for not recognizing the unrealized gains and losses is that they could reverse prior to realization and, in any case, will be realized very soon. Merrill Lynch should recognize revenue from fee-based services as it provides the services.

Rockwell—The absence of research and development expense from the income statement suggests that Rockwell charges all such costs to specific contracts. These costs become expenses as Rockwell recognizes revenue from the contracts. The multi-year nature of its contracts and the credit quality of the U.S. government suggest use of the percentage-of-completion method of income recognition. One difficulty encountered in applying the percentage-of-completion method is that Rockwell's contracts for projects such as the space shuttle get continually renewed. This procedure makes it difficult to identify a single contract price and accumulate costs for a single contract, which the percentage-of-completion method envisions.

b. **Amgen**—Amgen realized the highest profit margin of the seven companies. Its biotechnology products are protected by patents. It therefore maintains a monopoly position. Note that the cost of manufacturing its products is a small percent of revenues. Amgen's major cost is for research and development. Sales of its existing products are not only sufficient to cover its high, on-going research work but to provide a substantial profit margin as well. Its relatively low revenue to assets percentage is somewhat unexpected, given that its major "assets" are patents and research scientists. The reason for this low percentage (reason not provided in the case) is that cash and marketable securities comprise approximately 25 percent of its assets.

6.37 b. continued.

These assets generated a return of approximately 3 percent during the year. This rate of return decreased the overall ratio of revenues to assets for Amgen.

Brown Forman—Brown Forman realized the third highest profit margin among the seven companies. If one views the excise taxes as a reduction in revenues rather than as an expense, its profit margin is 10.4 percent [= 8.8%/(100.0% − 15.4%)]. Concerns about excess alcoholic drinking in recent years have resulted in some exodus of companies from the industry, leaving the remaining companies with a larger share of a smaller market. The products of Brown Forman carry brand name recognition, permitting the firm to obtain attractive prices.

Deere—Deere's relatively low profit margin reflects (1) weaknesses in the farming industry in recent years, which puts downward pressure on margins, and (2) decreased interest rates, which lowers profit margins. The revenue-to-assets percentage of Deere reflects its capital-intensive manufacturing operations and the low interest rate on outstanding loans to dealers and customers.

Fluor—The low profit margin of Fluor reflects the relatively low value added of construction services. It may also reflect recessionary conditions when construction activity is weak and profit margins are thin.

Golden West—The 12 percent profit margin (ignoring an addback for interest expense, which is common for financial services firms) seems high, relative to interest rates in recent years. Recall though that Golden West pays short-term interest rates on its deposits but obtains long-term interest rates on its loans. An upward-sloping yield curve provides a positive differential. Also, the existence of shareholders' equity funds in the capital structure means that Golden West has assets earning returns for which it recognizes no expense in its income statement (that is, firms do not recognize an expense for the implicit cost of shareholders' funds). Note also that the ratio of revenue to assets is only .1. Thus, the assets of Golden West earned a return of only 1.2 percent (= 12.0% X .1) during the year.

Merrill Lynch—The lower profit margin for Merrill Lynch relative to Golden West reflects in part the fact that both the investments and financing of Merrill Lynch are short term. Merrill Lynch, however, realizes revenue from fee-based services. Firms like Merrill Lynch can differentiate these services somewhat and realize attractive profit margins. However, such services have been quickly copied by competitors in recent years, reducing the profit margins accordingly.

6.37 b. continued.

> **Rockwell**—Rockwell's profit margin is in the middle of the seven companies. Factors arguing for a high profit margin include Rockwell's technological know-how and its role in long-term contracts with the U.S. government. Factors arguing for a lower profit margin include cutbacks in defense expenditures and excess capacity in the aerospace industry.

6.38   (Meaning of Allowance for Uncollectible Accounts account.)

a.   This characterization of the allowance account is incorrect. The allowance account normally has a credit balance and assets have debit balances. Firms do not set aside assets in an amount equal to the credit balance in the allowance account.

b.   This characterization of the allowance account is incorrect for the same reasons as in Part a. above. Firms do not set aside cash in an amount equal to the balance in the allowance account.

c.   This characterization of the allowance account is incorrect. The balance in the allowance accounts is an estimate of the amount from sales on account in all periods, not just the current period, that firms have not yet collected nor expect to collect.

d.   This characterization of the allowance account is incorrect. There is no need to provide for uncollectible accounts if customers have already paid.

e.   This characterization of the allowance account is correct.

f.   This characterization of the allowance account is incorrect. Although the allowance account normally has a credit balance, like liabilities, firms do not owe amounts to anyone if customers fail to pay.

g.   This characterization of the allowance account is incorrect for the same reasons as in Part f. above.

h.   This characterization is incorrect. The balance in the allowance account is an estimate of the amount of sales in all periods, not just the current period, that firms have not yet collected and never expect to collect. A portion of the balance in the allowance account does likely result from recognizing bad debt expense during the current period. However, the balance also includes portions of bad debt expense of earlier periods as well. There is no way to know how much of the balance in the allowance account relates to provisions made during the current period versus earlier periods.

6.38 continued.

i. This characterization is incorrect. Deferred revenues, commonly called advances from customers, have credit balances and are liabilities. The firm owes cash to those making advances if the firm does not deliver the goods and services as promised. The firm does not receive cash when it credits the allowance for uncolletibles account, nor does it owe cash to customers.

j. This characterization is incorrect. When firms credit the allowance account, they debit bad debt expense, a part of the retained earnings account. Thus, the allowance account indirectly links with retained earnings but is not an accurate characterization of its nature.

6.39 (Understanding the purpose of the Allowance for Uncollectible Accounts account.)

This case has the following history. Over the last several years, we have lectured to audit committee, and other board members, about the meaning of the requirement that audit committee members be financially literate, as specified by the New York Stock Exchange and the NASDAQ in its listing requirements. Many experienced members suggest our criteria for literacy are too stringent, because, they say, I do not need to know all that accounting stuff, as I know how to ask the tough questions. We believe that being able to ask tough questions is not enough, if the questioner cannot evaluate the answers, recognizing incorrect answers and being able to ask follow-up questions for correct, but only partial, answers. We devised a Tough Questions Quiz virtually identical to this case. Of the audit committee members who have taken the quiz [as you might imagine, its hard to get them to do so], the median number of correct responses is just under half. Former SEC Commissioner Arthur Levitt contributed to the malaise of the financially illiterate audit committee room by saying in a speech that he wanted board members to be able to ask the tough questions, without adding and be able to evaluate the answers.

a. This response does not address the question. Judging the adequacy of the allowance account focuses on estimating the portion of accounts receivable that a firm does not expect to collect. Thus, the question concerns the valuation of accounts receivable net of estimated uncollectibles. The CFO in essence is saying that even if the firm has more uncollectibles than the amount in the allowance account the firm will survive. The CFO's response does not demonstrate an understanding of the purpose of the allowance account.

b. This response demonstrates an understanding of the need to match estimated uncollectibles with sales of the period. Although the amount of bad debt expense this period may reflect accurately the expected amount of the current period's sales that a firm does not expect to col-

6.39 b. continued.

lect, it does not say anything about the adequacy of prior period's provisions to cover estimated uncollectibles from those periods' sales.

c. This response demonstrates an understanding that the allowance account should reflect the estimated amounts of accounts receivable that the firm does not expect to collect. It also shows that the CFO knows to use an aging of accounts receivable to judge the adequacy of the balance in the account. The misunderstanding is that the allowance account reflects the estimated amounts from sales of all periods, not just the current period, that the firm does not expect to collect.

d. This response demonstrates an accurate understanding of the purpose of the allowance account and the approach a firm should follow to judge the adequacy of the amount in the allowance account.

e. This response does not address the question. The CFO addresses the appropriateness of writing off accounts that were written off. It does not address the adequacy of the balance in the allowance account to cover accounts not yet written off.

f. The confirmation of receivables simply evidences that a valid receivable exists. It does not provide evidence about what portion of these receivables the firm does and does not expect to collect, which is the question asked.

g. This response demonstrates an understanding that the allowance account should carry a sufficient balance to equal amounts from the current and prior period's sales that the firm does not expect to collect. It also shows a need to assess the adequacy of the balance in the allowance account each period. Finally, it shows the use of external benchmarks to assess the adequacy of the amount of bad debt expense. The one remaining response that would have demonstrated even more understanding about the adequacy of the balance in the allowance account was for the CFO to state that the benchmark percentages from the credit reporting agencies have historically matched the firm's credit loss experience.

6.40 (Sage Department Stores; ethical issues in accounting for uncollectible accounts.)

A central question in this setting is the principal motivation of the chief financial officer (CFO) in recognizing the higher percentage of sales as bad debt expense. If the firm conducted a careful study of recent collection experience and the quality of uncollected receivables and concluded that it needed a 5-percent provision to adequately provide for uncollectible accounts, then ethical issues would not appear to arise. The firm's history

6.40 continued.

involved ongoing aging and assessments of receivables and the current year's assessment maintained this pattern. Understanding the possible future impact on earnings and recognizing that competitors might play such earnings games do not, in themselves, evidence unethical behavior. One difficulty in this case, however, is disentangling perhaps legitimate increases in bad debt expense due to the recession conditions from the other considerations mentioned. Each of these other considerations was obviously on the CFO's mind. Only the CFO can assess the relative weight each played in the decision. External users of financial statements usually cannot get into the mind of the CFO to make ethical judgments. In this case, however, the problem provides hints about the motivation of the CFO. The CFO apparently looked to see if security analysts noticed the increased provision, perhaps evidencing guilt of being caught. The CFO prepared a defense ahead of time in the event that security analysts questioned the provision, perhaps evidencing defensive behavior to counter the CFO's aggressive behavior. The wording of the CFO's reasoning about the decision suggests a calculating state of mind. Using such terms as "even more earnings growth," playing "this earnings game," and remaining "competitive" suggest that more than just adequately providing for uncollectible accounts influenced the CFO.

6.41 (Halliburton Company; ethical issues in accounting for long-term contracts.)

Some people take the position that an action must at least not violate any law or regulation to be ethical. Thus, the first question addressed is whether including revenues and costs from change orders into the income recognition from contracts meets GAAP's requirements for revenue recognition. Halliburton Company had worked on multi-year contracts for many years and should have historical data to support estimates of the likely amount of revenue and costs from change orders. It likely performs the work requested by the change orders as it performs work on the original contract. It must receive cash or recognize a receivable on the original contract work in order to use the percentage-of-completion method. Thus, it appears that GAAP would allow income recognition from change orders using the percentage-of-completion method in this case. One might point out, however, that such action likely reduces the quality of earnings. The percentage-of-completion method for regular contract work is already subject to numerous estimates, particularly with respect to costs. Recognizing revenue from change order on a percentage-of-completion basis requires estimates of both revenues and costs. Some people might argue that actions that reduce the quality of earnings present ethical issues. The remaining issue in this case is the manner in which Halliburton Company disclosed information about the change. The accounting is unusual. It appears that Halliburton Company did not disclose information about the change in an easy-to-understand manner, raising questions as to whether management intended to either mislead users or, at a minimum, discourage users from asking more questions.

6.42   (Qwest Communications International; ethical issues in income recognition.)

GAAP require firms to separate the recognition of revenue into parts if the firm can provide reliable evidence of the selling price of each part. It is likely that Qwest would have little difficulty providing such evidence, since it provided just the telecommunication services for some of its customers.

The facts of this case suggest that the sale of the equipment and its installation were interrelated activities. The Arizona School Facilities Board desired Internet access for its schools. It presumably purchased the equipment from Qwest, instead of from another supplier, because the package price provided by Qwest was lower than if it had purchased the equipment and installation separately. The fact that Qwest initially planned to recognize revenue for the sale of the equipment and for its installation as a unit provides support that the Board viewed the two parts as a single, unified product—the equipment without the installation being worthless to them. The agreement that the State would not pay for the equipment until Qwest had installed it and linked it with the Internet further indicates the customer's view of the two parts as a unit. Thus, it would appear that separating the recognition of revenue into the two parts in this case violates GAAP, although others would disagree. Qwest's auditor disagreed with our interpretation, and the auditor surely has more information on these matters than we do.

The manner in which Qwest obtained the necessary backing of the Arizona School Facilities Board to support its change in revenue recognition may raise ethical questions. The crafting of the letter, its hasty airport signing, and the pressure to sign it, or else, suggest that the content of the letter differed from the initial understanding of the parties to the contract. Was the deviation sufficient to suggest an intention to mislead the auditor and users of the financial statements? Some would say "yes." Others would say, "no." The auditor can stipulate the necessary conditions for the separation of the two types of revenue. Management can ask the customer to alter the original arrangement to suit the auditor's requirements. The signed letter by the head of the Board provides the necessary evidence to satisfy the auditor that the parties agree to the change. This is just the way businesses do business. The last-minute subtle coercion may suggest unethical behavior, but asking the customer to change an initial understanding is likely ethical behavior.

Ethical issues arise for the auditor as well. The auditor's request for a letter from the Board indicates awareness that Qwest changed its initial plan for recognizing revenues. The auditor seemed more concerned with such a letter to cover his or her risk than to carefully consider the appropriateness of the new revenue recognition method. The fact that Qwest received no payments until it completed both delivery and installation of the equipment suggests the inseparability of the two elements of revenue. The accounting likely violated GAAP. The process of obtaining a letter in this case appears to be a sham.

CHAPTER 7

INVENTORIES: THE SOURCE OF OPERATING PROFITS

Questions, Short Exercises, Exercises, Problems, and Cases: Answers and Solutions

7.1 See the text or the glossary at the end of the book.

7.2 The underlying principle is that acquisition cost includes all costs required to prepare an asset for its intended use. Assets provide future services. Costs that a firm must incur to obtain those expected services add value to the asset. Accountants therefore include such costs in the acquisition cost valuation of the asset.

7.3 Depreciation on manufacturing equipment is a product cost and remains in inventory accounts until the firm sells the manufactured goods. Depreciation on selling and administrative equipment is a period expense, because the use of such equipment does not create an asset with future service potential.

7.4 Both the Merchandise Inventory and Finished Goods Inventory accounts include the cost of completed units ready for sale. A merchandising firm acquires the units in finished form and debits Merchandise Inventory for their acquisition cost. A manufacturing firm incurs direct material, direct labor, and manufacturing overhead costs in transforming the units to a finished, salable condition. The Raw Materials Inventory and Work-in-Process Inventory accounts include such costs until the completion of manufacturing operations. Thus, the accountant debits the Finished Goods Inventory account for the cost of producing completed units. The accountant credits both the Merchandise Inventory and Finished Goods Inventory accounts for the cost of units sold and reports them as current assets on the balance sheet.

7.5 The accountant allocates the total income (cash inflow minus cash outflow) over the periods between purchase and sale. The inventory valuation method dictates this allocation. The acquisition cost valuation method allocates all of the income to the period of sale. A current cost valuation method allocates holding gains and losses to the periods when a firm holds inventory and an operating margin (sales minus replacement cost of goods sold) to the period of sale. A lower-of-cost-or-market valuation allocates holding losses to the periods when a firm holds inventory and holding gains plus operating margins to the period of sale.

7.6   Income increases in the year of change because of the recognition of the unrealized holding gains. Cost of goods sold in the next year will increase by the same amount, so that income in the second year will be less by the same amount as it was greater in the year of change. Over long enough time spans, accounting income equals cash inflows minus cash outflows; the valuation method affects the timing of income recognition, not its amount.

7.7   Accounting reports cost flows, not flows of physical quantities. Cost flow assumptions trace costs, not physical flows of goods. With specific identification, management manipulates cost flows by controlling goods flows.

7.8   Rising Purchase Prices:
        Higher Inventory Amount: FIFO
        Lower Inventory Amount: LIFO

        Falling Purchase Prices:
        Higher Inventory Amount: LIFO; LIFO results in a constant inventory amount so long as quantities do not change.
        Lower Inventory Amount: FIFO; FIFO results in an even lower inventory than does the weighted-average assumption.

7.9   a. Higher cost of goods sold amount: LIFO
            Lower cost of goods sold amount: FIFO

        b. Higher cost of goods sold amount: FIFO
            Lower cost of goods sold amount: LIFO

7.10   LIFO provides cost of goods sold closer to current costs than does FIFO so long as inventory quantities do not decrease and a firm does not liquidate old LIFO layers. Some would say, then, that LIFO does provide more meaningful income data when quantities do not decrease. The LIFO balance sheet always reflects older costs than does the FIFO balance sheet.

7.11   a. FIFO typically uses older acquisition costs for cost of goods sold than LIFO (except during a period of dipping into a LIFO layer), whereas LIFO uses older acquisition costs for ending inventory than FIFO. The larger the rate of change in the acquisition cost of inventory items, the more the older costs will differ from current costs and the larger will be the difference in cost of goods sold and ending inventory values between FIFO and LIFO.

        b. As the rate of inventory turnover increases, purchases during a period comprise an increasing proportion of cost of goods sold for that period under both FIFO and LIFO and differences in the beginning or ending inventory values under FIFO and LIFO play a decreasing role. Be-

7.11 b. continued.

cause purchases are the same regardless of the cost flow assumption, cost of goods sold under FIFO and LIFO should not differ significantly (unless the firm experienced dips into old LIFO layers).

c. The inventory turnover ratio relates cost of goods sold to average inventories. A faster inventory turnover means a smaller level of inventories in the denominator relative to cost of goods sold in the numerator. The difference between FIFO and LIFO amounts in the denominator depends on the age of a firm's LIFO layers and the rate of change in the cost of inventory items since the firm adopted LIFO. These latter items relate to the passage of time rather than to the rate of turnover within a period of time.

7.12 Dipping into an old LIFO layer may not be within a firm's control, such as when shortages prevent the firm from replacing a particular raw material. A dip may be partially within a firm's control, such as when a labor strike by employees forces the firm to reduce its finished goods inventory. A dip may be fully within a firm's control, such as when it delays purchases toward the end of the period in an effort to decrease cost of goods sold and increase net income. A firm may also implement more effective inventory control systems and, thereby, reduce the quantity of inventory on hand at any time.

7.13 Firms that maintain a relatively constant relation between the replacement cost of inventory items and selling prices will show a constant operating margin percentage (that is, operating margin/sales) each period. The operating margin will be the same under FIFO and LIFO. Both firms also include a realized holding gain or loss in their gross margins. The realized holding gain or loss reflects the change in the replacement cost of inventory items between the time of acquisition and the time of sale. The assumed holding period for FIFO is longer than for LIFO. Thus, FIFO likely includes more price changes (both increases and decreases) in the realized holding gain or loss than LIFO. If prices change at a constant rate and in a constant direction, then both FIFO and LIFO produce a smooth gross margin trend over time. If either the rate or direction of price change varies over time, FIFO more fully reflects these variations in the gross margin than LIFO.

7.14 Assuming a period of rising purchase prices, the firm might prefer to report higher earnings to shareholders and give up the tax savings that LIFO provides. Management's compensation often uses reported earnings as a base in its computation. Management obtains higher compensation by reporting higher earnings under FIFO. The firm might be experiencing operating difficulties and need to report higher earnings to keep shareholders happy. We question the rationality of such thinking but don't doubt that such reasoning occurs.

7.14 continued.

The firm might be experiencing decreasing prices (costs) for its inventory items and obtains the maximum tax benefits by using FIFO. Note, however, that the Internal Revenue Code does not preclude a firm from using FIFO for tax purposes and LIFO for financial reporting. This combination minimizes taxes but maximizes earnings reported to shareholders.

If prices are not changing much or if inventory turns over rapidly, then FIFO and LIFO do not differ significantly in terms of their effects on earnings or balance sheet amounts. The record keeping costs and fears of dipping into very old LIFO layers might lead a firm to use FIFO under these circumstances.

7.15 The firm saved taxes in earlier years when it created its LIFO layers and must pay the taxes in the year that it dips. It has at least delayed paying the taxes relative to FIFO, even if it must pay the same amount of taxes over time under both cost flow assumptions. Thus, the present value of the taxes saved under LIFO exceeds the present value under FIFO.

If tax rates were to rise dramatically during the period of the dip, the higher tax rate might overwhelm the effect of interest rates. Suppose the interest rate is 10 percent per period. Assume LIFO defers $100 at the end of Period 1, which the firm repays at the end of Period 3. The tax deferral is worth $21 [= (1.10 x 1.10 x $100) − $100]. If the income tax rate has increased by more than 21 percent between the end of Period 1 and the end of Period 3, then the deferral will not have saved present value dollars.

7.16 (Intervest Corporation; identifying inventory cost inclusions.)

Intervest should include all costs incurred to acquire and prepare the land for its intended use, but not costs to sell the land. Thus, the cost of the land inventory prior to sale totals $1,173,900 (= $450,000 + $12,000 + $22,900 + $689,000).

7.17 (Selby Corporation; effect of inventory valuation on net income.)

Year	Acquisition Cost	Lower of Cost or Market	Market Value
6	$ 0	$ (80,000)	$ (80,000)
7	0	0	260,000
8	220,000	300,000	40,000
Total	$ 220,000	$ 220,000	$ 220,000

7.18 (Fun-in-the Sun Tanning Lotion Company; income computation for a manufacturing firm.)

Manufacturing Costs Incurred during the Year:

Raw Materials	$ 56,300
Direct Labor	36,100
Manufacturing Overhead	26,800
Total Manufacturing Costs Incurred	$ 119,200
Less Manufacturing Costs Assigned to Work-in-Process Inventory	(12,700)
Cost of Units Completed during the Year	$ 106,500
Less Cost of Ending Inventory of Finished Goods	(28,500)
Cost of Goods Sold	$ 78,000

7.19 (Sun Health Foods; computations involving different cost flow assumptions.)

	Units	a. FIFO	b. Weighted Average	c. LIFO
Goods Available for Sale	2,500	$10,439	$10,439	$ 10,439
Less Ending Inventory	(420)	(1,722)[a]	(1,754)[c]	(1,806)[e]
Goods Sold	2,080	$ 8,717[b]	$ 8,685[d]	$ 8,633[f]

[a](420 x $4.10) = $1,722.
[b](460 x $4.30) + (670 x $4.20) + (500 x $4.16) + (450 x $4.10) = $8,717.
[c]($10,439/2,500) x 420 = $1,754.
[d]($10,439/2,500) x 2,080 = $8,685.
[e](420 x $4.30) = $1,806.
[f](870 x $4.10) + (500 x $4.16) + (670 x $4.20) + (40 x $4.30) = $8,633.

7.20 (Harmon Corporation; effect on LIFO on financial statements over several periods.)

a. Year	Ending Inventory	
8	19,000 x $20	$380,000
9	10,000 x $20	$200,000
10	(10,000 x $20) + (10,000 x $30)	$500,000

7.20 continued.

b.

Year	Cost of Goods Sold	
8	64,000 x $20	$ 1,280,000
9	(92,000 x $25) + (9,000 x $20)	$ 2,480,000
10	110,000 x $30	$ 3,300,000

Year	Income	
8	$2,048,000 – $1,280,000	$ 768,000
9	$4,040,000 – $2,480,000	$ 1,560,000
10	$5,280,000 – $3,300,000	$ 1,980,000

7.21 (Robertson Company; effect of dipping into LIFO inventories.)

If Robertson Company had not dipped into its LIFO layers, it would have had to make purchases of merchandise to keep inventory quantities at the end of the year the same as at the beginning of the year. It would have paid more for this merchandise than the acquisition cost embedded in the LIFO layers that it liquidated. The acquisition cost embedded in the LIFO layers liquidated was $6,300 (= $48,900 – $42,600). The increase in income before taxes that resulted from using $6,300 from the LIFO layers instead of the higher current purchase prices is $2,700. Thus, the additional units would cost $9,000 (= $6,300 + $2,700).

7.22 (United States Steel Corporation; conversion from LIFO to FIFO.)

	LIFO	Difference	FIFO
Beginning Inventory	$ 1,030	$ 310	$ 1,340
Production Costs	8,722	--	8,722
Goods Available for Sale	$ 9,752	$ 310	$ 10,062
Less Ending Inventory	(1,283)	(270)	(1,553)
Cost of Goods Sold	$ 8,469	$ 40	$ 8,509

7.23 (Miller Corporation; separating operating margins and holding gains.)

Sales Revenue (9,000 x $100)	$ 900,000
Less Replacement Cost of Goods Sold (9,000 x $82)	(738,000)
Operating Margin	$ 162,000
Realized Holding Gain [9,000 x ($82 – $80)]	18,000
Conventionally Reporting Gross Margin	$ 180,000
Unrealized Holding Gain [1,000 x ($84 – $80)]	4,000
Economic Profit	$ 184,000

7.24 (Trembly Department Store; identifying inventory cost inclusions.)

a.	Purchase Price	$ 300,000
b.	Freight Cost	13,800
c.	Salary of Purchasing Manager	3,000
d.	Depreciation, Taxes, Insurance and Utilities on Warehouse	27,300
e.	Salary of Warehouse Manager	2,200
f.	Merchandise Returns	(18,500)
g.	Cash Discounts Taken	(4,900)
	Acquisition Cost	$ 322,900

The underlying principle is that inventories should include all costs required to get the inventory ready for sale. The purchase of the inventory items (items a., c., f., and g.) provides the physical goods to be sold, the freight cost (item b.) puts the inventory items in the place most convenient for sale, and the storage costs (items d. and e.) keep the inventory items until the time of sale. Economists characterize these costs as providing form, place, and time utility, or benefits. Although accounting theory suggests the inclusion of each of these items in the valuation of inventory, some firms might exclude items c., d., e., and g. on the basis of lack of materiality.

7.25 (General Mills; income computation for a manufacturing firm.)

Sales	$ 6,700.2
Less Cost of Goods Sold	(2,697.6)
Less Selling and Administrative Expenses	(2,903.7)
Less Interest Expense	(151.9)
Income before Income Taxes	$ 947.0
Income Tax Expense at 35%	(331.5)
Net Income	$ 615.5
Work-in-Process Inventory, June 1, Year 10	$ 100.8
Plus Manufacturing Costs Incurred during Fiscal Year	2,752.0
Less Work-in-Process Inventory, May 30, Year 11	(119.1)
Cost of Goods Completed during Fiscal Year	$ 2,733.7
Plus Finished Goods Inventory, June 1, Year 10	286.2
Less Finished Goods Inventory, May 30, Year 11	(322.3)
Cost of Goods Sold	$ 2,697.6

7.26 (Dow Chemical Corporation; income computation for a manufacturing firm.)

Sales	$ 32,632
Less Cost of Goods Sold	(28,177)
Less Marketing and Administrative Expenses	(2,436)
Less Interest Expense	(828)
Income before Income Taxes	$ 1,191
Income Tax Expense at 35%	(417)
Net Income	$ 774
Work-in-Process Inventory, January 1	$ 843
Plus Manufacturing Costs Incurred during Year	28,044
Less Work-in-Process Inventory, December 31	(837)
Cost of Goods Completed during Year	$ 28,050
Plus Finished Goods Inventory, January 1	2,523
Less Finished Goods Inventory, December 31	(2,396)
Cost of Goods Sold	$ 28,177

7.27 (Duggan Company; over sufficiently long spans, income is cash in less cash out; cost basis for inventory.)

a. **Lower of Cost or Market:**

	Year 1	Year 2	Year 3
Sales	$ 200,000	$ 300,000	$ 400,000
Inventories, January 1	--	$ 50,000	$ 65,000
Purchases	$ 210,000	271,000	352,000
Goods Available for Sale	$ 210,000	$ 321,000	$ 417,000
Less Inventories, December 31	(50,000)	(65,000)	(115,000)
Cost of Goods Sold	$ 160,000	$ 256,000	$ 302,000
Gross Profit on Sales	$ 40,000	$ 44,000	$ 98,000

b. **Acquisition Cost:**

	Year 1	Year 2	Year 3
Sales	$ 200,000	$ 300,000	$ 400,000
Inventory, January 1	--	$ 60,000	$ 80,000
Purchases	$ 210,000	271,000	352,000
Goods Available from Sale	$ 210,000	$ 331,000	$ 432,000
Less Inventory, December 31	(60,000)	(80,000)	(115,000)
Cost of Goods Sold	$ 150,000	$ 251,000	$ 317,000
Gross Profit on Sales	$ 50,000	$ 49,000	$ 83,000

c. The lower-of-cost-or-market basis recognizes lower income in years when acquisition costs are falling. However, when that trend is reversed, it produces higher reported income figures than the acquisition cost basis. Over long enough time periods, income is constant, equal to cash inflows minus cash outflows. Compare the total gross profit over all three years, a constant $182,000.

7.28   (Cypres; When goods available for sale exceed sales, firms can manipulate income even when they use specific identification.)

	Revenue	− Cost of Goods Sold =	Gross Margin
a. FIFO Cost Flow:	200 x $600 = $120,000	100 x $300 + 100 x $400 = $70,000	$50,000
b. Minimum Income:	200 x $600 = $120,000	100 x $400 + 100 x $350 = $75,000	$45,000
c. Maximum Income:	200 x $600 = $120,000	100 x $300 + 100 x $350 = $65,000	$55,000

7.29   (Arnold Company; computations involving different cost flow assumptions.)

	Pounds	a. FIFO	b. Weighted Average	c. LIFO
Raw Materials Available for Use	10,700	$24,384	$24,384	$ 24,384
Less Ending Inventory	(3,500)	(8,110)[a]	(7,976)[c]	(7,818)[e]
Raw Materials Issued to Production	7,200	$16,274[b]	$16,408[d]	$ 16,566[f]

[a](3,000 x $2.32) + (500 x $2.30) = $8,110.

[b](1,200 x $2.20) + (2,200 x $2.25) + (2,800 x $2.28) + (1,000 x $2.30) = $16,274.

[c]($24,384/10,700) x 3,500 = $7,976.

[d]($24,384/10,700) x 7,200 = $16,408.

[e](1,200 x $2.20) + (2,200 x $2.25) + (100 x $2.28) = $7,818.

[f](3,000 x $2.32) + (1,500 x $2.30) + (2,700 x $2.28) = $16,566.

7.30   (Howell Corporation; effect of LIFO on financial statements over several periods.)

a.

Year	Ending Inventory	
7	8,000 x $10.00	$ 80,000
8	(8,000 x $10.00) + (2,000 x $10.50)	$101,000
9	7,000 x $10.00	$ 70,000
10	(7,000 x $10.00) + (1,000 x $12.40)	$ 82,400

7.30 continued.

b. Year | Sales | | – | Cost of Goods Sold | | = Income

7   28,000 X $12.00 = $336,000   28,000 X $10.00 = $280,000 $56,000
8   38,000 X $12.60 = $478,800   38,000 X $10.50 = $399,000 $79,800
9   48,000 X $13.23 = $635,040   45,000 X $11.30 +
                                 2,000 X $10.50 +
                                 1,000 X $10.00 = $539,500 $95,540
10 52,000 X $13.89 = $722,280   52,000 X $12.40 = $644,800 $77,480

c.

Year	Income	Sales	Rate of Income to Sales
7	$56,000	$336,000	16.67%
8	79,800	478,800	16.67%
9	95,540	635,040	15.00%
10	77,480	722,280	10.73%

d. Howell Corporation increased selling prices 5 percent [= ($12.60/$12.00) – 1] between Year 7 and Year 8 in line with the 5 percent [= ($10.50/$10.00) – 1] increase in acquisition costs. During Year 9, acquisition costs increased 7.6 percent [= ($11.30/$10.50) – 1] but the firm again increased selling prices only 5 percent [= ($13.23/$12.60) – 1]. Thus, the income to sales percentage declined. During Year 10, acquisition costs increased 9.7 percent [= ($12.40/$11.30) – 1] but the firm again increased selling prices only 5 percent [= $13.89/$13.23) – 1]. The income to sales percentage decreased even further.

7.31 (Chan Company; reconstructing financial statement data from information on effects of liquidations of LIFO layers.)

a. $8. Cost of goods sold was $900,000 lower than it would have been had the firm maintained inventories at 200,000 units. The average cost of the 50,000 units removed from the beginning inventory was $18 (= $900,000/50,000 units) less than current cost: $26 – $18 = $8.

b. $1,000,000. Derived as follows: $8 X 50,000 units = $400,000 decline in inventory during the year. Beginning inventory must have been $400,000 + $600,000 (ending inventory) = $1,000,000.

7.32 (EKG Company; LIFO provides opportunity for income manipulation.)

a. Largest cost of goods sold results from producing 70,000 (or more) additional units at a cost of $22 each, giving cost of goods sold of $1,540,000.

b. Smallest cost of goods sold results from producing no additional units, giving cost of goods sold of $980,000 [= ($8 X 10,000) + ($15 X 60,000)].

7.32 continued.

c.

	Income Reported	
	Minimum	**Maximum**
Revenues ($30 x 70,000)...............................	$2,100,000	$2,100,000
Less Cost of Goods Sold	(1,540,000)	(980,000)
Gross Margin..	$ 560,000	$1,120,000

7.33 (Sears; analysis of annual report; usage of LIFO.)

a. Reported pretax income would have been higher by $230 million (= $670 million – $440 million).

b. After taxes, net income would increase $230 million x .65 = $149.5 million. $149.5/$606.0 = .25; so net income would be 25 percent larger than shown, or $755.5 million.

7.34 (Giles Computer Store; separating operating margin from holding gains.)

	FIFO	LIFO
a.		
Beginning Inventory (200 x $300)	$ 60,000	$ 60,000
Purchases (2,500 x $400)	1,000,000	1,000,000
Goods Available for Sale	$1,060,000	$1,060,000
Less Ending Inventory:		
(400 x $400)	(160,000)	
(200 x $300) + (200 x $400)		(140,000)
Cost of Goods Sold	$ 900,000	$ 920,000
b.		
Revenues (2,300 x $800)	$1,840,000	$1,840,000
Less Cost of Goods Sold	(900,000)	(920,000)
Gross Margin on Sales	$ 940,000	$ 920,000
c.		
Revenues	$1,840,000	$1,840,000
Less Replacement Cost of Goods Sold (2,300 x $400)	(920,000)	(920,000)
Operating Margin	$ 920,000	$ 920,000
Realized Holding Gains:		
Replacement Cost of Goods Sold	$ 920,000	$ 920,000
Less Historical Cost of Goods Sold	(900,000)	(920,000)
Realized Holding Gain	20,000	-0-
Gross Margin on Sales	$ 940,000	$ 920,000
d		
Unrealized Holding Gains:		
Replacement Cost of Ending Inventory (400 x $500)	$ 200,000	$ 200,000
Less Historical Cost of Ending Inventory:		
(400 x $400)	(160,000)	
(200 x $300) + (200 x $400)		(140,000)
Unrealized Holding Gains	40,000	60,000
Total Realized Gross Margin and Unrealized Holding Gains	$ 980,000	$ 980,000

e. Not a coincidence. Total increase in wealth includes both realized and unrealized holding gains and the sum of those two does not depend on the cost flow assumption. The cost flow assumption determines the split of total holding gain between realized and unrealized, not their total.

7.35   (Warren Company; effect of inventory errors.)

   a. None.   f. Understatement by $1,000.
   b. None.   g. Understatement by $1,000.
   c. Understatement by $1,000.   h. None.
   d. Overstatement by $1,000.   i. None.
   e. Overstatement by $1,000.

7.36   (Best Furniture, Inc.; preparation of journal entries and income statement
        for a manufacturing firm.)

   a. (1) Raw Materials Inventory (Asset Increase)   667,200
            Accounts Payable (Liability Increase)   667,200

       (2) Work-in-Process Inventory (Asset Increase) ..   689,100
            Raw Materials Inventory (Asset De-
               crease)...   689,100

       (3) Work-in-Process Inventory (Asset Increase) ..   432,800
            Retained Earnings (Selling Expenses) (Share-
               holders' Equity Decrease)   89,700
            Retained Earnings (Administrative Expenses)
               (Shareholders' Equity Decrease).....................   22,300
            Cash (Asset Decrease)...............................   544,800

       (4) Work-in-Process Inventory (Asset Increase) ..   182,900
            Retained Earnings (Selling Expenses) (Share-
               holders' Equity Decrease)   87,400
            Retained Earnings (Administrative Expenses)
               (Shareholders' Equity Decrease).....................   12,200
            Accumulated Depreciation (Asset De-
               crease)   282,500

       (5) Work-in-Process Inventory (Asset Increase) ..   218,500
            Retained Earnings (Selling Expenses) (Share-
               holders' Equity Decrease)   55,100
            Retained Earnings (Administrative Expenses)
               (Shareholders' Equity Decrease).....................   34,700
            Cash (Asset Decrease)...............................   308,300

       (6) Finished Goods Inventory (Asset Increase) 1,564,500
            Work-in-Process Inventory (Asset De-
               crease)...   1,564,500

       (7) Accounts Receivable (Asset Increase) 2,400,000
            Retained Earnings (Sales) (Shareholders'
               Equity Increase)   2,400,000

7.36 a. continued.

(8) Retained Earnings (Cost of Goods Sold)
    (Shareholders' Equity Decrease)...................... 1,536,600
      Finished Goods Inventory (Asset De-
        crease).. 1,536,600
    $182,700 + $1,564,500 − $210,600 =
    $1,536,600.

b.

BEST FURNITURE, INC.
Income Statement
For the Month of January

Sales		$2,400,000
Less Expenses:		
Cost of Goods Sold	$1,536,600	
Selling	232,200	
Administrative	69,200	(1,838,000)
Net Income		$ 562,000

Note: Instead of using a functional classification of expenses (that is, selling, administrative), classification by their nature (salary, depreciation, other operating) is acceptable.

7.37 (Cornell Company; flow of manufacturing costs through the accounts.)

a.

Beginning Raw Materials Inventory	$ 46,900
Raw Materials Purchased	429,000
Raw Materials Available for Use	$ 475,900
Subtract Ending Raw Materials Inventory	(43,600)
Cost of Raw Materials Used	$ 432,300
Beginning Factory Supplies Inventory	$ 7,600
Factory Supplies Purchased	22,300
Factory Supplies Available for Use	$ 29,900
Subtract Ending Factory Supplies Inventory	(7,700)
Cost of Factory Supplies Used	$ 22,200

7.37 continued.

b.
Beginning Work-in-Process Inventory	$ 110,900
Cost of Raw Materials Used (from Part *a.*)	432,300
Cost of Factory Supplies Used (from Part *a.*)	22,200
Direct Labor Costs Incurred	362,100
Heat, Light, and Power Costs	10,300
Insurance	4,200
Depreciation of Factory Equipment	36,900
Prepaid Rent Expired	3,600
Total Beginning Work-in-Process and Manufacturing Costs Incurred	$ 982,500
Subtract Ending Work-in-Process Inventory	(115,200)
Cost of Units Completed and Transferred to Finished Goods Storeroom	$ 867,300

c.
Beginning Finished Goods Inventory	$ 76,700
Cost of Units Completed and Transferred to Finished Goods Storeroom (from Part *b.*)	867,300
Subtract Ending Finished Goods Inventory	(71,400)
Cost of Goods Sold	$ 872,600

d. Net Income is $110,040 [= (1 − .40)($1,350,000 − $872,600 − $246,900 − $47,100)].

7.38   (Hickory Industries; flow of manufacturing costs through the accounts.)

a.
Beginning Raw Materials Inventory	$ 50,600
Raw Materials Purchased	182,600
Raw Materials Available for Use	$ 233,200
Subtract Ending Raw Materials Inventory	(54,400)
Cost of Raw Materials Used	$ 178,800

b.
Beginning Work-in-Process Inventory	$ 156,200
Cost of Raw Materials Used (from Part *a.*)	178,800
Direct Labor Costs Incurred	144,800
Heat, Light, and Power Costs	6,200
Depreciation	35,600
Total Beginning Work-in-Process and Manufacturing Costs Incurred	$ 521,600
Subtract Ending Work-in-Process Inventory	(153,800)
Cost of Units Completed and Transferred to Finished Goods Storeroom	$ 367,800

c.
Beginning Finished Goods Inventory	$ 76,800
Cost of Units Completed and Transferred to Finished Goods Storeroom (from Part *b.*)	367,800
Subtract Ending Finished Goods Inventory	(79,400)
Cost of Goods Sold	$ 365,200

7.38 continued.

    d. Net Income is $46,320 [= $(1 - .40)($525,000 - $365,200 - $82,600)$].

7.39   (Hartison Corporation; detailed comparison of various choices for inventory accounting.)

	FIFO	LIFO	Weighted Average
Inventory, 1/1/Year 1......................	$ 0	$ 0	$ 0
Purchases for Year 1......................	25,600	25,600	25,600
Goods Available for Sale During Year 1.....................................	$ 25,600	$ 25,600	$ 25,600
Less Inventory, 12/31/Year 1........	(6,400)[1]	(5,000)[2]	(5,565)[3]
Cost of Goods Sold for Year 1	$ 19,200	$ 20,600	$ 20,035
Inventory, 1/1/Year 2......................	$ 6,400 [1]	$ 5,000 [2]	$ 5,565 [3]
Purchases for Year 2......................	42,600	42,600	42,600
Goods Available for Sale During Year 2.....................................	$ 49,000	$ 47,600	$ 48,165
Less Inventory, 12/31/Year 2........	(5,400)[4]	(3,000)[5]	(4,661)[6]
Cost of Goods Sold for Year 2	$ 43,600	$ 44,600	$ 43,504

[1]$(400 \times \$13) + (100 \times \$12) = \$6,400$.
[2]$500 \times \$10 = \$5,000$.
[3]$(\$25,600/2,300) \times 500 = \$5,565$.
[4]$300 \times \$18 = \$5,400$.
[5]$300 \times \$10 = \$3,000$.
[6]$(\$48,165/3,100) \times 300 = \$4,661$.

    a. $19,200.   d. $43,600.
    b. $20,600.   e. $44,600.
    c. $20,035.   f. $43,504.

    g.

	Cost of Goods Sold for Two Years
FIFO..	$62,800
LIFO..	65,200

    The FIFO cost flow assumption results in reported pretax income which is higher by $2,400 (= $65,200 - $62,800) over the two-year period. After taxes, the difference is reduced to .60 x $2,400 = $1,440.

    h. Management might prefer to report the higher net income from FIFO of $1,440. To do so, however, requires $960 (= .40 x $2,400) of extra income tax payments currently that could be postponed until Hartison Corporation dips further into its January Year 1 purchases. We think

7.39 h. continued.

management should use LIFO for tax purposes and, because financial reports must conform to tax reporting, in this case the firm should use LIFO for financial reporting.

7.40 (Hartison Corporation; continuation of preceding problem introducing current cost concepts.)

a.

	FIFO	LIFO	Weighted Average
Sales (1,800 x $18)..................	$32,400	$32,400	$ 32,400
Less Cost of Goods Sold at Average Current Replacement Cost (1,800 x $12).....	(21,600)	(21,600)	(21,600)
Operating Margin	$10,800	$10,800	$ 10,800
Realized Holding Gain:			
Cost of Goods Sold at Current Replacement Cost..	$21,600	$21,600	$ 21,600
Less Cost of Goods Sold at Acquisition Cost..............	(19,200)	(20,600)	(20,035)
Total Realized Holding Gain.....................	$ 2,400	$ 1,000	$ 1,565
Conventional Gross Margin....	$13,200	$11,800	$ 12,365
Unrealized Holding Gain:			
Ending Inventory at Current Replacement Cost (500 x $14).......................	$ 7,000	$ 7,000	$ 7,000
Less Ending Inventory at Acquisition Cost..............	(6,400)	(5,000)	(5,565)
Total Unrealized Holding Gain..............	$ 600	$ 2,000	$ 1,435
Less Unrealized Holding Gain at Beginning of Period	--	--	--
Total Profit Including Holding Gain[a].............................	$13,800	$13,800	$ 13,800

[a]Total of operating margin, realized holding gain, and unrealized holding gain.

7.40 continued.

b.

	FIFO	LIFO	Weighted Average
Sales (2,800 x $24).....................	$67,200	$67,200	$ 67,200
Less Cost of Goods Sold at Average Current Replacement Cost (2,800 x $16).....	(44,800)	(44,800)	(44,800)
Operating Margin	$22,400	$22,400	$ 22,400
Realized Holding Gain:			
Cost of Goods Sold at Current Replacement Cost..	$44,800	$44,800	$ 44,800
Less Cost of Goods Sold at Acquisition Cost..............	(43,600)	(44,600)	(43,504)
Total Realized Holding Gain	$ 1,200	$ 200	$ 1,296
Conventional Gross Margin....	$23,600	$22,600	$ 23,696
Unrealized Holding Gain:			
Ending Inventory at Current Replacement Cost (300 x $18)........................	$ 5,400	$ 5,400	$ 5,400
Less Ending Inventory at Acquisition Cost..............	(5,400)	(3,000)	(4,661)
Total Unrealized Holding Gain..............	$ 0	$ 2,400	$ 739
Less Unrealized Holding Gain at Beginning of Period (see Part a.)..............	(600)	(2,000)	$ (1,435)
Increase (Decrease) in Unrealized Holding Gain during Year 2........................	$ (600)	$ 400	$ (696)
Total Profit Including Holding Gain	$23,000	$23,000	$ 23,000
c. Operating Margin—Year 1	$10,800	$10,800	$10,800
—Year 2.....	22,400	22,400	22,400
Realized Holding Gain—			
Year 1.....................................	2,400	1,000	1,565
Year 2.....................................	1,200	200	1,296
Unrealized Holding Gain at the End of Year 2	0	2,400	739
Total Profit Including Holding Gain..................	$36,800	$36,800	$36,800

7.41 (Burton Corporation; detailed comparison of various choices for inventory accounting.)

	FIFO	LIFO	Weighted Average
Inventory, 1/1/Year 1......................	$ 0	$ 0	$ 0
Purchases for Year 1......................	14,400	14,400	14,400
Goods Available for Sale During Year 1..	$14,400	$14,400	$ 14,400
Less Inventory, 12/31/Year 1........	(3,000)[1]	(3,000)[2]	(2,400)[3]
Cost of Goods Sold for Year 1	$11,400	$12,400	$ 12,000
Inventory, 1/1/Year 2......................	$ 3,000 [1]	$ 2,000 [2]	$ 2,400 [3]
Purchases for Year 2......................	21,000	21,000	21,000
Goods Available for Sale During Year 2..	$24,000	$23,000	$ 23,400
Less Inventory, 12/31/Year 2........	(5,000)[4]	(6,200)[5]	(5,850)[6]
Cost of Goods Sold for Year 2	$19,000	$16,800	$ 17,550

[1] 200 x $15 = $3,000.
[2] 200 x $10 = $2,000.
[3] ($14,400/1,200) x 200 = $2,400.
[4] 500 x $10 = $5,000.
[5] (200 x $10) + (300 x $14) = $6,200.
[6] ($23,400/2,000) x 500 = $5,850.

a. $11,400.
b. $12,400.
c. $12,000.

d. $19,000.
e. $16,800.
f. $17,550.

g. FIFO results in higher net income for Year 1. Purchase prices for inventory items increased during Year 1. FIFO uses older, lower purchase prices to measure cost of goods sold, whereas LIFO uses more recent, higher prices.

h. LIFO results in higher net income for Year 2. Purchase prices for inventory items decreased during Year 2. LIFO uses more recent, lower prices to measure cost of goods sold, whereas FIFO uses older, higher prices.

7.42   (Burton Corporation; continuation of preceding problem introducing current cost concepts.)

a.

	FIFO	LIFO	Weighted Average
Sales (1,000 x $25)....................	$25,000	$25,000	$ 25,000
Less Cost of Goods Sold at Average Current Replacement Cost (1,000 x $14).....	(14,000)	(14,000)	(14,000)
Operating Margin	$11,000	$11,000	$ 11,000
Realized Holding Gain:			
Cost of Goods Sold at Current Replacement Cost..	$14,000	$14,000	$ 14,000
Less Cost of Goods Sold at Acquisition Cost...............	(11,400)	(12,400)	(12,000)
Total Realized Holding Gain..........................	$ 2,600	$ 1,600	$ 2,000
Conventional Gross Margin....	$13,600	$12,600	$ 13,000
Unrealized Holding Gain:			
Ending Inventory at Current Replacement Cost (200 x $16)........................	$ 3,200	$ 3,200	$ 3,200
Less Ending Inventory at Acquisition Cost...............	(3,000)	(2,000)	(2,400)
Total Unrealized Holding Gain.............	$ 200	$ 1,200	$ 800
Total Profit Including Holding Gain[a].....................................	$13,800	$13,800	$ 13,800

[a]Total of operating margin, realized holding gain, and unrealized holding gain.

7.42 continued.

b.

	FIFO	LIFO	Weighted Average
Sales (1,500 x $22)..................	$33,000	$33,000	$ 33,000
Less Cost of Goods Sold at Average Current Replacement Cost (1,500 x $12).....	(18,000)	(18,000)	(18,000)
Operating Margin.....................	$15,000	$15,000	$ 15,000
Realized Holding Gain:			
Cost of Goods Sold at Current Replacement Cost..	$18,000	$18,000	$ 18,000
Less Cost of Goods Sold at Acquisition Cost..............	(19,000)	(16,800)	(17,550)
Total Realized Holding Gain (Loss)..............	$ (1,000)	$ 1,200	$ 450
Conventional Gross Margin ...	$14,000	$16,200	$ 15,450
Unrealized Holding Gain:			
Ending Inventory at Current Replacement Cost (500 x $10)......................	$ 5,000	$ 5,000	$ 5,000
Less Ending Inventory at Acquisition Cost..............	(5,000)	(6,200)	(5,850)
Total Unrealized Holding Gain (Loss).....................	$ 0	$ (1,200)	$ (850)
Less Unrealized Holding Gain at Beginning of Period (see Part a.)................................	(200)	(1,200)	(800)
Increase (Decrease) in Unrealized Holding Gain during Year 2.............................	$ (200)	$ (2,400)	$ (1,650)
Total Profit Including Holding Gain.................................	$13,800	$13,800	$ 13,800

c.

	FIFO	LIFO	Weighted Average
Operating Margin—Year 1......	$11,000	$11,000	$11,000
—Year 2......	15,000	15,000	15,000
Realized Holding Gain (Loss)			
Year 1....................................	2,600	1,600	2,000
Year 2....................................	(1,000)	1,200	450
Unrealized Holding Gain (Loss) at the End of Year 2.............	0	(1,200)	(850)
Total Profit Including Holding Gain (Loss).....	$27,600	$27,600	$27,600

7.43   (Hanover Oil Products; effect of FIFO and LIFO on income statement and balance sheet.)

a.

	FIFO	LIFO
Beginning Inventory	$ 0	$ 0
Purchases:		
1/1: 4,000 @ $1.40	$ 5,600	$ 5,600
1/13: 6,000 @ $1.46	8,760	8,760
1/28: 5,000 @ $1.50	7,500	7,500
Total Purchases	$ 21,860	$ 21,860
Available for Sale	$ 21,860	$ 21,860
Less Ending Inventory:		
FIFO: 2,000 x $1.50	(3,000)	
LIFO: 2,000 x $1.40		(2,800)
Cost of Goods Sold	$ 18,860	$ 19,060

b.

	FIFO	LIFO
Beginning Inventory	$ 3,000	$ 2,800
Purchases:		
2/5: 7,000 @ $1.53	$ 10,710	$ 10,710
2/14: 6,000 @ $1.47	8,820	8,820
2/21: 10,000 @ $1.42	14,200	14,200
Total Purchases	$ 33,730	$ 33,730
Available for Sale	$ 36,730	$ 36,530
Less Ending Inventory:		
FIFO: 3,000 x $1.42	(4,260)	
LIFO: (2,000 x $1.40) + (1,000 x $1.53)		(4,330)
Cost of Goods Sold	$ 32,470	$ 32,200

c.

	FIFO	LIFO
Beginning Inventory	$ 4,260	$ 4,330
Purchases:		
3/2: 6,000 @ $1.48	$ 8,880	$ 8,880
3/15: 5,000 @ $1.54	7,700	7,700
3/26: 4,000 @ $1.60	6,400	6,400
Total Purchases	$ 22,980	$ 22,980
Available for Sale	$ 27,240	$ 27,310
Less Ending Inventory:		
FIFO: 1,000 x $1.60	(1,600)	
LIFO: 1,000 x $1.40		(1,400)
Cost of Goods Sold	$ 25,640	$ 25,910

d. Acquisition costs increased during January. During such periods, LIFO generally provides larger cost of goods sold amounts than FIFO because LIFO uses the most recent higher cost. Acquisition costs decreased during February. Under these circumstances, FIFO generally results in higher cost of goods sold because it uses the higher older cost. During March, acquisition costs increased. There was a liquidation of LIFO layers, however, which makes it more difficult to generalize about which cost flow assumption results in the higher cost of goods sold. LIFO results in the higher cost of goods sold in this case because the effect of increasing purchase costs dominated the effect of the LIFO liquidation.

e.

	January		February		March	
	FIFO	**LIFO**	**FIFO**	**LIFO**	**FIFO**	**LIFO**
(1) Sales..........	$20,840	$20,840	$35,490	$35,490	$28,648	$28,648
(2) Cost of Goods Sold ...	18,860	19,060	32,470	32,200	25,640	25,910
(2)/(1)..............	90.5%	91.5%	91.5%	90.7%	89.5%	90.4%

f. LIFO provides the most stable cost of goods sold to sales percentage because LIFO cost of goods sold amounts reflects current replacement cost more fully than FIFO. The firm prices its gasoline at a 10 percent markup on current replacement cost, so the cost of goods sold to sales percentage under LIFO will be closer to 90.9 percent (= 1/1.1) than FIFO.

g.

Available for Sale (from Part c.).......................	$ 27,240	$ 27,310
Plus Additional Purchases: 2,000 x $1.60.....	3,200	3,200
Less Ending Inventory:		
FIFO: 3,000 x $1.60....................................	(4,800)	
LIFO: (2,000 x $1.40) + (1,000 x $1.53).....		(4,330)
Cost of Goods Sold...	$ 25,640	$ 26,180

Costs of goods sold will not change under FIFO because the additional purchases simply increase both the quantity and valuation of the ending inventory. Cost of goods sold increases under LIFO because the additional purchases increase the quantity of ending inventory but the purchase price paid substitutes for the LIFO layers liquidated in measuring cost of goods sold.

7.44   (The Back Store; dealing with LIFO inventory layers.)

a. 200,000 units purchased in Year 30 − 10,000 units purchased in Year 30 included in the 12/31/Year 30 inventory = 190,000 units.

b.
Revenue (300,000 Units @ $15)	$4,500,000
Replacement Cost of Goods Sold (300,000 Units @ $10)	3,000,000
Operating Margin on Sales	$1,500,000

c.
Replacement Cost of Goods Sold (Average)		$3,000,000
Less Acquisition Cost:		
250,000 x $10	$2,500,000	
10,000 x $9	90,000	
20,000 x $6	120,000	
20,000 x $3	60,000	2,770,000
Realized Holding Gain		$ 230,000

Thus: $1,500,000 + $230,000 = $1,730,000 (conventional gross margin).

d.
Conventional Gross Margin		$1,730,000
Unrealized Holding Gain:		
Replacement Cost at Period-End: 40,000 x $11	$ 440,000	
Acquisition Cost: 40,000 x $3	(120,000)	320,000
Less: Unrealized Holding Gain in Beginning Inventory:		
Replacement Cost on 12/31/Year 30: 90,000 x $8	$ 720,000	
Inventory Cost on 12/31/Year 30	390,000	(330,000)
Economic Profit		$1,720,000

e.
Sales (300,000 x $15)		$4,500,000
Less Acquisition Cost of Goods Sold:		
90,000 x $9	$ 810,000	
210,000 x $10	2,100,000	(2,910,000)
Conventional Gross Margin (FIFO)		$1,590,000

This equals the operating margin on sales of $1,500,000 (see Part b. above) plus the realized holding gain of $90,000 which is the replacement cost of goods sold of $3,000,000 less the acquisition cost of goods sold of $2,910,000.

7.45   (Burch Corporation; reconstructing underlying events from ending inventory amounts [adapted from CPA examination].)

a.   Down. Notice that lower of cost or market is lower than acquisition cost (FIFO); current market price is less than cost.

b.   Up. FIFO means last-in, still-here. The last purchases (FIFO = LISH) cost $44,000 and the earlier purchases (LIFO = FISH) cost $41,800. Also, lower-of-cost-or-market basis shows acquisition costs which are greater than or equal to current cost.

c.   LIFO Cost. Other things being equal, the largest income results from the method that shows the largest *increase* in inventory during the year.

Margin   = Revenues – Cost of Goods Sold
         = Revenues – Beginning Inventory – Purchases + Ending Inventory
         = Revenues – Purchases + Increase in Inventory.

Because the beginning inventory in Year 1 is zero, the method with the largest closing inventory amount implies the largest increase and hence the largest income.

d.   Lower of Cost or Market. The method with the "largest increase in inventory" during the year in this case is the method with the smallest decrease, because all methods show declines in inventory during Year 2. Lower of cost or market shows a decrease in inventory of only $3,000 during Year 2—the other methods show larger decreases ($3,800; $4,000).

e.   Lower of Cost or Market. The method with the largest increase in inventory: $10,000. LIFO shows a $5,400 increase while FIFO shows $8,000.

f.   LIFO Cost. The lower income for all three years results from the method that shows the smallest increase in inventory over the three years. Because all beginning inventories were zero under all methods, we need merely find the method with the smallest ending inventory at Year 3 year-end.

g.   FIFO lower by $2,000. Under FIFO, inventories increased $8,000 during Year 3. Under lower of cost or market, inventories increased $10,000 during Year 3. Lower of cost or market has a bigger increase—$2,000—and therefore lower of cost or market shows a $2,000 larger income than FIFO for Year 3.

7.46 (Wilson Company; LIFO layers influence purchasing behavior and provide opportunity for income manipulation.)

	Cost per Pound	Layer	Beginning Inventory Cost ($000)	+ Purchases Cost ($000)	− Ending Inventory Pounds	Cost ($000)	= Cost of Goods Sold ($000)
a.	(Controller)	Year 1	$ 60.0	---	2,000	$ 60.0	---
		Year 6	9.2	---	200	9.2	---
		Year 7	19.2	---	400	19.2	---
	7,000 @	Year 10	72.8	---	1,400	72.8	---
	$62/lb.	Year 11	---	$ 434.0	---	---	434.0
			$ 161.2	$ 434.0	4,000	$ 161.2	$ 434.0
b.	(Purchasing	Year 1	$ 60.0	---	600	$ 18.0	$ 42.0
	Agent)	Year 6	9.2	---	---	---	9.2
		Year 7	19.2	---	---	---	19.2
	3,600 @	Year 10	72.8	---	---	---	72.8
	$62/lb.	Year 11	---	$ 223.2	---	---	223.2
			$ 161.2	$ 223.2	600	$ 18.0	$ 366.4

c.
Controller's Policy COGS $62/lb... $ 434.00
Less Purchasing Agent's COGS... (366.40)
Controller's Extra Deductions... $ 67.60
Tax Rate: 40 Percent.. X .40
Controller's Tax Savings.. $ 27.04
Controller's Extra Cash Costs for Inventory: 3,400 @
$10/lb.. $ 34.00

d. The economically sound action is to follow the purchasing agent's advice. The controller's policy does save taxes but not as much in taxes as the extra inventory costs. This response presumes that allowing inventory quantities to decrease to 600 pounds does not negatively affect operations prior to replenishing the inventory. A quality of earnings issue arises because the increase in net income that results from the LIFO liquidations is nonrecurring. Except for the older cost in the base layer of 600 units, new LIFO layers will use higher current cost. Liquidating those new layers in later years will not likely increase earnings as much as the current year's liquidations produced. One might argue that following the purchasing agent's advice does not raise an ethical issue because it is the economically sound action. However, management does have some discretion (see Question e.) as to whether to deplete inventories to 600 units or to stop short of that amount of depletion. To the extent that management has an earning target in mind and can choose the amount of inventory depletion to achieve that level of earnings, some would argue that ethical issues arise.

7.46 continued.

e. To maximize income for Year 11, liquidate all our LIFO inventory layers, 4,000 lbs. with total cost $161,200, and purchase only 3,000 lbs. at $62 each during Year 11. To minimize income, acquire 7,000 lbs. at $62 each.

Policy	Cost of Goods Sold for Year 11
Minimum Income:	
7,000 lbs. x $62	$ 434,000
Maximum Income:	
4,000 lbs. of Old Layers	(161,200)
3,000 lbs. at $62	(186,000)
Income Spread before Taxes	$ 86,800
Taxes at 40 Percent	(34,720)
Income Spread after Taxes	$ 52,080

By manipulating purchases of expensium, Wilson Company reports aftertax income anywhere in the range from $50,000 (by following the controller's policy) up to $102,080 (= $50,000 + $52,080) by acquiring only 3,000 lbs. and liquidating all LIFO layers.

7.47 (Bethlehem Steel; assessing the effect of LIFO versus FIFO on financial statements.) (Amounts in Millions)

a.

	Year 9	Year 10	Year 11
Cost of Goods Sold: LIFO	$ 4,399.1	$ 4,327.2	$ 4,059.7
Plus Excess of FIFO Cost over LIFO Values, Beginning of Year	530.1	562.5	499.1
Less Excess of FIFO Cost over LIFO Values, End of Year	(562.5)	(499.1)	(504.9)
Cost of Goods Sold: FIFO	$ 4,366.7	$ 4,390.6	$ 4,053.9

b.

Cost of Goods Sold/Sales	Year 9	Year 10	Year 11
LIFO: $4,399.1/$5,250.9	83.8%		
$4,327.2/$4,899.2		88.3%	
$4,059.7/$4,317.9			94.0%
FIFO: $4,366.7/$5,250.9	83.2%		
$4,390.6/$4,899.2		89.6%	
$4,053.9/$4,317.9			93.9%

7.47 continued.

c. Inventory quantities increased during Year 9 (LIFO ending inventory exceeds LIFO beginning inventory) but it is difficult to conclude for sure the direction of the change in manufacturing costs. It appears, however, that manufacturing costs increased during the year because cost of goods sold using LIFO exceeds cost of goods sold using FIFO. Inventory quantities increased again during Year 10 but it appears that manufacturing costs decreased, resulting in a higher cost of goods sold using FIFO than using LIFO. Clues that manufacturing costs decreased include (1) the excess of FIFO cost over LIFO values declined during Year 10, despite an increase in inventory quantities, and (2) ending inventory using FIFO is less that beginning inventory using FIFO, despite an increase in inventory quantities. Inventory quantities decreased during Year 11 but it appears that manufacturing costs increased. The principal clue for the latter conclusion is that the excess of FIFO cost over LIFO values increased during the year, despite a decrease in inventory quantities. The slightly higher cost of goods sold percentage using LIFO results from using higher manufacturing costs toward the end of Year 11 as well as dipping into the Year 10 LIFO layer priced at the higher manufacturing cost at the beginning of Year 10.

d. **Inventory Turnover Ratio**   **Year 9**   **Year 10**   **Year 11**

	Year 9	Year 10	Year 11
LIFO: $4,399.1/.5($369.0 + $410.3)...	11.3		
$4,327.2/.5($410.3 + $468.3)...		9.9	
$4,059.7/.5($468.3 + $453.4)...			8.8
FIFO: $4,366.7/.5($899.1 + $972.8)...	4.7		
$4,390.6/.5($972.8 + $967.4)...		4.5	
$4,053.9/.5($967.4 + $958.3)...			4.2

e. The inventory turnover ratio for LIFO includes current cost data in the numerator and old cost data in the denominator, whereas this ratio under FIFO includes somewhat out-of-date cost data in the numerator and a mixture of out-of-date and current cost data in the denominator. The mismatching of cost data is less severe for FIFO than for LIFO because of the very old LIFO layers. Thus, the inventory turnover ratio using FIFO probably more accurately measures the actual rate of inventory turnover.

7.47 continued.

f. **Current Ratio**

	Year 8	Year 9	Year 10	Year 11
LIFO: $1,439.8/$870.1........	1.65			
$1,435.2/$838.0........		1.71		
$1,203.2/$831.4........			1.45	
$957.8/$931.0..........				1.03
FIFO: $1,439.8 + (.66 x				
$530.1)/$870.1........	2.06			
$1,435.2 + (.66 x				
$562.5)/$838.0........		2.16		
$1,203.2 + (.66 x				
$499.1/)/$831.4.......			1.84	
$957.8 + (.66 x				
$504.9)/$931.0........				1.39

g. The current ratio decreased between Year 9 and Year 11, suggesting increased short-term liquidity risk. The current ratio using a FIFO cost-flow assumption for inventories probably reflects better the potential of current assets to cover current liabilities because the FIFO inventory values use more recent cost data. The current ratio using FIFO inventory values still exceeds 1.0 at the end of Year 11, suggesting that short-term liquidity risk is not yet at a serious level. However, the sharp decrease during the three-year period coupled with a slower inventory turnover (see Part *d*. above) raise doubts about the future.

Note: The annual report indicates that the decreased current ratio occurs primarily because of reductions in cash that Bethlehem Steel Company needed to help finance its deteriorating operating position.

7.48 (Dupont; interpreting inventory disclosures.)

a. $19,476 + ($4,853 − $4,409) − ($4,407 − $4,107) = $19,620.

b. The quantities of inventories decreased because the ending inventory under LIFO is less than the beginning inventory under FIFO. Thus, Dupont dipped into LIFO layers during the year.

c. The cost of goods under FIFO exceeds cost of goods sold under LIFO, leading one to conclude that manufacturing costs decreased during the year. This is an improper conclusion in this case, however, because of the LIFO liquidation. One cannot determine how much of the lower cost of goods sold under LIFO is due to lower manufacturing costs this year and how much might be due to lower manufacturing costs in the LIFO layers liquidated.

7.48 continued.

    d. LIFO: $19,476/.5($4,409 + $4,107) = 4.6.
       FIFO: $19,620/.5($4,853 + $4,407) = 4.2.

    e. The difference in the rate of inventory turnover occurs because LIFO uses old costs in computing inventory amounts whereas FIFO uses more up-to-date costs. Both cost flow assumptions use relatively recent costs in the numerator of the ratio, although those for LIFO are more up-to-date.

    f. The amount for purchases in the numerator of the accounts payable turnover ratio should not differ between LIFO and FIFO, unless the firm accelerates purchases or production at the end of a year to avoid dipping into its LIFO layers. The average balance for accounts payable in the denominator of the ratio should not differ between LIFO and FIFO, unless the extra income taxes paid under FIFO (rising acquisition costs) or LIFO (falling acquisition costs) constrains a firm's ability to repay its suppliers.

7.49 (Eli Lilly; analyzing inventory disclosures.)

    a.

	Year 8	Year 9	Year 10
Cost of Goods Sold using LIFO	$ 2,015.1	$ 2,098.0	$ 2,055.7
Plus (Minus) Excess of FIFO (LIFO) over LIFO (FIFO) Beginning Inventory	11.7	(2.7)	(7.1)
Less (Minus) Excess of FIFO (LIFO) over LIFO (FIFO) Ending Inventory	2.7	7.1	(11.9)
Cost of Goods Sold using FIFO	$ 2,029.5	$ 2,102.4	$ 2,036.7

    b. The inventory at the end of Year 8 under LIFO exceeded the inventory at the end of Year 9, suggesting that Eli Lilly dipped into LIFO layers during Year 9. Likewise, the inventory at the end of Year 9 under LIFO exceeded the inventory at the end of Year 10, suggesting that Eli Lilly dipped into LIFO layers during Year 10.

    c. Manufacturing likely increased during some years and decreased in other years. Manufacturing costs likely decreased during Year 8. Cost of goods sold under FIFO exceeded cost of goods sold under LIFO during Year 8. Eli Lilly did not appear to dip into LIFO layers during Year 8 since its ending inventory exceeded its beginning inventory. The ending inventory under LIFO exceeds the ending inventory under FIFO, providing further evidence that manufacturing costs decreased during the year.

7.49 c. continued.

Manufacturing costs likely decreased further during Year 9. Cost of goods sold under FIFO again exceeds cost of goods sold under LIFO. However, it appears that Eli Lilly dipped into LIFO layers of earlier years. If these layers had a lower cost than the manufacturing costs incurred during Year 9, then part of the reason for the lower LIFO cost of goods sold could relate to the LIFO liquidations. The ending inventory under LIFO exceeds the ending inventory under FIFO. Despite lower inventory levels at the end of Year 9 than at the end of Year 8. The excess of LIFO ending inventory over FIFO ending inventory increased during Year 9, lending further support to the conclusion that manufacturing costs decreased during Year 9.

Manufacturing costs likely increased during Year 10. Cost of goods sold under LIFO exceeds cost of goods sold under FIFO. This occurred despite Eli Lilly dipping into LIFO layers during the year. The ending inventory under FIFO exceeds that under LIFO, lending further support for an increase in manufacturing costs during Year 10.

d.
	LIFO	**FIFO**
Year 8	$2,015.1/$9,236.8 = 21.8%	$2,029.5/$9,236.8 = 22.0%
Year 9	$2,098.0/$10,002.6 = 21.0%	$2,102.4/$10,002.6 = 21.0%
Year 10	$2,055.7/$10,862.2 = 18.9%	$2,036.7/$10,862.2 = 18.8%

e.
	LIFO	**FIFO**
Year 8	$2,015.1/.5($900.7 + $999.9) = 2.1	$2,029.5/.5($912.4 + $997.2) = 2.1
Year 9	$2,098.0/.5($999.9 + $899.6) = 2.2	$2,102.4/.5($997.2 + $892.5) = 2.2
Year 10	$2,055.7/.5($899.6 + $883.1) = 2.3	$2,036.7/.5($892.5 + $895.0) = 2.3

f.
	Year 8	**Year 9**	**Year 10**
Cost of Goods Sold...................	$ 2,029.5	$ 2,102.4	$ 2,036.7
Plus Ending Finished Goods Inventory..............................	236.3	224.7	284.3
Less Beginning Finished Goods Inventory..................	(191.0)	(236.3)	(224.7)
Cost of Goods Manufactured during the Year....................	$ 2,074.8	$ 2,090.8	$ 2,096.3

g. **Year 8:** $2,029.5/.5($191.0 + $236.3) = 9.5
   Year 9: $2,102.4/.5($236.3 + $224.7) = 9.1
   Year 10: $2,036.7/.5($224.7 + $284.3) = 8.0

h. **Year 8:** $2,074.8/.5($459.4 + $435.8) = 4.6
   Year 9: $2,090.8/.5($435.8 + $372.7) = 5.2
   Year 10: $2,096.3/.5($372.7 + $380.6) = 5.6

7.49 continued.

i. The decrease in the cost of goods sold to sales percentage between Year 8 and Year 9 relates in part to lower manufacturing costs. Sales increased 8.3 percent [= ($10,002.6/$9,236.8) − 1]. Perhaps the firm spread the relatively fixed costs of its manufacturing facilities over a larger sales base, reducing its average per unit costs. The firm may also have raised its prices, thereby reducing its cost of goods sold to sales percentage. Note that the percentage decreased on both a LIFO and a FIFO basis, so the cost flow assumption and the dipping into LIFO layers does not change this trend. The decrease in the cost of goods sold to sales percentage between Year 9 and Year 10 likely results from increased selling prices. Manufacturing costs increased during the year.

The increase in the inventory turnover ratio suggests more effective inventory control. The analysis in Parts g. and h. suggests that the improvement relates to an increase in the work-in-process inventory turnover, offset by a decrease in the finished goods inventory turnover.

7.50 (Ethical issues in accounting for inventory.)

a. Firm A appears to have met the criteria for the recognition of revenue. It has received cash and performed substantially all that the customer expected of it. There appears to be no obvious effort on the part of Firm A to mislead its auditors. The firm did all within its control to ship the items on December 31. Assuming that the auditor viewed the recognition of revenue as within GAAP standards, one might conclude that no ethical issue arises. Another issue, though, is whether Firm A typically recognizes revenue at the time of delivery for custom-made goods. If so, this action deviates from previous policy, presumably with the intention of overstating earnings. An intent to deceive would, thereby, appear to be present, raising an ethical issue.

b. The action of Firm B is contrary to GAAP and with an intention to deceive. There are both legal and ethical issues. The fact that the action "corrects itself" by the end of the second year does not change the misstatement of the time pattern of earnings.

c. This action is perhaps more egregious than the preceding two because of the extent of the actions perpetrated to mislead the auditors. The action is also contrary to GAAP.

CHAPTER 8

LONG-LIVED TANGIBLE AND INTANGIBLE ASSETS:
THE SOURCE OF OPERATING CAPACITY

Questions, Short Exercises, Exercises, Problems, and Cases: Answers and Solutions

8.1   See the text or the glossary at the end of the book.

8.2   Maintenance services provided for selling and administrative activities appear as expenses of the current period. Maintenance services provided for manufacturing activities accumulate in Work-in-Process and Finished Goods Inventory accounts. These costs become expenses in the period of sale. Expenditures from any of these activities that increase the service life or service potential of assets beyond that originally expected increase the assets' depreciable base. Such expenditures become expenses as the firm recognizes depreciation during future years.

8.3   Generally accepted accounting principles use acquisition costs in the valuation of most assets. Accounting gives no recognition to the fact that some firms can acquire a particular asset for a lower price than other firms can acquire it. Part of the explanation relates to measuring the relevant cost savings. There is seldom a single, unique alternative price. Additionally, accounting views firms as generating income from using assets in operations, not from simply purchasing them.

The income effect of both recording procedures is a net expense of $250,000, the cash outflow to self-construct the warehouse. The generally accepted procedure recognizes $250,000 as depreciation expense over the life of the warehouse. The unacceptable procedure recognizes revenue of $50,000 upon completion of the warehouse and depreciation expense of $300,000 over the life of the warehouse.

8.4   a.   Over the life of the project, income is cash-in less cash-out. Capitalizing and then amortizing interest versus expensing it affects the timing but not the total amount of income. Capitalizing interest defers expense from the construction period to the periods of use, increasing income in the early years of construction and decreasing it in the periods of use, when depreciation charges are larger.

b.   The "catch-up" described in the preceding part is indefinitely delayed. Reported income in each year increases by the policy of capitalizing interest. When the self-construction activity declines, then the reported income declines as a result of reduced capitalization of interest, but not before.

8.5   a. If the life of an asset is shorter than the accounting period (or that portion of the period remaining after the purchase of the asset), depreciation, as an accounting measurement problem, disappears. The difficulties increase as it becomes necessary to spread the cost of an asset over a number of periods of time. If the accounting period were ten years, fewer items would have to be spread, or "depreciated." If no asset lasted more than a year or two, accountants could make even annual depreciation calculations with considerable accuracy.

        b. Depreciation accounting allocates the cost of long-lived assets to the periods of use in an orderly, reasonable manner. Recognizing depreciation does not "provide funds" for the firm. Selling the firm's products to customers provides funds.

8.6   a. Depreciation life is: $100,000/$10,000 per year = 10 years.

            Age of the asset is: $60,000 accumulated depreciation charge divided by $10,000 depreciation per year = 6 years.

        b. Age of the asset in years = accumulated depreciation at the end of a year divided by depreciation charge for the year.

8.7   Depreciation for years prior to the change in estimate is larger or smaller than it would have been if the firm had originally used the revised estimate. Depreciation for the current and future years is also smaller or larger than it would be if the firm corrected for the original misestimate retroactively. Thus, depreciation in no year of the assets' service life will show the appropriate depreciation for the actual depreciable life of assets.

8.8   The small amounts of certain expenditures often do not justify the record keeping cost of capitalization and depreciation or amortization. Firms therefore expense all expenditures below a certain threshold amount.

8.9   The relevant question to apply generally accepted accounting principles is whether the expenditure maintained the originally expected useful life or extended that useful life. Firms should expense, as maintenance or repairs, expenditures that maintain the originally expected five-year life. In this case, the expenditure both maintains and extends the useful life. A portion of the expenditure should appear as an expense immediately (perhaps two-thirds) and a portion (perhaps one-third) should increase the depreciable base for the asset.

8.10   Accounting views sales of equipment as peripheral to a firm's principal business activities. Revenues and expenses from a firm's principal business activities appear as sales revenue and cost of goods sold. Accounting nets the revenues and expenses from peripheral activities to show only the gain or loss.

8.11   Generally accepted accounting principles compares the undiscounted cash flows from an asset to its book value to determine if an impairment loss has occurred. The rationale is that an impairment loss has not occurred if a firm will receive cash flows in the future at least equal to the book value of the asset. Receiving such cash flows will permit the firm to recover the book value. This criterion ignores the time value of money. Cash received earlier has more economic value than cash received later, but this criterion ignores such differences.

8.12   Some critics of the required expensing of research and development (R & D) costs argue that there is little difference to justify the different accounting treatments. One possible explanation for the different treatment is the greater tangible nature of mineral resources relative to most R & D expenditures. Yet, some R & D expenditures result in tangible prototypes or products. Another possible explanation for the difference is the established market for most mineral resources versus the more unknown market potential for R & D expenditures.

8.13   Critics of the required expensing of research and development (R & D) costs argue that there is little rationale to justify the different accounting. One difference between the two cases is that firms make R & D expenditures for an uncertain future result (that is, the possibility of a patent), whereas less uncertainty exists for the purchase of a completed patent. A market transaction between an independent buyer and seller establish the existence and value of future benefits in the case of a purchased patent. Similar expenditures for R & D simply establish that a firm has made an expenditure.

8.14   (Outback Steakhouse; calculating acquisition costs of long-lived assets.)

The relative market values of the land and building are 20 percent (= $52,000/$260,000) for the land and 80 percent (= $208,000/$260,000) for the building. We use these percentages to allocate joint cost of the land and building.

	Land	**Building**
Purchase Price of Land and Building.........	$ 52,000	$ 208,000
Legal Costs Split 20% and 80%..................	2,520	10,080
Renovation Costs.......................................	--	35,900
Property and Liability Costs during Renovation Split 20% and 80%...........	800	3,200
Property Taxes during Renovation Split 20% and 80%..	1,000	4,000
Total..	$ 56,320	$ 261,180

Note: One might argue that the split of the insurance and property taxes should recognize the increase in market value of the building as a result of the renovation and use some other percentages besides 20 percent and 80 percent. Note also that the insurance and property taxes for the period after opening are expenses of the first year of operation.

8.15   (Target Stores; calculating interest capitalized during construction.)

Capitalized Interest on Borrowing Directly Related to Con-
       struction: .06 x $2,000,000 .... $ 120,000
Capitalized Interest of Other Borrowing: .07 x $1,400,000   98,000
       Total Interest Capitalized .... $ 218,000

8.16   (Office Depot; computing depreciation expense.)

Straight-Line Method: ($40,000 − $4,000)/6 = $6,000.

Double-Declining-Balance Method: 2/6 x $40,000 = $13,333.

Sum-of-the-Years'-Digits Method: 6/21 x ($40,000 − $4,000) = $10,286.

8.17   (Thomson Financial; change in depreciable life and salvage value.)

Book Value on January 1, Year 14: $10,000,000 − {2 x [($10,000,000 − $1,000,000)/6]} = $7,000,000. Depreciation expense for Year 14 based on the new depreciable life and salvage value is $3,200,000 [= ($7,000,000 − $600,000)/2].

8.18   (Disney World; distinguishing repairs versus betterments.)

Repair: (.80 x $30,200) + $86,100 + (.75 x $26,900) + $12,600) = $143,035.

Betterment: (.20 x $30,200) + (.25 x $26,900) = $12,765.

8.19   (Wildwood Properties; computing the amount of an impairment loss on tangible long-lived assets.)

The undiscounted cash flows total $12,400,000 [= ($1,400,000 x 6) + $4,000,000]. The book value of the building of $15,000,000 exceeds the undiscounted estimated cash flows, so an impairment loss has occurred. The present value of the expected cash flows when discounted at 10 percent is $8,355,244 [= ($1,400,000 x 4.35526) + ($4,000,000 x .56447) = $6,097,364 + $2,257,880]. The impairment loss is, therefore, $6,644,756 (= $15,000,000 − $8,355,244).

8.20   (Federal Express; computing the gain or loss on sale of equipment.)

Annual depreciation is $7,000 [= ($48,000 − $6,000)/6].   Depreciation expense for the first six months of Year 14 is $3,500.

Retained Earnings (Depreciation Expense) (Share-
       holders' Equity Decrease) 3,500
       Accumulated Depreciation (Asset Decrease)   3,500

8.20 continued.

The book value of the delivery truck after the entry above is $16,500 [= $48,000 − (4.5 x $7,000)]. The accumulated depreciation totals $31,500 (= 4.5 x $7,000). The entry to record the sale is:

Cash (Asset Increase)...	14,000	
Accumulated Depreciation (Asset Increase)...................	31,500	
Retained Earnings (Loss on Sale of Delivery Truck)		
(Shareholders' Equity Decrease)..................................	2,500	
Delivery Truck (Asset Decrease).............................		48,000

8.21 (Classifying expenditure as asset or expense.)

a. (3) Expense.

b. (3) Expense.

c. (3) Expense.

d. (1) Noncurrent asset (machine).

e. (3) Expense.

f. (3) Expense.

g. (2) Current asset (inventory).

h. (1) Noncurrent asset (equipment).

i. (3) Expense.

j. (1) Noncurrent asset (ore deposit).

k. (1) Current asset (prepayment).

l. (1) Current asset (marketable securities).

m. (2) Current asset product cost (inventories).

n. (1) Noncurrent asset (trademark).

o. (1) Noncurrent asset (copyright).

p. (1) Noncurrent asset (computer software).

q. (3) Expense.

8.22 (Bolton Company; cost of self-constructed assets.)

Land: $70,000 + $2,000 (14) = $72,000.

Factory Building: $200,000 (1) + $12,000 (2) + $140,000 (3) + $6,000 (5) − $7,000 (7) + $10,000 (8) + $8,000 (9) + $3,000[a] (10) + $8,000 (11) + $4,000 (13) + $1,000[a] (15) = $385,000.

Office Building: $20,000 + $13,000 (4) = $33,000.

Site Improvements: $5,000 (12).

> [a]The firm might expense these items. It depends on the rationality of the firm's "self-insurance" policy.
>
> Item (6) is omitted because of *SFAS No. 34*.
>
> Item (16) is omitted because no arm's length transaction occurred in which the firm earned a profit.

8.23 (Duck Vehicle Manufacturing Company; cost of self-developed product.)

The first four items qualify as research and development costs which the firm must expense in the year incurred. It might appear that the firm should capitalize the cost of the prototype because it acquires the prototype from an external contractor. However, completion of a prototype does not signify a viable product. Purchasing the prototype externally versus constructing it internally does not change the accounting.

The firm should capitalize the legal fees to register and establish the patent as part of the cost of the patent. The firm might consider this cost as sufficiently immaterial to warrant treatment as an asset and expense it immediately.

The firm should capitalize the cost of the castings and amortize them over the expected useful life of the vehicle. The cost of the manufacturing permits and the cost of manufacturing the first vehicle are product costs that increase work-in-process inventory.

8.24 (Nucor; amount of interest capitalized during construction.)

a. Average Construction = ($30,000,000 + $60,000,000)/2 = $45,000,000.

Relevant Loans	Interest Anticipated
$ 25,000,000 at .08	$ 2,000,000
20,000,000 at .06	1,200,000
$ 45,000,000	$ 3,200,000

8.24 continued.

    b.   Retained Earnings (Interest Expense) (Share-
            holders' Equity Decrease) 8,000,000
               Interest Payable (Liability Increase) 8,000,000
       ($25,000,000 x .08) + ($100,000,000 x .06).

       Construction in Process (Asset Increase) 3,200,000
          Retained Earnings (Interest Expense)
            (Shareholders' Equity Increase)................. 3,200,000

    c.   Retained Earnings (Interest Expense) (Share-
            holders' Equity Decrease) 8,000,000
               Interest Payable (Liability Increase) 8,000,000
       ($25,000,000 x .08) + ($100,000,000 x .06).

       Construction in Process (Asset Increase) 7,100,000
          Retained Earnings (Interest Expense)
            (Shareholders' Equity Increase)................. 7,100,000
       ($25,000,000 x .08) + ($85,000,000 x .06).

8.25   (Nebok Company; capitalizing interest during construction.) (Amounts in Thousands)

    a.   Weighted average interest rate: $5,480/.5($51,500 + $49,700) = 10.83 percent.

       Weighted average balance in Construction in Process: .5($23,186 + $68,797) = $45,992.

       Interest Capitalized: .1083 x $45,992 = $4,981.

    b.   Retained Earnings (Interest Expense) (Share-
            holders' Equity Decrease) 5,480
               Interest Payable (Liability Increase) 5,480

       Construction in Process (Asset Increase) 4,981
          Retained Earnings (Interest Expense) (Share-
            holders' Equity Increase).................................. 4,981

c. Income before Interest Expense and Income Taxes	$ 16,300
Interest Expense ($5,480 – $4,981)	(499)
Income before Income Taxes...	$ 15,801
Income Tax Expense at 35 Percent...	(5,530)
Net Income..	$ 10,271

8.25 continued.

      d. $16,300/$499 = 32.67 times.

      e. $16,300/$5,480 = 2.97 times.

      f. The interest coverage ratio in Part *e.* indicates the interest that the firm must pay and therefore provides a better measure for assessing risk.

8.26   (Alcoa; calculations for various depreciation methods.)

	Year 1	Year 2	Year 3
a. Straight-Line Method..................... ($88,800 − $4,800)/6 = $14,000.	$14,000	$14,000	$14,000
b. Sum-of-the-Years'-Digits Method... (6 X 7)/2 = 21 sum-of-the-years'-digits.	$24,000	$20,000	$16,000
c. Declining-Balance Method............. 33 percent rate.	$29,304	$19,634	$13,154
d. Production Method.......................... $84,000/30,000 = $2.80 per hour.	$12,600	$14,000	$15,400

8.27   (Luck Delivery Company; calculations for various depreciation methods.)

a.

	Depreciation Charge (Straight-Line)
Year 8......................	$ 6,000 (30,000/5)
Year 9......................	6,000
Year 10....................	6,000
Year 11....................	6,000
Year 12....................	6,000
	$30,000

b.

	Depreciation Charge (Double-Declining-Balance)
Year 8......................	$12,000 ($30,000 X .40)
Year 9......................	7,200 ($18,000 X .40)
Year 10....................	4,320 ($10,800 X .40)
Year 11....................	3,240 ($6,480/2)
Year 12....................	3,240 (balance)
	$30,000

8.27 continued.

c.

	Depreciation Charge (Sum-of-the-Years'-Digits)	
Year 8	$10,000	($30,000 × 5/15)
Year 9	8,000	($30,000 × 4/15)
Year 10	6,000	($30,000 × 3/15)
Year 11	4,000	($30,000 × 2/15)
Year 12	2,000	($30,000 × 1/15)
	$30,000	

d.

	MACRS (5-Year Class)	
Year 8	$ 6,000	(= $30,000 × .20)
Year 9	9,600	(= $30,000 × .32)
Year 10	5,760	(= $30,000 × .192)
Year 11	3,450	(= $30,000 × .115)
Year 12	3,450	(= $30,000 × .115)
Year 13	1,740	(= $30,000 × .058)
	$30,000	

e.

	Depreciation Charge (Sum-of-the-Years'-Digits)	
Year 8	3/4 × $10,000	= $ 7,500
Year 9	3/4 × $ 8,000 + 1/4 × $10,000 =	8,500
Year 10	3/4 × $ 6,000 + 1/4 × $ 8,000 =	6,500
Year 11	3/4 × $ 4,000 + 1/4 × $ 6,000 =	4,500
Year 12	3/4 × $ 2,000 + 1/4 × $ 4,000 =	2,500
Year 13	1/4 × $ 2,000 =	500
		$ 30,000

8.28 (Slow Poke Delivery Company; revision of estimated service life changes depreciation schedule.)

Summary of the depreciation charges under the two methods:

	a. Straight-Line	b. Sum-of-the-Years'-Digits
Year 12	$ 7,200[a]	$13,091[c]
Year 13	7,200[a]	11,782[d]
Year 14	9,600[b]	13,465[e]
Year 15	9,600[b]	11,221[f]
	$33,600	$49,559

[a]($80,000 − $8,000)/10 = $7,200.

[b]($80,000 − $7,200 − $7,200 − $8,000)/6 = $9,600.

[c][($80,000 − $8,000) × 10/55] = $13,091.

[d][($80,000 − $8,000) × 9/55] = $11,782.

[e]($80,000 − $13,091 − $11,782 − $8,000) × 6/21 = $13,465.

[f]($80,000 − $13,091 − $11,782 − $8,000) × 5/21 = $11,221.

8.29 (Florida Manufacturing Corporation; journal entries for revising estimate of life.)

a. Work-in-Process Inventory (Asset Increase) 2,400
    Accumulated Depreciation (Asset Decrease)...... 2,400
    ($180,000 − $7,200)/144 = $1,200 per month.

b. Work-in-Process Inventory (Asset Increase) 14,400
    Accumulated Depreciation (Asset Decrease)...... 14,400
    12 × $1,200 = $14,400.

c. Depreciation to 1/1/Year 20 = 62 × $1,200 = $74,400.
   Remaining depreciation = $180,000 − $74,400 − $3,840 = $101,760.
   Remaining life = 168 months − 62 months = 106 months as of
       1/1/Year 20.
   Depreciation charge per month = $101,760/106 = $960.

    Work-in-Process Inventory (Asset Increase) 11,520
        Accumulated Depreciation (Asset Decrease)...... 11,520
    12 × $960 = $11,520.

d. By March 31, Year 25, the machine has been on the new depreciation schedule for Year 20 through Year 24 plus 3 months or 63 months altogether. Accumulated depreciation is $74,400 + (63 × $960) = $74,400 + $60,480 = $134,880.

   Book value is $180,000 − $134,880 = $45,120; loss is $5,120.

   Journal entries are:

    Work-in-Process Inventory (Asset Increase) 2,880
        Accumulated Depreciation (Asset Decrease)...... 2,880
    3 × $960 = $2,880; to bring depreciation up to date
    as of 3/31/Year 25.

    Cash (Asset Increase) 40,000
    Accumulated Depreciation (Asset Increase) 134,880
    Retained Earnings (Loss on Disposal of Machin-
        ery) (Shareholders' Equity Decrease)................... 5,120
            Machinery (Asset Decrease) 180,000

8.30 (Wilcox Corporation; working backwards to derive proceeds from disposition of plant assets.)

Cost of Equipment Sold: $400,000 + $230,000 − $550,000 = $80,000.
Accumulated Depreciation
   on Equipment Sold: $180,000 + $50,000 − $160,000 = $70,000.
Book Value of Equipment
   Sold: $80,000 − $70,000 = $10,000.
Proceeds of Sale: $10,000 + $4,000 = $14,000.

8.31   (Kieran Corporation; computing the amount of impairment loss.)

	Book Value	Undis- counted Cash Flows	Impair- ment Loss Recog- nized	Market Value	Amount of Loss
Land	$ 550,000	$ 575,000	No	$ 550,000	$ 0
Buildings.....................	580,000	600,000	No	580,000	0
Equipment	1,200,000	950,000	Yes	800,000	400,000
Goodwill.......................	500,000	--	Yes	270,000	230,000
Total.....................	$2,830,000			$2,200,000	$630,000

After recognizing the impairment losses on the property, plant, and equipment, the book value of Kieran Corporation is $2,430,000 (= $550,000 for land + $580,000 for buildings + $800,000 for equipment + $500,000 for goodwill). The book value of $2,430,000 exceeds the market value of the entity of $2,200,000, so a goodwill impairment loss may have occurred (Step 1 of goodwill impairment test). The market value column above shows the allocation of the $2,200,000 market value to identifiable assets, with the residual of $270,000 attributed to goodwill. The book value of the goodwill of $500,000 exceeds its implied market value of $270,000, so Kieran Corporation recognizes an impairment loss on the goodwill of $230,000 (Step 2 of goodwill impairment test).

8.32   (Journal entries to correct accounting errors.)

a. Retained Earnings (Depreciation Expense)
      (Shareholders' Equity Decrease)............................   375
          Accumulated Depreciation (Asset De-
              crease)   375
      $3,000 X .25 X 6/12 = $375.

   Accumulated Depreciation (Asset Increase)...........   1,875
   Retained Earnings (Loss on Disposal of Equip-
       ment) (Shareholders' Equity Decrease)................   325
          Equipment (Asset Decrease)..............................   2,200
      $3,000 X .25 X 2.5 = $1,875. $3,200 + $3000 –
      $4,000 = $2,200.

b. Accumulated Depreciation (Asset Increase)...........   5,000
          Truck (Asset Decrease)   5,000

8.32 continued.

c. Retained Earnings (Depreciation Expense)
(Shareholders' Equity Decrease)............................ 60
    Accumulated Depreciation (Asset De-
        crease)... 60
$1,200 x .10 x 6/12 = $60.

Accumulated Depreciation (Asset Increase)........... 270
    Retained Earnings (Theft Loss) (Shareholders'
        Equity Increase).. 270
$1,200 x .10 x 27/12 = $270.

8.33   (Effects of transactions on statement of cash flows.)

a. The journal entry to record this transaction is as follows:

Cash (Asset Increase)... 3,000
Accumulated Depreciation (Asset Increase)........... 6,000
Retained Earnings (Loss on Sale of Machine)
    (Shareholders' Equity Decrease)........................... 1,000
    Machine (Asset Decrease) 10,000

This transaction does not provide an operating source of cash, so Lines
(1) and (2) do not change. The debit to the Cash account means that
Line (11) increases by $3,000. Sales of plant assets are investing
transactions, so Line (6) increases by $3,000. The loss on the sale
reduces net income, so Line (3) decreases by $1,000. Because we show
the full cash proceeds of $3,000 on Line (6), we must offset the effect of
the $1,000 reduction on Line (3). Thus, Line (4) increases by $1,000.
The net effect of the entries on Lines (3) and (4) is zero.

b. The journal entry to record this transaction is as follows:

Cash (Asset Increase)... 5,000
Accumulated Depreciation (Asset Increase).......... 6,000
    Machine (Asset Decrease)................................... 10,000
    Retained Earnings (Gain on Sale of Machine)
        (Shareholders' Equity Increase)....................... 1,000

This transaction does not provide an operating source of cash, so Lines
(1) and (2) do not change. The debit to the Cash account means that
Line (11) increases by $5,000. Sales of plant assets are investing
transactions, so Line (6) increases by $5,000. The gain on the sale
increases net income, so Line (3) increases by $1,000. Because we
show the full cash proceeds of $5,000 on Line (6), we must offset the
effect of the $1,000 increase on Line (3). Thus, Line (5) increases by
$1,000. The net effect of the entries on Lines (3) and (5) is zero.

8.33 continued.

    c.   The journal entry to record this transaction is as follows:

Machine (New) (Asset Increase)	8,000	
Accumulated Depreciation (Old) (Asset In-		
crease)	6,000	
Machine (Old) (Asset Decrease)		10,000
Cash (Asset Decrease)		4,000

Acquisitions of machinery are investing, not operating, activities, so Lines (1) and (2) do not change. The credit to the Cash account reduces Line (11) by $4,000. Acquisitions of plant assets are investing transactions, so Line (7) increases by $4,000. Because this entry does not involve an income statement account, there is no effect on the Operating section of the statement of cash flows.

    d.   The journal entry to record this transaction is as follows:

Retained Earnings (Loss from Fire) (Shareholders'		
Equity Decrease)	50,000	
Accumulated Depreciation (Asset Increase)	40,000	
Warehouse (Asset Decrease)		90,000

Because this entry does not involve an entry to the Cash account, there is no effect on Lines (1), (2), or (11). The loss from the fire reduces net income, so Line (3) decreases by $50,000. We must offset this loss if the net effect on Line (11) is to be zero. Thus, Line (4) increases by $50,000 for the loss that does not use cash.

    e.   The journal entry to record this transaction is as follows:

Retained Earnings (Loss from Fire) (Shareholders'		
Equity Decrease)	60,000	
Inventory (Asset Decrease)		60,000

This entry does not involve a debit or credit to the Cash account so Lines (1), (2), and (11) are not affected. The loss from the fire reduces net income, so Line (3) decreases by $60,000. We must offset this loss if the net effect on Line (11) is to be zero. Thus, Line (4) increases by $60,000 for the decrease in inventories.

8.34   (May Department Stores; improvements versus repairs or maintenance.)

    a.   **January 2**

Building (or Entrances) (Asset Increase)	28,000	
Cash (Asset Decrease)		28,000
To record cost of new entrances.		

8.34 a. continued.

> **December 31**
> Retained Earnings (Depreciation Expense)
>   (Shareholders' Equity Decrease)............................ 24,000
>   Accumulated Depreciation on Building
>   (Asset Decrease)..   24,000
> $24,000 = 1/7 \times [(\$800,000 - \$660,000 +$
> $\$28,000)] = 1/40 \times \$800,000 + 1/7 \times \$28,000.$

b. **January 2**
   Retained Earnings (Loss from Flood) (Share-
        holders' Equity Decrease)..................................... 28,000
             Building (or Accumulated Depreciation on
                  Building) (Asset Decrease)............................   28,000
   Recognize loss from destruction.

   Building (or Accumulated Depreciation on
        Building) (Asset Increase)..................................... 28,000
             Cash (Asset Decrease)......................................   28,000
   To recognize cost of new entrance facilities.

   These two entries are equivalent to, and could be replaced by:

   Retained Earnings (Loss from Flood) (Share-
        holders' Equity Decrease)..................................... 28,000
             Cash (Asset Decrease)......................................   28,000

   December 31
   Retained Earnings (Depreciation Expense)
        (Shareholders' Equity Decrease)......................... 20,000
             Accumulated Depreciation (Asset De-
                  crease)...   20,000
   Depreciation for year on remaining $140,000
   over 7 years = $800,000/40 years.

c. Same as *b.* above.

d. Opinions differ on this one. Some favor the treatment in Part *a.* (capitalize and amortize), while others favor the treatment in Part *b.* or Part *c.* (immediate loss). Those favoring Part *a.* point to the voluntary nature of the decision to replace the entrances rather than to close down. Presumably, society as a whole benefits from use of handicapped-accessible entrances or else regulations would not require them. If future benefits to society as a whole result and the firm decides to make the expenditure, an asset results, which the firm will depreciate over its estimated service life. It would be improper, some say, to charge the entire cost of making future operations possible to

8.34 d. continued.

this year. They cite the enormous expenditures for antipollution equipment as being similar.

Those favoring the treatment in Part *b.* argue that regulators require this expenditure to maintain the service potential of the building assets at the same level as before passage of the law. They see no essential difference between the economic effects of destruction by natural disaster (Part *b.*), human disaster (Part *c.*), and another form of human "disaster" (Part *d.*). It may seem antisocial to say that the passage of a law results in damage no different from vandalism, but the economic consequences to the owner of the business are the same in Parts *c.* and *d.*, and so they urge immediate expensing. They agree that the enormous expenditures for antipollution equipment are also a loss (at least to the degree that costs exceed firm-specific benefits) even though most firms do not expense such items.

The holders of the opposing (capitalize) view see a significant difference between natural (or human) disasters and democratic social decisions, which they view as not being " human disasters."

    e.   If you believe that Part *d.* is like Part *a.*, then so is Part *e.* like Part *a.* If you believe that Part *d.* is like Parts *b.* and *c.*, then the loss here should be only \$21,000 (= \$28,000 − \$7,000). Depreciation expense for each of the last seven years is \$21,000 [= (\$140,000 + \$7,000)/7 years].

8.35   (Capitalizing versus expensing; if capitalized, what amortization period?)

    a.   If the firm makes this expenditure to secure future benefits, then there is an argument for capitalizing it. The entries would be:

Building (or Fire Escapes) (Asset Increase)............	28,000	
Cash (Asset Decrease)...		28,000
To capitalize improvements.		

Retained Earnings (Depreciation Expense)		
(Shareholders' Equity Decrease)..........................	4,000	
Accumulated Depreciation (Asset De-		
crease)		4,000
One year's amortization of improvements based		
on a seven-year life.		

A somewhat more logical view is that the firm made the expenditure to maintain the service potential that it had planned previously. It obtains no additional benefits beyond those planned. See the discussion in Part *d.* of Problem 8.34 above. The expenditure is a result of new legislation, so this view results in the following entry at the time the law is passed:

8.35 a. continued.

Retained Earnings (Loss from New Legislation)
    (Shareholders' Equity Decrease).......................... 28,000
      Building (or Accumulated Depreciation)
        (Asset Decrease)... 28,000
To recognize loss.

When the expenditure is made, the entry is:

Building (or Fire Escapes) (Asset Increase)............ 28,000
    Cash (Asset Decrease)....................................... 28,000
To capitalize expenditure for fire escapes.

This second treatment results in immediate recognition of the loss, and subsequent depreciation of the building improvements and fire escapes is the same as before the law was passed.

b. Building (Asset Increase)..1,050,000
    Investment in General Electric Stock (Asset
      Decrease).. 100,000
    Retained Earnings (Gain on Disposal of Invest-
      ment) (Shareholders' Equity Increase)............. 950,000

In the case of widely traded stock, the stock market valuation is probably a better guide than is the appraisal value of a single building.

c. Building (Asset Increase)..1,000,000
    Investment in Small Timers Stock (Asset
      Decrease).. 100,000
    Retained Earnings (Gain on Disposal of Invest-
      ment) (Shareholders' Equity Increase)............. 900,000

For thinly traded issues, the appraisal value of the building may be a more reliable guide. Many people think that investors cannot sell large blocks of such stock at once, except at a discount from the quoted price per share. We would not argue with the same answer as Part *b.* above.

d. Garages (Asset Increase)... 18,000
    Cash (Asset Decrease)....................................... 18,000
To capitalize improvements to garages.

Retained Earnings (Depreciation Expense)
    (Shareholders' Equity Decrease).......................... 900
      Accumulated Depreciation (Asset De-
        crease)... 900
$18,000/20 years = $900 per year.

8.35 d. continued.

The useful life of the improvements in this case is likely to be as long as the useful lives of the garages. A case can be made, however, for amortization over five or ten years.

e. Retained Earnings (Advertising Expense)
   (Shareholders' Equity Decrease)........................... 400,000
       Cash (Asset Decrease) 400,000

Firms generally immediately expense expenditures on advertising. Theoretically, the firm should capitalize some portion of the expenditures as an asset because the company probably would not spend on advertising unless it expected future benefits. However, firms seldom follow the more theoretically sound procedure in practice due to the difficulty of identifying and measuring the future benefits.

f. Retained Earnings (Research Expense) (Share-
   holders' Equity Decrease) 1,500,000
       Cash (Asset Decrease) 1,500,000

This is the treatment required by FASB *Statement No. 2*, although we criticize it. The company has a proven record of success with its research and it would not continue the research expenditures unless it expected future benefits. Capitalization of these benefits on the balance sheet and subsequent amortization is at least a theoretically superior treatment.

g. Retained Earnings (Charitable Contribution–
   Expense) (Shareholders' Equity Decrease).......... 250,000
       Cash (Asset Decrease) 250,000

Although some indirect future benefit may come to the company, it is too indefinite to justify recognition of an asset. We wonder, though, if companies give away money without some expectation of future benefit.

h. Machine Tools (Asset Increase)................................6,000,000
       Cash (Asset Decrease).. 6,000,000
   To set up asset account.

   Work-in-Process Inventory (Asset Increase)..........2,000,000
       Accumulated Depreciation (Asset Decrease)...... 2,000,000
   Depreciate over 3 years, the life of the automobile
   model.

The tools will be obsolete in three years; their physical life of six years is irrelevant. For some reason, automobile manufacturers do not show accumulated depreciation on special tools in published statements; credits appear to go directly to the asset account.

8.35 continued.

    i.   (Dollar Amounts in Millions)

Start of Year

Plant Assets (Airplanes) (Asset Increase)..............	100	
Cash (Asset Decrease)...		100

To record purchase of airplanes.

Plant Assets (Spare Parts) (Asset Increase)..........	20	
Cash (Asset Decrease)...		20

To record spare parts as plant assets, not as inventory. This is the point of the question. Because the spare parts are giving up their future benefits as the firm uses the airplanes, we treat their cost as plant assets. At the end of the useful life of the airplanes, the spare parts will be worthless. We think they should be depreciated over the life of the airplanes, not accounted for like an inventory of parts which the firm can use in various alternative ways. Nothing in the chapter alerts the student to this treatment and many, if not most, will set up the asset as inventory.

(Dollar Amounts in Millions)

End of Year

Retained Earnings (Depreciation Expense) (Shareholders' Equity Decrease)............................	12	
Accumulated Depreciation (Asset Decrease)		12

Depreciation on plant assets for 1/10 of useful life costing $120 (= $100 + $20) in total. This treatment is consistent with that described in the preceding entry.

Whether or not the instructor or students agree with us, the point is worth discussing. Is the cost of spare parts acquired solely for use with a plant asset and therefore treated like plant assets or like inventory?

8.35 continued.

j. (Dollar Amounts in Millions)

End of Year
Retained Earnings (Depreciation Expense)
   (Shareholders' Equity Decrease)..........................   12
     Accumulated Depreciation (Asset De-
       crease)   12
The entry made for the same reason as in the
preceding question. We think the following entries,
which result from treating the spare parts as
inventory, are wrong:

Retained Earnings (Depreciation Expense)
   (Shareholders' Equity Decrease).........................   10
     Accumulated Depreciation (Asset De-
       crease)   10

Retained Earnings (Repair Expense) (Share-
   holders' Equity Decrease)   1
     Spare Parts Inventory (Asset Decrease)   1

8.36 (Epstein Company; accounting for intangibles.)

a. The issue here is whether the firm must amortize the trademark. Even though the registration terminates in three years, Epstein Company can re-register the trademark. Because the firm intends to continue making and selling the product, the trademark has an indefinite life and need not be amortized.

b. The same problem and reasoning above leads us to use a five-year life.

c. The amortization period here is theoretically indefinite, so FASB *Statement No. 142* does not require amortization.

d. In Year 2, we should debit expense and credit asset for the diminution in the value of the trade secret. This amount will be hard to estimate. The auditor may argue that the secret has lost all of its value and will require the write off of the remaining book value.

e. The firm should capitalize the film as an asset and write it off over its economic life. This is an easy statement to make, but the estimate of life might be as short as three years or as long as the firm sells thyristors, which appears to be the indefinite future. The firm will pick a number and be prepared to give in to the auditor who asks for a shorter life. Management will lack any sound arguments as to what the life should be. We would argue only with the immediate expensing of the film's cost.

8.36 continued.

Sheldon L. Epstein, former patent counsel of Brunswick Corporation, suggested this question to us. His reaction to the above answers is as follows:

a. The trademark registration is simple proof of ownership in the United States which the company could renew again and again for twenty-year periods. Because trademark rights will continue to exist as long as the company properly uses the mark, the amortization period is theoretically indefinite. FASB *Statement No. 142* requires no amortization. In the event that the company discontinues the use of the mark or loses the exclusive right to use the mark, the firm should write off the unamortized amount in the year in which the event occurs as an impairment loss. Where the company owns a foreign trademark, the right to exclusive use may be dependent on a valid registration, and loss or expiration of the registration could require complete write off in the year when such an event occurs. Note that trademarks receive a different accounting treatment from that given patents because trademarks can have an indefinite life while patents expire on a known date.

b. The design patent grants the company the right to exclude others from manufacturing, using or selling the same or similar containers for 5 years. After that, anyone is free to copy the design. Therefore, the privilege of exclusivity diminishes with time and the value should be amortized over the remaining life of the patent.

c. I agree with your answer.

d. I agree with your answer but with the caveat that its value depends on what the competitor does with its knowledge of the trade secret. If it does nothing, then there is little or no loss of value. If it uses it for the purpose of competition, then its value diminishes by the present value of anticipated lost profits and the accountant should recognize the value lost in the year the event occurs. If a competitor publishes the trade secret, then all of its value is lost.

e. The answer is generally correct; however, note that the accounting treatment for copyrights lies somewhere between that used for patents and that used for trademarks. Under the copyright law, it is possible for the copyright to extend for periods well beyond 40 years or for a substantially shorter period (as would be the case for an old work). The important point is to ask what the remaining life of the exclusive privilege is and, in the case of a work licensed by the company from an individual, when the right reverts to the author (35 years). For example, copyrights in new works last for the life of the author plus 50 years except for anonymous or pseudonymous works for which the period is the first of 75 years from publication or 100 years from crea-

8.36 e. continued.

tion. For older works, many expired on December 31, 2002; however, there are a number of exceptions.

8.37 (The Mead Corporation; interpreting disclosures regarding property, plant and equipment.) (Amounts in Millions)

a.

Property, Plant and Equipment (Asset Increase)..	315.6	
Cash (Asset Decrease)..		315.6

Retained Earnings (Depreciation Expense) (Shareholders' Equity Decrease)........................	188.1	
Accumulated Depreciation (Asset Decrease)...		188.1

Cash (Given) (Asset Increase).................................	38.7	
Retained Earnings (Loss on Sale of Property, Plant and Equipment) (Shareholders' Equity Decrease) (Plug)...	19.9	
Accumulated Depreciation ($1,803.7 + $188.1 − x = $1,849.3; x = $142.5) (Asset Increase)............	142.5	
Property, Plant and Equipment ($3,824.0 + $315.6 − y = $3,938.5; y = $201.1) (Asset Decrease)...		201.1

b. $.5(\$3,824.0 + \$3,938.5)/\$188.1 = 20.6$ years.

c. $.5(\$1,803.7 + \$1,849.3)/\$188.1 = 9.7$ years.

d. $\$4,557.5/.5(\$2,020.3 + \$2,089.2) = 2.2$.

e. $\$4,557.5/.5(\$1,013.8^a + \$1,108.0^b) = 4.3$.

[a]$3,824.0 − $2,810.2 = $1,013.8.
[b]$3,938.5 − $2,830.5 = $1,108.0.

8.38 (PepsiCo; interpreting disclosures regarding property, plant and equipment.) (Amounts in Millions)

a.

Property, Plant and Equipment (Asset Increase)..	2,253.2	
Cash (Asset Decrease)..		2,253.2

Retained Earnings (Depreciation Expense) (Shareholders' Equity Decrease)........................	1,200.0	
Accumulated Depreciation (Asset Decrease)...		1,200.0

8.38 a. continued.

Cash (Asset Increase)	55.3	
Accumulated Depreciation ($5,394.4 + $1,200.0		
$\quad$ − x = $6,247.3; x = $347.1) (Asset Increase)	347.1	
$\quad$ Property, Plant and Equipment ($14,250.0 +		
$\qquad$ $2,253.2 − y = $16,130.1; y = 373.1)		
$\qquad$ (Asset Decrease)		373.1
$\quad$ Retained Earnings (Gain on Sale of Property,		
$\qquad$ Plant and Equipment) (Shareholders'		
$\qquad$ Equity Increase) (Plug)		29.3

b. .5($14,250.0 + $16,130.1)/$1,200.0 = 12.7 years.

c. .5($5,394.4 + $6,247.3)/$1,200.0 = 4.9 years.

d. $28,472.4/.5($8,855.6 + $9,882.8) = 3.0.

e. $28,472.4/.5($7,231.2[a] + $8,393.4[b]) = 3.6.

[a]$14,250.0 − $7,018.8 = $7,231.2.
[b]$16,130.1 − $7,736.7 = $8,393.4.

8.39 (American Airlines; effect on net income of changes in estimates for depreciable assets.)

Income has been about $180 million (= .06 × $3 billion) per year.

Reconciliation of Plant Data:

Airplanes Cost	$ 2,500,000,000
$\quad$ Less Salvage Value (10%)....................................	250,000,000
$\quad$ Depreciable Basis	$ 2,250,000,000
Divided by 10-Year Life Equals Yearly Depreciation	
$\quad$ Charges..	$ 225,000,000
Times 4 Years Equals Accumulated Depreciation..............	$ 900,000,000
Plus Net Book Value..	1,600,000,000
Airplanes Cost	$ 2,500,000,000

New Depreciation Charge:

Net Book Value...	$ 1,600,000,000
$\quad$ Less Salvage Value (12% of Cost).............................	300,000,000
$\quad$ Depreciation Basis..	$ 1,300,000,000
Divided by 10 (= 14 − 4) Years Equals Revised Yearly	
$\quad$ Depreciation Charge...	$ 130,000,000

8.39 continued.

Increase in Pretax Income:

Old Depreciation Charges		$ 225,000,000
New Depreciation Charges		130,000,000
		$ 95,000,000
Multiplied by (1 − tax rate) = 1 − .35 = .65		X .65
Increase in Aftertax Income		$ 61,750,000

Income will rise by about 34.3 percent (= $61.75/$180.0).

Note that a modest change in depreciation parameters can significantly affect net income. The analyst will want to study the basis for any changes in such parameters.

8.40   (Moon Macrosystems; recording transactions involving tangible and intangible assets.)

a.   Office Equipment (Asset Increase) 400,000
      Computer Software (Asset Increase) 40,000
         Cash (Asset Decrease) 440,000

b.   Office Equipment (Asset Increase) 20,000
      Computer Software (Asset Increase) 10,000
         Cash (Asset Decrease) 30,000

c.   **Year 6 and Year 7**
      Retained Earnings (Depreciation Expense)
      [($400,000 + $20,000 − $40,000)/10] (Share-
      holders' Equity Decrease) 38,000
      Retained Earnings (Amortization Expense)
      [($40,000 + $10,000)/4] (Shareholders' Equity
      Decrease) 12,500
         Accumulated Depreciation (Asset De-
         crease) 38,000
         Computer Software (Asset Decrease) 12,500

d.   Retained Earnings (Impairment Loss of Compu-
      ter Software) ($40,000 + $10,000 − $12,500 −
      $12,500) (Shareholders' Equity Decrease) 25,000
         Computer Software (Asset Decrease) 25,000

e.   Retained Earnings (Depreciation Expense)
      [($400,000 + $20,000 − $38,000 − $38,000 −
      $56,000)/12] (Shareholders' Equity Decrease) 24,000
         Accumulated Depreciation (Asset De-
         crease) 24,000

f.   Retained Earnings (Depreciation Expense)
      (Shareholders' Equity Decrease) 24,000
         Accumulated Depreciation (Asset De-
         crease) 24,000

8.40 f. continued.

Cash (Asset Increase)	260,000	
Accumulated Depreciation ($38,000 + $38,000 + $24,000 + $24,000) (Asset Increase)	124,000	
Retained Earnings (Loss on Sale of Office Equipment) (Shareholders' Equity Decrease)	36,000	
Office Equipment (Asset Decrease)		420,000

8.41   (Recognizing and measuring impairment losses.)

a.   The loss occurs because of an adverse action by a governmental entity. The undiscounted cash flows of $50 million are less than the book value of the building of $60 million. An impairment loss has therefore occurred. The market value of the building of $32 million is less than the book value of $60 million. Thus, the amount of the impairment loss is $28 million (= $60 million – $32 million). The journal entry to record the impairment loss is (in millions):

Retained Earnings (Loss from Impairment) (Shareholders' Equity Decrease)	28	
Accumulated Depreciation (Asset Increase)	20	
Building (Asset Decrease)		48

This entry records the impairment loss, eliminates the accumulated depreciation, and writes down the building to its market value of $32 million (= $80 – $48).

b.   The undiscounted cash flows of $70 exceed the book value of the building of $60 million. Thus, no impairment loss occurs according to the definition in FASB *Statement No. 144*. An *economic* loss occurred but GAAP do not permit it to be recognized.

c.   The loss arises because the accumulated costs significantly exceed the amount originally anticipated. The book value of the building of $25 million exceeds the undiscounted future cash flows of $22 million. Thus, an impairment loss has occurred. The impairment loss recognized equals $9 million (= $25 million – $16 million). The journal entry is (in millions):

Retained Earnings (Loss from Impairment) (Shareholders' Equity Decrease)	9	
Construction in Process (Asset Decrease)		9

d.   The loss occurs because of a significant decline in the market value of the patent. FASB *Statement No. 142* requires calculation of the impairment loss on the patent before computing the value loss on goodwill. The undiscounted future cash flows of $18 million are less than the book value of the patent of $20 million. Thus, an impairment

8.41 d. continued.

loss occurred. The amount of the loss is $8 million (= $20 million − $12 million). The journal entry to record the loss is:

Retained Earnings (Loss from Impairment)
(Shareholders' Equity Decrease)............................   8
    Patent (Asset Decrease)   8

The second step is to determine if an impairment loss on the goodwill occurred. The market value of the entity is $25 million. The book value after writing down the patent is $27 million (= $12 million for patent and $15 million for goodwill). Thus, a goodwill impairment loss occurred. If the market value of the patent is $12 million, the market value of the goodwill is $13 million. The impairment loss on goodwill is therefore $2 million (= $15 million − $13 million). The journal entry is:

Retained Earnings (Loss from Impairment)
(Shareholders' Equity Decrease)............................   2
    Goodwill (Asset Decrease)..................................   2

e. The loss occurs because of a significant change in the business climate for Chicken Franchisees. One might question whether this loss is temporary or permanent. Evidence from previous similar events (for example, Tylenol) suggests that consumers soon forget or at least forgive the offending company. The FASB reporting standard discusses but rejects the use of a permanency criterion in identifying impairment losses. Thus, an impairment loss occurs in this case because the future undiscounted cash flows of $6 million from the franchise rights are less than the book value of the franchise rights of $10 million. The amount of the impairment loss is $7 million (= $10 million − $3 million). The journal entry is (in millions):

Retained Earnings (Impairment Loss) (Share-
holders' Equity Decrease)   7
    Franchise Rights (Asset Decrease)...................   7

This entry assumes that Chicken Franchisees does not use an Accumulated Amortization account.

8.42 (Pfizer; expensing versus capitalizing research and development costs.) (Amounts in Millions)

a. **Expense Costs as Incurred**

	Year 1	Year 2	Year 3	Year 4
Other Income	$ 30	$ 30	$ 30	$ 30
Additional Income from R&D:				
First Year's R&D	36	36	36	
Second Year's R&D		36	36	36
Third Year's R&D			36	36
Fourth Year's R&D				36
R&D Expense	(90)	(90)	(90)	(90)
Income (Loss) before Taxes	$ (24)	$ 12	$ 48	$ 48

b. **Capitalize and Amortize Over 3 Years (Including Year of Occurrence)**

	Year 1	Year 2	Year 3	Year 4
Other Income	$ 30	$ 30	$ 30	$ 30
Additional Income from R&D:				
First Year's R&D	36	36	36	
Second Year's R&D		36	36	36
Third Year's R&D			36	36
Fourth Year's R&D				36
R&D Amortization Expense:				
First Year's R&D	(30)	(30)	(30)	
Second Year's R&D		(30)	(30)	(30)
Third Year's R&D			(30)	(30)
Fourth Year's R&D				(30)
Income before Taxes	$ 36	$ 42	$ 48	$ 48
Deferred R&D Asset on Balance Sheet:				
First Year's R&D	$ 60	$ 30		
Second Year's R&D		60	$ 30	
Third Year's R&D			60	$ 30
Fourth Year's R&D				60
Total	$ 60	$ 90	$ 90	$ 90

c. The expensing policy leads to higher expenses and lower income before income taxes, in the first two years. After that, the two policies are the same. When the firm ceases to spend on R&D, the policy of expensing will show higher income in the two years when the benefits of prior R&D continue, but there are no matching expenses. There are no expenses under Policy (1), but Policy (2) continues to show amortization expense. Thus, Policy (1) is more conservative in the sense that it results in smaller cumulative income before taxes until the firm ceases to spend on R&D. Policy (1) also results in smaller assets on the balance sheet because, unlike Policy (2), it shows no asset for Deferred R&D Costs.

d. The pre-tax income under the two policies will continue to be the same if there is no growth or change in policy. Policy (2) will show a lower rate of return on total assets and a lower rate of return on stockholders' equity than will Policy (1) because the asset and equity totals are larger under Policy (2) than under Policy (1).

8.43 (Ross Laboratories; valuation of brand name.) (Dollar amounts in millions.)

	Part a.	Part b.
(1) Operating Margin	$ 600.0	$ 600.0
Employed Physical Capital $500.0		
Subtract Pretax Profit on Physical Capital Required at 10 (Part *a.*) or 20 (Part *b.*)	(50.0)	(100.0)
(2) Profit Generated by Brand	$ 550.0	$ 500.0
Subtract Income Taxes at 40 Percent	(220.0)	(200.0)
(3) Net Brand Profits	$ 330.0	$ 300.0
Multiply by Aftertax Capitalization Factor	17.0	8.0
(4) Estimate of Brand Value	$5,610.0	$2,400.0

8.44   (WorldCom; ethical issues in capitalization versus expense policy.)

a.   To justify capitalization of any cost, a firm must demonstrate that the cost provides future benefits and is not simply a charge for services already received. WorldCom might have argued that the costs helped it establish a telecommunications network that would permit it to gain market share in the future. If these charges were in the nature of a front-end fee for multi-year access to the telecommunication lines of other carriers, then capitalizing these costs and subsequently amortizing them makes sense. In this case, however, the access fees related directly to access each period (the fixed fee part) and to usage (the variable fee part).

b.   The access fee was for services received each period for which WorldCom, in turn, recognized revenue from customers. Proper matching of access fees with revenues requires the immediate expensing of these costs.

c.   WorldCom might have argued that it was using the flexibility within GAAP for capitalization versus expensing and, therefore, did not confront ethical concerns. The case for treating these access fees as an asset is so weak, some would say nonexistent, that the management of WorldCom had to have known that its action was contrary to GAAP. The action was likely done to mislead financial statement users in the hope that it would not be discovered. Disclosures of such costs in the financial statements and notes are generally not sufficient for a user to detect management's actions. Thus, management likely knew that someone inside the firm would have to reveal the action, which is what happened.

CHAPTER 9

LIABILITIES: INTRODUCTION

Questions, Short Exercises, Exercises, Problems, and Cases: Answers and Solutions

9.1   See the text or the glossary at the end of the book.

9.2   a. Yes; amount of accrued interest payable.

       b. Yes. In spite of the indefiniteness of the time of delivery of the goods or services and the amount, the balance sheet reports a liability in the amount of the cash received.

       c. No; accounting does not record executory promises.

       d. Yes; at the present value, calculated using the yield rate at the time of issue, of the remaining coupon and principal payments.

       e. Yes; at the expected, undiscounted value of future service costs arising from all sales made prior to the balance sheet date. The income statement includes warranty expense because of a desire to match all expenses of a sale with the sale; presumably one reason the firm sold the product was the promise of free repairs. When recognizing the expense, the accountant credits a liability account to recognize the need for the future expenditures.

       f. No. If the firm expected to lose a reasonably estimable amount in the suit, then it would show an estimated liability.

       g. Yes, assuming statutes or contracts require the restoration. The present value of an estimate of the costs is the theoretically correct answer, but many accountants would use the full amount undiscounted.

       h. No; viewed as executory.

       i. Airlines recognize an expense and a liability for the estimated costs of providing the free flight during the periods when customers use flight services at regular fares. The airlines accrue either the incremental cost of the free flight, which is a relatively small amount, or a portion of the average cost of a flight. The incremental cost is small because customers use otherwise unused capacity.

9.3   The expected value of the liability is $90,000 in both cases (.90 x $100,000 = $90,000; .09 x $1 x 1,000,000 = $90,000). Accounting would probably report the liability from the lawsuit as $100,000 and the liability for the coupons as $90,000. This inconsistency seems curious since the two situations differ only with respect to the number of possible outcomes (that is, all or nothing with respect to the lawsuit, whereas the coupon redemption rate conceivably ranges from one to one million).

9.4   Suppliers often grant a discount if customers pay within a certain number of days after the invoice date, in which case this source of funds has an explicit interest cost. Suppliers who do not offer discounts for prompt payment often include an implicit interest change in the selling price of the product. Customers in this second category should delay payment as long as possible because they are paying for the use of the funds. Firms should not delay payment to such an extent that it hurts their credit rating and raises their cost of financing.

9.5   The Parker School should accrue the salary in ten monthly installments of $360,000 each at the end of each month, September through June. It will have paid $300,000 at the end of each of these months, so that by the end of the reporting year, it reports a current liability of $600,000 [= $3,600,000 − (10 x $300,000)].

9.6   There are two principal explanations. First, the obligation to customers in the event the firm does not publish the magazines is $45,000. Second, recognition of a liability of $32,000 requires a remaining credit of $13,000 to some other account. Recognizing the $13,000 as income is inappropriate because the publisher has not yet rendered the required services. Including the $13,000 is some type of Deferred Income account (a liability) has the same effect on total liabilities as reporting the Advance from Customers at $45,000.

9.7   It is cheaper (and, therefore, more profitable) to repair a few sets than to have such stringent quality control that the manufacturing process produces zero defectives. An allowance is justified when firms expect to have warranty costs. Manufacturers of TV sets for use on space ships or heart pacemakers should strive for zero defects.

9.8   **Similarities:** The accountant makes estimates of future events in both cases. The accountant charges the cost of estimated uncollectibles or warranties to income in the period of sale, not in the later period when specific items become uncollectible or break down. The income statement reports the charge against income as an expense in both cases, although some accountants report the charge for estimated uncollectibles as a revenue contra (and we prefer it that way).

Differences: The balance sheet account showing the expected costs of future uncollectibles reduces an asset account, while that for estimated warranties appears as a liability.

9.9 The coupon rate and par value of the bonds, the market rate of interest, and the market's opinion of the firm as a borrower. If the coupon rate is 8 percent, the market rate is 12 percent and the market views the firm as a relatively poor credit risk, the bonds will sell at a price to yield say, 15 percent. This means that the firm will receive less than the par value of the bonds it issues. We are told that when bonds are brought to the market, the investment banker attempts to set the coupon rate so the bonds will sell close to par.

9.10 a. Par value and face value are always synonymous.

b. Par value appears on the bond certificate and serves as the base for computing the periodic coupon interest payment. The book value is the same as the par value whenever the market-required interest rate on the date of issue equals the coupon interest rate. The book value will exceed the par value when the coupon rate exceeds the market rate at the time of issue. The par value will exceed the book value when the market rate exceeds the coupon rate at the time of issue.

c. Book value equals the present value of future cash flows on a bond discounted at the market-required interest rate at the time of issue. Current market value equals the present value of future cash flows on a bond discounted at the interest rate the market currently requires to induce purchase of the bond. The book value exceeds the current market value when the market interest rate at the time of issue was lower than the current market interest rate. The current market value will exceed the book value when the current market interest rate is lower than the market interest rate at the time of issue.

9.11 Generally, accountants initially record assets at acquisition cost and then allocate this amount to future periods as an expense. Changes in the market value of most assets (except for use of the lower-of-cost-or-market method for inventories; the market value method for marketable securities and investments in securities; and impairments) do not appear in the accounting records. Similarly, using the market interest rate at the time of issue to account for bonds results in an initial liability equal to the amount of cash received and a subsequent liability that reflects amortization of this initial amount. Changes in the market value of bonds do not appear in the accounting records.

9.12 With bond financing, the firm borrows the entire principal, $1 million, for the entire term of the loan. With lease or mortgage financing, the firm repays part of the principal with each payment. Thus, the effective amount borrowed decreases over time and interest expenses should also decrease, even though the borrowings use the same rate.

9.13   Zero coupon bonds offer no cash payments to the investor until maturity. The issuer benefits by delaying cash payments. The issuer also gets a tax deduction for interest expense (that is, amortization of bond discount) during the period the bonds are outstanding even though it has no immediate cash outflow for interest. The investor locks in a yield at the time of purchase. The investor need not worry about having to invest periodic coupon payments during the life of the bonds. Thus, the investor avoids the risk of interest rate changes. The disadvantage to the investor is that the amortization of bond discount during the life of the bonds is taxable income even though the investor receives no cash. Most investors in zero coupon bonds do not pay taxes (for example, pension funds).

9.14   The call premium, which typically declines as bonds approach maturity, compensates bondholders for the loss of interest payments when a firm calls, or buys back, some of its outstanding bonds before the maturity date. The call premium protects the bondholder from redemption by the issuer if interest rates in the market decline by reasonably small amounts.

9.15   When market interest rates change, so do market values of bonds. When interest rates rise, bond prices decline, but book values of bonds remain unchanged. Firms can issue new bonds at current market rates and use the proceeds to retire outstanding bonds previously issued when rates were lower, and accountants record this transaction as a gain. The gain actually occurred as market rates rose and the burden of the debt fell. This is an unrealized holding gain in historical cost accounting. Because management can time bond retirements, management can time income recognition. This possibility explains in part the former requirement, no longer part of GAAP, that firms report gains and losses on bond retirements as extraordinary items in the income statement.

9.16   (Recognition of a loss contingency.)

The store should recognize the loss as soon as it is probable that it has incurred a liability and it can reasonably estimate the amount of the loss. Whether the store recognizes a loss at the time of the injury on July 5, Year 6, depends on the strength of the case the store feels it has against the customer's claims. If the floor was wet because a broken bottle had remained on the floor for several hours and was not cleaned up, then the store may feel it is probable that it has incurred a liability. If, on the other hand, the customer fell while running down a dry, uncluttered aisle while trying to shop quickly, then the store may feel that it is probable that it has not incurred a liability. Attorneys, not accountants, must make these probability assessments.

If the store does not recognize a loss at the time of the injury, the next most likely time is June 15, Year 7, when the jury renders its verdict. Unless attorneys for the store feel that it is highly probable that the court will reverse the verdict on appeal, the store should recognize the loss at this time.

9.16 continued.

If attorneys feel that the grounds for appeal are strong, then the next most likely time is on April 20, Year 8, when the jury in the lower court reaches the same verdict as previously. This is the latest time in this case at which the store should recognize the loss. If the store had recognized a loss on June 15, Year 7, it would recognize only the extra damage award in Year 8.

9.17   (McGee Associates; journal entries for payroll.)

a.   Retained Earnings (Wage and Salary Expense)
        (Shareholders' Equity Decrease)........................... 700,000
            Withholding and FICA Taxes Payable (Lia-
                bility Increase).. 210,000
            Wages and Salaries Payable (Liability
                Increase)... 490,000
        Amounts payable to and for employees.

    Retained Earnings (Wage and Salary Expense)
        (Shareholders' Equity Decrease)........................... 114,800
            Taxes Payable (Liability Increase)................. 70,000
            Payable to Profit Sharing Fund (Liability
                Increase)... 28,000
            Vacation Liability (Liability Increase)............ 16,800
        Employer's additional wage expense; estimated
        vacation liability is $16,800 (= 1.20 x $14,000).

b. $814,800 = $700,000 + $114,800.

9.18   (Allowance method for uncollectibles and warranties.)

$19,000. The aging analyses tell us the required ending balances in the balance sheet accounts. We plug for the expense required to achieve those balance sheet amounts. The percentage of sales method approximates the final number, but must yield to the analysis of the actual expected uncollectibles embedded in the current receivables and of the actual expected warranty costs embedded in the current obligations for warranties.

9.19   (Blaydon Company; amortization schedule for note where explicit interest differs from market rate of interest.)

a. **Amortization Schedule for a Three-Year Note with a Maturity Value of $40,000, Calling for 8-Percent Annual Interest Payments, Yield of 12 Percent per Year**

Year (1)	Book Value Start of Year (2)	Interest Expense for Period (3)[a]	Payment (4)	Interest Added to (Subtracted from) Book Value (5)	Book Value End of Year (6)
0					$ 36,157
1	$ 36,157	$ 4,339	$ 3,200	$ 1,139	37,296
2	37,296	4,476	3,200	1,276	38,572
3	38,572	4,628	43,200	(38,572)	-0-

[a](3) = (2) X .12, except in Year 3 where it is a plug.

b. Computer (Asset Increase) 36,157
      Note Payable (Liability Increase).......................... 36,157
    To record purchase.

Annual Journal Entry for Interest and Principal

Retained Earnings
    (Interest Expense)
    (Shareholders'
    Equity Decrease)........   Amount in Col. (3)
      Cash (Asset De-
          crease) ....   Amount in Col. (4)
      Note Payable (Lia-
          bility Increase)...   Amount in Col. (5)*

*In third year, the firm debits Note Payable for $38,572.

9.20   (Computing the issue price of bonds.)

a. $10,000,000 X .09722[a]... $ 972,200

[a]Present value of $1 for 40 periods at 6%.

b. $500,000 X 23.11477[a]... $ 11,557,385

[a]Present value of annuity for 40 periods at 3%.

9.21   (Florida Edison Company; using bond tables; computing interest expense.)

a. $885,301; see Table 5, 10-year row, 12-percent column.

b. $53,118 = .06 X $885,301.

c. $53,305 = .06 X $888,419; see Table 5, 9.5-year row, 12-percent column.

d. $926,399; see Table 5, 5-year row, 12-percent column.

e. $55,584 = .06 X $926,399.

9.22   (Womack Company; amortization schedule for bonds.)

a. $100,000 X .67556[a] .... $ 67,556

$5,000 X 8.11090[b]   40,555

Issue Price... $ 108,111[c]

[a]Table 2, 4-percent column and 10-period row.
[b]Table 4, 4-percent column and 10-period row.
[c]Also, see Table 5.

b.

Six-Month Period	Liability at Start of Period	Interest at 4 Percent for Period	Coupon at 5% of Par	Decrease in Book Value of Liability	Liability at End of Period
0					$ 108,111
1	$ 108,111	$ 4,324	$ 5,000	$ 676	107,435
2	107,435	4,297	5,000	703	106,732
3	106,732	4,269	5,000	731	106,001
4	106,001	4,240	5,000	760	105,241
5	105,241	4,210	5,000	790	104,451
6	104,451	4,178	5,000	822	103,629
7	103,629	4,145	5,000	855	102,774
8	102,774	4,111	5,000	889	101,885
9	101,885	4,075	5,000	925	100,960
10	100,960	4,040[a]	5,000	960	100,000
Total		$ 41,889	$ 50,000	$ 8,111	

[a]Does not equal .04 X $100,960 due to rounding.

9.22 continued.

  c. Book Value of Bonds: $10,363.

Bonds Payable (Liability Decrease)......................	10,363	
Retained Earnings (Gain on Bond Retirement)		
(Shareholders' Equity Increase)......................		63
Cash (Asset Decrease)...		10,300

9.23 (Hurley Corporation; accounting for uncollectible accounts and warranties.)

  a. **Allowance for Uncollectible Accounts**

Balance, December 31, Year 8...	$	355
Plus Bad Debt Expense for Year 9: .02 x $18,000..............		360
Less Accounts Written Off (Plug).......................................		(310)
Balance, December 31, Year 9...	$	405
Plus Bad Debt Expense for Year 10: .02 x $16,000............		320
Less Accounts Written Off (Plug).......................................		(480)
Balance, December 31, Year 10...	$	245

  b. **Estimated Warranty Liability**

Balance, December 31, Year 8...	$	1,325
Plus Warranty Expense for Year 9: .06 x $18,000..............		1,080
Less Actual Warranty Costs (Plug).....................................		(870)
Balance, December 31, Year 9...	$	1,535
Plus Warranty Expense for Year 10: .06 x $16,000...........		960
Less Actual Warranty Costs (Plug).....................................		(775)
Balance, December 31, Year 10...	$	1,720

9.24 (Morrison's Cafeteria; journal entries for coupons.)

  a. **January**

Cash (Asset Increase)..	50,100	
Retained Earnings (Sales Revenue) (Share-holders' Equity Increase)		48,000
Coupon Liability (Liability Increase)....................		2,100
Coupon Liability (Liability Decrease)......................	1,600	
Retained Earnings (Sales Revenue) (Share-holders' Equity Increase).................................		1,600

      February

Cash (Asset Increase)..	50,700	
Retained Earnings (Sales Revenue) (Share-holders' Equity Increase)		48,500
Coupon Liability (Liability Increase)....................		2,200

9.24 continued.

Coupon Liability (Liability Decrease)	2,300	
Retained Earnings (Sales Revenue) (Share- holders' Equity Increase)		2,300

March

Cash (Asset Increase)..	52,400	
Retained Earnings (Sales Revenue) (Share- holders' Equity Increase)		50,000
Coupon Liability (Liability Increase)...................		2,400

Coupon Liability (Liability Decrease)	2,100	
Retained Earnings (Sales Revenue) (Share- holders' Equity Increase)		2,100

b. The Coupon Liability account has a balance of $4,700 (= $4,000 + $2,100 – $1,600 + $2,200 – $2,300 + $2,400 – $2,100) on March 31.

9.25   (Abson Corporation; journal entries for service contracts.)

a. **1/31–3/31**

Cash (Asset Increase)..	180,000	
Service Contract Fees Received in Advance (Liability Increase)..		180,000
To record sale of 300 annual contracts.		

3/31

Service Contract Fees Received in Advance (Liability Decrease)..	22,500	
Retained Earnings (Contract Revenues) (Shareholders' Equity Increase)		22,500
To recognize revenue on 300 contracts sold during the first quarter; 1.5/12 x $180,000.		

1/01–3/31

Retained Earnings (Service Expenses) (Share- holders' Equity Decrease)....................................	32,000	
Cash [and Other Assets (Asset Decrease) and Liabilities (Liability Increase)]..............		32,000

4/01–6/30

Cash (Asset Increase)..	300,000	
Service Contract Fees Received in Advance (Liability Increase)..		300,000
To record sale of 500 annual contracts.		

9.25 a. continued.

6/30

Service Contract Fees Received in Advance
(Liability Decrease)... 82,500
    Retained Earnings (Contract Revenues)
    (Shareholders' Equity Increase) 82,500
To recognize revenue on 500 contracts sold and
300 contracts outstanding:
  First Quarter:
    3/12 x $180,000 = $45,000
  Second Quarter:
    1.5/12 x $300,000 =   37,500
                      $82,500

4/01–6/30

Retained Earnings (Service Expenses) (Share-
holders' Equity Decrease)...................................... 71,000
    Cash [and Other Assets (Asset Decrease)
    and Liabilities Liability Increase)] 71,000

7/01–9/30

Cash (Asset Increase)... 240,000
    Service Contract Fees Received in Advance
    (Liability Increase)...................................... 240,000
To record sale of 400 annual contracts.

9/30

Service Contract Fees Received in Advance
(Liability Decrease)... 150,000
    Retained Earnings (Contract Revenues)
    (Shareholders' Equity Increase) 150,000
To recognize revenue on 400 contracts sold and
800 contracts outstanding from prior sales.
  First Quarter Sales:
    3/12 x $180,000 = $ 45,000
  Second Quarter Sales:
    3/12 x $300,000 =   75,000
  Third Quarter Sales:
    1.5/12 x $240,000 =   30,000
                 = $150,000

7/01–9/30

Retained Earnings (Service Expenses) (Share-
holders' Equity Decrease)...................................... 105,000
    Cash [and Other Assets (Asset Decrease)
    and Liabilities (Liability Increase)].............. 105,000

9.25 continued.

   b. Balances in Service Contract Fees Received in Advance Account:

   January 1..   --
   Less First Quarter Expirations.. $ (22,500)
   Plus First Quarter Sales...   180,000
   March 31... $ 157,500
   Less Second Quarter Expirations...   (82,500)
   Plus Second Quarter Sales...   300,000
   June 30.. $ 375,000
   Less Third Quarter Expirations ....   (150,000)
   Plus Third Quarter Sales   240,000
   September 30.. $ 465,000
   Less Fourth Quarter Expirations ....   (195,000)
   Plus Fourth Quarter Sales   120,000
   December 31 .... $ 390,000

OR

Contracts	x	Balance Remaining	x	$600	=	Amount
300	x	1.5/12	x	$600	= $	22,500
500	x	4.5/12	x	$600	=	112,500
400	x	7.5/12	x	$600	=	150,000
200	x	10.5/12	x	$600	=	105,000
						$ 390,000

9.26   (Maypool Corporation; journal entries for estimated warranty liabilities and subsequent expenditures.)

   a. **Year 1**
   Accounts Receivable (Asset Increase).................... 1,200,000
       Retained Earnings (Sales) (Shareholders'
       Equity Increase)..   1,200,000

   Estimated Warranty Liability (Liability De-
       crease)...   12,000
       Cash (Asset Decrease)....................................   12,000
   Expenditures actually made.

   Retained Earnings (Warranty Expense) (Share-
       holders' Equity Decrease)...................................   48,000
       Estimated Warranty Liability (Liability
       Increase)..   48,000
   .04 x $1,200,000.

9.26 a. continued.

Year 2

Accounts Receivable (Asset Increase)..................... 1,500,000
    Retained Earnings (Sales Revenue) (Share-
        holders' Equity Increase)   1,500,000

Estimated Warranty Liability (Liability De-
    crease)...   50,000
        Cash (Asset Decrease)....................................   50,000
Expenditures actually made.

Retained Earnings (Warranty Expense) (Share-
    holders' Equity Decrease).....................................   60,000
        Estimated Warranty Liability (Liability
        Increase)...   60,000
.04 x $1,500,000.

b. $46,000 = $48,000 − $12,000 + $60,000 − $50,000.

9.27   (Global Motors Corporation; journal entries for estimated warranty liabilities and subsequent expenditures.)

a. **Year 1**

Cash (Asset Increase)...   800,000
    Retained Earnings (Sales Revenue) (Share-
        holders' Equity Increase)   800,000

Estimated Warranty Liability (Liability De-
    crease)...   22,000
        Cash (Asset Decrease)....................................   13,200
        Parts Inventory (Asset Decrease)...................   8,800

Retained Earnings (Warranty Expense) (Share-
    holders' Equity Decrease).....................................   48,000
        Estimated Warranty Liability (Liability
        Increase)...   48,000
.06 x $800,000 = $48,000.

Year 2

Cash (Asset Increase)... 1,200,000
    Retained Earnings (Sales Revenue) (Share-
        holders' Equity Increase)   1,200,000

Estimated Warranty Liability (Liability De-
    crease)   55,000
        Cash (Asset Decrease)....................................   33,000
        Parts Inventory (Asset Decrease)...................   22,000

9.27 a. continued.

Retained Earnings (Warranty Expense) (Share-holders' Equity Decrease)..	72,000
Estimated Warranty Liability (Liability Increase)...	72,000

.06 x $1,200,000 = $72,000.

Year 3

Cash (Asset Increase)..	900,000
Retained Earnings (Sales Revenue) (Share-holders' Equity Increase)	900,000

Estimated Warranty Liability (Liability De-crease)..	52,000
Cash (Asset Decrease)..	31,200
Parts Inventory (Asset Decrease).....................	20,800

Retained Earnings (Warranty Expense) (Share-holders' Equity Decrease)..	54,000
Estimated Warranty Liability (Liability Increase)...	54,000

.06 x $900,000 = $54,000.

b. $48,000 − $22,000 + $72,000 − $55,000 + $54,000 − $52,000 = $45,000.

9.28 (Sung Company; journal entry for short-term note payable.)

a. **12/01**

Cash (Asset Increase)..	50,000
Notes Payable (Liability Increase).......................	50,000

12/31

Retained Earnings (Interest Expense) (Share-holders' Equity Decrease)..	250
Interest Payable (Liability Increase)..............	250

$50,000 x .06 x 30/360 = $250.

1/30

Retained Earnings (Interest Expense) (Share-holders' Equity Decrease)..	250
Interest Payable (Liability Increase)..............	250

9.28 a. continued.

1/30

Notes Payable (Liability Decrease) (Original Note)...	50,000	
Interest Payable (Liability Decrease)......................	500	
Notes Payable (Liability Increase) (New Note)..		50,000
Cash (Asset Decrease)......................................		500

> *Note:* Omitting the entries to the Notes Payable account above is also acceptable.

3/2

Notes Payable (Liability Decrease)..........................	50,000	
Retained Earnings (Interest Expense) (Shareholders' Equity Decrease)....................................	250	
Cash (Asset Decrease)......................................		50,250

b. The entry to complete the accrual of interest (30 days) is the first entry under both alternatives. It is:

Retained Earnings (Interest Expense) (Shareholders' Equity Decrease)	250	
Interest Payable (Liability Increase)......		250

(1) **1/30**

Notes Payable (Liability Decrease) (Original Note)...	50,000	
Interest Payable (Liability Decrease).............	500	
Cash (Asset Decrease)...........................		50,500

(2) **1/30**

Notes Payable (Liability Decrease) (Original Note)...	50,000	
Interest Payable (Liability Decrease).............	500	
Notes Payable (Liability Increase) (New Note)..		50,500

9.29 (Computing the issue price of bonds.)

a. $1,000,000 x .09722[a].. $ 97,220

[a]Present value of $1 for 40 periods at 6%.

b. $50,000 x 23.11477[a].. $ 1,155,739

[a]Present value of annuity for 40 periods at 3%.

9.29 continued.

   c. $50,000 x 19.79277[a] .... $ 989,639
       $1,000,000 x .20829[b]   208,290
                                                                                  $ 1,197,929

[a]Present value of annuity for 40 periods at 4%.
[b]Present value of $1 for 40 periods at 4%.

   d. $30,000 x 12.46221[a] .... $ 373,866
       $70,000 x 12.46221[a] x .37689[b]   328,782
       $1,000,000 x .14205[c]   142,050
                                                                                $ 844,698

[a]Present value of annuity for 20 periods at 5%.
[b]Present value of $1 for 20 periods at 5%.
[c]Present value of $1 for 40 periods at 5%.

9.30   (Huergo Dooley Corporation; accounting for bonds.)

   a. $2,000,000 x .61391[a] .... $ 1,227,820
       $80,000 x 7.72173[b]   617,738
                                                                                $ 1,845,558

[a]Present value of $1 for 10 periods at 5%.
[b]Present value of an annuity for 10 periods at 5%.

   b. Retained Earnings (Interest Expense) (.05 x
       $1,845,558) (Shareholders' Equity Decrease)   92,278
          Cash (.04 x $2,000,000) (Asset Decrease)   80,000
          Bonds Payable (Liability Increase) (Plug).......   12,278

   c. Retained Earnings (Interest Expense) [.05 x
       ($1,845,558 + $12,278)] (Shareholders' Equity
       Decrease)...   92,892
          Cash (.04 x $2,000,000) (Asset Decrease)   80,000
          Bonds Payable (Liability Increase) (Plug).......   12,892

9.30 continued.

d. Bonds Payable [.20 x ($1,845,558 + $12,278 +
$12,892)] (Liability Decrease) 374,146
    Retained Earnings (Loss on Repurchase of Bonds)
    (Shareholders' Equity Decrease) 53,933
        Cash (Asset Decrease)...................................... 428,079

$2,000,000 x .78941[a].. $ 1,578,820
$80,000 x 7.01969[b].. 561,575
                                                                            $ 2,140,395
    Total.. X .20
Purchase Price.. $ 428,079

[a]Present value of $1 for 8 periods at 3%.
[b]Present value of an annuity for 8 periods at 3%.

9.31   (O'Brien Corporation; computing the issue price of bonds and interest
        expense.)

a. $8,000,000 x .30656[a] .... $ 2,452,480
   $320,000 x 23.11477[b]... 7,396,726
       Issue Price.. $ 9,849,206

[a]Table 2, 3-percent column and 40-period row.
[b]Table 4, 3-percent column and 40-period row.

b. .03 x $9,849,206 = $295,476.

c. .03($9,849,206 + $295,476 – $320,000) = $294,740.

d. Book Value: ($9,849,206 + $295,476 – $320,000 +
   $294,740 – $320,000)... $ 9,799,422

e. $8,000,000 x .32523[a]... $ 2,601,840
   $320,000 x 22.49246[b] 7,197,587
       Present Value... $ 9,799,427

[a]Table 2, 3-percent column and 38-period row.
[b]Table 4 3-percent column and 38-period row.

The difference between the book value in Part *d.* and the present value
in Part *e.* results from rounding present value factors.

9.32 (Robinson Company; computing the issue price of bonds and interest expense.)

a.
$5,000,000 X .37689[a]	$ 1,884,450
$200,000 X 12.46221[b]	2,492,442
Issue Price	$ 4,376,892

[a]Table 2, 5-percent column and 20-period row.
[b]Table 4, 5-percent column and 20-period row.

b. .05 X $4,376,892 = $218,845.

c. .05($4,376,892 + $218,845 − $200,000) = $219,787.

d. $4,376,892 + $218,845 − $200,000 + $219,787 − $200,000 = $4,415,524.

e.
$5,000,000 X .41552[a]	$ 2,077,600
$200,000 X 11.68959[b]	2,337,918
Present Value	$ 4,415,518

[a]Table 2, 5-percent column and 18-period row.
[b]Table 4, 5-percent column and 18-period row.

The difference between the book value in Part *d.* and the present value in Part *e.* results from rounding present value factors.

9.33 (Centrix Company; using bond tables.)

Refer to Table 6.

a. $1,084,658; 25-year row; 11-percent column.

b. $1,080,231; 20-year row; 11-percent column.

c. $1,072,669; 15-year row; 11-percent column.

d. $1,072,669; same answer is *not* coincidental.

e. ($1,000,000 X .06) − ($1,004,739 − $1,000,000) = $60,000 − $4,739 = $55,261; 0.5-year row; 11-percent column.

f. $934,707; 15-year row; 13-percent column.

g. 10 percent compounded semiannually; scan 10-year row to find 112.46.

9.34   (Mendoza Corporation; journal entries for bond coupon payments and retirements.)

a. **7/1/Year 7**
    Retained Earnings (Interest Expense) (.05 X
        $1,124,622) (Shareholders' Equity Decrease)....   56,231
            Bonds Payable (Liability Decrease) (Plug)......   3,769
            Cash (.06 X $1,000,000) (Asset Decrease).....   60,000

    12/31/Year 7
    Retained Earnings (Interest Expense[a]) (Share-
        holders' Equity Decrease)...................................   56,043
    Bonds Payable (Liability Decrease) (Plug)..............   3,957
            Cash (Asset Decrease) (as above)...................   60,000

    [a].05 X ($1,124,622 − $3,769) = $56,043.

b. Bonds Payable ($1,116,896/2) (Liability De-
        crease)   558,448
            Retained Earnings (Gain on Retirement)
                (Shareholders' Equity Increase) (Plug)........   108,743
            Cash[a] (Asset Decrease)   449,705

    [a]$500,000 X .899409 = $449,705 (value in a 14 percent market).

c. It would appear as a gain on the income statement.

9.35   (Seward Corporation; amortization schedule for bonds.)

a. $100,000 X .74622[a] .... $ 74,622
    $4,000 X 5.07569[b]...   20,303
        Issue Price... $ 94,925

    [a]Table 2, 5-percent column and 6-period row.
    [b]Table 4, 5-percent column and 6-period row.

9.35 continued.

b.

Six-Month Period	Liability at Start of Period	Interest at 5 Percent for Period	Coupon at 4% of Par	Increase in Book Value of Liability	Liability at End of Period
0					$ 94,925
1	$ 94,925	$ 4,746	$ 4,000	$ 746	95,671
2	95,671	4,784	4,000	784	96,455
3	96,455	4,823	4,000	823	97,278
4	97,278	4,864	4,000	864	98,142
5	98,142	4,907	4,000	907	99,049
6	99,049	4,951	4,000	951	100,000
Total		$ 29,075	$ 24,000	$ 5,075	

c. **January 2, Year 1**

Cash (Asset Decrease)..	94,925	
Bonds Payable (Liability Increase)		94,925

June 30, Year 1

Retained Earnings (Interest Expense) (Shareholders' Equity Decrease)	4,746	
Interest Payable (Liability Increase).............		4,000
Bonds Payable (Liability Increase)................		746

July 1, Year 1

Interest Payable (Liability Decrease).....................	4,000	
Cash (Asset Decrease)..		4,000

December 31, Year 1

Retained Earnings (Interest Expense) (Shareholders' Equity Decrease)	4,784	
Interest Payable (Liability Increase).............		4,000
Bonds Payable (Liability Increase)		784

d.

Bonds Payable (.20 x $98,142) (Liability Decrease)	19,628	
Retained Earnings (Loss on Retirement of Bonds) (Shareholders' Equity Decrease).........................	772	
Cash (Asset Decrease)....................................		20,400

9.36 (Brooks Corporation; journal entries to account for bonds.)

a.

$100,000 x .55368[a]	$	55,368
$4,000 x 14.87747[b]		59,510
Issue Price...	$	114,878

[a]Table 2, 3-percent column and 20-period row.
[b]Table 4, 3-percent column and 20-period row.

9.36 continued.

    b. **January 2, Year 2**

Cash (Asset Increase)...	114,878	
Bonds Payable (Liability Increase)......................		114,878

        June 30, Year 2

Retained Earnings (Interest Expense) (.03 x		
$114,878) (Shareholders' Equity Decrease)........	3,446	
Bonds Payable (Liability Decrease)	554	
Cash (Asset Decrease).......................................		4,000

        December 31, Year 2

Retained Earnings (Interest Expense) [.03 x		
($114,878 – $554)] (Shareholders' Equity		
Decrease)..	3,430	
Bonds Payable (Liability Decrease)	570	
Cash (Asset Decrease).......................................		4,000

    c. Book Value: $114,878 – $554 – $570 = $113,754.

       Market Value:

$100,000 x .41552[a]..	$ 41,552
$4,000 x 11.68959[b]...	46,758
Total Market Value...	$ 88,310

[a]Table 2, 5-percent column and 18-period row.

[b]Table 4, 5-percent column and 18-period row.

Bonds Payable (Liability Decrease).........................	113,754	
Cash (Asset Decrease)...		88,310
Retained Earnings (Gain on Bond Retirement)		
(Shareholders' Equity Increase)........................		25,444

9.37   (Central Appliance; allowance method for warranties; reconstructing transactions.)

    a. $720,000 = $820,000 (Goods Available for Sale) – $100,000 (Beginning Inventory).

    b. $700,000 = $820,000 (Goods Available for Sale) – $120,000 (Ending Inventory).

    c. $21,000 = $6,000 (Cr. Balance) + $15,000 (Dr. Balance).

    d. $20,000 = $5,000 (Required Cr. Balance) + $15,000 (Existing Dr. Balance).

9.37 continued.

 e. Estimated Liability for Warranty Repairs (Liability Decrease).. 21,000

   Various Assets Used for Repairs (Asset Decrease)...   21,000

  Repairs made during Year 2.

  Retained Earnings (Warranty Expense) (Shareholders' Equity Decrease).................................... 20,000

   Estimated Liability for Warranty Repairs (Liability Increase).....................................   20,000

  Expense recognition for Year 2.

  Retained Earnings (Cost of Goods Sold) (Shareholders' Equity Decrease).................................... 700,000

   Merchandise Inventory (Asset Decrease).....   700,000

  Cost of goods sold is goods available for sale less ending inventory.

9.38 (Time Warner, Inc.; accounting for zero-coupon debt; see *The Wall Street Journal* for December 8, 1992.)

 a. $483 million = $1,550 million/3.20714; see table 1, 6-percent column, 20-period row.

 b. 5.8 percent = ($1,550/$500)$^{1/20}$ − 1 = 3.10$^{1/20}$ − 1. That is, for each dollar of the initial issue proceeds (of the $500 million), Time Warner must pay $3.10 (= $1,550/$500) at maturity of the notes. You can find the periodic interest rate to make $1.00 grow to $3.10 in 20 periods by trial and error or by using the exponential function on your computer or calculator. Note that you can state an equation to solve, as follows:

$$(1 + r)^{20} = 3.10; \text{ solve for } r.$$

You can see from Table 1 that 5.8 percent is approximately correct.

 c. $28 million = .07 × $400 million.

 d. $101.4 million. Ask, first, what must the book value of the notes be at the end of Year 19. Then, compute interest for the year on that amount. The book value of the loan at the end of Year 19 must be $1,448.6 (= $1,550/1.07) million. Interest for one year at 7 percent on $1,448.6 million is $101.4 (= .07 × $1,448.6 = $1,550.0 − $1,448.6) million. You can check this approach to finding the answer by noting that:

$$\$1,448.6 \times 1.07 = \$1,550.0.$$

9.39   (Aggarwal Corporation; accounting for long-term bonds.)

a. **Interest Expense**
First Six Months: .05 x $301,512 = $15,076.
Second Six Months: .05($301,512 + $15,076) = $15,829.
Book value of bonds on December 31, Year 4: $301,512 + $15,076 + $15,829 = $332,417.

b. **Book Value of Bonds on December 31, Year 3**
Interest:
$35,000 x 8.11090 = $ 283,882   (Table 4, 10 periods and 4%)
Principal:
$1,000,000 x .67556 = ___675,560   (Table 2, 10 periods and 4%)
    Total............................ $ 959,442

Book Value of Bonds, December 31, Year 3.............................	$ 959,442
Add Interest Expense for Year 4..	x
Subtract Coupon Payments during Year 4..............................	(70,000)
Book Value of Bonds, December 31, Year 4...........................	$ 966,336

Interest expense for Year 4 is $76,894.

c. **Book Value of Bonds on July 1, Year 4**

Book Value of Bonds, December 31, Year 3.........................	$ 1,305,832
Plus Interest Expense for First Six Months of Year 4: .03 x $1,305,832..	39,175
Subtract Coupon Payment during First Six Months of Year 4...	(45,000)
Book Value of Bonds, July 1, Year 4....................................	$ 1,300,007
Book Value of One-Half of Bonds...	$ 650,004

Bonds Payable (Liability Decrease)........................	650,004	
Cash (Asset Decrease)..		526,720
Retained Earnings (Gain on Bonds Retirement)		
(Shareholders' Equity Increase)........................		123,284

d. **Interest Expense for Second Six Months**
.03 x $650,004 = $19,500.

9.40   (Wal-Mart Stores; accounting for long-term bonds.)

a.	.06 x $83,758,595...	$ 5,025,516
	.06($83,758,595 + $5,025,516 − $4,500,000)....................	5,057,047
		$ 10,082,563

9.40 continued.

b.

	Interest Expense..	$ 10,082,563
	Interest Payable..	9,000,000
	Increase in Bonds Payable...	$ 1,082,563
	Book Value, January 31, Year 11.................................	83,758,595
	Book Value, January 31, Year 12.................................	$ 84,841,158

c. Present Value = Maturity Value x Present Value Factors.
$162,395,233 = Maturity Value x (4 percent, 11 periods).
$175,646,684 = Maturity Value x (4 percent, 9 periods).
Maturity Value = $250,000,000.

d. The book value equals the par value, so the initial market yield is the stated interest yield of 9.25 percent compounded semiannually.

9.41 (IBM Credit Corporation; comparison of straight-line and effective interest methods of amortizing debt discount.)

a. $58,173,000. See Table 2, 14-period column, 7-percent row, where the factor is .38782.

.38782 x $150,000,000 = $58,173,000.

b. $4,072,110 = $58,173,000 x .07.

c. $6,559,071 = ($150,000,000 − $58,173,000)/14.

$2,623,628 = .40 x $6,559,071.

d. $87,754,890 = $150,000,000 − $58,173,000 − $4,072,110
= $150,000,000 − (1.07 x $58,173,000).

e. Issuers like not having to pay the cash for coupons during the life of the issue, but this fact is reflected in the original issue price of the bonds, so it is hard to justify this as being an economic advantage.
Some purchasers like zero coupon bonds, because there is no need to consider uncertainty about future interest rates and the reinvesting of interest coupons. If one wants a fixed sum some years in the future, then zero coupon notes may be a more useful instrument than coupon bonds. Investment advisors understand this advantage. Another advantage to the purchaser, but one not so well understood by the press, accountants, and even some investment bankers, is the extra call protection in a zero coupon note. Because the issuer can call the bonds at par value (and no other cash interest payments will occur over the entire life of the bond), it will never pay the issuer to call them unless interest rates drop to zero. Thus, the lender has more protection than in a callable coupon-bearing bond against interest rate declines. Of course, such protection has a price, and the lack of an "option" fea-

9.41 e. continued.

ture to the issuer may account for much of the apparently lower cost of borrowing via zero coupon notes.

As to the loophole, the Treasury might take offense that the tax rules, generally cash-based, allow the current deduction and current tax savings for an item whose cash flows occur seven years in the future. Note from the preceding part that the only cash effect of the interest and related tax transactions is IBMCC's saving $2,623,628 in income tax payments it would otherwise have made.

The Wall Street Journal story indicated, however, that the Treasury had in mind as a "loophole" the $2,486,961 difference between the $6,559,071 interest deduction resulting from using the straight-line method and the $4,072,110 interest computed "correctly" with the effective interest method. Using the straight-line method resulted in cash savings in taxes of $994,784 (= .40 X $2,486,961) as compared to the effective interest method.

The Tax Equity and Fiscal Reform Act (TEFRA) of 1982 did indeed change the tax law so that issues must amortize original-issue discount for tax purposes using the effective interest method, not the straight-line method.

However, the Treasury position overlooks the symmetry in the tax treatment of zero coupon bonds to the issuer and the holder. While the issuer is entitled to deduct interest on a straight-line basis, the holder is taxable on a straight-line basis. The Treasury might respond to such arguments by noting that the issuer is generally a taxable entity, while the holder of zero-coupon notes is often tax-exempt (a pension fund, for example).

If we choose to interpret the words "interest expense" in a precise mathematical fashion, the mathematics of compound interest seems to favor the effective interest method, as does Accounting Principles Board *Opinion No. 21*. The straight-line method is easier to compute, but the availability of low cost computing largely obviates this advantage. An alternative point of view, of course, is that the words "interest expense" mean whatever Congress and the courts define them to mean, insofar as taxes are concerned.

A more important economic issue is the symmetry of the tax laws. If both lender and borrower are taxed at the same rate, the total proceeds to the Treasury are the same under either method, so long as the lender and borrower are treated symmetrically. Of course, the *incidence* of the tax will be affected, holding all other things constant (i.e., in a partial equilibrium analysis). Switching to the effective interest method for both parties would shift taxes from the lender to the borrower. In a general equilibrium analysis, however, the subsequent readjustment of bond prices is much harder to compute. If, on the other hand, many of the lenders are tax exempt, revenues to the Treasury would be increased by the effective interest method, because it raises the present value of the borrower's tax liability. But again, the ultimate equilibrium that would be obtained after such a change is not readily apparent, at least to us.

9.42   (Quaker Oats Company; ethical issues of managing income and the debt-equity ratio through bond retirement.)

a. $25,200,000 = .63 x $40,000,000 of cash must be raised to retire old issue.

	Dollars in Thousands	
Cash (Asset Increase)......................................	25,200	
Bonds Payable—9 Percent (Liability Increase)...		25,200
Issue of new bonds.		
Bonds Payable—5 Percent (Liability Decrease)...	40,000	
Cash (Asset Decrease)...........................		25,200
Retained Earnings (Gain on Bond Retirement) (Shareholders' Equity Increase)......................		14,800
Retained Earnings (Income Tax Expense) (Shareholders' Equity Decrease)....................................	5,920	
Cash (Asset Decrease)...........................		5,920
.40 x $14,800.		

b.   Income increases by $8,880,000 [= (1 − .40) x $14,800,000], or by about 110 percent (= $8,880/$8,000) to about $17 million. Retained Earnings increases by $8,880,000.

c.   Debt-equity ratio ($ in 000):

$$\frac{\$5,000 + \$25,200}{\$5,000 + \$25,200 + \$35,000 + \$8,880} = \frac{\$30,200}{\$74,080} = 40.8\%.$$

d.   Gains on refinancing transactions, such as this one, do, indeed, appear in income with no special labeling. The transactions are acceptable under GAAP, even though such refinancings serve little purpose except to manage income. Without the refinancing, the firm would enjoy the boost to income each year from having interest expense a bit lower than it would be if based on market rates closer to current rates. The transactions are permissible, but management ought to be clear in disclosing to readers how much of the income of the year results from these refinancings. The rules for disclosure will require management to make some disclosure, but the disclosures need not be clear. We think the disclosure rules are inadequate.

9.43   (FNB/OOPS; accounting for bonds in a troubled-debt restructuring.)

a.   Present value of newly-promised cash flows at 20 percent, compounded semiannually = $2,563,903.

9.43 a. continued.

        Present value of 50 semiannual payments of $1 discounted at 10 percent per period = 9.91481; see Table 4, 50-period row, 10-percent column.
9.91481 x $250,000.. $2,478,703

        Present value of $1 paid 50 periods hence, discounted at 10 percent per period = .00852; see Table 2, 50-period row, 10-percent column.
.00852 x $10,000,000.. <u>   85,200</u>
                                                   <u>$2,563,903</u>

b.   Present value of newly-promised cash flows at 12 percent, compounded semiannually = $4,483,365.

        Present value of 50 semiannual payments of $1 discounted at 6 percent per period = 15.76186; see Table 4, 50-period row, 6-percent column.
15.76186 x $250,000.. $3,940,465

        Present value of $1 paid 50 periods hence, discounted at 6 percent per period = .05429; see Table 2, 50-period row, 6-percent column.
.05429 x $10,000,000.. <u> 542,900</u>
                                                   <u>$4,483,365</u>

c.   FNB would recognize a loss of $7,436,097 (= $10,000,000 – $2,563,903) under the first method. This would be followed by interest revenue of $12,500,000 (= 50 x $250,000) from cash receipts plus interest revenue from amortization of debt discount of $7,436,097. Total income under the first method would be equal to the following:
$–7,436,097 for write down in 2005 plus $12,500,000 for cash receipts plus $7,436,097 for interest revenue from amortization; total income equal to $12,500,000.
    Under the second method, FNB would recognize a loss of $5,516,635 (= $10,000,000 – $4,483,365). This would be followed by interest revenue of $12,500,000 (= 50 x $250,000) from cash receipts plus interest revenue from amortization of discount of $5,516,635. Total income under the second method would be $12,500,000 which equals $–5,516,635 + $12,500,000 + $5,516,635.
    Under the third method, income over the next twenty-five years would be $12,500,000 (= 50 x $250,000) for cash receipts.
    Over long enough time spans, accounting income is equal to cash receipts. But note that the timing of income recognition varies drastically as a function of the treatment chosen.

d.   We prefer the first method, because we think the troubled-debt restructuring results from an arm's length transaction. FASB *Statement No. 114*, however, requires the use of the second method.

9.44   (Discounting warranty obligations.)

a. **Year 1**
    Retained Earnings (Warranty Expense) (Share-
         holders' Equity Decrease).. 2,000,000
            Estimated Warranty Liability (Liability
                 Increase)..   2,000,000

    Year 2
    Estimated Warranty Liability (Liability De-
         crease)... 500,000
            Cash and Other Accounts (Asset De-
                 crease)...   500,000

    Year 3
    Estimated Warranty Liability (Liability De-
         crease)... 600,000
            Cash and Other Accounts (Asset De-
                 crease)...   600,000

    Year 4
    Estimated Warranty Liability (Liability De-
         crease)... 900,000
            Cash and Other Accounts (Asset De-
                 crease)...   900,000

b. The present value of the future cost amounts on December 31, Year 1,
    discounted at 10 percent, is $1,626,594, computed as follows:

    Year 2: $500,000 x .90909.. $ 454,545
    Year 3: $600,000 x .82645..   495,870
    Year 4: $900,000 x .75131..   676,179
                 Total .... $ 1,626,594

    Year 1
    Retained Earnings (Warranty Expense) (Share-
         holders' Equity Decrease).....................................1,626,594
            Estimated Warranty Liability (Liability
                 Increase)..   1,626,594

    Year 2
    Retained Earnings (Interest Expense) (Share-
         holders' Equity Decrease)..................................... 162,659
            Estimated Warranty Liability (Liability
                 Increase)..   162,659
    .10 x $1,626,594 = $162,659.

9.44 b. continued.

Year 2

Estimated Warranty Liability (Liability Decrease)...	500,000	
Cash and Other Accounts (Asset Decrease)..		500,000

Year 3

Retained Earnings (Interest Expense) (Shareholders' Equity Decrease).......................................	128,925	
Estimated Warranty Liability (Liability Increase)..		128,925

.10($1,626,594 + $162,659 − $500,000) = $128,925.

Year 3

Estimated Warranty Liability (Liability Decrease)...	600,000	
Cash and Other Accounts (Asset Decrease)..		600,000

Year 4

Retained Earnings (Interest Expense) (Shareholders' Equity Decrease).......................................	81,818	
Estimated Warranty Liability (Liability Increase)..		81,818

.10($1,626,594 + $162,659 − $500,000 + $128,925 − $600,000) = .10 x $818,178 = $81,818.

Year 4

Estimated Warranty Liability (Liability Decrease)...	899,996	
Retained Earnings (Interest Expense) (Shareholders' Equity Decrease).......................................	4	
Cash and Other Accounts (Asset Decrease)..		900,000

There is a rounding error of $4 in the Estimated Warranty Liability account at the end of Year 4. Interest expense for Year 4, therefore, increases by $4.

c. The firm must first acquire for cash the goods and services provided under the warranty plan. Thus, even though customers will receive goods and services, the firm must expend cash at some point. To be consistent with monetary liabilities, accounting would discount these amounts to their present value.

9.45   (Effects on statement of cash flows.)

a.   The journal entry to record this transaction is:

Cash (Asset Increase) 100,000
    Bonds Payable (Liability Increase)   100,000

The debit to the Cash account results in an increase of $100,000 in Line (11). Issuing debt is a financing activity, so Line (8) increases by $100,000.

b.   The journal entry for this transaction is:

Building (Asset Increase) 100,000
    Bonds Payable (Liability Increase)   100,000

The transaction does not affect the Cash account, so Line (11) does not change. This transaction does not affect net income, so Line (3) does not change. This transaction does not appear in the statement of cash flows but in a note to the financial statements.

c.   The journal entry to record this transaction is:

Bonds Payable (Liability Decrease) 100,000
    Cash (Asset Decrease)   90,000
    Retained Earnings (Gain on Bond Retirement)
        (Shareholders' Equity Increase)   10,000

The Cash account decreases, so Line (11) decreases by $90,000. Retiring bonds is a financing activity, so Line (9) increases by $90,000. The gain increases net income, so Line (3) increases by $10,000. Because this gain does not provide an operating source of cash, Line (5) increases by $10,000 to offset the gain and result in a zero net effect on cash flow from operations.

9.45 continued.

    d.   The journal entry for this transaction is:

Bonds Payable (Liability Decrease) 100,000
Retained Earnings (Loss on Bond Retirement)
   (Shareholders' Equity Decrease) 5,000
      Cash (Asset Decrease).....................................   105,000

The Cash account decreases, so Line (11) decreases by $105,000. Calling bonds is a financing activity, so Line (9) increases by $105,000. The loss reduces net income, so Line (3) decreases by $5,000. Because this loss does not use an operating cash flow, Line (4) increases by $5,000 to offset the loss and result in a zero net effect on cash flow from operations.

    e.   The journal entry to record this transaction is:

Retained Earnings (Interest Expense) (= .06 x
   $90,000) (Shareholders' Equity Decrease).......... 5,400
      Cash (= .05 x $100,000) (Asset Decrease)   5,000
      Bonds Payable (Liability Increase)   400

The Cash account decreases by $5,000, so Line (11) decreases by $5,000. Line (2) shows a subtraction larger by $5,000. Net income decreases by $5,400 for interest expense, so Line (3) decreases by $5,400. Because the firm uses only $5,000 cash for this expense, Line (4) increases by $400 for the portion of the expense that does not use cash.

    f.   The journal entry to record this transaction is:

Retained Earnings (Interest Expense) (= .05 x
   $105,000) (Shareholders' Equity Decrease)........ 5,250
Bonds Payable Liability Decrease).......................... 750
      Cash (= .06 x $100,000) (Asset Decrease)   6,000

The Cash account decreases by $6,000, so Line (11) decreases by $6,000. The amount subtracted on Line (20 increases by $5,250. Net income decreases by $5,250, so Line (3) decreases by $5,250. Because the firm uses more cash than the amount of interest expense, Line (9) increases by $750 for debt retirement. The total effect on cash flow from operations is $5,250.

9.46   (Ethical Issues.)

This problem raises the same issues as does Problem 9.42, Part *d.* above. This version requires no calculations.

Gains on refinancing transactions, such as this one do, indeed, appear in income with no special labeling. The transactions are acceptable under GAAP, even though such refinancings serve little purpose except to manage income. Without the refinancing, the firm would enjoy the boost to income each year from having interest expense a bit lower than it would be if based on market rates closer to current rates. The transactions are permissible, but management ought to be clear in disclosing to readers how much of the income of the year results from these refinancings. The rules for disclosure will require management to make some disclosure, but the disclosures need not be clear.

CHAPTER 10

LIABILITIES: OFF-BALANCE-SHEET FINANCING, LEASES, DEFERRED INCOME TAXES, AND RETIREMENT BENEFITS

Questions, Short Exercises, Exercises, Problems, and Cases: Answers and Solutions

10.1 See the text or the glossary at the end of the book.

10.2 One premise underlying this statement is that the notes provide sufficient information to permit the analyst to make an informed judgment about the nature of the obligation or commitment and its associated risks. Current disclosures of off-balance-sheet commitments aggregate similar transactions, making an informed judgment about individual items difficult. Even if the disclosure permitted an informed judgment, the question arises as to whether information processing costs for analysts would decrease if firms actually recognized these items as liabilities. The counter argument to recognition of off-balance-sheet liabilities is that they differ in their risk characteristics relative to liabilities appearing on the books; thus disclosure in the notes is more appropriate than recognition in the balance sheet.

10.3 Using an executory contract to achieve off-balance-sheet financing results in the recognition of neither an asset (for example, leased assets) nor a liability (for example, lease liability) on the balance sheet. Using an asset sale with recourse results in a decrease in an asset (for example, accounts receivable) and an increase in cash. In both cases, no liability appears on the balance sheet.

10.4 The party with the risks and rewards of ownership effectively owns the asset, whatever the legal niceties. The asset should appear on the balance sheet of the owner. The capital lease criteria attempt to state unambiguously who has economic ownership.

10.5 The distinction depends upon which criteria of the lease made it a capital lease. The major difference is that at the end of a lease term the asset reverts to the lessor in a capital lease, whereas at the end of the installment payments, the asset belongs to the purchaser. The criteria for capitalizing a lease are such that the expected value of the asset when it reverts to the lessor is small, but misestimates can occur. In most other respects, capital leases and installment purchases are similar in economic substance.

10.6   The differences are minor. The lessee's asset is Leased Asset on the one hand and Actual Asset (Plant or Fixed Assets) on the other. The liability will have different titles. The effect on income and balance sheet totals is the same for both transactions.

10.7   Expenses are gone assets. The measure of expense over the life of a lease is the total outflow of cash to discharge the obligation. The accounting for leases, either operating or capital, does not change the total cash outflow, only the timing of the recognition of asset expirations.

10.8   Disagree. Operating Lease: Rent revenue for the lessor will equal rent expense for the lessee on an operating lease, but lessor also has depreciation expense on leased assets. Capital Lease: Interest revenue for the lessor should equal interest expense for the lessee on a capital lease. The lessor recognizes its cost to acquire or manufacture the leased asset as cost of goods sold under a capital lease. The lessor also recognizes revenue under a capital lease equal to the "selling price" of the lease asset on the date of signing the lease.

10.9   Deferred tax accounting matches against pre-tax book income each period the income taxes a firm has to pay currently plus (minus) the income taxes the firm expects to pay (save) in the future when revenues and expenses that appear in book income now appear in tax returns later.

10.10   This statement is incorrect. In order for deferred taxes to be a loan, there must be a receipt of cash or other goods or services at the inception of the loan and a disbursement of cash or other goods or services at the maturity date. The entries for a deferred tax liability are as follows:

When Timing Differences Originate:

Retained Earnings (Income Tax Expense) (Share-holders' Equity Decrease)...	X	
Deferred Tax Liability (Liability Increase)...........		X

When Timing Differences Reverse:

Deferred Tax Liability (Liability Decrease).....................	X	
Retained Earnings (Income Tax Expense) (Share-holders' Equity Decrease)		X

There are no cash or other asset flows involved and, therefore, no loan.

Another approach is to raise the question: How would cash flows have differed if a firm used the same methods of accounting for book as it used for tax? The response is that cash flows would have been the same even though deferred income taxes would have been eliminated. Thus, recognizing or not recognizing deferred taxes has no incremental effect on cash or other asset flows and, therefore, cannot represent a loan.

10.11   The Congress defines the manner in which firms calculate taxable income and income taxes payable. Corporations pay the income taxes each year that the income tax law legally requires them to pay. The amount shown for Deferred Tax Liability is not a liability. It may become a liability if the firm earns taxable income in the future. It represents the cumulative tax savings from using different methods of accounting for financial reporting and income tax purposes. The Congress and the FASB permit such differences in accounting methods because the objectives of income taxation and financial reporting differ. The income taxation system attempts to raise revenues in an equitable manner. Generally accepted accounting principles attempt to measure operating performance and financial position. If the Congress feels that it should not permit such differences, it should legislate either (1) that firms prepare their financial statements in conformance with the accounting methods used for tax purposes, or (2) that they compute taxable income in accordance with the accounting methods used for financial reporting purposes. Both approaches result in eliminating the Deferred Tax Liability account. Given the differences in objectives of the two reporting systems, it seems undesirable for Congress to take either of the actions indicated above. Congress should merely recognize that Deferred Tax Liability is not a liability but the result of accountants' attempts to obtain meaningful measures of operating performance over time.

10.12   Unlike Accounts Payable or Bonds, which "roll over" and new obligations replace them, the deferred tax liability does not arise from specific transactions. A firm computes taxes on operations as a whole, not on specific transactions. The analyst should attempt to ascertain when the firm is likely to pay the deferred taxes. Then the analyst should use the present value of those payments as the amount of the debt. If, as is likely, a stable or growing firm is never likely to pay the deferred taxes (for example, as with deferred taxes arising from depreciation charges for a growing firm), then the present value of the payments is zero, and the analyst should exclude the "liability" from the amount of debt. (This results in larger shareholders' equity.)

10.13   Deferred tax assets (liabilities) arise when a firm recognizes revenue (expense) earlier for tax purposes than book purposes or expenses (revenues) later for tax purposes than for book purposes. Deferred tax assets (liabilities) provide for lower (higher) taxable income in the future relative to book income and, therefore, future tax savings (costs).

10.14   The difference arises for two principal reasons: tax rate differences and permanent differences. The income tax rate on state, municipal and foreign income likely differs from the statutory U.S. tax rate. Also, firms recognize various revenues and expenses for book purposes that never appear (for example, interest on state and municipal bonds) or appear in smaller amounts (for example, dividends received from domestic subsidiaries) in taxable income.

10.15   The matching convention suggests that firms recognize as expenses each period all costs actually incurred currently or expected to be incurred in the future to generate the current period's revenues. Employees provide labor services each period in return for both current compensation (salary, health care benefits) and compensation deferred until retirement (pensions, health care benefits). The absence of deferred compensation arrangements would presumably lead employees to demand higher current compensation to permit them to fund their own retirement plans. Thus, firms must match current compensation and the present value of deferred compensation against the current period's revenues.

10.16   Laws require firms to contribute funds to an independent trustee to manage on behalf of employees. The employer cannot use these funds for its general corporate purposes. Firms must, however, report some underfunded pension obligations on the balance sheet as a liability.

10.17   One defines outputs (defined benefit) whereas the other defines inputs (defined contribution). Actuaries can design both to have the same expected costs with the same payment patterns by the company.

Immediate funding for defined-contribution plans transfers all accounting problems subsequent to funding to the plan trustee. The defined-benefit plan could similarly transfer obligations to the pension fund by immediate cash payments, but the company would ultimately be responsible for making up any shortages caused by deviations of earnings or mortality from expectations.

10.18   Pension fund assets appear when a firm funds its pension plan faster than it expenses it. Pension fund liabilities appear when a firm expenses its pension plan faster than it funds it.

10.19   (Cypres Appliance Store; using accounts receivable to achieve off-balance sheet financing.)

   a. (1) **January 2, Year 2**
      Cash (Asset Increase)..................................... 89,286
         Bank Loan Payable (Liability Increase).....   89,286
      To record bank loan.

      December 31, Year 2
      Cash (Asset Increase)..................................... 100,000
         Accounts Receivable (Asset Decrease)......   100,000
      To record collections from customers.

      Interest Expense (= .12 X $89,286) (Share-
         holders' Equity Decrease)............................. 10,714
      Bank Loan Payable (Liability Decrease)........ 89,286
         Cash (Asset Decrease).............................   100,000
      To record interest expense on loan for
      Year 2 and repayment of the loan.

10.19 a. continued.

(2) Cash (Asset Increase).. 89,286
Retained Earnings (Loss from Sale of Ac-
counts Receivable) (Shareholders Equity
Decrease).. 10,714
Accounts Receivable (Asset Decrease).. 100,000
To record sale of accounts receivable; alter-
native title for the loss account is interest
expense.

b. Both transactions result in an expense of $10,714 for Year 2 for this financing. Both transactions result in an immediate increase in cash. Liabilities increase for the collateralized loan, whereas an asset decreases for the sale.

c. Cypres Appliance Store must attempt to shift credit and interest rate risk to the bank. The bank should have no rights to demand additional receivables if interest rates increase or uncollectible accounts appear. Likewise, Cypres Appliance Store should have no rights to buy back the accounts receivable if interest rates decline. The bank of course will not both lend on the receivables and purchase the receivables at the same price because it incurs different amounts of risk in each case.

10.20 (P. J. Lorimar Company; using inventory to achieve off-balance sheet financing.)

a. (i) **January 2, Year 5**
Cash (Asset Increase).. 300,000
Bank Loan Payable (Liability Increase)..... 300,000
To record bank loan.

December 31, Year 5
Retained Earnings (Interest Expense) (= .10
x $300,000) (Shareholders' Equity De-
crease)... 30,000
Bank Loan Payable (Liability
Increase)... 30,000
To record interest expense for Year 5.

December 31, Year 6
Cash (Asset Increase).. 363,000
Retained Earnings (Sales Revenue)
(Shareholders' Equity Increase).............. 363,000
To record sale of tobacco inventory.

10.20 a. continued.

Retained Earnings (Cost of Goods Sold)
  (Shareholders' Equity Decrease)................... 200,000
    Inventory (Asset Decrease)...................... 200,000
  To record cost of tobacco inventory sold.

Retained Earnings (Interest Expense)
  (= .10 x $330,000) (Shareholders' Equity
  Decrease)....................................... 33,000
Bank Loan Payable (Liability Decrease).......... 330,000
  Cash (Asset Decrease).......................... 363,000
  To record interest expense for Year 6 and
  repayment of loan.

(ii) **January 2, Year 5**

Cash (Asset Increase)........................... 300,000
  Retained Earnings (Sales Revenue)
    (Shareholders' Equity Increase)............... 300,000
  To record "sale" of tobacco to bank.

Retained Earnings (Cost of Goods Sold)
  (Shareholders' Equity Decrease)................... 200,000
    Inventory (Asset Decrease)...................... 200,000
  To record cost of tobacco "sold".

b. Both transactions result in a total of $100,000 income for the two years combined. The collateralized loan shows $163,000 gross profit from the sale in Year 6 and interest expense of $30,000 in Year 5 and $33,000 in Year 6. The "sale" results in $100,000 gross profit in Year 5. Cash increases by $300,000 in both transactions. Liabilities increase for the collateralized loan, whereas an asset decreases for the "sale".

c. P. J. Lorimar Company must shift the risk of changes in storage costs for Year 5 and Year 6 and the selling price for the tobacco at the end of Year 6 to the bank. The firm should not guarantee a price or agree to cover insurance and other storage costs. Of course, the bank will not both lend on the inventory and "purchase" the inventory for $300,000 because it incurs different amounts of risk in each case.

10.21 (FedUp Delivery Services; preparing lessee's journal entries for an operating and a capital lease.)

a. This lease is a capital lease because the present value of the lease payments of $22,581 (= $750 x 30.10751) exceeds 90 percent of the market value of the leased asset (.90 x $24,000 = $21,600). The life of the lease is less than 75 percent of the life of the leased property and the property reverts to GM at the end of the lease period, so the lease fails these criteria for a capital lease.

10.21 continued.

b. **Time of Signing Lease**
No Entry.

End of Each Month

Retained Earnings (Rent Expense) (Shareholders' Equity Decrease)	750	
Cash (Asset Decrease)		750

To record monthly rental expense and payment.

c. **Time of Signing Lease**

Leased Asset (Asset Increase)	22,581	
Lease Liability (Liability Increase)		22,581

To record capital lease.

End of First Month

Retained Earnings (Interest Expense) (= .01 X $22,581) (Shareholders' Equity Decrease)	225.81	
Lease Liability (Liability Decrease)	524.19	
Cash (Asset Decrease)		750.00

To record interest expense and cash payment for first month; the book value of the lease liability is now $22,056.81 (= $22,581.00 – $524.19).

Retained Earnings (Depreciation Expense) (Shareholders' Equity Decrease)	627.25	
Accumulated Depreciation (Asset Decrease)		627.25

To record depreciation expense for the first month of $627.25 (= $22,581/36).

End of Second Month

Retained Earnings (Interest Expense) (= .01 X $22,056.81) (Shareholders' Equity Decrease)	220.57	
Lease Liability (Liability Decrease)	529.43	
Cash (Asset Decrease)		750.00

To record interest expense and cash payment for the second month.

Retained Earnings (Depreciation Expense) (Shareholders' Equity Decrease)	627.25	
Accumulated Depreciation (Asset Decrease)		627.25

To record depreciation expense for the second month.

10.22   (Sun Microsystems; preparing lessor's journal entries for an operating lease and a capital lease.)

a.   This lease is a capital lease. The life of the lease equals the expected useful life of the property. The present value of the lease payments of $12,000 [= $4,386.70 + ($4,386.70 x 1.73554)] equals the market value of the leased asset.

b.   **Beginning of Each Year**

Cash (Asset Increase)	4,386.70	
Rental Fees Received in Advance (Liability Increase)		4,386.70
To record cash received in advance from lessee.		

End of Each Year

Rental Fees Received in Advance (Liability Decrease)	4,386.70	
Retained Earnings (Rent Revenue) (Shareholders' Equity Increase)		4,386.70
To record rent revenue for each year.		
Retained Earnings (Depreciation Expense) (Shareholders' Equity Decrease)	2,400.00	
Accumulated Depreciation (Asset Decrease)		2,400.00
To record annual depreciation (= $7,200/3).		

c.   **January 2, Year 2**

Cash (Asset Increase)	4,386.70	
Lease Receivable (= $4,386.70 x 1.73554) (Asset Increase)	7,613.30	
Retained Earnings (Sales Revenue) (Shareholders' Equity Increase)		12,000.00
To record "sale" of work station.		
Retained Earnings (Cost of Goods Sold) (Shareholders' Equity Decrease)	7,200.00	
Inventory (Asset Decrease)		7,200.00
To record cost of workstation "sold".		

December 31, Year 2

Lease Receivable (= .10 x $7,613.30) (Asset Increase)	761.33	
Retained Earnings (Interest Revenue) (Shareholders' Equity Increase)		761.33
To record interest revenue for Year 2.		

10.22 c. continued.

January 2, Year 3
Cash (Asset Increase).. 4,386.70
    Lease Receivable (Asset Decrease)...................... 4,386.70
To record cash received at the beginning of
Year 3. The book value of the receivable is now
$3,987.93 (= $7,613.30 + $761.33 – $4,386.70).

December 31, Year 3
Lease Receivable (= .10 x $3,987.93) (Asset
    Increase)... 398.77
    Retained Earnings (Interest Revenue)
        (Shareholders' Equity Increase) 398.77
To record interest revenue for Year 3. Interest
revenue is slightly less than .10 x $3,987.93 due
to rounding of present value factors. The book
value of the receivable is now $4,386.70 (=
$3,987.93 + $398.77).

January 2, Year 4
Cash (Asset Increase).. 4,386.70
    Lease Receivable (Asset Decrease)...................... 4,386.70
To record cash received for Year 4.

10.23   (Ingersoll-Rand; preparing journal entries for income tax expense.)

a. **Year 9**
Retained Earnings (Income Tax Expense) (Share-
    holders' Equity Decrease)..................................... 67,400
Deferred Tax Liability (Liability Decrease).............. 43,575
    Cash or Income Tax Payable (Asset De-
        crease or Liability Increase)......................... 110,975

Year 10
Retained Earnings (Income Tax Expense) (Share-
    holders' Equity Decrease)..................................... 90,000
Deferred Tax Liability (Liability Decrease).............. 15,537
    Cash or Income Tax Payable (Asset De-
        crease or Liability Increase)......................... 105,537

Year 11
Retained Earnings (Income Tax Expense) (Share-
    holders' Equity Decrease)..................................... 118,800
    Deferred Tax Liability (Liability Increase)...... 14,185
    Cash or Income Tax Payable (Asset De-
        crease or Liability Increase)......................... 104,615

10.23 continued.

    b.   Taxable income exceeds book income for Year 9 and Year 10 but taxable income was less than book income for Year 11. Ingersoll-Rand probably reduced its expenditures on new depreciable assets during Year 9 and Year 10 so that depreciation expense for financial reporting exceeded depreciation deducted in computing taxable income. Ingersoll-Rand increased its capital expenditures during Year 11 so that depreciation deducted in computing taxable income exceeded depreciation expense recognized for financial reporting.

10.24   (Sung Company; computations and journal entries for income taxes with both temporary and permanent differences.)

    a. **Year 1**

Retained Earnings (Income Tax Expense) (.40 x $560,000) (Shareholders' Equity Decrease)	224,000	
Deferred Tax Liability (.40 x $40,000) (Liability Decrease)	16,000	
Income Tax Payable—Current (.40 x $600,000) (Liability Increase)		240,000

        Year 2

Retained Earnings (Income Tax Expense) (.40 x $500,000) (Shareholders' Equity Decrease)	200,000	
Deferred Tax Liability (.40 x $50,000) (Liability Increase)		20,000
Income Tax Payable—Current (.40 x $450,000) (Liability Increase)		180,000

        Year 3

Retained Earnings (Income Tax Expense) (.40 x $620,000) (Shareholders' Equity Decrease)	248,000	
Deferred Tax Liability (.40 x $6,000) (Liability Increase)		24,000
Income Tax Payable—Current (.40 x $560,000) (Liability Increase)		224,000

    b. **Year 1**

Retained Earnings (Income Tax Expense) [.40 x ($560,000 – $10,000)] (Shareholders' Equity Decrease)	220,000	
Deferred Tax Liability (.40 x $50,000) (Liability Decrease)	20,000	
Income Tax Payable—Current (.40 x $600,000) (Liability Increase)		240,000

10.24 b. continued.

Year 2

Retained Earnings (Income Tax Expense) [.40 × ($500,000 − $10,000)] (Shareholders' Equity Decrease)...	196,000	
Deferred Tax Liability (.40 × $40,000) (Liability Increase)..		16,000
Income Tax Payable—Current (.40 × $450,000) (Liability Increase)......................		180,000

Year 3

Retained Earnings (Income Tax Expense) [.40 × ($620,000 − $10,000)] (Shareholders' Equity Decrease)...	244,000	
Deferred Tax Liability (.40 × $50,000) (Liability Increase)..		20,000
Income Tax Payable—Current (.40 × $560,000) (Liability Increase)		224,000

10.25 (Pownall Company; deriving permanent and temporary differences from financial statement disclosures.)

a.

Income Tax Expense	=	Income Taxes Currently Payable	+	Change in Deferred Tax Liability
$156,000	=	$48,000	+	x
x	=	$108,000		

Temporary Differences	=	Changes in Deferred Tax Liability/.40
	=	$108,000/.40
	=	$270,000

Because income tax expense exceeds income taxes payable, book income exceeded taxable income.

b.

Taxable Income: $48,000/.40..	$120,000
Temporary Differences	270,000
Book Income before Taxes Excluding Permanent Differences	$390,000
Permanent Differences (Plug)...	72,000
Book Income before Taxes (Given)...	$318,000

10.26 (Boeing and American; applying the capital lease criteria.)

a. This lease is a capital lease because the lease period of 20 years exceeds 75 percent of the expected life of the aircraft. The lease does not meet any other capital lease criteria. The aircraft reverts to Boeing at the end of 20 years. The present value of the lease payments when discounted at 10 percent is $51.1 million ($6 million X 8.51356), which is less than $54 million (= 90 percent of the fair market value of $60 million).

b. This lease is a capital lease because the present value of the lease payments of $54.8 million (= $7.2 million X 7.60608) exceeds 90 percent of the $60 million fair market value of the aircraft.

c. The lease is not a capital lease. The present value of the required lease payments of $36.9 million (= $5.5 million X 6.71008) is less than $54 million (= 90 percent of the market value of the aircraft). The life of the lease is less than 75 percent of the expected useful life of the aircraft. The purchase option price coupled with the rental payments provides Boeing with a present value of all cash flows exceeding $62.4 million [= ($5.5 million X 6.71008) + ($55 million X .46319)]. This amount exceeds the usual sales price of $60 million, so there does not appear to be a bargain purchase option.

d. This lease is not a capital lease. The present value of the minimum required lease payments is $50.9 million (= $6.2 million X 8.20141). The fee contingent on usage could be zero, so the calculations exclude it. The life of the lease is less than 75 percent of the useful life of the aircraft. The aircraft reverts to Boeing at the end of the lease period.

10.27 (Baldwin Products; preparing lessee's journal entries for an operating lease and a capital lease.)

a. This lease does not satisfy any of the criteria for a capital lease, so it is an operating lease. The leased asset reverts to the lessor at the end of the lease period. The life of the lease (3 years) is less than 75 percent of the expected useful life of the leased asset (5 years). The present value of the lease payments of $24,018 (= $10,000 X 2.40183) is less than 90 percent of the market value of the leased asset of $30,000.

b. **December 31, of Each Year**
Retained Earnings (Rent Expense) (Shareholders'
    Equity Decrease)... 10,000
        Cash (Asset Decrease) 10,000
To record annual rent expense and cash payment.

10.27 continued.

c. **January 2, Year 6**
Leased Asset (Asset Increase)................................. 24,018
    Lease Liability (Liability Increase)......................   24,018
To record capital lease.

December 31, Year 6
Retained Earnings (Interest Expense) (= .12 X
    $24,018) (Shareholders' Equity Decrease)........... 2,882
Lease Liability (Liability Decrease)........................... 7,118
    Cash (Asset Decrease)......................................   10,000
To record interest expense and cash payment for
Year 6. The book value of the lease liability is now
$16,900 (= $24,018 − $7,118).

Retained Earnings (Depreciation Expense or
    Work-in-Process Inventory) ($24,018/3)
    (Shareholders' Equity Decrease or Asset In-
    crease).. 8,006
    Accumulated Depreciation (Asset De-
        crease)..   8,006
To record depreciation expense for Year 6.

December 31, Year 7
Retained Earnings (Interest Expense) (= .12 X
    $16,900) (Shareholders' Equity Decrease)........... 2,028
Lease Liability (Liability Decrease)........................... 7,972
    Cash (Asset Decrease)......................................   10,000
To record interest expense and cash payment for
Year 7. The book value of the lease liability is now
$8,928 (= $16,900 − $7,972).

Retained Earnings (Depreciation Expense or
    Work-in-Process Inventory) (Shareholders'
    Equity Decrease or Asset Increase)..................... 8,006
    Accumulated Depreciation (Asset De-
        crease)..   8,006
To record depreciation expense for Year 7.

December 31, Year 8
Retained Earnings (Interest Expense) (= .12 X
    $8,928) (Shareholders' Equity Decrease)............. 1,072
Lease Liability (Liability Decrease)........................... 8,928
    Cash (Asset Decrease)......................................   10,000
To record interest expense and cash payment for
Year 8. Interest expense does not precisely equal
.12 X $8,928 due to rounding. Book value of the lia-
bility is now zero.

10.27 c. continued.

> Retained Earnings (Depreciation Expense or
> Work-in-Process Inventory) (Shareholders'
> Equity Decrease or Asset Increase).................... 8,006
>   Accumulated Depreciation (Asset De-
>   crease).. 8,006
> To record depreciation expense for Year 8.

d. Operating Lease Method: Rent Expense (= $10,000 × 3)...... <u>$ 30,000</u>

Capital Lease Method: Interest Expense (= $2,882 +
$2,028 + $1,072)... $ 5,982
Depreciation (= $8,006 × 3).. <u>24,018</u>
   Total Expenses.. <u>$ 30,000</u>

10.28   (L.A. Gear; preparing journal entries for income tax expense.)

a. **Year 4**
> Retained Earnings (Income Tax Expense)
> (Shareholders' Equity Decrease).......................... 34,364
> Deferred Tax Asset (Asset Increase)....................... 3,555
>   Cash or Income Tax Payable (Asset De-
>   crease or Liability Increase)......................... 37,919

Year 5
> Retained Earnings (Income Tax Expense)
> (Shareholders' Equity Decrease).......................... 9,392
> Deferred Tax Asset (Asset Increase)....................... 3,492
>   Cash or Income Tax Payable (Asset De-
>   crease or Liability Increase)......................... 12,884

Year 6
> Cash or Income Tax Receivable (Asset In-
> crease).. 17,184
> Deferred Tax Asset (Asset Increase)....................... 5,543
>   Retained Earnings (Income Tax Expense)
>   (Credit) (Shareholders' Equity Increase)..... 22,727

b. Book income and taxable income were both positive for Years 4 and 5. Taxable income exceeded book income. The deferred tax asset related to uncollectible accounts increased, suggesting an increased sales level for each year.

Book income and taxable income were both negative in Year 6. The loss for book purposes exceeded the loss for tax purposes. The increase in the deferred tax asset related to uncollectible accounts suggests increasing sales but decreasing profits on those sales.

10.29 (Woodward Corporation; effect of temporary differences on income taxes.)

a.

	Year 1	Year 2	Year 3	Year 4
Other Pre-Tax Income	$35,000	$35,000	$35,000	$35,000
Income before Depreciation from Machine..........................	25,000	25,000	25,000	25,000
Depreciation Deduction:				
.33 x $50,000..........................	(16,500)			
.44 x $50,000..........................		(22,000)		
.15 x $50,000			(7,500)	
.08 x $50,000..........................				(4,000)
Taxable Income	$43,500	$38,000	$52,500	$56,000
Tax Rate	.40	.40	.40	.40
Income Taxes Payable..............	$17,400	$15,200	$21,000	$22,400

b.

Financial Reporting	Year 1	Year 2	Year 3	Year 4
Book Value, January 1	$50,000	$37,500	$25,000	$ 12,500
Depreciation Expense	(12,500)	(12,500)	(12,500)	(12,500)
Book Value, December 31........	$37,500	$25,000	$12,500	$ --
Tax Reporting				
Tax Basis, January 1................	$50,000	$33,500	$11,500	$ 4,000
Depreciation Deduction............	(16,500)	(22,000)	(7,500)	(4,000)
Tax Basis, December 31...........	$33,500	$11,500	$ 4,000	$ --

c.

Financial Reporting	Year 1	Year 2	Year 3	Year 4
Income before Depreciation.....	$60,000	$60,000	$60,000	$ 60,000
Depreciation Expense ($50,000/4)............................	(12,500)	(12,500)	(12,500)	(12,500)
Pretax Income	$47,500	$47,500	$47,500	$ 47,500
Income Tax Expense at .40	$19,000	$19,000	$19,000	$ 19,000

d.

	Year 1	Year 2	Year 3	Year 4
Income Tax Payable (from Part *a*.)—Cr.	$17,400	$ 15,200	$ 21,000	$22,400
Change in Deferred Tax Liability (Plug): Cr. if Positive Dr. if Negative	1,600	3,800	(2,000)	(3,400)
Income Tax Expense—Dr.	$19,000	$ 19,000	$ 19,000	$19,000

Year 1

Retained Earnings (Income Tax Expense) (Shareholders' Equity Decrease)......................................	19,000	
Cash or Income Tax Payable (Asset Decrease or Liability Increase).........................		17,400
Deferred Tax Liability (Liability Increase)......		1,600

10.29 d. continued.

Year 2

Retained Earnings (Income Tax Expense) (Shareholders' Equity Decrease).................................	19,000	
Cash or Income Tax Payable (Asset Decrease or Liability Increase)........................		15,200
Deferred Tax Liability (Liability Increase)......		3,800

Year 3

Retained Earnings (Income Tax Expense) (Shareholders' Equity Decrease).................................	19,000	
Deferred Tax Liability (Liability Decrease)..............	2,000	
Cash or Income Tax Payable (Asset Decrease or Liability Increase)........................		21,000

Year 4

Retained Earnings (Income Tax Expense) (Shareholders' Equity Decrease).................................	19,000	
Deferred Tax Liability (Liability Decrease)..............	3,400	
Cash or Income Tax Payable (Asset Decrease or Liability Increase)........................		22,400

10.30   (Lilly Company; reconstructing information about income taxes.)

LILLY COMPANY
Illustrations of Timing Differences and Permanent Differences

	Financial Statements	Type of Difference	Income Tax Return
Operating Income Except Depreciation........................	$ 427,800 (6)	--	$ 427,800 (4)
Depreciation.............................	(322,800) (g)	Timing	(358,800) (3)
Municipal Bond Interest...........	85,800 (5)	Permanent	--
Taxable Income..........................	--		$ 69,000 (2)
Pretax Income...........................	$ 190,800 (g)		
Income Taxes Payable at 40 Percent..............................			$ 27,600 (g)
Income Tax Expense at 40 Percent of $105,000 = $427,800 – $322,800, Which Is Book Income Excluding Permanent Differences...........................	(42,000) (g)		
Net Income................................	$ 148,800 (1)		

10.30 continued.

Order and derivation of computations:
(g) Given.
(1) $148,800 = $190,800 − $42,000.
(2) $69,000 = $27,600/.40.
(3) Timing difference for depreciation is ($42,000 − $27,600)/.40 = $36,000. Because income taxes payable are less than income tax expense, we know that depreciation deducted on tax return exceeds depreciation expense on financial statements. Thus, the depreciation deduction on the tax return is $358,800 = $322,800 + $36,000.
(4) $427,800 = $358,800 + $69,000.
(5) Taxable income on financial statements is $105,000 = $42,000/.40. Total financial statement income before taxes, including permanent differences, is $190,800. Hence, permanent differences are $190,800 − $105,000 = $85,800.
(6) $190,800 + $322,800 − $85,800 = $427,800. See also (4), for check.

10.31   (Effects of leases on statement of cash flows.)

a.   The journal entry to record this transaction is:

Retained Earnings (Depreciation Expense)
    (Shareholders' Equity Decrease) 10,000
        Accumulated Depreciation (Asset De-
            crease).. 10,000

Because this entry does not involve a debit or credit to the Cash account, Line (11) does not change. Depreciation expense reduces net income, so Line (3) decreases by $10,000. The recognition of depreciation expense does not affect cash, so Line (4) increases by $10,000.

b.   The journal entry for this transaction is:

Cash (Asset Increase)... 19,925
    Retained Earnings (Rent Revenue) (Share-
        holders' Equity Increase) 19,925

The debit to Cash results in an increase of $19,925 in Line (11). The receipt of $19,925 increases Line (1). The credit to Rent Revenue increases Line (3), net income, by $19,925.

10.31 continued.

   c.   The journal entry to record this transaction is:

Retained Earnings (Rent Expense) (Shareholders'
     Equity Decrease) 19,925
        Cash (Asset Decrease)...................................... 19,925

The credit to Cash results in a decrease of $19,925 in Line (11) and an increase in the expenditure subtracted on Line (2). The debit to Rent Expense reduces Line (3), net income, by $19,925.

   d.   The journal entry for this transaction is:

Leased Asset (Asset Increase)................................. 100,000
     Lease Liability (Liability Increase)....................... 100,000

This transaction does not involve a change in cash, so Line (11) does not change. The entry does not affect net income, so Line (3) does not change. This transaction is an investing and financing activity that would not appear in the statement of cash flows but in a supplementary schedule or note to the financial statements.

   e.   The journal entry to record this transaction is:

Retained Earnings (Interest Expense) (Share-
     holders' Equity Decrease)..................................... 15,000
Lease Liability (Liability Decrease) 4,925
        Cash (Asset Decrease)...................................... 19,925

This entry results in a reduction in Cash, so Line (11) decreases by $19,925 and the subtraction on Line (2) increases by $19,925. Line (3) decreases by $15,000 for interest expense and Line (9) increases by $4,925 for the reduction in the lease liability. Thus, $15,000 of the reduction in cash appears in the operating section and $4,925 appears in the financing section of the statement of cash flows.

10.32   (Effects of income taxes on statement of cash flows.)

   a.   The entry to record this event is:

Retained Earnings (Income Tax Expense) (.4 x
     $200,000) (Shareholders' Equity Decrease)........ 80,000
     Income Tax Payable (.4 x $150,000) (Lia-
        bility Increase) 60,000
     Deferred Tax Liability (.4 x $50,000) (Lia-
        bility Increase) 20,000

10.32 a. continued.

This entry does not involve a change in Cash, so Line (11) does not change. The debit to income tax expense reduces Line (3), net income, by $80,000. Line (4) increases by $60,000 for the increases in a current operating liability. Line (4) also increases by $20,000 for the addback of an expense that does not use cash. Thus, the effect on cash flow from operations is zero.

b. The journal entry for this event is:

Retained Earnings (Income Tax Expense) (.4 X
$300,000) (Shareholders' Equity Decrease)........ 120,000
Deferred Tax Asset (.4 X $40,000) (Asset
Increase)... 16,000
    Cash (.4 X $340,000) (Asset Decrease)........... 136,000

This entry reduces Cash, so Line (11) decreases by $136,000. Expenditure for tax expense increases the subtraction on Line (2) by $120,000. The recognition of income tax expense reduces Line (3), net income, by $120,000. Line (5) increases by $16,000 for the acquisition of the noncurrent deferred tax asset.

c. The journal entry and explanation for this part are the same as in Part b. above. Line (2) subtraction increases by $120,000. Line (3) decreases by $120,000, Line (5) increases by $16,000, and Line (11) decreases by $136,000.

d. The journal entry is:.

Cash (Asset Increase)... 10,000
    Retained Earnings (Interest Revenue) (Share-
    holders' Equity Increase) 10,000

Interest on municipal bonds is nontaxable, so recognition of income taxes on the interest revenue is inappropriate (a permanent difference). The Cash account increases, so Lines (1) and (11) increase by $10,000. The recognition of interest revenue increases Line (3), net income, by $10,000.

10.33 (Wal-Mart Stores; financial statement effects of operating and capital leases.)

a. Retained Earnings (Interest Expense) (= .11 X
$1,694.2) (Shareholders' Equity Decrease)..... 186.4
Lease Liability (Plug) (Liability Decrease).......... 18.3
    Cash (Given) (Asset Decrease) 204.7

10.33 continued.

b. Retained Earnings (Rent Expense) (Share-
holders' Equity Decrease).................................. 249.3
    Cash (Asset Decrease)......................................   249.3

c. **January 31, Year 9**
Leased Asset (Asset Increase)........................... 1,586.5
    Lease Liability (Liability Increase)...................   1,586.5
To capitalize operating leases.

January 31, Year 10
Retained Earnings (Interest Expense) (= .12 x
    $1,586.5) (Shareholders' Equity Decrease)..... 190.4
Lease Liability (Liability Decrease) 58.9
    Cash (Asset Decrease)......................................   249.3
To record interest expense and cash payment
on capitalized operating leases.

Retained Earnings (Depreciation Expense)
    (Shareholders' Equity Decrease) 105.8
    Accumulated Depreciation (Asset De-
      crease)...   105.8
To record depreciation expense on capitalized
operating leases; $105.8 = $1,586.5/15.

10.34 (American Airlines; financial statement effect of operating and capital
leases.)

(Amounts in Millions)
a. Capital Lease Liability, December 31, Year 10............................ $ 2,233
    Interest Expense for Year 11 (= .08 x $2,233)............................... 179
    Cash Payment for Year 11.. (268)
    New Leases Signed during Year 11 (Plug).................................... 259
    Capital Lease Liability, December 31, Year 11............................ $ 2,403

b. Leasehold Asset, December 31, Year 10...................................... $ 1,716
    New Leases Capitalized during Year 11 (from Part a.)................ 259
    Depreciation Expense for Year 11 (Plug)...................................... (97)
    Leasehold Asset, December 31, Year 11.. $ 1,878

c. **December 31, Year 11**
Retained Earnings (Interest Expense) (Share-
    holders' Equity Decrease)... 179
Lease Liability (Liability Decrease) 89
    Cash (Asset Decrease)......................................   268

10.34 c. continued.

	Retained Earnings (Depreciation Expense) (Shareholders' Equity Decrease)...	97	
	Accumulated Depreciation (Asset Decrease)....		97
	Leased Asset (Asset Increase)......................................	259	
	Lease Liability (Liability Increase).........................		259

d. **December 31, Year 11**

	Retained Earnings (Rent Expense) (Shareholders' Equity Decrease)	946	
	Cash (Asset Decrease)..		946

e. **December 31, Year 10**

	Leased Asset (Asset Increase)......................................	7,793	
	Lease Liability (Liability Increase).........................		7,793

To capitalize operating leases as if they were capital leases.

December 31, Year 11

Retained Earnings (Interest Expense) (= .10 x $7,793) (Shareholders' Equity Decrease)	779	
Lease Liability (Liability Decrease)	167	
Cash (Asset Decrease)..		946

To record interest expense and cash payment for capitalized operating leases.

Retained Earnings (Depreciation Expense) (Shareholders' Equity Decrease).....................................	354	
Accumulated Depreciation (Asset Decrease)....		354

To record depreciation for Year 11; ($354 = $7,793/22).

Leased Asset (Asset Increase)......................................	538	
Lease Liability (Liability Increase).........................		538

To record present value of new leases; $7,793 + x − $167 = $8,164; x = $538.

10.35   (Carom Sports Collectibles Shop; comparison of borrow/buy with operating and capital leases.)

a. $100,000/3.79079 = $26,379.725 = $26,380.

Carom Sports Collectibles Shop Amortization Schedule

Year	Start of Year Balance	Interest (10%)	Payment	Reduction	End of Year Balance
1	$ 100,000	$10,000	$26,380	$16,380	$83,620
2	83,620	8,362	26,380	18,018	65,602
3	65,602	6,560	26,380	19,820	45,782
4	45,782	4,578	26,380	21,802	23,980
5	23,980	2,398	26,380	23,982	(2)

b.   (1) Asset—Cash.
Asset—Computer System.
Asset Contra—Accumulated Depreciation on Computer System.
Liability—Bonds Payable and Interest Payable.

(2) None.

(3) Asset—Cash.
Asset—Leased Computer System.
Asset Contra—Accumulated Depreciation.
Liability—Lease Liability.

c. $150,000 = $100,000 + (.10 X $100,000 X 5).

d.   (1) Operating: $131,900 = $26,380 X 5.
(2) Capital: $131,900.

e.   The method of accounting for a lease affects only the timing of expenses, not their total. Expenses under Plan (1) are larger because the firm borrows $100,000 for the entire 5 years, whereas under Plan (2) it pays the loan with part of each lease payment; with smaller average borrowing, interest expense is smaller.

f.   (1) $30,000 = $20,000 depreciation plus $10,000 bond interest.
(2) Operating-lease Method: $26,380.
Capital-lease Method: $30,000 = $20,000 amortization +
$10,000 lease interest.

By convention, we use the word *depreciation* for plant assets and the word *amortization* for the intangible asset leasehold.

g.   (1) $30,000.
(2) Operating: $26,380.
Capital: $22,400 (or $22,398) = $20,000 + $2,400 (or $2,398).

10.35 g. continued.

CAROM SPORTS COLLECTIBLES SHOP SUMMARY
(Not Required)

	Year 1	Year 2	Year 3	Year 4	Year 5	Total
Plan 1						
Depreciation Expense............	$20,000	$20,000	$20,000	$20,000	$20,000	$100,000
Interest Expense............	10,000	10,000	10,000	10,000	10,000	50,000
Total..............	$30,000	$30,000	$30,000	$30,000	$30,000	$150,000
Plan 2 (Operating)						
Lease Expense...	$26,380	$26,380	$26,380	$26,380	$26,380	$131,900
Plan 2 (Financing)						
Depreciation Expense............	$20,000	$20,000	$20,000	$20,000	$20,000	$100,000
Interest Expense............	10,000	8,362	6,560	4,578	2,400*	31,900
Total..............	$30,000	$28,362	$26,560	$24,578	$22,400	$131,900

*Plug to correct for rounding errors. By computations, this number is $2,398 = [$26,380 – ($26,380/1.10)].

10.36 (IBM and Adair Corporation; accounting for lease by lessor and lessee.)

a. **January 1, Year 11**

Cash (Asset Increase)...	10,000	
Note Payable (Liability Increase)........................		10,000
Computer (Asset Increase).....................................	10,000	
Cash (Asset Decrease)...		10,000

December 31, Year 11

Retained Earnings (Depreciation Expense) (Shareholders' Equity Decrease).........................	3,333	
Accumulated Depreciation (Asset Decrease)...		3,333
Retained Earnings (Interest Expense) (.08 X $10,000) (Shareholders' Equity Decrease)..........	800	
Note Payable (Plug) (Liability Decrease)................	3,080	
Cash ($10,000/2.57710) (Asset Decrease).....		3,880

December 31, Year 12

Retained Earnings (Depreciation Expense) (Shareholders' Equity Decrease).........................	3,333	
Accumulated Depreciation (Asset Decrease)...		3,333

10.36 a. continued.

Retained Earnings (Interest Expense) [.08 x ($10,000 – $3,080)] (Shareholders' Equity Decrease)..	554	
Note Payable (Plug) (Liability Decrease).................	3,326	
Cash (Asset Decrease).....................................		3,880

b. **January 1, Year 11**
No entry.

December 31, Year 11

Retained Earnings (Rent Expense) (Shareholders' Equity Decrease)..	3,810	
Cash (Asset Decrease).....................................		3,810

December 31, Year 12

Retained Earnings (Rent Expense) (Shareholders' Equity Decrease)..	3,810	
Cash (Asset Decrease).....................................		3,810

c. **January 1, Year 11**

Leased Asset (Asset Increase)................................	10,000	
Lease Liability (Liability Increase).....................		10,000

December 31, Year 11

Retained Earnings (Depreciation Expense) (Shareholders' Equity Decrease).....................................	3,333	
Accumulated Depreciation (Asset Decrease).		3,333

Retained Earnings (Interest Expense) (.07 x $10,000) (Shareholders' Equity Decrease)..........	700	
Lease Liability (Plug) (Liability Decrease)...............	3,110	
Cash ($10,000/2.62432) (Asset Decrease).....		3,810

December 31, Year 12

Retained Earnings (Depreciation Expense) (Shareholders' Equity Decrease)	3,333	
Accumulated Depreciation (Asset Decrease)..		3,333

Retained Earnings (Interest Expense) [.07 x ($10,000 – $3,110)] (Shareholders' Equity Decrease)..	482	
Lease Liability (Plug) (Liability Decrease)...............	3,328	
Cash (Asset Decrease).....................................		3,810

10.36 continued.

d. **January 1, Year 11**
Cash (Asset Increase)... 10,000
    Retained Earnings (Sales Revenue) (Share-
    holders' Equity Increase) 10,000

Retained Earnings (Cost of Goods Sold) (Shareholders' Equity Decrease)................................. 6,000
    Inventory (Asset Decrease)............................... 6,000

e. **January 1, Year 11**
Computer Equipment (Asset Increase) 6,000
    Inventory (Asset Decrease) 6,000

December 31, Year 11
Retained Earnings (Depreciation Expense)
(Shareholders' Equity Decrease) 2,000
    Accumulated Depreciation (Asset De-
    crease).. 2,000

Cash (Asset Increase)... 3,810
    Retained Earnings (Rent Revenue) (Share-
    holders' Equity Increase) 3,810

December 31, Year 12
Retained Earnings (Depreciation Expense)
(Shareholders' Equity Decrease) 2,000
    Accumulated Depreciation (Asset De-
    crease).. 2,000

Cash (Asset Increase)... 3,810
    Retained Earnings (Rent Revenue) (Share-
    holders' Equity Increase) 3,810

f. **January 1, Year 11**
Lease Receivable (Asset Increase).......................... 10,000
    Retained Earnings (Sales Revenue) (Share-
    holders' Equity Increase) 10,000

Retained Earnings (Cost of Goods Sold) (Shareholders' Equity Decrease)................................. 6,000
    Inventory (Asset Decrease)............................... 6,000

December 31, Year 11
Cash (Asset Increase)... 3,810
    Retained Earnings (Interest Revenue) (see
    Part c.) (Shareholders' Equity Increase).......... 700
    Lease Receivable (Asset Decrease)..................... 3,110

10.36 f. continued.

December 31, Year 12
Cash (Asset Increase)... 3,810
   Retained Earnings (Interest Revenue) (see
      Part *c*.) (Shareholders' Equity Increase)......... 482
   Lease Receivable (Asset Decrease).................... 3,328

g. **Lessee**

	Year 11	Year 12	Year 13	Total
Borrow and Purchase				
Depreciation Expense.....	$ 3,333	$ 3,333	$ 3,334	$ 10,000
Interest Expense............	800	554	286	1,640
	$ 4,133	$ 3,887	$ 3,620	$ 11,640
Operating Lease				
Rent Expense..................	$ 3,810	$ 3,810	$ 3,810	$ 11,430
Capital Lease				
Depreciation Expense.....	$ 3,333	$ 3,333	$ 3,334	$ 10,000
Interest Expense............	700	482	248	1,430
	$ 4,033	$ 3,815	$ 3,582	$ 11,430

h. **Lessor**

	Year 11	Year 12	Year 13	Total
Sale				
Sales Revenue.................	$10,000	$ --	$ --	$ 10,000
Cost of Goods Sold...........	(6,000)	--	--	(6,000)
	$ 4,000	$ --	$ --	$ 4,000
Operating Lease				
Rent Revenue..................	$ 3,810	$ 3,810	$ 3,810	$ 11,430
Depreciation Expense.....	(2,000)	(2,000)	(2,000)	(6,000)
	$ 1,810	$ 1,810	$ 1,810	$ 5,430
Capital Lease				
Sales Revenue.................	$10,000	$ --	$ --	$ 10,000
Cost of Goods Sold...........	(6,000)	--	--	(6,000)
Interest Revenue............	700	482	248	1,430
	$ 4,700	$ 482	$ 248	$ 5,430

10.37 (Various U.S. airlines; financial statement effects of capitalizing operating leases.)

	American	Delta	United
a. $7,878/($7,878 + $3,380).......................	70.0%		
$3,121/($3,121 + $1,827).......................		63.1%	
$3,617/($3,617 − $267)...........................			108.0%

10.37 continued.

b. ($7,878 + $8,164)/($7,878 + $8,164 +
    $3,380) 82.6%
    ($3,121 + $7,307)/($3,121 + $7,307 +
    $1,827) 85.1%
    ($3,617 + $10,645)/($3,617 + $10,645
    − $267) 101.9%

c. The airlines have high debt ratios without including operating leases. Inclusion of the operating leases in liabilities probably violates debt covenants of these airlines.

d. The lease period probably runs for less than 75 percent of the useful life of their equipment or the lessor incurs the salvage value risk.

e. The airlines often operate at a loss and are unable to take advantage of depreciation deductions. The airlines hope to obtain lower lease payments by allowing the lessor to claim the depreciation deductions for tax purposes.

10.38   (Deere & Company; interpreting income tax disclosures.) (Amounts in Millions)

a. **Year 10**
    Retained Earnings (Income Tax Expense) (Share-
      holders' Equity Decrease) 182
    Deferred Tax Asset (= $82 − $77) (Asset
      Increase) 5
        Deferred Tax Liability (= $375 − $312)
          (Liability Increase)... 63
        Income Tax Payable or Cash (Liability In-
          crease or Asset Decrease)............................ 124

b. Book income before income taxes exceeded taxable income because income tax expense exceeds income taxes currently payable. Also, the deferred tax accounts on the balance sheet experienced a net credit change of $58 million (= $63 − $5) during Year 10, suggesting larger book income than taxable income.

c. **Year 11**
    Deferred Tax Asset (= $149 − $82) (Asset
      Increase) 67
    Deferred Tax Liability (= $342 − $375) (Liability
      Decrease) 33
        Income Tax Payable (Liability Increase)......... 95
        Retained Earnings (Income Tax Expense—
          Credit) (Shareholders' Equity Increase) 5

10.38 continued.

d. Book loss before income taxes was smaller than taxable income. Also, the deferred tax accounts on the balance sheet experienced a net debit change of $100 million (= $67 + $33) during Year 11, suggesting smaller book income (loss) than taxable income.

e. The decline in book income before income taxes between Year 10 and Year 11 suggests the possibility of a slowdown in sales growth. Revenue recognized for tax purposes using the installment method exceeds revenue recognized at the time of sale for book purposes, resulting in a decrease in the deferred tax liability relating to installment sales. The increase in the deferred tax assets relating to uncollectible accounts and sales rebates and allowances suggest weak economic conditions, causing Deere to increase its provisions for these items for book purposes.

f. Change in Deferred Tax Liability Relating to Depreciable
   Assets (= $215 – $208) .... $ 7
   Income Tax Rate .... ÷ .35
   Temporary Difference for Year 11 .... $ 20
   Book Depreciation   209
   Tax Depreciation .... $ 229

10.39 (Sun Microsystems; interpreting income tax disclosures.) (Amounts in Millions)

a. **Year 5**
   Retained Earnings (Income Tax Expense) (Share-
      holders' Equity Decrease) 67
   Deferred Tax Asset (= $150 – $142) (Asset Increase) ... 8
   Deferred Tax Liability (= $7 – $14) (Liability De-
      crease) 7
         Income Tax Payable or Cash (= $38 + $38 + $6)
         (Liability Increase or Asset Decrease) 82

b. Book income before income taxes was less than taxable income because there is a net debit change (= $8 + $7) in the deferred tax accounts on the balance sheet.

c. **Year 6**
   Retained Earnings (Income Tax Expense) (Share-
      holders' Equity Decrease) 88
   Deferred Tax Asset (= $174 – $150) (Asset Increase) ... 24
      Deferred Tax Liability (= $27 – $7) (Liability
         Increase) 20
      Income Tax Payable or Cash (= $28 + $60 + $4)
         (Liability Increase or Asset Decrease) 92

10.39 continued.

d. Book income before income taxes was less than taxable income because there is a net debit change (= $24 − $20) in the deferred tax accounts on the balance sheet.

e. **Year 7**

Retained Earnings (Income Tax Expense) (Share-holders' Equity Decrease)..	167
Deferred Tax Asset (= $195 − $174) (Asset Increase)...	21
Deferred Tax Liability (= $25 − $27) (Liability De-crease)..	2
Income Tax Payable or Cash (= $123 + $57 + $10) (Liability Increase or Asset Decrease).......	190

f. Taxable income exceeds book income before income taxes. The deferred tax accounts on the balance sheet experienced a net debit change (= $21 + $2) during Year 7.

g. Sun probably decreased its capital expenditures during Year 7 because depreciation for book purposes exceeded depreciation for tax purposes (that is, the deferred tax liability relating to depreciation temporary differences decreased during Year 7).

10.40 (General Products Company; interpreting income tax disclosures.)

a. Book income was likely less than taxable income because the deferred tax accounts on the balance sheet experienced a net debit change during Year 3.

b. Book income was likely larger than taxable income because the deferred tax accounts on the balance sheet experienced a net credit change during Year 4.

c. The sales of products on account and under warranty plans increased continually during the three-year period. Estimated bad debt expense on each year's sales exceeded actual write-off of uncollectible accounts arising from the current and previous years' sales. Estimated warranty expense on products sold each year exceeded actual expenditures for warranties and products sold during the current and previous years.

d.

Change in Deferred Tax Liability Relating to Temporary Depreciable Assets (= $213 − $155)...................................	$ 58
Income Tax Rate..	÷ .35
Excess of Tax Depreciation Over Book Depreciation............	$ 165.7

10.41 (Equilibrium Company; behavior of deferred income tax account when a firm acquires new assets every year.)

Year	Units Acquired							
		1	**2**	**3**	**4**	**5**	**6**	**7**
1	1	$2,400	$3,840	$2,280	$1,440	$1,320	$720	$0
2	1		2,400	3,840	2,280	1,440	1,320	720
3	1			2,400	3,840	2,280	1,440	1,320
4	1				2,400	3,840	2,280	1,440
5	1					2,400	3,840	2,280
6	1						2,400	3,840
7	1							2,400

TAX DEPRECIATION (AMCRS)

	1	**2**	**3**	**4**	**5**	**6**	**7**
a. Annual Depreciation	$2,400	$6,240	$8,520	$9,960	$11,280	$12,000	$12,000
b. Straight Line Depreciation = $2,000 per Machine per Year	2,000	4,000	6,000	8,000	10,000	12,000	12,000
c. Difference	$400	$2,240	$2,520	$1,960	$1,280	$0	$0
d. Increase in Deferred Tax (40%)	$160	$896	$1,008	$784	$512	$0	$0
e. Balance of Deferred Income Taxes	$160	$1,056	$2,064	$2,848	$3,360	$3,360	$3,360

f. The Deferred Income Taxes account balance will remain constant at $3,360 so long as the firm continues this replacement policy. If asset prices increase or physical assets increase, or both, the Deferred Tax Liability will continue to grow.

10.42　(Shiraz Company; attempts to achieve off-balance-sheet financing.)

[The chapter does not give sufficient information for the student to know the GAAP answers. The six items are designed to generate a lively discussion.]

Transfer of Receivables with Recourse *SFAS No. 77* (1983) sets out the following criteria to treat a transfer of receivables with recourse as a sale: (1) the seller (Shiraz) surrenders control of the future economic benefits and risks of the receivables, and (2) the purchaser of the receivables (Credit Company) cannot require the seller to repurchase the receivables except as set out in the original provision, and (3) the seller can estimate its obligation under the recourse provision.

Shiraz Company retains control of the future economic benefits. If interest rates decrease, Shiraz can borrow funds at the lower interest rate and repurchase the receivables. Because the receivables carry a fixed interest return, Shiraz enjoys the benefit of the difference between the fixed interest return on the receivables and the lower borrowing cost. If interest rates increase, Shiraz will not repurchase the receivables. Credit Company bears the risk of interest rate increases because of the fixed interest return on the receivables. The control of who benefits from interest rate changes and who bears the risk resides with Shiraz Company. Shiraz Company also bears credit risk in excess of the allowance. Thus, this transaction does not meet the first two criteria as a sale. Shiraz Company should report the transaction as a collateralized loan.

Product Financing Arrangement *SFAS No. 49* (1981) provides that firms recognize product financing arrangements as liabilities if (1) the arrangement requires the sponsoring firm (Shiraz) to purchase the inventory at specified prices and (2) the payments made to the other entity (Credit Company) cover all acquisition, holding, and financing costs.

Shiraz Company agrees to repurchase the inventory at a fixed price, thereby incurring the risk of changing prices. The purchase price formula includes a fixed interest rate, so Shiraz enjoys the benefits or incurs the risk of interest rate changes. Shiraz also controls the benefits and risk of changes in storage costs. Thus, Shiraz treats this product financing arrangement as a collateralized loan.

Throughput Contract *SFAS Statement No. 49* (1981) treats throughput contracts as executory contracts and does not require their recognition as a liability. Note, however, the similarity between a product financing arrangement (involving inventory) and a throughput contract (involving a service). Shiraz Company must pay specified amounts each period regardless of whether it uses the shipping services. The wording of the problem makes it unclear as to whether the initial contract specifies a selling price (railroad bears risk of operating cost increases) or whether the selling price is the railroad's current charges for shipping services each period (Shiraz bears risk of operating cost increases). It seems unlikely that the railroad would accept a fixed price for all ten years. Thus, it appears that Shiraz incurs a commitment to make highly probable future cash payments in amounts that cover the railroad's operating and financing costs. This transaction has the economic characteristics of a collateralized loan, even though GAAP permit treatment as an executory contract.

Construction Joint Venture The construction loan will likely appear as a liability of the books of Shiraz, as well as on the books of Chemical, the joint entity. Shiraz and Mission each own 50 percent but Shiraz appears to have the residual owners' equity because in return for guaranteeing the debt of Chemical, it can buy out Mission for a fixed cost-based price if the venture turns out well. (Chapter 11 discusses consolidated financial statements and variable interest entities.)

GAAP treat the commitment to pay one-half of the operating and debt service costs as an executory contract, similar to the throughput contract. Even though the probability of making future cash payments is high, GAAP conclude that a liability does not arise until the firm receives future benefits from Chemical.

Shiraz will recognize a liability because of its debt guarantee and right to capture the upside if the venture succeeds.

Research and Development Partnership *SFAS No. 68* (1982) requires firms to recognize financings related to research and development (R & D) as liabilities if (1) the sponsoring firm (Shiraz) must repay the financing regardless of the outcome of the R & D work, or (2) the sponsoring firm, even in the absence of a loan guarantee, bears the risk of failure of the R & D effort.

Shiraz guarantees the bank loan in this case regardless of the outcome of the R & D effort and therefore must recognize a liability (satisfies first criterion above). It does not matter whether Shiraz has an option or an obligation to purchase the results of the R & D effort.

If Shiraz did not guarantee the bank loan, then the second criterion above determines whether Shiraz recognizes a liability. If Shiraz has the option to purchase the results of the R & D work, it does not bear the risk of failure and need not recognize a liability. If Shiraz has the obligation to purchase the results, it recognizes a liability for the probable amount payable. The problem does not make it clear whether the amount payable includes the unpaid balance of the loan or merely the value of the R & D work (which could be zero). It seems unlikely that the bank would lend funds for the R & D work without some commitment or obligation by Shiraz to repay the loan.

10.42 continued.

Hotel Financing Shiraz Company will recognize a liability for the hotel financing only if its debt guarantee satisfies the criteria for a loss contingency. It appears in this case that the probability of Shiraz having to make payments under the loan guarantee is low. The hotel is profitable and probably generating cash flows. In addition, the bank can sell the hotel in the event of loan default to satisfy the unpaid balance of the loan. Thus, Shiraz's loan guarantee is a third level of defense against loan default. If default does occur and the first two lines of defense prove inadequate to repay the loan in full, then Shiraz would recognize a liability for the unpaid portion.

10.43   (Xerox Corporation; bundled leases and related earnings quality and ethical issues.)

a. $11,616.12 = $14,816.12 total annual collection − $2,000 for service/maintenance − $1,200 for supplies.

b. $48,328 is the present value of $11,616.12 received annually at the end of each year for seven years; $11,616.12 x 4.16042 [Table 4, 7-period row, 15% column].

c.   Derivation of total interest revenue over life of lease.

End of Year	[1] BV at Start of Year	[2] Interest Revenue	[3] Collection for Equipment and Interest	[4] BV of Lease Receivable at End of Year
0				$48,328
1	$48,328	$7,249.17	$11,616.12	43,961
2	43,961	6,594.13	11,616.12	38,939
3	38,939	5,840.83	11,616.12	33,164
4	33,164	4,974.54	11,616.12	26,522
5	26,522	3,978.30	11,616.12	18,884
6	18,884	2,832.63	11,616.12	10,101
7	10,101	1,515.11	11,616.12	(0)

Total Interest Revenue..... $32,984.72

[1] = [4], preceding year
[2] = [1] x interest rate; 15% in Part *c.* and 12% in Part *f.*
[3] = annual payment; given
[4] = [1] + [2] - [3]

10.43 continued.

d. Gross profit is: $25,328 (= $48,328 – $23,000).

e. As interest rate estimated by Ford decreases, total interest revenue decreases and present value of lease receivable increases, which increases the gross profit recorded at the time of sale.

f. Present value of payments is: $53,013.14 = $11,616.12 x Table 4, 7-period row, 12% column.

   Discount rate = 12% $53,013.14 = $11,616.12 x 4.56376.

End of Year	[1] BV at Start of Year	[2] Interest Revenue	[3] Collection for Equipment and Interest	[4] BV of Lease Receivable at End of Year
0				$53,013
1	$53,013	$6,361.58	$ 11,616.12	47,759
2	47,759	$5,731.03	11,616.12	41,874
3	41,874	$5,024.82	11,616.12	35,282
4	35,282	$4,233.87	11,616.12	27,900
5	27,900	$3,347.99	11,616.12	19,632
6	19,632	$2,355.82	11,616.12	10,372
7	10,372	$1,244.58	11,616.12	(0)

Total Interest Revenue.. $28,299.69

Gross profit is: $30,013 (= $53,013 – $23,000).

The 20 percent decrease in interest rate, from 15% to 12% increases gross profit by about: 18.5% [= ($30,013/$25,328) – 1].

g. Xerox's total cash receipts for the equipment and interest are $81,312 (= 7 x $11,616), which is the total cash receipts for these items. Total revenues equal total cash inflows.

   Xerox's procedures allocate this fixed cash amount between interest and equipment. Total revenue must equal total cash receipts, but Xerox recognizes all revenue (and profit) from equipment at the inception of the lease, while the interest revenue spreads over seven years. Xerox management, if tempted to boost current period income, could shade downward its estimate of Ford's borrowing costs.

10.43 g. continued.

The SEC alleged that Xerox did choose the lessee's borrowing rate with an eye toward managing earnings. Xerox managers claimed that they refined their methods over time to derive better estimates of lessees' borrowing rates, but that the refinements improved the process, and the managers had not designed them to manipulate income. Ultimately, Xerox settled the issues with the SEC by paying a fine and restating earnings, reducing them for the years of lease inception.

The bundled nature of the transactions requires Xerox to estimate either the interest rate or the separate price of the equipment alone. Both these estimates give latitude to the financial manager. It is not clear that the quality of earnings is reduced when Xerox estimates the lessees' borrowing rate than when it estimates the stand-alone price of equipment it rarely, if ever, sells alone in comparable markets. Xerox must estimate one or the other.

Bundled lease transactions offer opportunity for earnings management, so potentially lower the quality of earnings.

Does Xerox confront an ethical issue when unbundling its leasing transactions, as GAAP require? One view argues that ethical issues do not arise so long as Xerox makes its estimates to comply with GAAP. GAAP set the rules and Xerox complies. Another view argues that ethical issues do arise because Xerox has the opportunity to manage income through estimates. The SEC was suspicious that each of Xerox's changes in estimation procedures resulted in shifting income forward to the date of signing the lease.

Ironically, by the time the SEC and Xerox settled their issues, and Xerox restated some of its lease numbers, the result was to increase income in the period of settlement. The result stemmed from restatement of earlier periods' income downwards, for gross profit at lease inception, which resulted in higher interest income over the subsequent years of the lease.

CHAPTER 11

MARKETABLE SECURITIES, DERIVATIVES, AND INVESTMENTS

Questions, Short Exercises, Exercises, Problems, and Cases: Answers and Solutions

11.1   See the text or the glossary at the end of the book.

11.2   Securities that a firm intends to sell within approximately one year of the date of the balance sheet appear as current assets. All other securities appear as noncurrent assets.

11.3   a.   Debt securities that a firm intends to hold to maturity (for example, to lock in the yield at acquisition for the full period to maturity) and has the ability to hold to maturity (for example, the firm has adequate liquid assets and borrowing capacity such that it need not sell the debt securities prior to maturity to obtain cash) appear as "debt held to maturity." All other debt securities appear in the "available for sale" category. The latter includes short-term investments in government debt securities that serve as a liquid investment of excess cash and short-and long-term investments in government and corporate debt securities that serve either as hedges of interest rate, exchange rate, or similar risks or as sources of cash at a later date to pay debt coming due.

   b.   The classification as "trading securities" implies a firm's active involvement in buying and selling securities for profit. The holding period of trading securities is typically measured in minutes or hours instead of days. The classification as "available for sale" implies less frequent trading and usually relates to an operating purpose other than profit alone (for example, to generate income while a firm has temporarily excess cash, to invest in a firm with potential new technologies). The holding period of securities available for sale is typically measured in days, months, or years.

   c.   Amortized acquisition cost equals the purchase price of debt securities plus or minus amortization of any difference between acquisition cost and maturity value. Amortized acquisition cost bears no necessary relation to the market value of the debt security during the periods subsequent to acquisition. The market value of a debt security depends on the risk characteristics of the issuer, the provisions of the debt security with respect to interest rate, term to maturity, and similar factors, and the general level of interest rates in the economy.

11.3 continued.

    d. Unrealized holding gains and losses occur when the market value of a security changes while the firm holds the security. The unrealized holding gain or loss on trading securities appears in the income statement each period, whereas it appears in Accumulated Other Comprehensive Income, a separate shareholders' equity account, each period for securities available for sale.

    e. Realized gains and losses appear in the income statement when a firm sells a security. The realized gain or loss on trading securities equals the selling price minus the market value of the security on the most recent balance sheet. The realized gain or loss on securities available for sale equals the selling price minus the acquisition cost of the security.

11.4   Firms acquire trading securities primarily for their short-term profit potential. Including the unrealized holding gain or loss in income provides the financial statement user with relevant information for assessing the performance of the trading activity. Firms acquire securities available for sale to support an operating activity (for example, investment of temporarily excess cash) instead of primarily for their profit potential. Deferring recognition of any gain or loss until sale treats securities available for sale the same as inventories, equipment and other assets. Excluding the unrealized gain or loss from earnings also reduces earnings volatility.

11.5   The realized gain or loss for a security classified as available for sale equals the selling price minus the acquisition cost of the security. The realized gain or loss for a trading security equals the selling price minus the market value on the date of the most recent balance sheet. GAAP allocate all of the income from a security classified as available for sale to the period of sale, whereas GAAP allocate this same amount of income on a trading security to all periods between purchase and sale.

11.6   The required accounting does appear to contain a degree of inconsistency. One might explain this seeming inconsistency by arguing that the balance sheet and income statement serve different purposes. The balance sheet attempts to portray the resources of a firm and the claims on those users by creditors and owners. Market values for securities are more relevant than acquisition cost or lower-of-cost-or-market for assessing the adequacy of resources to satisfy claims. The income statement reports the results of operating performance. One might argue that operating performance from investing in marketable securities available for sale is not complete until the firm sells the securities. Another argument for excluding at least unrealized gains on marketable securities from earnings is that it achieves consistency with the delayed recognition of unrealized gains on inventories, equipment, and other assets.

    As for earnings quality and ethical issues, the unrealized holding gains can be realized at management whim, which means management can bring

11.6 continued.

the gains from accumulated other comprehensive income into net income. Management cannot manipulate other comprehensive income, only net income. When analysts become accustomed to analyzing other comprehensive income, the manipulation of net income will be less of an earnings quality issue.

11.7　a.　These accounts are both part of accumulated other comprehensive income, a shareholders' equity account, and reflect the change in the market value of securities since acquisition.

　　　b.　Dividend Revenue is an income statement account. It reflects the revenue recognized when a firm uses the market-value method. Equity in Earnings of Unconsolidated Affiliates is also an income statement account. It reflects the revenue recognized when a firm uses the equity method.

　　　c.　Equity in Earnings of Unconsolidated Affiliate is an income statement account. It reflects the revenue earned by a minority, active investor in an investee accounted for using the equity method. Minority Interest in Earnings of Consolidated Subsidiary is an account appearing on the consolidated income statement of a parent and its majority-owned, active investee. It represents the external, minority interest in the earnings of the investee.

　　　d.　Minority Interest in Earnings of Consolidated Subsidiary is an income statement account. It reflects the external, minority interest in the earnings of a majority-owned consolidated subsidiary. Minority Interest in Net Assets of Consolidated Subsidiary is a balance sheet account. It reflects the external, minority interest in the net assets of a consolidated subsidiary.

11.8　Dividends represent revenues under the market-value method and a return of capital under the equity method.

11.9　Under the equity method, the change each period in the net assets, or shareholders' equity, of the subsidiary appears on the one line, Investment in Subsidiary, on the balance sheet. When the parent consolidates the subsidiary, changes in the individual assets and liabilities that comprise the net asset change appear in the individual consolidated assets and liabilities. Likewise, under the equity method, the investor's interest in the investee's earnings appears in one line on the income statement, Equity in Earnings of Unconsolidated Subsidiary. When the parent consolidates the subsidiary, the individual revenues and expenses of the subsidiary appear in consolidated revenues and expenses.

11.10　A derivative is a hedge for a firm when the firm bears a risk such that the change in the value of the derivative attempts to offset the change in the value of the firm as time passes. We can distinguish an attempt at hedging

11.10 continued.

from an effective hedge or even from a partially effective hedge. A firm attempting to hedge by holding a derivative has a hedge, even though that hedge may be only partially effective. When the firm acquires a derivative that is completely ineffective, that is, zero correlated with the hedged item, then we would say the firm does not hold a hedge, even though the firm says it attempts to reduce risk.

Under this interpretation, a derivative is not a hedge when changes in the fair value of the derivative do not at least partially offset other changes in firm value occurring at the same time.

If the firm chooses not to use hedge accounting when it could, the fluctuations in the market value of the derivative appear in income, not offset by the changes in market value of the hedged item. We would say that choosing not to use hedge accounting reduces opportunity for manipulation rather than that it increases it because firms cannot offset gains and losses on the derivative against losses and gains on the hedged item.

11.11   A *fair-value hedge* is a hedge of an exposure to changes in the fair value of a recognized asset or liability or of an unrecognized firm commitment. A *cash-flow hedge* is a hedge of an exposure to variability in the cash flows of a recognized asset or liability, such as variable interest rates, or of a forecasted transaction, such as expected future foreign sales.

11.12   The firm has an effective cash-flow hedge. The change in value of the derivative appears both in the balance sheet valuation of the derivative, which is market value, and in other comprehensive income. However, the firm does not restate to market value the hedged item, so the change in the market value of the hedged item does not appear in income nor in other comprehensive income.

11.13   If Company A owns less than, or equal to, 50 percent of Company B's voting stock, it is a minority investor in Company B. If Company A owns more than 50 percent of Company C, it is a majority investor in Company C. The entities holding the remainder of the voting stock of Company C are minority investors. Their minority interest appears on the consolidated balance sheet of Company A and Company C.

11.14   When the investor uses the equity method, total assets include the Investment in Subsidiary account. The investment account reflects the parent's interest in the *net* assets (assets minus liabilities) of the subsidiary. When the investor consolidates the subsidiary, total consolidated assets include all of the subsidiary's assets. Consolidated liabilities include the liabilities of the subsidiary. Thus, total assets on a consolidated basis exceed total assets when the investor uses the equity method.

11.15 Buildings and equipment have a determinable useful life, whereas the expected useful life of goodwill is indefinite.

11.16 (Accounting principles for marketable securities.)

  a. (4) Firm has option to use hedge accounting, deferring income effects until realization and reporting changes in fair value in periodic other comprehensive income, or not use hedge accounting and reporting holding gains and losses, like trading securities gains and losses, in current period income.

  b. (1) This is a speculative position, so gains and losses appear in current income.

  c. (1) Because not both ability and intent to hold to maturity are present, it will appear at market value. Because the firm trades securities such as this, the classification is as a trading security. If the firm were not a trader, then Treatment (3) would apply.

  d. (3) Standard treatment for securities available for sale.

11.17 (Fischer/Black Co.; working backwards from data on marketable securities transaction.)

  a. $21,000 = $18,000 + $3,000.

  b $18,000, the amount credited to Marketable Securities in the journal entry which the student might think of as $21,000 acquisition cost, derived above, less $3,000 of Unrealized Holding Loss.

  c. $5,000 loss from the debit for Realized Loss.

11.18 (Canning/Werther; working backwards from data on marketable securities transaction.)

  a. $15,000 = $18,000 proceeds − $4,000 realized gain + $1,000 loss previously recognized because they are trading securities.

  b. $14,000 = $18,000 proceeds − $4,000 realized gain which is selling price less acquisition cost because they are securities available for sale.

11.19 (Reconstructing events from journal entries.)

  a. The market value of a marketable security is $4,000 less than its book value and the firm increases the Unrealized Holding Loss account on the balance sheet.

  b. A firm sells marketable securities for an amount that is $200 (= $1,100 − $1,300) less than was originally paid for them.

11.19 continued.

   c. The market value of marketable securities is $750 more than its book value and the firm increases the Unrealized Holding Gain account on the balance sheet.

   d. A firm sells marketable securities for an amount that is $100 (= $1,800 − $1,700) more than was originally paid for them.

11.20   (Hanna Company; equity method entries.)

Investment in Stock of Denver Company (Asset Increase)	550,000	
Cash (Asset Decrease)		550,000
To record acquisition of common stock.		

Investment in Stock of Denver Company (Asset Increase)	120,000	
Retained Earnings (Equity in Earnings of Denver Company) (Shareholders' Equity Increase)		120,000
To accrue 100 percent share of Denver Company's earnings.		

Cash or Dividends Receivable (Asset Increase)	30,000	
Investment in Stock of Denver Company (Asset Decrease)		30,000
To accrue dividends received or receivable.		

11.21   (Laesch Company; working backwards to consolidation relations.)

   a. $70,000 = ($156,000 − $100,000)/.80.

   b. 72.7 percent = ($156,000 − $100,000)/$77,000.

   c. $56,000 = ($156,000 − $100,000).

11.22   (Dealco Corporation; working backwards from consolidated income statements.) (Amounts in Millions)

   a. $56/$140 = 40 percent.

   b. [.40 X (1 − .25) X $140] = $42.

   c. [1 − ($42/$280)] = 1 − .15 = 85 percent.

11.23 (Classifying securities.)

    a. Securities available for sale; current asset.

    b. Debt securities held to maturity; noncurrent asset.

    c. Securities available for sale; current asset.

    d. Securities available for sale; noncurrent asset.

    e. Trading securities; current asset.

    f. Securities available for sale; noncurrent asset (although a portion of these bonds might appear as a current asset).

11.24 (Vermont Company; journal entries to apply the market value method to short-term investments in securities.)

8/21

Marketable Securities (Asset Increase)..........................	45,000	
Cash (Asset Decrease)...		45,000

To record the cost of purchases in asset account: (1,000 x $45) = $45,000.

9/13

No entry because September 13 is not the end of an accounting period.

9/30

Dividends Receivable (Asset Increase)...........................	500	
Retained Earnings (Dividend Revenue) (Shareholders' Equity Increase)...		500

To record declaration of dividend as revenue: 1,000 x $0.50 = $500.

10/25

Cash (Asset Increase)...	500	
Dividends Receivable (Asset Decrease)......................		500

To record receipt of dividend in cash.

12/31

Marketable Securities (Asset Increase)..........................	6,000	
Accumulated Other Comprehensive Income (Unrealized Holding Gain on Securities Available for Sale) (Shareholders' Equity Increase)....................		6,000

To record increase in market price: 1,000 x ($51 – $45) = $6,000.

11.24 continued.

1/20

Cash (600 x $55) (Asset Increase)	33,000	
Marketable Securities (600 x $45) (Asset Decrease)		27,000
Realized Earnings (Realized Gain on Sale of Securities Available for Sale) [600 x ($55 – $45)] (Shareholders' Equity Increase)		6,000

To record sale of 600 shares of Texas Instruments.

Accumulated Other Comprehensive Income (Unrealized Holding Gain on Securities Available for Sale) [600 x ($51– $45)] (Shareholders' Equity Decrease)	3,600	
Marketable Securities (Asset Decrease)		3,600

To eliminate changes previously recorded in the market value of Texas Instruments.

11.25 (Elston Corporation; journal entries to apply the market value method for short-term investments in securities.)

10/15/Year 4

Marketable Securities (Security A) (Asset Increase)	28,000	
Cash (Asset Decrease)		28,000

To record acquisition of shares of Security A.

11/02/Year 4

Marketable Securities (Security B) (Asset Increase)	49,000	
Cash (Asset Decrease)		49,000

To record acquisition of shares of Security B.

12/31/Year 4

Cash (Asset Increase)	1,000	
Retained Earnings (Dividend Revenue) (Shareholders' Equity Increase)		1,000

To record dividend received from Security B.

12/31/Year 4

Accumulated Other Comprehensive Income (Unrealized Holding Loss on Security A Available for Sale) (Shareholders' Equity Decrease)	3,000	
Marketable Securities (Security A) (Asset Decrease)		3,000

To record unrealized holding loss on Security A.

11.25 continued.

12/31/Year 4

Marketable Securities (Security B) (Asset Increase)...	6,000	
Accumulated Other Comprehensive Income (Unrealized Holding Gain on Security B Available for Sale) (Shareholders' Equity Increase)............		6,000

To record unrealized holding gain on Security B.

2/10/Year 5

Cash (Asset Increase)..	24,000	
Retained Earnings (Realized Loss on Sale of Securities Available for Sale) ($24,000 − $28,000) (Shareholders' Equity Decrease)...............................	4,000	
Marketable Securities (Security A) (Asset Decrease)..		28,000

To record sale of Security A.

Marketable Securities (Security A) (Asset Increase)...	3,000	
Accumulated Other Comprehensive Income (Unrealized Holding Loss on Security A Available for Sale) (Shareholders' Equity Increase)..............		3,000

To eliminate the effects of changes previously recorded in the market value of Security A.

12/31/Year 5

Cash (Asset Increase)...	1,200	
Retained Earnings (Dividend Revenue) (Shareholders' Equity Increase)...		1,200

To record dividend received from Security B.

12/31/Year 5

Accumulated Other Comprehensive Income (Unrealized Holding Gain on Security B Available for Sale) (Shareholders' Equity Decrease)......................	2,000	
Marketable Securities (Security B) ($53,000 − $55,000) (Asset Decrease)................................		2,000

To revalue Security B to market value.

7/15/Year 6

Cash (Asset Increase)...	57,000	
Marketable Securities (Security B) (Asset Decrease)..		49,000
Retained Earnings (Realized Gain on Sale of Securities Available for Sale) ($57,000 − $49,000) (Shareholders' Equity Increase).............................		8,000

To record sale of Security B.

11.25 continued.

Accumulated Other Comprehensive Income (Unrealized Holding Gain on Security B Available for Sale) ($6,000 – $2,000) (Shareholders' Equity Decrease) 4,000

    Marketable Securities (Security B) (Asset Decrease)   4,000

To eliminate the effects of changes previously recorded in the market value of Security B.

11.26   (Simmons Corporation; journal entries to apply the market value method to short-term investments in securities.)

6/13/Year 6

Marketable Securities (Security S) (Asset Increase).... 12,000
Marketable Securities (Security T) (Asset Increase).... 29,000
Marketable Securities (Security U) (Asset Increase)... 43,000
    Cash (Asset Decrease)   84,000

To record acquisition of marketable equity securities as a temporary investment.

10/11/Year 6

Cash (Asset Increase) 39,000
Retained Earnings (Realized Loss on Sale of Security U Available for Sale) (Shareholders' Equity Decrease) 4,000
    Marketable Securities (Security U) (Asset Decrease)   43,000

To record sale of Security U.

12/31/Year 6

Marketable Securities (Security S) ($13,500 – $12,000) (Asset Increase) 1,500
    Accumulated Other Comprehensive Income (Unrealized Holding Gain on Security S Available for Sale) (Shareholders' Equity Increase)   1,500

To revalue Security S to market value.

12/31/Year 6

Accumulated Other Comprehensive Income (Unrealized Holding Loss on Security T Available for Sale) (Shareholders' Equity Decrease) 2,800
    Marketable Securities (Security T) ($26,200 – $29,000) (Asset Decrease)   2,800

To revalue Security T to market value.

11.26 continued.

12/31/Year 7

Marketable Securities (Security S) ($15,200 – $13,500) (Asset Increase)	1,700	
Accumulated Other Comprehensive Income (Unrealized Holding Gain on Security S Available for Sale) (Shareholders' Equity Increase)		1,700

To revalue Security S to market value.

12/31/Year 7

Marketable Securities (Security T) ($31,700 – $26,200) (Asset Increase)	5,500	
Accumulated Other Comprehensive Income (Unrealized Holding Loss on Security T Available for Sale) (from 12/31/Year 6 Entry) (Shareholders' Equity Increase)		2,800
Accumulated Other Comprehensive Income (Unrealized Holding Gain on Security T Available for Sale) (Shareholders' Equity Increase)		2,700

To revalue Security T to market value.

2/15/Year 8

Cash (Asset Increase)	14,900	
Marketable Securities (Security S) (Asset Decrease)		12,000
Retained Earnings (Realized Gain on Sale of Security S Available for Sale) ($14,900 – $12,000) (Shareholders' Equity Increase)		2,900

To record sale of Security S.

Accumulated Other Comprehensive Income (Unrealized Holding Gain on Security S Available for Sale) ($1,500 + $1,700) (Shareholders' Equity Decrease)	3,200	
Marketable Securities (Security S) (Asset Decrease)		3,200

To eliminate the effects of changes previously recorded in the market value of Security S.

8/22/Year 8

Cash (Asset Increase)	28,500	
Retained Earnings (Realized Loss on Sale of Securities Available for Sale) (Security T) ($28,500 – $29,000) (Shareholders' Equity Decrease)	500	
Marketable Securities (Security T) (Asset Decrease)		29,000

To record sale of Security T.

11.26 continued.

> Accumulated Other Comprehensive Income (Unrealized Holding Gain on Security T Available for Sale) (Shareholders' Equity Decrease)...................... 2,700
> > Marketable Securities (Security T) (Asset Decrease)... 2,700
>
> To eliminate the effects of changes previously recorded in the market value of Security T.

11.27 (Apollo Corporation; amount of income recognized under various methods of accounting for investments.)

a. and b.

> $3.0 million = .15 x $20 million. Increase in market value has no effect on income.

c. $24 million = .30 x $80 million.

11.28 (Trusco; balance sheet and income effects of alternative methods of accounting for investments.)

Part	Investment	Net Income
a.	$40 million	$3 million
b.	$39 million	$3 million
c.	$45 million	$3 million
d.	$126 million[a]	$15 million[b]
e.	$166 million[c]	$15 million[d]

[a]$120 million + .30($50 million – $30 million) = $126 million.
[b].30 x $50 million = $15 million.
[c]$160 million + .30($50 million – $30 million) = $166 million.
[d].30 x $50 million = $15 million.

11.29 (Randle Corporation; journal entries to apply the market value method for long-term investments in securities.)

April 10, Year 1
Investment in Securities (M) (Asset Increase)............... 37,000
> Cash (Asset Decrease).. 37,000

July 11, Year 1
Investment in Securities (N) (Asset Increase)............. 31,000
> Cash (Asset Decrease).. 31,000

September 29, Year 1
Investment in Securities (O) (Asset Increase) 94,000
> Cash (Asset Decrease).. 94,000

11.29 continued.

December 31, Year 1
Cash (Asset Increase)... 7,900
    Retained Earnings (Dividend Revenue) (Share-
        holders' Equity Increase) 7,900

December 31, Year 1
Accumulated Other Comprehensive Income (Unre-
    alized Holding Loss on Investments in Securities)
    (M) (Shareholders' Equity Decrease)........................... 2,000
    Investment in Securities (M) (Asset Decrease).. 2,000

December 31, Year 1
Investment in Securities (N) (Asset Increase).............. 7,000
    Accumulated Other Comprehensive Income (Un-
        realized Holding Gain on Investment in Secur-
        ities) (N) (Shareholders' Equity Increase)........... 7,000

December 31, Year 1
Accumulated Other Comprehensive Income (Unre-
    alized Holding Loss on Investment in Securities)
    (O) (Shareholders' Equity Decrease) 7,000
    Investment in Securities (O) (Asset Decrease).. 7,000

October 15, Year 2
Cash (Asset Increase)... 43,000
    Investment in Securities (M) (Asset Decrease)....... 37,000
    Retained Earnings (Realized Gain on Sale of In-
        vestment in Securities) (Shareholders' Equity
        Increase) 6,000

October 31, Year 2 or December 31, Year 2
Investment in Securities (M) (Asset Increase).............. 2,000
    Accumulated Other Comprehensive Income (Un-
        realized Holding Loss on Investment in Secur-
        ities) (M) (Shareholders' Equity Increase)........... 2,000

December 31, Year 2
Cash (Asset Increase)... 5,600
    Retained Earnings (Dividend Revenue) (Share-
        holders' Equity Increase) 5,600

December 31, Year 2
Investment in Securities (N) (Asset Increase).............. 7,000
    Accumulated Other Comprehensive Income (Un-
        realized Holding Gain on Investment in Secur-
        ities) (N) (Shareholders' Equity Increase)........... 7,000

11.29 continued.

December 31, Year 2

Investment in Securities (O) (Asset Increase)	2,000	
Accumulated Other Comprehensive Income (Unrealized Holding Loss on Investment in Securities) (O) (Shareholders' Equity Increase)		2,000

11.30   (Blake Company; journal entries to apply the market value method to long-term investments in securities.)

July 2, Year 4

Investment in Securities (G) (Asset Increase)	42,800	
Cash (Asset Decrease)		42,800

October 19, Year 4

Investment in Securities (H) (Asset Increase)	29,600	
Cash (Asset Decrease)		29,600

October 29, Year 4

Cash (Asset Increase)	89,700	
Retained Earnings (Realized Loss on Sale of Investments in Securities) (Shareholders' Equity Decrease)	4,000	
Investment in Securities (F) (Asset Decrease) ...		93,700

October 29, Year 4 or December 31, Year 4

Investment in Securities (F) (Asset Increase)	2,500	
Accumulated Other Comprehensive Income (Unrealized Holding Loss on Investment in Securities) (F) (Shareholders' Equity Increase)		2,500

December 31, Year 4

Accumulated Other Comprehensive Income (Unrealized Holding Loss on Investment in Securities) (G) (Shareholders' Equity Decrease)	4,500	
Investment in Securities (G) (Asset Decrease)		4,500

December 31, Year 4

Investment in Securities (H) (Asset Increase)	2,000	
Accumulated Other Comprehensive Income (Unrealized Holding Gain on Investment in Securities) (H) (Shareholders' Equity Increase)		2,000

February 9, Year 5

Investment in Securities (I) (Asset Increase)	18,100	
Cash (Asset Decrease)		18,100

11.30 continued.

September 17, Year 5

Cash (Asset Increase)..	32,300	
Investment in Securities (H) (Asset Decrease).......		29,600
Retained Earnings (Realized Gain on Sale of Investment in Securities) (Shareholders' Equity Increase)..		2,700

September 17, Year 5 or December 31, Year 5

Accumulated Other Comprehensive Income (Unrealized Holding Gain on Investment in Securities) (H) (Shareholders' Equity Decrease)..........................	2,000	
Investment in Securities (H) (Asset Decrease)...		2,000

December 31, Year 5

Accumulated Other Comprehensive Income (Unrealized Holding Loss on Investment in Securities) (G) (Shareholders' Equity Decrease)..........................	1,400	
Investment in Securities (G) (Asset Decrease)...		1,400

December 31, Year 5

Investment in Securities (I) (Asset Increase).................	2,600	
Accumulated Other Comprehensive Income (Unrealized Holding Gain on Investment in Securities) (I) (Shareholders' Equity Increase)........................		2,600

11.31   (Wood Corporation; journal entries to apply the equity method of accounting for investments in securities.)

January 2

Investment in Securities (Knox) (Asset Increase).........	350,000	
Investment in Securities (Vachi) (Asset Increase)........	196,000	
Investment in Securities (Snow) (Asset Increase)........	100,000	
Cash (Asset Decrease)...		646,000

December 31

Investment in Securities (Knox) (Asset Increase).........	35,000	
Investment in Securities (Vachi) (Asset Increase)........	12,000	
Investment in Securities (Snow) (Asset Decrease)...		4,800
Retained Earnings (Equity in Earnings of Affiliates) (Shareholders' Equity Increase)..................		42,200

$(.50 \times \$70,000) + (.30 \times \$40,000) - (.20 \times \$24,000) = \$42,200.$

11.31 continued.

December 31
Cash (Asset Increase).. 19,500
    Investment in Securities (Knox) (Asset Decrease)..   15,000
    Investment in Securities (Vachi) (Asset De-
       crease)..   4,500
(.50 x $30,000) + (.30 x $15,000) = $19,500.

11.32   (Stebbins Corporation; journal entries to apply the equity method of accounting for investments in securities.)

a. **January 1, Year 1**
Investment in Securities (R) (Asset Increase)........ 250,000
Investment in Securities (S) (Asset Increase)........ 325,000
Investment in Securities (T) (Asset Increase)........ 475,000
    Cash (Asset Decrease).....................................   1,050,000

December 31, Year 1
Investment in Securities (R) (Asset Increase)........ 50,000
Investment in Securities (S) (Asset Increase)........ 48,000
    Investment in Securities (T) (Asset Decrease)...   75,000
    Retained Earnings (Equity in Earnings of Affil-
       iates) (Shareholders' Equity Increase).............   23,000
(.25 x $200,000) + (.40 x $120,000) − (.50 x
$150,000) = $23,000.

December 31, Year 1
Cash (Asset Increase)... 63,250
    Investment in Securities (R) (Asset De-
       crease)..   31,250
    Investment in Securities (S) (Asset Decrease)..   32,000
(.25 x $125,000) + (.40 x $80,000) = $63,250.

December 31, Year 1
Retained Earnings (Depreciation Expense) (Share-
    holders' Equity Decrease)......................................   4,000
    Investment in Securities (R) (Asset De-
       crease)...   4,000

The cost of the investment in Company R exceeds the book value of the net assets acquired by $50,000 [= $250,000 − (.25 x $800,000)]. Stebbins Corporation attributes $40,000 of the excess to buildings and must depreciate $4,000 (= $40,000/10) each year. The firm attributes the remaining excess to goodwill, which it need not depreciate.

The cost of the investment in Company S exceeds its book value by $25,000 [= $325,000 − (.40 x $750,000)]. Stebbins Corporation attributes this excess to goodwill. The acquisition cost of the investment in Security T equals the book value of the net assets acquired.

11.32 a. continued.

December 31, Year 2
Investment in Securities (R) (Asset Increase)........ 56,250
Investment in Securities (S) (Asset Increase)........ 30,000
Investment in Securities (T) (Asset Increase)........ 25,000
    Retained Earnings (Equity in Earnings of Affil-
    iates) (Shareholders' Equity Increase).............   111,250
(.25 x $225,000) + (.40 x $75,000) + (.50 x
$50,000) − $111,250

December 31, Year 2
Cash (Asset Increase)...................................... 64,500
    Investment in Securities (R) (Asset Decrease)..   32,500
    Investment in Securities (S) (Asset Decrease)...   32,000
(.25 x $130,000) + (.40 x $80,000).

December 31, Year 2
Retained Earnings (Depreciation Expense) (Share-
    holders' Equity Decrease)....................................... 4,000
    Investment in Securities (R) (Asset De-
    crease)...   4,000

b.   Cash (Asset Increase)... 275,000
    Retained Earnings (Loss on Sale of Investments)
    (Shareholders' Equity Decrease)......................... 9,500
       Investment in Securities (R) (Asset De-
       crease)...   284,500
    $250,000 + $50,000 − $31,250 − $4,000 +
    $56,250 − $32,500 − $4,000 = $284,500.

11.33   (Mulherin Corporation; journal entries under various methods of accounting
for investments.)

January 2
Investment in Hanson (Asset Increase)...................... 320,000
Investment in Maloney (Asset Increase).................... 680,000
Investment in Quinn (Asset Increase)......................... 2,800,000
    Cash (Asset Decrease)...   3,800,000
To record acquisition of investments.

December 31
Cash (Asset Increase)... 6,000
    Retained Earnings (Dividend Revenue) (Share-
    holders' Equity Increase)......................................   6,000
To record dividend from Hanson: .15 x $40,000 =
$6,000.

11.33 continued.

December 31
Accumulated Other Comprehensive Income (Unrealized Holding Loss on Investment in Secur-
ities) (Shareholders' Equity Decrease).................... 15,000
    Investment in Hanson (Asset Decrease)............ 15,000
To apply the market value method to the investment
in Hanson.

December 31
Investment in Maloney (Asset Increase)...................... 150,000
    Retained Earnings (Equity in Earnings of
        Maloney) (Shareholders' Equity Increase).......... 150,000
To recognize share of Maloney's earnings; .30 x
$500,000 = $150,000.

December 31
Cash (Asset Increase)... 54,000
    Investment in Maloney (Asset Decrease).............. 54,000
To recognize share of Maloney's dividends; .30 x
$180,000 = $54,000.

December 31
Retained Earnings (Amortization Expense)
    (Shareholders' Equity Decrease)............................. 8,000
        Investment in Maloney (Asset Decrease).......... 8,000
To amortize excess acquisition cost for Maloney;
$680,000 − (.30 x $2,000,000) = $80,000; $80,000/
10 = $8,000.

December 31
Investment in Quinn (Asset Increase) 600,000
    Retained Earnings (Equity in Earnings of
        Quinn) (Shareholders' Equity Increase) 600,000
To recognize share of Quinn's earnings.

December 31
Cash (Asset Increase)... 310,000
    Investment in Quinn (Asset Decrease) 310,000
To recognize share of Quinn's dividends.

11.34   (CAR Corporation; consolidation policy and principal consolidation
concepts.)

   a.   CAR Corporation should consolidate Alexandre du France Software
        Systems and R Credit Corporation or, under exceptional
        circumstances, use the market value method.

11.34 continued.

b.

Charles Electronics	(.75 X $120,000) =	$	90,000
Alexandre du France Software Systems....	(.80 X 60,000) =		48,000
R Credit Corporation	(.90 X 144,000) =		129,600
Total Income from Subsidiaries		$	267,600

c.   Minority Interest shown under accounting assumed in problem:

Charles Electronics	(.25 X $120,000) =	$	30,000
Alexandre du France Software Systems....	(None) =		--
R Credit Corporation	(None) =		--
		$	30,000

CAR Corporation subtracts the minority interest in computing net income.

d.   Charles Electronics, no increase because already consolidated.

Alexandre du France Software Systems increase by 80 percent of net income less dividends:

.80 X ($96,000 − $60,000) = $28,800.

R Credit Corporation, no increase because equity method results in the same income statement effects as do consolidated statements. Net income of CAR Corporation would be:

$1,228,800 = $1,200,000 (as reported) + $28,800 (increase).

e.   Minority Interest shown if CAR Corporation consolidated all companies:

Charles Electronics	(.25 X $120,000) =	$	30,000
Alexandre du France Software Systems..	(.20 X 96,000) =		19,200
R Credit Corporation	(.10 X 144,000) =		14,400
		$	63,600

11.35   (Bush Corporation; equity method entries, earnings quality, and ethics.) (Amounts in Millions.)

a.   Investment in Stock of Cheney Computer (Asset
        Increase) 100
            Cash (Asset Decrease)   100
        To record acquisition of shares of common stock.

11.35 a. continued.

Investment in Stock of Cheney Computer (Asset Increase)	20	
Retained Earnings (Equity in Earnings of Cheney Computer) (Shareholders' Equity Increase)		20

To accrue Cheney Computer's earnings for the year.

Cash (Asset Increase) (or Dividends Receivable) ...	6	
Investment in Stock of Cheney Computer (Asset Decrease) ..		6

To recognize dividends received or receivable.

Retained Earnings (Amortization Expense) (Shareholders' Equity Decrease)	1.6	
Investment in Stock of Cheney Computer (Asset Decrease)		1.6

To amortize patent; $1.6 = [.20 \times (\$500 - \$420)/10]$.
Investment is now $112.4 = \$100 + \$20 - \$6 - \$1.6$.

b. GAAP provide a rebuttable presumption that less than 20 percent ownership means no need to use the equity method, but the primary test is that of significant influence. Firms should not be able to manipulate their use, or not, of the equity method by small changes in ownership percentage because small changes likely do not alter the ability, or not, to exert influence. Still, companies toy with the percentage and auditors seem to acquiesce.

11.36 (Joyce Company and Vogel Company; equity method entries.)

Joyce Company's Books

(1) Investment in Stock of Vogel Company (Asset Increase)	420,000	
Cash (Asset Decrease)		420,000

To record acquisition of common stock.

(2) Accounts Receivable (Asset Increase)	29,000	
Retained Earnings (Sales Revenue) (Shareholders' Equity Increase)		29,000

To record intercompany sales on account.

(2) Retained Earnings (Cost of Goods Sold) (Shareholders' Equity Decrease)	29,000	
Inventories (Asset Decrease)		29,000

To record cost of intercompany sales.

11.36 continued.

(3) Advance to Vogel Company (Asset Increase).........   6,000
    Cash (Asset Decrease)...   6,000
    To record advance to Vogel Company.

(4) Cash (Asset Increase)...   16,000
    Accounts Receivable (Asset Decrease)...............   16,000
    To record collections on account from Vogel Com-
    pany.

(5) Cash (Asset Increase)...   4,000
    Advance to Vogel Company (Asset Decrease)....   4,000
    To record collection of advance from Vogel Com-
    pany.

(6) Cash (Asset Increase)...   20,000
    Investment in Stock of Vogel Company (Asset
      Decrease)...   20,000
    To record dividend from Vogel Company.

(7) Investment in Stock of Vogel Company (Asset
      Increase)...   30,000
    Retained Earnings (Equity in Earnings of
      Vogel Company) (Shareholders' Equity
      Increase)...   30,000
    To accrue 100 percent share of Vogel Company's
    net income.

(8) Retained Earnings (Amortization Expense)
      (Shareholders' Equity Decrease)...........................   4,000
    Investment in Stock of Vogel Company
      (Asset Decrease)...   4,000
    To record amortization of patent; $4,000 =
    ($420,000 − $380,000)/10.

Vogel Company's Books

(1) No entry.

(2) Inventories (Asset Increase)...................................   29,000
    Accounts Payable (Liability Increase)................   29,000
    To record intercompany purchase of materials on
    account.

(3) Cash (Asset Increase)...   6,000
    Advance from Joyce Company (Liability In-
      crease)...   6,000
    To record advance from Joyce Company.

11.36 continued.

    (4) Accounts Payable (Liability Decrease)..................... 16,000
          Cash (Asset Decrease)... 16,000
       To record payment for purchases on account.

    (5) Advance from Joyce Company (Liability De-
        crease).. 4,000
          Cash (Asset Decrease) 4,000
       To record repayment of advance.

    (6) Retained Earnings (Shareholders' Equity De-
        crease).. 20,000
          Cash (Asset Decrease) 20,000
       To record declaration and payment of dividend.

11.37   (Alpha/Omega; working backwards from data which has eliminated intercompany transactions.)

    a. $80,000 = $450,000 + $250,000 – $620,000.

    b. $30,000 is Omega's cost; $20,000 is Alpha's cost; $20,000 original cost to Alpha.

        Markup on the goods sold from Alpha to Omega, which remain in Omega's inventory, is $10,000 (= $60,000 + $50,000 – $100,000).
        Because Alpha priced the goods with markup 50 percent over its costs, the cost to Alpha to produce goods with markup of $10,000 is $20,000 and the total sales price from Alpha to Omega is $30,000 (= $10,000 + $20,000).

11.38   (Homer/Tonga; working backwards from purchase data.)

    a. $1,060,000 = $80,000 + $980,000.

    b.   Book Value of Total Assets (from Part *a.*)............................ $1,060,000
        Less Book Value of Current Assets.. (210,000)
        Less Book Value of Goodwill 0
        Book Value of Depreciable Assets.. $ 850,000

11.39 (Bristol-Myers and Squibb; financial statement effects of the revaluations required by the purchase method.)

a. (Amounts in Millions)

	Purchase Method
Assets, Except Goodwill	$ 17,173[c]
Goodwill	2,569[d]
Total Assets	$ 19,742
Liabilities	$ 3,325[b]
Shareholders' Equity	16,417[a]
Total Equities	$ 19,742

[a]$3,547 + $12,870 = $16,417.
[b]$1,643 + $1,682 = $3,325.
[c]$5,190 + $3,083 + $2,500 + $6,400 = $17,173.
[d]$12,870 − $1,401 − $2,500 − $6,400 = $2,569.

b. (Amounts in Millions)

	Purchase Method
Precombination Projected Consolidated Net Income	$ 1,748
Building and Equipment Depreciation: $2,500/10	(250)
Patent Amortization: $6,400/5	(1,280)
Revised Projected Net Income	$ 218

11.40 (Effects of transactions involving the market value methods on the statement of cash flows.)

a. The journal entry to record this transaction is as follows:

Marketable Securities (Asset Increase)	59,800	
Cash (Asset Decrease)		59,800

Because this entry involves a credit to the Cash account, Line (11) decreases by $59,800. The purchase of marketable securities (whether trading or, as here, securities available for sale) is an Investing activity, so Line (7) increases by $59,800. Note that Line (7) carries a negative sign, so increasing it reduces cash.

b. The journal entries to record this transaction are as follows:

Cash (Asset Increase)	47,900	
Marketable Securities (Asset Decrease)		42,200
Retained Earnings (Realized Gain on Sale of Securities Available for Sale) (Shareholders' Equity Increase)		5,700

11.40 b. continued.

Accumulated Other Comprehensive Income
(Unrealized Holding Gain on Securities Available for Sale) (Shareholders' Equity Decrease)... 1,800
    Marketable Securities ($44,000 − $42,200)
      (Asset Decrease) 1,800

Because the first entry involves a debit to the Cash account, Line (11) increases by $47,900. The sale of securities available for sale is an Investing activity, so Line (6) increases by $47,900 and there is no effect on Cash Flow from Operations. Because the realized gain is an income statement account, Line (3) increases by $5,700. We show all of the cash proceeds of sale ($47,900) on Line (6). Under the indirect method, we double count cash in the amount of the gain if we do not eliminate $5,700 from the Operations section of the statement of cash flows. Thus, Line (5) increases by $5,700 to offset the realized gain. The net effect of the entries on Line (3) and Line (5) is zero. The second entry does not involve an income statement account or the Cash account and therefore would not appear on the statement of cash flows.

c. The journal entries to record this transaction are as follows:

Cash (Asset Increase) 18,700
Retained Earnings (Realized Loss on Sale of Se-
  curities Available for Sale) (Shareholders'
  Equity Decrease) 6,400
    Marketable Securities (Asset Decrease) 25,100

Marketable Securities ($25,100 − $19,600)
  (Asset increase) 5,500
    Accumulated Other Comprehensive Income
      (Unrealized Holding Loss on Securities
      Available for Sale) (Shareholders' Equity
      Increase) 5,500

Because the first entry involves a debit to the Cash account, Line (11) increases by $18,700. The sale of securities available for sale is an Investing activity, so Line (6) increases by $18,700 and there is no effect on Cash Flow from Operations. Because the realized loss is an income statement account, Line (3) decreases by $6,400. The loss used no cash so Line (4) shows an addback of $6,400. The second entry does not involve the Cash account, nor any income statement account, so it does not affect the statement of cash flows.

d. The journal entry is as follows:

Accumulated Other Comprehensive Income (Unrealized Holding Loss on Securities Available
  for Sale) (Shareholders' Equity Decrease)............   19,000
    Marketable Securities ($220,500 –
      $201,500) (Asset Decrease).........................   19,000

This entry does not involve a debit or credit to the Cash account, so
Line (11) is not affected. This entry also does not affect an income
statement account (the Unrealized Holding Loss on Securities Available for Sale account is part of other comprehensive income), so Line
(3) is not affected. Thus, this entry does not appear on the statement
of cash flows. The firm would disclose this event in a supplementary
schedule or note if the amount were material.

e. The journal entry is as follows:

Marketable Securities (Asset Increase).................   7,400
  Accumulated Other Comprehensive Income
    (Unrealized Holding Gain on Securities
    Available for Sale) (Shareholders' Equity
    Increase)..   7,400

For the same reasons given in Part d. above, this entry does not appear
on the statement of cash flows. The firm would disclose this event in a
supplementary schedule or note if the amount were material.

f. The journal entry to record this transaction is:

Cash (Asset Increase)...   8,000
  Retained Earnings (Dividend Revenue) (Share-
    holders' Equity Increase)....................................   8,000

The Cash account increases, so Line (11) increases by $8,000. Line (1)
increases by $8,000. Net income increases, so Line (3) increases by
$8,000.

g. The journal entry to record this event is:

Accumulated Other Comprehensive Income (Unrealized Holding Loss on Securities Available
  for Sale) (Shareholders' Equity Decrease)............   2,000
    Investments in Securities (Asset Decrease)....   2,000

The Cash account does not change so there is no effect on Line (11).
Net income does not change so there is no effect on Line (3). The firm
would disclose this event in a supplementary schedule or note if the
amount were material.

11.41   (Effects of transactions involving the equity method on the statement of cash flows.)

a.   The journal entry to record this transaction is:

Cash (.40 x $10,000) (Asset Increase).....................	4,000	
Investment in Affiliate [.40 x ($25,000 – $10,000)]		
(Asset Increase)...	6,000	
Retained Earnings (Equity in Earnings of		
Affiliate) (.40 x $25,000) (Shareholders'		
Equity Increase)...		10,000

The Cash account increases in the amount of the dividend, so Lines (1) and (11) increase $4,000. Net income on Line (3) increases by $10,000 for the equity in earnings. Because the firm recognizes more revenue ($10,000) than the cash received ($4,000), it must increase Line (5) by $6,000 to convert net income to cash flow from operations.

b.   The journal entry to record this event is:

Retained Earnings (Equity in Loss of Affiliate)		
(.40 x $12,500) (Shareholders' Equity De-		
crease)...	5,000	
Investment in Affiliate (Asset Decrease)........		5,000

There is no effect on the Cash account so Line (11) does not change. Net income decreases for the share of the loss so Line (3) decreases by $5,000. Because the loss does not use cash, Line (4) increases by $5,000 when converting net income to cash flow from operations.

c.   The journal entry to record this event is:

Retained Earnings (Amortization Expense)		
(Shareholders' Equity Decrease)...........................	3,000	
Investment in Affiliate (Asset Decrease)........		3,000

There is no effect on the Cash account so Line (11) does not change. Net income on Line (3) decreases for amortization expense. Because the amortization expense does not reduce cash, Line (4) increases by $3,000 when converting net income to cash flow from operations.

11.42 (Effect of errors involving securities available for sale on financial statement ratios.)

		Rate of Return on Assets	Debt Equity Ratio
a.	Accumulated Other Comprehensive Income (Unrealized Holding Loss on Securities Available for Sale) (Shareholders' Equity Decrease)............ X	$\dfrac{NO}{O/S} = U/S$	$\dfrac{NO}{O/S} = U/S$
	Marketable Securities (Asset Decrease)............ X		
b.	Investment in Securities (Asset Increase)............ X	$\dfrac{NO}{U/S} = O/S$	$\dfrac{NO}{U/S} = O/S$
	Accumulated Other Comprehensive Income (Unrealized Holding Gain on Securities Available for Sale) (Shareholders' Equity Increase)............ X		
c.	Cash (Asset Increase)............ X	$\dfrac{U/S}{U/S} = U/S$	$\dfrac{NO}{U/S} = O/S$
	Retained Earnings (Dividend Revenue) (Shareholders' Equity Increase)............ X		
d.	Cash (Asset Increase)............ X	$\dfrac{O/S}{O/S} = O/S$	$\dfrac{NO}{O/S} = U/S$
	Investment Account (Asset Decrease)............ X		
e.	Retained Earnings (Depreciation Expense) (Shareholders' Equity Decrease)............ X	$\dfrac{O/S}{O/S} = O/S$	$\dfrac{NO}{O/S} = U/S$
	Investment Account (Asset Decrease)............ X		

Note: This problem asks only for the net effect of each error on the two financial ratios. The journal entries and the numerator and denominator effects appear to show the reason for the net effect.

11.43 (Effect of errors on financial statements.)

	Assets	Liabilities	Shareholders' Equity	Net Income
a.	U/S	No	U/S	U/S
b.	O/S	No	O/S	No
c.	O/S	No	O/S	O/S
d.	O/S	No	O/S	O/S
e.	No	No	No	No
f.	O/S	O/S	No	No
g.	No	U/S	O/S	O/S

11.44 (Dostal Corporation; journal entries and financial statement presentation of short-term securities available for sale.)

a. **2/05/Year 1**

Marketable Securities (Security A) (Asset Increase)	60,000	
Cash (Asset Decrease)		60,000

8/12/Year 1

Marketable Securities (Security B) (Asset Increase)	25,000	
Cash (Asset Decrease)		25,000

12/31/Year 1

Marketable Securities (Security A) ($66,000 − $60,000) (Asset Increase)	6,000	
Accumulated Other Comprehensive Income (Unrealized Holding Gain on Security A Available for Sale) (Shareholders' Equity Increase)		6,000

Accumulated Other Comprehensive Income (Unrealized Holding Loss on Security B Available for Sale) (Shareholders' Equity Decrease)	5,000	
Marketable Securities (Security B) ($20,000 − $25,000) (Asset Decrease)		5,000

1/22/Year 2

Marketable Securities (Security C) (Asset Increase)	82,000	
Cash (Asset Decrease)		82,000

2/25/Year 2

Marketable Securities (Security D) (Asset Increase)	42,000	
Cash (Asset Decrease)		42,000

11.44 a. continued.

3/25/Year 2

Marketable Securities (Security E) (Asset Increase)......	75,000	
Cash (Asset Decrease)......		75,000

6/05/Year 2

Cash (Asset Increase)......	72,000	
Marketable Securities (Security A) (Asset Decrease)......		60,000
Retained Earnings (Realized Gain on Sale of Securities Available for Sale) (Shareholders' Equity Increase)......		12,000

Accumulated Other Comprehensive Income (Unrealized Holding Gain on Security A Available for Sale) (Shareholders' Equity Decrease)......	6,000	
Marketable Securities (Security A) (Asset Decrease)......		6,000

6/05/Year 2

Cash (Asset Increase)......	39,000	
Retained Earnings (Realized Loss on Sale of Securities Available for Sale) (Shareholders' Equity Decrease)......	3,000	
Marketable Securities (Security D) (Asset Decrease)......		42,000

12/31/Year 2

Marketable Securities (Security B) ($23,000 – $20,000) (Asset Increase)......	3,000	
Accumulated Other Comprehensive Income (Unrealized Holding Loss on Security B Available for Sale) (Shareholders' Equity Increase)......		3,000

12/31/Year 2

Accumulated Other Comprehensive Income (Unrealized Holding Loss on Security C Available for Sale) (Shareholders' Equity Decrease)......	3,000	
Marketable Securities (Security C) ($79,000 – $82,000) (Asset Decrease)......		3,000

11.44 a. continued.

12/31/Year 2
Marketable Securities (Security E) ($80,000 –
$75,000) (Asset Increase) 5,000
    Accumulated Other Comprehensive Income
    (Unrealized Holding Gain on Security E
    Available for Sale) (Shareholders' Equity
    Increase) 5,000

b. **Balance Sheet on December 31, Year 1**
Marketable Securities at Market Value .... $ 86,000
Net Unrealized Holding Gain on Securities Available for
    Sale ($6,000 – $5,000) .... $ 1,000

Footnote
Marketable Securities on December 31, Year 1 had an acquisition cost of $85,000 and a market value of $86,000. Gross unrealized gains total $6,000 and gross unrealized losses total $5,000.

c. **Balance Sheet on December 31, Year 2**
Marketable Securities at Market Value .... $ 182,000
Net Unrealized Holding Loss on Securities Available for
    Sale.. -0-

Footnote
Marketable Securities on December 31, Year 2 had an acquisition cost of $182,000 and a market value of $182,000. Gross unrealized gains total $5,000 and gross unrealized losses total $5,000. Proceeds from sales of marketable securities totaled $111,000 during Year 2. These sales resulted in gross realized gains of $12,000 and gross realized losses of $3,000. The net unrealized holding loss on securities available for sale changed as follows during Year 2:

Balance, December 31, Year 1 .... $ 1,000 Cr.
Accumulated Other Comprehensive Income (Unre-
    alized Holding Gain on Securities Sold) .... (6,000) Dr.
Change in Net Unrealized Loss on Securities Held at
    Year End ($3,000 – $3,000 + $5,000) .... 5,000 Cr.
Balance, December 31, Year 2 .... $ --

11.45 (Rice Corporation; journal entries and financial statement presentation of long-term securities available for sale.)

a. **3/05/Year 1**
Investments in Securities (Security A) (Asset
    Increase) 40,000
        Cash (Asset Decrease) 40,000

11.45 a. continued.

5/12/Year 1

Investments in Securities (Security B) (Asset Increase)..	80,000	
Cash (Asset Decrease).......................................		80,000

12/31/Year 1

Investments in Securities (Security A) ($45,000 – $40,000) (Asset Increase).................	5,000	
Accumulated Other Comprehensive Income (Unrealized Holding Gain on Security A Available for Sale) (Shareholders' Equity Increase)..		5,000

12/31/Year 1

Accumulated Other Comprehensive Income (Un-realized Holding Loss on Security B Available for Sale) (Shareholders' Equity Decrease)...........	10,000	
Investments in Securities (Security B) ($70,000 – $80,000) (Asset Decrease).......		10,000

3/22/Year 2

Investments in Securities (Security C) (Asset Increase)..	32,000	
Cash (Asset Decrease).......................................		32,000

5/25/Year 2

Investments in Securities (Security D) (Asset Increase)..	17,000	
Cash (Asset Decrease).......................................		17,000

5/25/Year 2

Investments in Securities (Security E) (Asset Increase)..	63,000	
Cash (Asset Decrease).......................................		63,000

10/05/Year 2

Cash (Asset Increase)...	52,000	
Investments in Securities (Security A) (Asset Decrease)...		40,000
Retained Earnings (Realized Gain on Sale of Securities Available for Sale) (Shareholders' Equity Increase)...		12,000

11.45 a. continued.

Accumulated Other Comprehensive Income (Unrealized Holding Gain on Security A Available
for Sale) (Shareholders' Equity Decrease)........... 5,000
    Investments in Securities (Security A)
    (Asset Decrease)................................. 5,000

10/05/Year 2
Cash (Asset Increase)................................. 16,000
Retained Earnings (Realized Loss on Sale of Se-
curities Available for Sale) (Shareholders'
Equity Decrease) 1,000
    Investments in Securities (Security D)
    (Asset Decrease)................................. 17,000

12/31/Year 2
Investments in Securities (Security B) ($83,000
  – $70,000) (Asset Increase)............................. 13,000
    Other Comprehensive Income (Unrealized
    Holding Loss on Security B Available for
    Sale) (Shareholders' Equity Increase)......... 10,000
    Accumulated Other Comprehensive Income
    (Unrealized Holding Gain on Security B
    Available for Sale) (Shareholders' Equity
    Increase)... 3,000

12/31/Year 2
Accumulated Other Comprehensive Income (Unrealized Holding Loss on Security C Available
for Sale) (Shareholders' Equity Decrease)
($27,000 – $32,000)................................. 5,000
    Investments in Securities (Security C)
    (Asset Decrease)................................. 5,000

12/31/Year 2
Investments in Securities (Security E) ($67,000
  – $63,000) (Asset Increase)............................. 4,000
    Accumulated Other Comprehensive Income
    (Unrealized Holding Gain on Security E
    Available for Sale) (Shareholders' Equity
    Increase)... 4,000

11.45 continued.

 b. **Balance Sheet on December 31, Year 1**

  Investments in Securities at Market Value............................ $ 115,000
  Net Unrealized Holding Loss on Securities Available for
   Sale ($5,000 − $10,000).. $ (5,000)

  Footnote
  Investments in Securities on December 31, Year 1 had an acquisition cost of $120,000 and a market value of $115,000. Gross unrealized gains total $5,000 and gross unrealized losses total $10,000.

 c. **Balance Sheet on December 31, Year 2**

  Investments in Securities at Market Value............................ $ 177,000
  Net Unrealized Holding Gain on Securities Available for
   Sale.. $ 2,000

  Footnote
  Investments in Securities on December 31, Year 2 had an acquisition cost of $175,000 and a market value of $177,000. Gross unrealized gains total $7,000 (= $3,000 + $4,000) and gross unrealized losses total $5,000. Proceeds from sales of investments in securities totaled $68,000 during Year 2. These sales resulted in gross realized gains of $12,000 and gross realized losses of $1,000. The net unrealized holding loss on securities available for sale changed as follows during Year 2:

  Balance, December 31, Year 1... $ (5,000) Dr.
  Unrealized Holding Gain on Securities Sold....................... (5,000) Dr.
  Change in Net Unrealized Loss on Securities Held at
   Year End ($13,000 − $5,000 + $4,000)........................... <u>12,000</u> Cr.
  Balance, December 31, Year 2 .... <u>$ 2,000</u> Cr.

11.46 (Zeff Corporation; reconstructing transactions involving short-term securities available for sale.)

 a. Sale of marketable securities during Year 2: Proceeds of $14,000; gain on sale is $4,000 = $14,000 − $10,000, so original cost was $10,000.

 b. Book value at time of sale was $13,000, so unrealized holding gain at time of sale was $3,000 = $13,000 − $10,000.

 c. The ending balance of Net Unrealized holding Gains was $2,000 less at the end of Year 2 than at the beginning, while the unrealized holding gain on the securities sold was $3,000. The sale reduced the balance by $3,000. Since the ending balance declined by only $2,000, the securities on hand must have increased during the year by $1,000, so the net decline is $2,000 = $3,000 − $1,000.

11.46 continued.

    d. The Marketable Securities account increased by $9,000 = $196,000 − $187,000 during Year 2. The sale reduced the account by $13,000 and the unrealized holding gain on the securities held at the end of the year increased the balance by $1,000; see Part *c*. A net increase of $9,000 after a reduction of $12,000 means the cost of new securities is $21,000 = $9,000 + $12,000.

11.47 (Sunshine Mining Company; analysis of financial statement disclosures for securities available for sale.) (Amounts in Thousands)

    a. $10,267 loss = $11,418 − $21,685.

    b. $2,649 gain = $8,807 − $6,158.

    c. $12,459 = $21,685 − $6,158 − $3,068.

    d. None. The unrealized holding loss on current marketable securities of $2,466 (= $4,601 − $7,067) and the unrealized holding gain on noncurrent marketable securities of $2,649 (= $8,807 − $6,158) appear in the shareholders' equity section of the balance sheet.

11.48 (Callahan Corporation; effect of various methods of accounting for marketable equity securities.)

    a. **Trading Securities**

	Year 1	Year 2
Income Statement:		
Dividend Revenue	$ 3,300	$ 2,200
Unrealized Holding Gain (Loss):		
($54,000 − $55,000)	(1,000)	--
($17,000 − $14,000)	--	3,000
Realized Holding Gain (Loss) ($14,500 +		
$26,000) − ($16,000 + $24,000)	--	500
Total	$ 2,300	$ 5,700
Balance Sheet:		
Current Assets:		
Marketable Securities at Market Value	$54,000	$ 17,000

11.48 continued.

   b. **Securities Available for Sale (Current Asset)**

	Year 1	Year 2
Income Statement:		
Dividend Revenue	$ 3,300	$ 2,200
Realized Holding Gain (Loss): [$40,500 −		
($18,000 + $25,000)].....................................	--	(2,500)
Total..	$ 3,300	$ (300)
Balance Sheet:		
Current Assets:		
Marketable Securities at Market Value	$54,000	$ 17,000
Shareholders' Equity:		
Net Unrealized Holding Gain (Loss) on Se-		
curities Available for Sale (Part of Accu-		
mulated Other Comprehensive Income):		
($54,000 − $55,000).....................................	(1,000)	--
($17,000 − $12,000).....................................	--	5,000

   c. Same as Part *b.* except that the securities appear as Investments in Securities in the noncurrent assets section of the balance sheet.

   d.

	Trading Securities	Securities Available for Sale	
		Current Assets	Noncurrent Assets
Year 1	$ 2,300	$ 3,300	$ 3,300
Year 2	5,700	(300)	(300)
Total..............................	$ 8,000	$ 3,000	$ 3,000

The unrealized gain on Security I of $5,000 (= $17,000 − $12,000) at the end of Year 2 appears in income if these securities are trading securities but in a separate shareholders' equity account if these securities are securities available for sale (either a current asset or a noncurrent asset). Total shareholders' equity is the same. Retained earnings (pretax) are $5,000 larger if these securities are trading securities and the unrealized holding gain account is $5,000 larger if these securities are classified as securities available for sale.

11.49   (Citibank; analysis of financial statement disclosures related to marketable securities and quality of earnings.) (Amounts in Millions)

   a.

Cash (Asset Increase)	37,600
Retained Earnings (Realized Loss on Sale of Se-	
curities Available for Sale) (Shareholders'	
Equity Decrease)...	113
Retained Earnings (Realized Gain on Secur-	
ities Available for Sale) (Shareholders'	
Equity Increase)...	443
Marketable Securities (Asset Decrease)	37,270[a]

    [a]$14,075 + $37,163 − $13,968 = $37,270.

11.49 a. continued.

Marketable Securities (Asset Increase)..................	262	

Accumulated Other Comprehensive Income
  (Unrealized Holding Loss on Securities
  Available for Sale) ($37,270 – $37,008)
  (Shareholders' Equity Increase)........................
		262

b.
Balance, December 31, Year 10 ($957 – $510)................	$	447 Cr.
Net Unrealized Holding Loss on Securities Sold (from Part a.)..		262 Cr.
Increase in Net Unrealized Holding Gain on Securities Held on December 31, Year 11 (Plug)...........................		518 Cr.
Balance, December 31, Year 11 ($1,445 – $218).............	$	1,227 Cr.

c.
Interest and Dividend Revenue	$	1,081

Net Realized Gain on Securities Sold from Market
  Price Changes Occurring During Year 11:
  ($37,600 – $37,008)...
		592

Net Unrealized Holding Gain on Securities Held on December 31, Year 11 (from Part b.)............................		518
Total Income...	$	2,191

d. Citibank sold marketable securities during Year 11 which had net unrealized holding losses of $262 million as of December 31, Year 10. The sale of these securities at a gain suggests that market prices increased substantially ($592 million) during Year 11. The substantial increase in the net unrealized holding gain of $518 lends support to this conclusion about market price increases. Citibank could have increased its income still further by selecting securities for sale that had unrealized holding *gains* as of December 31, Year 10. If prices continued to increase on such securities during Year 11 prior to sale, the realized gain would have been even larger than the reported net realized gain of $330 million (= $443 – $113). Firms with securities available for sale with unrealized holding gains can manage income by choosing which items to sell. This will not affect Comprehensive Income, but until analysts focus on Comprehensive Income, rather than Net Income, managements will be tempted to manage the Net Income figure. Most would not consider such earnings management a breach of ethics.

11.50 (Rockwell Corporation; journal entries for various methods of accounting for intercorporate investments.)

a.
Investment in Stock of Company R (Asset Increase)...	648,000	
Cash (Asset Decrease)		648,000
To record acquisitions of shares of Company R.		

11.50 a. continued.

Cash and Dividends Receivable (Asset Increase) .. 48,000
   Retained Earnings (Dividend Revenue) (Share-
      holders' Equity Increase) 48,000
To record dividends received or receivable.

Accumulated Other Comprehensive Income (Unrealized Holding Loss on Investment in Securities) (Shareholders' Equity Decrease) 24,000
   Investment in Stock of Company R (Asset
     Decrease)... 24,000
To write down investment in stock of Company R
account to market value; $24,000 = $648,000 –
$624,000.

b. Investment in Stock of Company S (Asset
    Increase)... 2,040,000
     Cash (Asset Decrease)................................. 2,040,000
To record acquisitions of shares of Company S.

Investment in Stock of Company S (Asset
    Increase)... 360,000
     Retained Earnings (Equity in Earnings of
      Company S) (Shareholders' Equity
      Increase)... 360,000
To accrue share of Company S's earnings;
$360,000 = .30 x $1,200,000.

Cash and Dividends Receivable (Asset Increase) .. 144,000
   Investment in Stock of Company S (Asset
     Decrease) 144,000
To record dividends received or receivable.

c. Investment in Stock of Company T (Asset
    Increase)... 6,000,000
     Cash (Asset Decrease)................................. 6,000,000
To record acquisitions of shares of Company T.

Investment in Stock of Company T (Asset
    Increase)... 1,200,000
     Retained Earnings (Equity in Earnings of
      Company T) (Shareholders' Equity
      Increase)... 1,200,000
To accrue earnings of Company T; $1,200,000 =
100% x $1,200,000.

11.50 c. continued.

Cash and Dividends Receivable (Asset Increase).. 480,000

    Investment in Stock of Company T (Asset Decrease)... 480,000

    To record dividends received or receivable.

11.51   (Coke and Pepsi; effect of intercorporate investment policies on financial statements.)

a. Coke as Reported: $[\$1,364 + (1 - .34)(\$231)]/\$9,280 = 16.3\%.$
Coke's Bottlers: $[\$290 + (1 - .34)(\$452)]/\$11,110 = 5.3\%.$
Coke and Bottlers
  Consolidated: $[\$1,364 + (1 - .34)(\$231 + \$452) + .51(\$290)]/\$18,675 = 10.5\%.$

Pepsi as Reported: $[\$1,091 + (1 - .34)(\$689)/\$15,637 = 9.9\%.$

b. Coke as Reported: $(\$4,296 + \$1,133)/\$9,280 = 58.5\%.$
Coke's Bottlers: $(\$2,752 + \$4,858)/\$11,110 = 68.5\%.$
Coke and Bottlers
  Consolidated: $(\$7,048 + \$5,991)/\$18,675 = 69.8\%.$

Pepsi as Reported: $(\$3,264 + \$7,469)/\$15,637 = 68.6\%.$

c. The rate of return on assets using reported amounts suggests that Coke is considerably more profitable than Pepsi. This measure of the rate of return on assets includes Coke's 49 percent interest in the earnings of its bottlers but does not include Coke's 49 percent interest in the assets of these bottlers. Coke's rate of return on assets with its bottlers consolidated includes 100 percent of the net income and assets of these bottlers. Thus, Coke appears only slightly more profitable than Pepsi during Year 8.

Coke's liabilities to assets ratio is less than the corresponding ratio for its bottlers. On a comparable measurement basis with Pepsi, Coke has slightly more debt in its capital structure instead of approximately 14.7 percent less debt as indicated by the reported amounts [14.7% = (68.6% − 58.5%)/68.6%].

d. Coke's intercorporate investment policy permits it to report higher profitability and lower debt ratios than if it held a sufficient ownership percentage to consolidate its bottlers. Coke's 49 percent ownership probably permits it to exert control over its bottlers because (1) the remaining 51 percent is widely-held by many individuals and institutions, and (2) Coke maintains exclusive contracts with its bottlers that tie their success to Coke's success. Thus, one might argue that consolidation reflects the economic reality of the relationship better than use of the equity method.

11.52 (Interaction of regulation and accounting rules for financial institutions, particularly banks.)

Effects of Changing Market Value of Assets on a Bank's Activities
Bank Has Capital Ratio of 5 Percent

Step [1]: Market Value of Assets Increases, Also Increasing Owners' Equity
Step [2]: Bank Increases Lending to Maintain Capital (Leverage) Ratio at 5 Percent
Step [3]: Market Value of Original Bank Decreases, Decreasing Owners' Equity
Step [4]: Bank Decreases Lending to Maintain Capital (Leverage) Ratio at 5 Percent
Operating Income Excludes Gains and Losses in Market Value of Assets Held

Balance Sheet				Partial Income Statement		Rate of Return On:	
Original Bank, Before Market Value Changes							
Assets		Equities		Revenues as			
		Liabilities:		% of Assets			
$1,000 Original		Borrowings............	$950	7.0%	$70.0		
				Interest Expense			
				5.5%	(52.3)		
		Owners' Equity		Operating Expense			
		Contributed Capital ...	50	% of Assets			
		Retained Earnings....	0	0.4%	(4.0)		
		Total Owners' Equity.	$50	Fixed Costs.....	(1.0)	Assets...	1.3%
						Owners'	
$1,000		Totals	$1,000	Operating Income	$12.8	Equity...	25.5%

Balance Sheet				Partial Income Statement		Rate of Return On:	
Market Value of Assets							
Increases 4.0%							
Assets		Equities		Revenues as			
		Liabilities:		% of Assets			
$1,000 Original		Original Borrowings..	$950	7.0%	$126.0		
				Interest Expense			
[1] 40 Market Value Increase				5.5%	(94.1)		
[2] 760 New Lending	[2]	New Borrowing.......	760	Operating Expense			
				% of Assets			
		Owners' Equity:		0.4%	(7.2)		
		Contributed Capital...	50	Fixed Costs.....	(1.0)		
	[1]	Retained Earnings....	40				
		Total Owners' Equity.	$90			Assets....	1.3%
						Owners'	
$1,800		Totals	$1,800	Operating Income	$23.8	Equity...	26.4%

Balance Sheet				Partial Income Statement		Rate of Return On:	
Market Value of Assets							
Decreases -4.0%							
Assets		Equities		Revenues as			
		Liabilities:		% of Assets			
$1,000 Original		Original Borrowings..	$950	7.0%	$14.0		
				Interest Expense			
[3] (40) Market Value Decline				5.5%	(10.5)		
[4] (760) Reduce Lending	[4]	Reduce Borrowing....	(760)	Operating Expense			
				% of Assets			
		Owners' Equity:		0.4%	(0.8)		
		Contributed Capital...	50	Fixed Costs.......	(1.0)		
	[3]	Retained Earnings....	(40)				
		Total Owners' Equity.	$10			Assets....	0.9%
						Owners'	
$200		Totals	$200	Operating Income	$1.8	Equity...	17.5%

CHAPTER 12

SHAREHOLDERS' EQUITY: CAPITAL CONTRIBUTIONS, DISTRIBUTIONS, AND EARNINGS

Questions, Short Exercises, Exercises, Problems, and Cases: Answers and Solutions

12.1 See the text or the glossary at the end of the book.

12.2 The common shareholders would not likely receive an amount equal to the amounts in the common shareholders' equity accounts. The amounts in these accounts reflect acquisition cost valuations for assets. The firm might sell assets for more or less than their book values, with the common shareholders thereby receiving more or less than the amount in the common shareholders' equity accounts. Furthermore, the bankruptcy and liquidation process requires legal and other costs not now reflected on the balance sheet. The asset sales must generate sufficient cash to pay these costs before the common shareholders receive any residual cash.

12.3 The accounting for each of these transactions potentially involves transfers between contributed capital and retained earnings accounts and clouds the distinction between capital transactions and operating transactions. The market value method of accounting for stock options results in a reduction in net income and retained earnings and an increase in contributed capital. The accounting for stock dividends results in a reduction in retained earnings and an increased in contributed capital. The purchase of treasury stock represents a reduction in both contributed capital and accumulated earnings. The reissuance of treasury stock at a "loss" may result in a debit to both contributed capital and retained earnings. Thus, the Common Stock and Additional Paid-in Capital accounts do not reflect just capital transactions and Retained Earnings does not reflect just operating transactions.

12.4 The three provisions provide different benefits and risks to the issuing firm and the investor and should sell at different prices. Callable preferred stock should sell for less than convertible preferred stock. The issuing firm gains benefits with an option to call, or repurchase, the preferred stock and must thereby accept a lower issue price. The investor gains benefits with an option to convert into common stock and must pay a higher price. The mandatory redemption requirement makes the preferred stock more like debt than shareholders' equity. Its market price depends on market interest rates for similar maturity debt (versus the 4 percent yield on the preferred stock) and the rank-ordering priority of the preferred stock in bankruptcy.

12.5   All three items permit their holder to acquire shares of common stock at a set price. Their values depend on the difference between the market price and the exercise price on the exercise date and the length of the exercise period. Firms grant stock options to employees, grant stock rights to current shareholders and either sell stock warrants on the open market or attach them to a debt or preferred stock issue. The issuance of stock options and stock rights does not result in an immediate cash inflow, whereas the issuance of a stock warrant usually does. Accountants amortize the cost of stock options to expense over the expected period of benefit. Accountants credit a Stock Warrant account if the value of the stock warrant is objectively measurable. At the time of exercise of all these items, the accountant records the cash proceeds as a capital contribution.

12.6   The greater the volatility of the stock price, the larger is the potential excess of the market price over the exercise price on the exercise date and the greater the benefit to the employee. The longer the time between the grant date and the exercise date, the more time that elapses for the market price to increase. Offsetting the value of this increased benefit element is the longer time to realize the benefit, which reduces the present value of the option. Stock option valuation models discount the expected benefit element in a stock option to a present value. The larger the discount rate, the smaller is the present value of the benefit.

12.7   The theoretical rationale is matching expenses of employee compensation with the benefit received in the form of higher revenues from employees' services.

12.8   In the case of a cash dividend, the shareholder now holds the investment in two parts—cash and stock certificates. The sum of the cash and the book value of the stock after the dividend declaration equals the book value of the stock before the firm declared the dividend. It is common to speak of a cash dividend as income, but it is merely the conversion of a portion of the shareholder's investment into a different form. In a sense, the shareholder earns income on the investment when the corporation earns its income. Because of the realization test for income recognition in accounting, however, the shareholders do not recognize income (except under the equity method discussed in Chapter 11) until the firm distributes cash. A stock dividend does not even improve the marketability of the investment, although when a firm issues preferred shares to common shareholders or vice versa, shareholders may view the situation as similar to a cash dividend. The stock dividend capitalizes a portion of retained earnings.

12.9   The managers of a firm have knowledge of the plans and risks of the firm that external investors may not possess. Although laws prevent firms from taking advantage of this "inside information," inclusion of gains from treasury stock transactions in net income might motivate firms to buy and sell treasury stock to improve reported earnings. Excluding these gains from net income removes this incentive. Also, the accounting for the acquisition of treasury stock (that is, a reduction from total shareholders'

12.9 continued.

> equity) has the same effect on shareholders' equity as a retirement of the capital stock. The reissue of the treasury stock for more than its acquisition cost does not result in a gain any more than the issue of common stock for more than par value represents a gain.

12.10   There are at least two issues here. First, the proposal gives management an opportunity to decide which income items are and are not likely to recur. Firms can manage earnings with their choice. Second, the proposal presumes that an analyst will not overlook certain income items that appear only in the statement of retained earnings. It also presumes that the firm will provide sufficient information about income items for the analyst to judge if it should be in earnings.

12.11   The FASB suggests that the distinction between performance-related (subject to significant influence by management) and non-performance-related (subject to external influences not controllable by management) items drives the exclusion. The real reason, however, we suspect, has to do with the volatility of some of the items of other comprehensive income. Including all holding gains and losses on securities held in earnings will cause reported earnings to fluctuate (in response to fluctuations in market prices) more than it would otherwise. Many, probably most, managers prefer to report stable earnings in contrast to fluctuating earnings. All else equal, the less risky the earnings stream—that is, the less volatile are reported earnings—the higher will be the market price of the firm's shares.

12.12   An error in previously-issued financial statements results from oversights or errors which the firm should not have made given reasonable diligence in accessing available information at the time. Accountants restate the previously-issued financial statements to correct the error. A change in accounting principles results either from a firm's choice to change accounting principles or from a mandated change by a standard-setting body. Firms retroactively restate previously-issued financial statements for the accounting change. A change in an accounting estimate results from *new* information that suggests that the original estimate was inaccurate as judged *ex post*. Accountants adjust for changes in estimates during the current and future periods instead of restating previously-issued financial statements.

12.13   (Office Depot; journal entry to issue common stock.) (Amounts in Millions)

Cash (= 10 million X $12.50) (Asset Increase) 125
  Common Stock (= 10 million X $2) (Shareholders'
    Equity Increase) 20
  Additional Paid-in Capital (= 10 million X $10.50)
    (Shareholders' Equity Increase) 105

12.14   (Intel; accounting for stock options.)

The value of the stock options on December 31, Year 13, is $1,200,000 (= 100,000 x $12). Intel amortizes this value as an expense of $400,000 (= $1,200,000/3) for Year 14, Year 15, and Year 16. Intel recognizes no additional expense when employees exercise their options in Year 18.

12.15   (Symantec; accounting for conversion of bonds.)

Book Value Method

Convertible Bonds Payable (Liability Decrease)	10,255,000	
Common Stock (100,000 x $10) (Shareholders' Equity Increase)		1,000,000
Additional Paid-in Capital (Plug) (Shareholders' Equity Increase)		9,255,000

Market Value Method

Convertible Bonds Payable (Liability Decrease)	10,255,000	
Retained Earnings (Loss on Conversion of Bonds) (Plug) (Shareholders' Equity Decrease)	245,000	
Common Stock (100,000 x $10) (Shareholders' Equity Increase)		1,000,000
Additional Paid-in Capital (100,000 x $95) (Shareholders' Equity Increase)		9,500,000

12.16   (Wyeth Corporation; accounting for declaration and payment of a dividend.)

December 10, Year 13

Retained Earnings (100,000 x $100 x .04) (Shareholders' Equity Decrease)	400,000	
Dividend Payable (Liability Increase)		400,000

January 10, Year 14

Dividend Payable (Liability Decrease)	400,000	
Cash (Asset Decrease)		400,000

12.17   (PepsiCo; accounting for treasury stock transactions.)

July 15, Year 13

Treasury Stock (Shareholders' Equity Decrease) (75,000 x $55)	4,125,000	
Cash (Asset Decrease)		4,125,000

February 10, Year 14

Cash (Asset Increase) (50,000 x $62)	3,100,000	
Treasury Stock (Shareholders' Equity Increase) (50,000 x $55)		2,750,000
Additional Paid-in Capital (Shareholders' Equity Increase) (Plug)		350,000

12.18   (Champion Enterprises; computation of net income and comprehensive income.) (Amounts in Millions)

Net Income: $126.7 – $26.9 – $10.3 = $89.5.
Comprehensive Income: $89.5 + $17.9 = $107.4.

12.19   (Treatment of accounting errors, changes in accounting principles, and changes in accounting estimates.)

   (1) Accounting Error:
         Year 12: $1,100 (= $1,500 – $400)
         Year 13: $1,800

   (2) Change in Accounting Principle:
         Year 12: $1,100 (= $1,500 – $400)
         Year 13: $1,800

   (3) Change in Accounting Estimate:
         Year 12: $1,500
         Year 13: $1,800

12.20   (Journal entries to record the issuance of capital stock.)

   a. Cash (= 50,000 x $30) (Asset Increase)............. 1,500,000
         Common Stock (= 50,000 x $5) (Share-
            holders' Equity Increase)   250,000
         Additional Paid-in Capital (= 50,000 x $25)
            (Shareholders' Equity Increase)..................   1,250,000

   b. Cash (= 20,000 x $100) (Asset Increase).......... 2,000,000
         Preferred Stock (Shareholders' Equity
            Increase)   2,000,000

   c. Patent (= 16,000 x $15) (Asset Increase)..........   240,000
         Common Stock (= 16,000 x $10) (Share-
            holders' Equity Increase)   160,000
         Additional Paid-in Capital (= 16,000 x $5)
            (Shareholders' Equity Increase)..................   80,000

   d. Convertible Preferred Stock (Shareholders'
         Equity Decrease)   400,000
         Common Stock (= 25,000 x $1) (Share-
            holders' Equity Increase)...........................   25,000
         Additional Paid-in Capital (= $400,000 –
            $25,000) (Shareholders' Equity
            Increase)...   375,000

12.20 continued.

e. Retained Earnings (Compensation Expense)
(= 5,000 x $12) (Shareholders' Equity De-
crease).. 60,000

    Common Stock (= 5,000 x $10) (Share-
    holders' Equity Increase)........................ 50,000

    Additional Paid-in Capital (= 5,000 x $2)
    (Shareholders' Equity Increase) 10,000

12.21 (Journal entries for the issuance of common stock.)

a. Inventory (Asset Increase).............................. 175,000
Land (Asset Increase)....................................... 220,000
Building (Asset Increase).................................. 1,400,000
Equipment (Asset Increase).............................. 405,000

    Common Stock (= 20,000 x $10) (Share-
    holders' Equity Increase) 200,000

    Additional Paid-in Capital (Shareholders'
    Equity Increase)...................................... 2,000,000

b. Cash (= 10,000 x $100) (Asset Increase).......... 1,000,000

    Redeemable Preferred Stock (Liability
    Increase) 1,000,000

c. Cash (= 5,000 x $24) (Asset Increase)............... 120,000
Common Stock Warrants (= 5,000 x $8)
(Shareholders' Equity Decrease) 40,000

    Common Stock (= 5,000 x $1) (Share-
    holders' Equity Increase)........................ 5,000

    Additional Paid-in Capital (Shareholders'
    Equity Increase) 155,000

d. Preferred Stock (= 10,000 x $50) (Share-
holders' Equity Decrease)............................... 500,000

    Common Stock (= 20,000 x $10) (Share-
    holders' Equity Increase)........................ 200,000

    Additional Paid-in Capital (Shareholders'
    Equity Increase) 300,000

12.22 (Morrissey Corporation; journal entries for employee stock options.)

December 31, Year 13
No entry.

12.22 continued.

December 31, Year 14 and December 31, Year 15

Retained Earnings (Compensation Expense) (= $400,000/2) (Shareholders' Equity Decrease)	200,000	
Additional Paid-in Capital (Stock Options) (Shareholders' Equity Increase)		200,000

June 30, Year 15

Cash (= 30,000 x $60) (Asset Increase)	1,800,000	
Additional Paid-in Capital (Stock Options) [= (30,000/50,000) x $400,000] (Shareholders' Equity Decrease)	240,000	
Common Stock (= 30,000 x $1) (Shareholders' Equity Increase)		30,000
Additional Paid-in Capital [= $240,000 + (30,000 x $59)] (Shareholders' Equity Increase)		2,010,000

November 15, Year 16

Cash (= 20,000 x $60) (Asset Increase)	1,200,000	
Additional Paid-in Capital (Stock Options) [= (20,000/50,000) x $400,000] (Shareholders' Equity Decrease)	160,000	
Common Stock (= 20,000 x $1) (Shareholders' Equity Increase)		20,000
Additional Paid-in Capital [= $160,000 + (20,000 x $59)] (Shareholders' Equity Increase)		1,340,000

12.23 (Watson Corporation; journal entries for employee stock options.)

December 31, Year 6, Year 7, and Year 8

Retained Earnings (Compensation Expense) (= $75,000/3) (Shareholders' Equity Decrease)	25,000	
Additional Paid-in Capital (Stock Options) (Shareholders' Equity Increase)		25,000

April 30, Year 9

Cash (= 15,000 x $25) (Asset Increase)	375,000	
Additional Paid-in Capital (Stock Options) [= (15,000/20,000) x $75,000] (Shareholders' Equity Decrease)	56,250	
Common Stock (= 15,000 x $10) (Shareholders' Equity Increase)		150,000
Additional Paid-in Capital [= $56,250 + (15,000 x $15)] (Shareholders' Equity Increase)		281,250

12.23 continued.

September 15, Year 10
Cash (= 5,000 x $25) (Asset Increase) 125,000
Additional Paid-in Capital (Stock Options) [= (5,000/
   20,000) x $75,000] (Shareholders' Equity De-
   crease) 18,750
     Common Stock (= 5,000 x $10) (Shareholders'
      Equity Increase) 50,000
     Additional Paid-in Capital [= $18,750 +
      (5,000 x $15)] (Shareholders' Equity
      Increase) 93,750

12.24   (Kiersten Corporation; journal entries for stock warrants.)

February 26, Year 12
Cash (Asset Increase) 240,000
   Common Stock Warrants (= 60,000 x $4)
     (Shareholders' Equity Increase) 240,000

June 6, Year 14
Cash (= 40,000 x $30) (Asset Increase) 1,200,000
Common Stock Warrants (= 40,000 x $4) (Share-
   holders' Equity Decrease) 160,000
     Common Stock (= 40,000 x $10) (Share-
      holders' Equity Increase) 400,000
     Additional Paid-in Capital (Shareholders'
      Equity Increase) 960,000

February 26, Year 16
Common Stock Warrants (= 20,000 x $4) (Share-
   holders' Equity Decrease) 80,000
     Additional Paid-in Capital (Shareholders'
      Equity Increase) 80,000

12.25   (Higgins Corporation; journal entries for convertible bonds.)

a. **1/02/Year 1**
    Cash (Asset Increase) 1,000,000
       Convertible Bonds Payable (Liability
        Increase) 1,000,000
    To record the issue of convertible bonds.

12.25 a. continued.

  1/02/Year 5
  Convertible Bonds Payable (Liability Decrease).. 1,000,000
     Common Stock—$1 Par (Shareholders'
       Equity Increase) 40,000
     Additional Paid-in Capital (Shareholders'
       Equity Increase) 960,000
  To record conversion using book value of bonds.

  b. **1/02/Year 1**
  Cash (Asset Increase)... 1,000,000
     Convertible Bonds Payable (Liability Increase) 685,140.50
     Additional Paid-in Capital (Shareholders'
       Equity Increase).. 314,859.50
  Issue of 10-percent semiannual coupon convertible bonds at a time when the firm could issue ordinary 10-percent bonds for $685,140.50 when the market interest rate is 15 percent compounded semiannually.

  Supporting Computations
  $50,000 X 12.59441... $ 629,720.50
  $1,000,000 X .05542.. 55,420.00
     Issue Price.. $ 685,140.50

  Also, see Table 5 at the back of the book.

12.26 (Uncertainty Corporation; journal entries to correct errors and adjust for changes in estimates.)

  a. Retained Earnings (Shareholders' Equity Decrease)... 12,000
     Patent (or Accumulated Amortization)
       (Asset Decrease)... 12,000
  To correct error from neglecting to amortize patent during previous year.

  b. Accumulated Depreciation (Asset Increase)........... 7,000
     Retained Earnings (Shareholders' Equity
       Increase) 4,000
     Retained Earnings (Shareholders' Equity
       Increase) 3,000
  To correct error in recording the sale of a machine by eliminating the balance in accumulated depreciation relating to the machine sold and converting a $4,000 loss on the sale to a $3,000 gain.

12.26 continued.

    c.   Retained Earnings (Depreciation Expense)
          (Shareholders' Equity Decrease) 50,000
             Accumulated Depreciation (Asset De-
                crease) 50,000
        Book value on January 1, Year 13 is $1,600,000
        [= $2,400,000 – ($80,000 x 10)]. The revised
        annual depreciation is $50,000 (= $1,600,000/32).

    d.   Retained Earnings (Bad Debt Expense) (Share-
          holders' Equity Decrease)................................... 10,000
             Allowance for Uncollectible Accounts (Asset
                Decrease)... 10,000
        To adjust the balance in the allowance account
        to the amount needed to cover estimated un-
        collectibles.

12.27   (Journal entries for dividends.)

    a.   Retained Earnings (Dividends Declared) (Share-
          holders' Equity Decrease).................................... 19,500
             Dividends Payable—Preferred Stock (Liabil-
                ity Increase)... 19,500
        Dividend of $1.50 per share on 13,000 shares.

    b.   Dividends Payable—Preferred Stock (Liability
          Decrease).. 19,500
             Cash (Asset Decrease).................................... 19,500

    c.   Retained Earnings (Stock Dividend) (Share-
          holders' Equity Decrease).................................... 300,000
             Common Stock (Shareholders' Equity
                Increase)... 300,000

    d.   No entry.

12.28   (Watt Corporation; journal entries for dividends.)

    a.   **March 31, Year 6**
        Retained Earnings (Dividend Declared) (Share-
          holders' Equity Decrease).................................... 10,000
             Dividends Payable (Liability Increase)............ 10,000
        $10,000 = 20,000 x $.50.

    b.   **April 15, Year 6**
        Dividends Payable (Liability Decrease)................... 10,000
             Cash (Asset Decrease)...................................... 10,000

12.28 continued.

 c. **June 30, Year 6**

Retained Earnings (= 2,000 x $20) (Stock Divi-
dend) (Shareholders' Equity Decrease)................ 40,000

  Common Stock (= 2,000 x $15) (Share-
  holders' Equity Increase)..............................   30,000

  Additional Paid-in Capital (Shareholders'
  Equity Increase)   10,000

 d. **September 30, Year 6**

Retained Earnings (Dividend Declared) (Share-
holders' Equity Decrease)..................................... 11,000

  Dividends Payable (Liability Increase)............   11,000

$11,000 = 22,000 x $.50.

 e. **October 15, Year 6**

Dividends Payable (Liability Decrease).................... 11,000

  Cash (Asset Decrease)......................................   11,000

 f. **December 31, Year 6**

Additional Paid-in Capital (Shareholders' Equity
Decrease)... 165,000

  Common Stock (= 11,000 x $15) (Share-
  holders' Equity Increase)..............................   165,000

12.29 (Danos Corporation; journal entries for treasury stock transactions.)

 a. Treasury Stock (Shareholders' Equity Decrease).. 300,000

  Cash (= 10,000 x $30) (Asset Decrease).............   300,000

 b. Cash (= 6,000 x $32) (Asset Increase)..................... 192,000

  Additional Paid-in Capital (Common Stock
  Options) (= 6,000 x $6) (Shareholders' Equity
  Decrease)... 36,000

   Treasury Stock (= 6,000 x $30) (Share-
   holders' Equity Increase)..............................   180,000

   Additional Paid-in Capital (Shareholders'
   Equity Increase)   48,000

 c. Treasury Stock (Shareholders' Equity Decrease).. 266,000

  Cash (= 7,000 x $38) (Asset Decrease)...............   266,000

 d. Land (Asset Increase)... 300,000

  Treasury Stock [= (4,000 x $30) + (4,000 x
  $38)] (Shareholders' Equity Increase)   272,000

  Additional Paid-in Capital (Shareholders'
  Equity Increase)...   28,000

12.29 continued.

 e. Cash (= 3,000 × $36) (Asset Increase)...................... 108,000
   Additional Paid-in Capital (Shareholders' Equity
    Decrease).. 6,000
     Treasury Stock (= 3,000 × $38) (Share-
      holders' Equity Increase)............................... 114,000

12.30 (Melissa Corporation; journal entries for treasury stock transactions.)

 a. Treasury Stock (Shareholders' Equity Decrease).. 120,000
   Cash (= 10,000 × $12) (Asset Decrease)............. 120,000

 b. Bonds Payable (Liability Decrease)........................ 72,000
   Treasury Stock (= 6,000 × $12) (Shareholders'
    Equity Increase).. 72,000

 c. Treasury Stock (Shareholders' Equity Decrease).. 300,000
   Cash (= 20,000 × $15) (Asset Decrease)............. 300,000

 d. Land (Asset Increase)... 540,000
   Treasury Stock [= (4,000 × $12) + (20,000 ×
    $15)] (Shareholders' Equity Increase)............. 348,000
   Common Stock (= 6,000 × $5) (Shareholders'
    Equity Increase).. 30,000
   Additional Paid-in Capital (Shareholders'
    Equity Increase).. 162,000

12.31 (Effects on statement of cash flows.)

 a. The journal entry to record this transaction is:

   Cash (Asset Increase)... 200,000
    Common Stock (Shareholders' Equity In-
     crease) 200,000

   The Cash account increases, so Line (11) increases by $200,000.
   Issuing common stock is a financing activity, so Line (8) increases by
   $200,000.

 b. The journal entry to record this transaction is:

   Common Stock (Shareholders' Equity Decrease)... 50,000
   Additional Paid-in Capital (Shareholders' Equity
    Decrease).. 25,000
    Cash (Asset Decrease)....................................... 75,000

12.31 b. continued.

The Cash account decreases, so Line (11) decreases by $75,000. Repurchasing common stock is a financing activity, so Line (9) increases by $75,000.

c. (1) The journal entry to record this transaction using the book value method is:

Convertible Bonds Payable (Liability Decrease)..	100,000	
Common Stock (Shareholders' Equity Increase)...		10,000
Additional Paid-in Capital (Shareholders' Equity Increase).......................		90,000

(2) The journal entry to record this transaction under the market value method is:

Convertible Bonds Payable (Liability Decrease)..	100,000	
Retained Earnings (Loss on Conversion of Bonds) (Shareholders' Equity Decrease).....	140,000	
Common Stock (Shareholders' Equity Increase)...		10,000
Additional Paid-in Capital (Shareholders' Equity Increase)		230,000

The Cash account does not change under either method of recording the transaction. The transaction does not appear on the statement of cash flows when the firm uses the book value method. When the firm uses the market value method, net income on Line (3) decreases for the loss. Line (4) increases to add back the loss to net income since it does not affect cash. The firm reports this financing transaction in a supplementary schedule or note.

d. The journal entry to record this transaction is:

Cash (Asset Increase)...	15,000	
Additional Paid-in Capital (Shareholders' Equity Decrease)..	5,000	
Treasury Stock (Shareholders' Equity Increase)...		20,000

The Cash account increases, so Line (11) increases by $15,000. Issuing treasury stock is a financing transaction, so Line (8) increases by $15,000.

12.31 continued.

e. The journal entry to record this transaction is:

Retained Earnings (Stock Dividend) (Share-
    holders' Equity Decrease).................................... 300,000
    Common Stock (Shareholders' Equity
        Increase).. 1,000
    Additional Paid-in Capital (Shareholders'
        Equity Increase) 299,000

Because this transaction does not affect the Cash account, it does not appear in the statement of cash flows.

f. The journal entry to record this transaction is:

Retained Earnings (Dividend Declared) (Share-
    holders' Equity Decrease)..................................... 70,000
    Dividends Payable (Liability Increase)............ 70,000

Because this transaction does not affect the Cash account, it does not appear in the statement of cash flows.

g. The journal entry to record this transaction is:

Dividends Payable (Liability Decrease).................... 70,000
    Cash (Asset Decrease).. 70,000

The Cash account decreases, so Line (11) decreases by $70,000. Paying dividends is a financing activity, so Line (10) increases by $70,000.

h. The journal entry to record this transaction is:

Cash (Asset Increase).. 20,000
    Common Stock (Shareholders' Equity
        Increase) 1,000
    Additional Paid-in Capital (Shareholders'
        Equity Increase)... 19,000

The Cash account increases, so Line (11) increases by $20,000. Issuing common stock under a stock rights plan is a financing activity, so Line (8) increases by $20,000.

12.32   (Wilson Supply Company; transactions to incorporate and run a business.)

a. **1/02**
Cash (Asset Increase).. 9,000
   Common Stock—$30 Stated Value (Share-
      holders' Equity Increase)   9,000
300 shares x $30 = $9,000.

h   **1/06**
Cash (Asset Increase).. 60,000
   Common Stock—$30 Stated Value (Share-
      holders' Equity Increase)   60,000
2,000 shares x $30 = $60,000.

c. **1/08**
Cash (Asset Increase).. 400,000
   Preferred Stock—Par (Shareholders' Equity
      Increase)   400,000
4,000 shares x $100 = $400,000.

d. **1/09**
No entry.

e. **1/12**
Inventories (Asset Increase) 50,000
Land (Asset Increase).. 80,000
Building (Asset Increase)....................................... 210,000
Equipment (Asset Increase).................................... 120,000
   Preferred Stock—Par (Shareholders' Equity
      Increase)   100,000
   Common Stock—$30 Stated Value (Share-
      holders' Equity Increase)   360,000

f. **7/03**
Retained Earnings (Dividend Declared) (Share-
   holders' Equity Decrease)................................... 20,000
   Dividends Payable on Preferred Stock (Lia-
      bility Increase)   20,000
$100 x (.08/2) x (4,000 + 1,000) shares = $20,000.

g. **7/05**
Cash (Asset Increase).. 825,000
   Common Stock—$30 Stated Value (Share-
      holders' Equity Increase)   750,000
   Additional Paid-in Capital (Shareholders' Equity
      Increase)   75,000
25,000 shares x $33 = $825,000.

12.32 continued.

    h. **7/25**
        Dividends Payable on Preferred Stock (Liability

Decrease)	20,000	
Cash (Asset Decrease)		20,000

    i. **10/02**
        Retained Earnings (Dividend Declared) (Share-

holders' Equity Decrease)	39,300	
Dividends Payable on Common Stock (Lia-bility Increase)		39,300

$1 × (300 + 2,000 + 12,000 + 25,000) shares = $39,300.

    j. **10/25**
        Dividends Payable on Common Stock (Liability

Decrease)	39,300	
Cash (Asset Decrease)		39,300

12.33 (Fisher Company; reconstructing transactions involving shareholders' equity.)

    a. $60,000 par value/$10 per share = 6,000 shares.

    b. $7,200/360 = $20 per share.

    c. 600 − 360 = 240 shares.

    d. If the Additional Paid-in Capital is $31,440, then $30,000 [= 6,000 × ($15 − $10)] represents contributions in excess of par value on original issue of 6,000 shares. Then, $1,440 (= $31,440 − $30,000) represents the credit to Additional Paid-in Capital when it reissued the treasury shares.

        The $1,440 represents 240 shares reissued times the excess of reissue price over acquisition price:

$$240(\$X - \$20) = \$1,440, \text{ or } X = \$26.$$

The shares were reissued for $26 each.

    e. (1)

Cash (6,000 × $15) (Asset Increase)	90,000	
Common Stock ($10 Par Value) (Share-holders' Equity Increase)		60,000
Additional Paid-in Capital (Shareholders' Equity Increase)		30,000

12.33 e. continued.

 (2) Treasury Shares (Shareholders' Equity Decrease).. 12,000
     Cash (600 x $20) (Asset Decrease).........   12,000

 (3) Cash (240 x $26) (Asset Increase).................. 6,240
    Treasury Shares (240 x $20) (Shareholders' Equity Increase)   4,800
    Additional Paid-in Capital (Shareholders' Equity Increase).................................   1,440

 (4) Cash (Asset Increase)...................................... 10,000
    Securities Available for Sale (Asset Decrease)   6,000
    Retained Earnings (Realized Gain on Sale of Securities Available for Sale) (Shareholders' Equity Increase)   4,000

 (5) Securities Available for Sale (Asset Increase).. 2,000
    Accumulated Other Comprehensive Income (Unrealized Holding Gain on Securities Available for Sale) (Shareholders' Equity Increase)......................   2,000

 f. Realized gain appears in Income (Earnings) Statement and the Unrealized Gain appears in Statement of Comprehensive Income or in reconciliation of Accumulated Other Comprehensive Income.

12.34 (Shea Company; reconstructing transactions involving shareholders' equity.)

 a. $100,000 par value/$5 per share = 20,000 shares.

 b. $33,600/1,200 = $28 per share.

 c. 2,000 – 1,200 = 800 shares.

 d. If the Additional Paid-in Capital is $509,600, then $500,000 [= 20,000 x ($30 – $5)] represents contributions in excess of par value on original issue of 20,000 shares. Then, $9,600 (= $509,600 – $500,000) represents the credit to Additional Paid-in Capital when it reissued the treasury shares.
  The $9,600 represents 800 shares reissued times the excess of reissue price over acquisition price:

$$800(\$X - \$28) = \$9,600, \text{ or } X = \$40.$$

The shares were reissued for $40 each.

12.34 continued.

    e. (1) Cash (Asset Increase).. 600,000

              Common Stock ($5 Par Value) (Share-
                 holders' Equity Increase) 100,000
              Additional Paid-in Capital (Shareholders'
                 Equity Increase)....................................... 500,000

       (2) Treasury Shares (Shareholders' Equity
             Decrease).. 56,000
                Cash (Asset Decrease)............................. 56,000

       (3) Cash (Asset Increase).. 32,000
             Treasury Shares (Shareholders' Equity
                Increase) 22,400
             Additional Paid-in Capital (Shareholders'
                Equity Increase)....................................... 9,600
             800 X $40 = $32,000.

       (4) Cash (Asset Increase).. 12,000
             Retained Earnings (Realized Loss on Sale of
             Securities Available for Sale) (Share-
             holders' Equity Decrease)............................ 2,000
                Securities Available for Sale (Asset
                Decrease)... 14,000

       (5) Accumulated Other Comprehensive Income
             (Unrealized Holding Loss on Securities
             Available for Sale) (Shareholders' Equity
             Decrease)... 7,000
                Securities Available for Sale (Asset
                Decrease)... 7,000
             Write down securities from $25,000 to
             $18,000.

    f. Realized Loss appears in Income (Earnings) Statement and the Unrealized Loss appears in Statement of Comprehensive Income or in reconciliation of Accumulated Other Comprehensive Income.

12.35 (Lowe Corporation; accounting for stock options.)

Year 1: zero compensation because all benefits occur after the granting of the stock option.

Year 2:	.5(5,000 X $2.40)..	$	6,000
Year 3:	[.5(5,000 X $2.40) + .5(6,000 X $3.00)].....................		15,000
Year 4:	[.5(6,000 X $3.00) + .5(7,000 X $3.14)].....................		19,990
Year 5:	[.5(7,000 X $3.14) + .5(8,000 X $3.25)].....................		23,990
Total	....	$	64,980

12.36 (Alex Corporation; comprehensive review of accounting for shareholders' equity.)

a.

	JOURNAL ENTRY			BOOK VALUE PER SHARE (Numerator is Total Book Value)

b.

(1) Retained Earnings (Shareholders' Equity Decrease)........ 150,000
  Common Stock (5,000 x $10) (Shareholders' Equity Increase)........ 50,000
  Additional Paid-in Capital (5,000 x $20) (Shareholders' Equity Increase)........ 100,000

$\frac{\$2,250,000}{50,000} = \$45.00$ per share.

(2) Common Stock ($10 Par Value) (Shareholders' Equity Decrease)........ 500,000
  Common Stock ($5 per Share) (Shareholders' Equity Increase)........ 500,000

$\frac{\$2,250,000}{55,000} = \$40.91$ per share.

$\frac{\$2,250,000}{100,000} = \$22.50$ per share.

(3) Treasury Stock (Shareholders' Equity Decrease)........ 125,000
  Cash (5,000 x $25) (Asset Decrease)........ 125,000

$\frac{\$2,125,000}{45,000} = \$47.22$ per share.

(4) Treasury Stock (Shareholders' Equity Decrease)........ 75,000
  Cash (5,000 x $15) (Asset Decrease)........ 75,000

$\frac{\$2,175,000}{45,000} = \$48.33$ per share.

(5) Cash (5,000 x $35) (Asset Increase)........ 175,000
  Treasury Stock (5,000 x $25) (Shareholders' Equity Increase)........ 125,000
  Additional Paid-in Capital (Shareholders' Equity Increase)........ 50,000

$\frac{\$2,300,000}{50,000} = \$46.00$ per share.

(6) Cash (5,000 x $20) (Asset Increase)........ 100,000
  Additional Paid-in Capital (Shareholders' Equity Decrease)........ 25,000
  Treasury Stock (5,000 x $25) (Shareholders' Equity Increase)........ 125,000

$\frac{\$2,225,000}{50,000} = \$44.50$ per share.

(7) Cash (5,000 x $15) (Asset Increase)........ 75,000
  Additional Paid-in Capital (Shareholders' Equity Decrease)........ 50,000
  Treasury Stock (5,000 x $25) (Shareholders' Equity Increase)........ 125,000

$\frac{\$2,200,000}{50,000} = \$44.00$ per share.

(8) Cash (5,000 x $15) (Asset Increase)........ 75,000
  Common Stock (5,000 x $10) (Shareholders' Equity Increase)........ 50,000
  Additional Paid-in Capital (Shareholders' Equity Increase)........ 25,000

$\frac{\$2,325,000}{55,000} = \$42.27$ per share.

(9) Cash (5,000 x $50) (Asset Increase)........ 250,000
  Common Stock (5,000 x $10) (Shareholders' Equity Increase)........ 50,000
  Additional Paid-in Capital (Shareholders' Equity Increase)........ 200,000

$\frac{\$2,500,000}{55,000} = \$45.45$ per share.

(10) Bonds Payable (Liability Decrease)........ 150,000
  Common Stock (10,000 x $10) (Shareholders' Equity Increase)........ 100,000
  Additional Paid-in Capital (Shareholders' Equity Increase)........ 50,000

$\frac{\$2,400,000}{60,000} = \$40.00$ per share.

(11) Bonds Payable (Liability Decrease)........ 150,000
  Retained Earnings (Loss on Conversion of Bonds) (Shareholders' Equity Decrease)........ 20,000
  Common Stock (Shareholders' Equity Increase)........ 100,000
  Additional Paid-in Capital (Shareholders' Equity Increase)........ 70,000

$\frac{\$2,400,000}{60,000} = \$40.00$ per share.

12.36 continued.

    c. (1) The acquisition of treasury shares, the declaration of dividends, and the incurrence of a net loss reduce total book value.

        (2) The issue of common shares for a price less than current book value per share (for example, under stock option plans), the acquisition of treasury shares for a price greater than current book value per share, and the sale or reissue of treasury shares at a price less than their acquisition cost (at a "loss") reduce book value per share.

12.37   (Neslin Company; reconstructing events affecting shareholders' equity.)

    a. (1) Issue of 20,000 shares of common stock at $52 per share for cash or other assets.

        (2) Acquisition of 4,000 shares of treasury stock for $55 per share.

        (3) Reissue of 3,000 shares of treasury stock for $48 per share.

        (4) Reissue of 1,000 shares of treasury stock for $60 per share.

        (5) Net income of $2,400,000 included in Retained Earnings.

        (6) A decline in value occurred during the year related to securities available for sale, derivatives, pensions, foreign currency translation, or some combination of those items.

        (7) Dividends declared of $10 per share.

    b. (1)

Cash (Asset Increase)	1,040,000	
Common Stock (Shareholders' Equity Increase)		200,000
Additional Paid-in Capital (Shareholders' Equity Increase)		840,000

        (2)

Treasury Stock (Shareholders' Equity Decrease)	220,000	
Cash (Asset Decrease)		220,000

        (3)

Cash (Asset Increase)	144,000	
Additional Paid-in Capital (Shareholders' Equity Decrease)	21,000	
Treasury Stock (Shareholders' Equity Increase)		165,000

12.37 b. continued.

    (4)   Cash (Asset Increase)................................   60,000
              Treasury Stock (Shareholders'
                Equity Increase)................................   55,000
               Additional Paid-in Capital (Share-
                holders Equity Increase)................   5,000

    (5)   No entry required because revenues and expenses are already included in retained earnings.

    (6)   Accumulated Other Comprehensive
               Income (Unrealized Holding Gain on
               Holdings of Securities Available for
               Sale) (Shareholders' Equity De-
               crease)...   150,000
                Securities Available for Sale
                  (Asset Decrease)...........................   150,000

    (7)   Retained Earnings (Dividend Declared)
               (Shareholders' Equity Decrease)........   1,200,000
                Cash or Dividends Payable (Asset
                Decrease or Liability In-
                crease)...   1,200,000

12.38   (Wal-Mart Stores; journal entries for changes in shareholders' equity.)

    (1)   No entry required because retained earnings already include revenues and expenses.

    (2)   Retained Earnings (Dividend Declared)
               (Shareholders' Equity Decrease)....................   158,889
                Cash (Asset Decrease)...............................   158,889

    (3)   Cash (Asset Increase).......................................   3,820
               Common Stock (Shareholders' Equity
                Increase)...   66
               Additional Paid-in Capital (Shareholders'
                Equity Increase)..............................   3,754

    Note: The credit to Additional Paid-in Capital is the net of a debit for the cost of the stock options previously amortized to expense and a credit for the excess of the issue price plus the cost of the stock options over the par value of the stock issued.

    (4)   Additional Paid-in Capital (Shareholders'
               Equity Decrease)...   56,680
                Common Stock (Shareholders' Equity
                Increase)..   56,680

12.38 continued.

    (5) Investment in Securities (Asset Increase)....... 274,696
            Common Stock (Shareholders' Equity
                Increase).. 1,037
            Additional Paid-in Capital (Shareholders'
                Equity Increase)... 273,659

    (6) Treasury Stock (Shareholders' Equity
            Decrease)... 25,826
            Cash (Asset Decrease)................................ 25,826

    (7) Accumulated Other Comprehensive Income
            (Unrealized Gains on Holdings of Securities
            Available for Sale) (Shareholders' Equity
            Decrease)... 57,086
            Securities Available for Sale (Asset
                Decrease)... 57,086

12.39   (Merck & Co.; treasury shares and their effects on performance ratios.)

    a. (1)   Cash (Asset Increase).. 714.1
                Treasury Stock (Shareholders' Equity
                    Increase).. 427.6
                Common Stock/Additional Paid-in Capital
                    (Shareholders' Equity Increase)................... 286.5

The common shares were issued at an option price of $49.28 per share
[= $714.1/(.307 + 14.183)]. The treasury shares issued were purchased
for $30.15 per share (= $427.6/14.183). The difference of $19.13 per
share (= $49.28 − $30.15) was credited to Additional Paid-in Capital.
This amount includes a debit to Additional Paid-in Capital for the cost of
stock options previously amortized and a credit for the difference
between the cash proceeds plus the cost of the stock options over the
par value of the shares issued. The remaining credits to Common
Stock and Additional Paid-in Capital were for the amounts received for
the .307 common shares issued net of any amounts debited and
credited to Additional Paid-in Capital as a result of recognizing the cost
of the options in the accounts.

    (2)   Treasury Stock (Shareholders' Equity
            Decrease... 2,572.8
            Cash (Asset Decrease)................................ 2,572.8

These treasury shares were purchased for an average price of $93.75
per share (= $2,572.8/27.444).

12.39 continued.

b.

	Year 3/Year 4	Year 4/Year 5
Net Income:		
[($3,870.5/$3,376.6) − 1]..............	+14.6%	
[($4,596.5/$3,870.5) − 1]..............		+18.8%
Earnings per Common Share:		
[($3.20/$2.70) − 1].........................	+18.5%	
[($3.83/$3.20) − 1].........................		+19.7%

Earnings per share increases faster than net income because Merck reduces the number of shares outstanding each year by repurchasing shares of treasury stock.

c.

	Year 3	Year 4	Year 5
Book Value per Share:			
$11,735.7/(1,483.463 − 254.615)....	$9.55		
$11,970.5/(1,483.619 − 277.017)....		$9.92	
$12,613.5/(1,483.926 − 290.278)....			$10.57
Percentage Change:			
[($9.92/$9.55) − 1]..............................		+3.9%	
[($10.57/$9.92) − 1]...........................			+6.6%

There are several reasons why book value per share increases more slowly than net income and earnings per share. First, dividends reduce shareholders' equity but not net income. Second, the repurchases of treasury shares reduce the numerator proportionally more than they reduce the denominator. The average repurchase price during Year 5 of $93.75 per share (see the answer to Part a.) had the effect of reducing book value per share. Book value per share increased overall in Year 5 because of net income.

d.

	Year 3	Year 4	Year 5
[$3,376.6/.5($11,139.0 + $11,735.7)]..	29.5%		
[$3,870.5/.5($11,735.7 + $11,970.5)]..		32.7%	
[$4,596.5/.5($11,970.5 + $12,613.5)]..			37.4%

e. No. Merck has purchased considerably more treasury shares than are needed for its stock option plans. Treasury shares do not receive dividends, so Merck does conserve cash. However, dividends have grown at approximately the same growth rate as net income. One purpose might have been to increase the return on common shareholders' equity. Cash generally earns a return of approximately 4 percent each year after taxes. By eliminating this low-yielding asset from the balance sheet, Merck's overall rate of return on common shareholders' equity increases. The market often interprets stock re-

12.39 e. continued.

purchases as a positive signal that management has inside information and thinks that the stock is undervalued. The positive signal results in an increase in the stock price. One can estimate the increase in market price by observing the average price at which Merck repurchased its shares each year:

Year 3: $1,570.9/33.377 = $47.07
Year 4: $2,493.3/38.384 = $64.96
Year 5: $2,572.8/27.444 = $93.75

Thus, the stock price doubled during the three-year period, whereas earnings increased by approximately 36 percent [= ($4,596.5/$3,376.6) − 1].

12.40   (Layton Ball Corporation; case introducing earnings-per-share calculations for a complex capital structure.)

a. $\dfrac{\$9,500}{2,500} = \$3.80$ per share.

b.   1,000 options x $15 = $15,000 cash raised.

$\dfrac{\$15,000 \text{ new cash}}{\$25 \text{ per share}} = 600$ shares.

Total number of shares increases by 400 (= 1,000 − 600).

$\dfrac{\$9,500}{2,500 + 400} = \$3.276$ per share.

c.   2,000 warrants x $30 = $60,000 cash raised.

$\dfrac{\$60,000 \text{ new cash}}{\$25 \text{ per share}} = 2,400$ shares purchased.

Total number of shares decreases by 400 (= 2,000 − 2,400).

$\dfrac{\$9,500}{2,500 - 400} = \$4.524$ per share.

d.   Before taxes, each converted bond saves $40 in annual interest expense. After taxes, the savings in expense and increase in income is only $24 [= (1 − .40) x $40].
There are 100 bonds outstanding; each is convertible into 10 shares. Thus, the new earnings per share figure is:

12.40 d. continued.

$$\frac{\$9,500 + \$24 \text{ savings per bond} \times 100 \text{ bonds}}{2,500 + 10 \text{ shares per bond} \times 100 \text{ bonds}} = \frac{\$11,900}{3,500 \text{ shares}} =$$

$3.40 per share.

e. The warrants are antidilutive and should be ignored if we seek the maximum possible dilution of earnings per share.

$$\frac{\$9,500 + \$2,500 \text{ (Increase from interest savings)}}{2,500 + 1,000 \text{ (bond conversion)} + 400 \text{ (option exercise)}} = \frac{\$12,000}{3,900} =$$

$3.077 per share.

f. Probably the *Wall Street Journal* should use the earnings per share that results in the maximum possible dilution. It should clearly ignore antidilutive securities. Do not conclude from the presentation in this problem that one can check the dilution characteristics of potentially dilutive securities one by one and know for sure which combination of assumed exercise and conversions lead to the minimum earnings per share figure. See S. Davidson and R. L. Weil, "A Shortcut in Computing Earnings per Share," *Journal of Accountancy*, December 1975, page 45.

12.41   (Case for discussion: value of stock options.)

The answer must be either *a.* or *b.* The cost per option cannot exceed one penny per share, for otherwise StartUp would merely buy the shares on the open market, rather than pay Goldman Sachs to relieve StartUp of the burden. The total cost of the options awarded to Bithead, then, cannot exceed $100 (= 10,000 shares × $.01 per share). We think the answer is likely to be in the range of $15–$40 for those shares, so we would answer *b.*

Within the last two decades, no subject has caused more controversy in accounting than the accounting for the cost of employee stock options. When it issued *SFAS No. 119* in 1995, FASB said that this issue threatened to end standard setting in the private sector and that the debate had ceased to be rational.

Some firms, such as GE, grant to employees the right to buy a specified number of shares of the firm's stock at a fixed price, called the *exercise price*, usually the price on the day the firm awards the options to the employee, say $10 per share. The employee, typically, has several years to decide whether to exercise the option—that is, give up the option and cash in return for the shares. If the stock price rises above the exercise price, say to $18 per share, then the employee can give up the option and $10 in return for a share with current market value of $18.

Such options have value to employees who receive them and many companies, particularly the high-tech Silicon Valley companies, award such options as part of their compensation in hopes that the employer's shares will skyrocket in value, enriching the employee.

12.41 continued.

The accounting issue has been: how much should the employer firm, such as GE, charge to expense in the period when it awards an option to its employees. The FASB's Exposure Draft outlines an approach for computing such amounts of expense and requiring that firms report such amounts as expense.

William H. Scott, Jr. of Scientific Applications International Corporation of San Diego, has studied the costs to the issuing firm. He found that under a wide variety of conditions, the cost to the firm issuing an option exercisable at the market price on the date of grant is, for most firms, about 10–20 percent of the market value of the shares on the date of the grant. The cost to the firm of awarding the option can never exceed the market value of the share itself on the date of the award. This is true because the firm can always, on that day, go out into the market to buy a share for the current market price, building that share until the employee exercises the option.

At the height of the debate, chief financial officers (CFOs) from Silicon Valley lobbied against the FASB proposal. We believed that many of those CFOs did not understand the FASB proposal, nor its consequences. Consequently, at a private seminar on the subject at which one of us taught, we administered the question in the text to the Silicon Valley CFOs.

The Silicon Valley CFOs answered as follows: $a. = 3$, $b. = 3$, $c. = 6$, $d. = 8$, $e. = 5$, and $f. = 1$. That is, only six of the 26 participating got the answer right, which means that 20 of the 26 got it wrong. In the discussion following, we pointed out that these officers should probably understand the cost of options better than they did before arguing so hard against the proposed accounting. It's no wonder that a CFO would dislike the proposed accounting for options which the CFO thinks cost $10,000 when they actually cost no more than $100. About 25 percent of the Silicon Valley CFOs had beliefs that much in error.

12.42   (Ethical issues in accounting for stock options.)

The recognition of an expense for stock options will likely make shareholders more aware of the cost of these options and examine new option plans more carefully. Recognizing an expense also depresses earnings. Uninformed investors may respond to the lower earnings by selling their share of stock, which could depress stock prices and reflect negatively on management. Although managers argue that stock options cannot be measured reliably, they must have some sense of the value of such options when accepting them instead of cash or other forms of compensation. Thus, managers clearly have a vested interest in not recognizing an expense for stock options. One might question the ethics of managers who use their positions to promote a method of reporting that clearly benefits them and that is contrary to the broad concepts of financial reporting and perhaps not in the best interest of shareholders as well.

APPENDIX

COMPOUND INTEREST: CONCEPTS AND APPLICATIONS

Questions, Short Exercises, Exercises, Problems, and Cases: Answers and Solutions

A.1   See the text or the glossary at the end of the book.

A.2   Rent paid or received for the use of the asset, cash.

A.3   In simple interest, only the principal sum earns interest. In compound interest, interest is earned on the principal plus amounts of interest not paid or withdrawn.

A.4   There is no difference; these items refer to the same thing.

A.5   The timing of the first payment for an annuity due is *now* (at the beginning of the first period) while that for an ordinary annuity is at the *end* of the first period. The future value of an annuity due is computed as of one year after the final payment, but for an ordinary annuity is computed as of the time of the last payment.

A.6   The discount rate that sets the net present value of a stream of payments equal to zero is the implicit rate for that stream.

(1) Guess a rate.

(2) Compute the net present values of the cash flows using the current guess.

(3) If the net present value in (2) is less than zero, then increase the rate guessed and go to Step (2).

(4) If the net present value in (2) is greater than zero, then reduce the rate guessed and go to Step (2).

(5) Otherwise, the current guess is the implicit rate of return.

The process will converge to the right answer only if one is systematic with the guesses, narrowing the range successively.

A.7   Present values increase when interest rates decrease and present values decrease when interest rates increase.

A.8   6 percent. The present value will be larger the smaller the discount rate.

A.9   The formula assumes that the growth [represented by the parameter g in the formula $1/(r - g)$] continues forever. That is a long time. The formula assumes also that the discount and growth rates remain constant. In our experience, more harm results from assuming the growth persists forever than from the other assumptions.

A.10   a. $5,000 x 3.20714 x 1.06 = $16,998.

       b. $5,000 x 10.06266 x 1.25971 = $63,380.

A.11   a. $150,000 x .62741 = $94,112.

       b. $150,000 x .54027 = $81,041.

A.12   a. $4,000 x 6.97532 = $27,901.

       b. $4,000 x 7.33593 = $29,344.

A.13   a.   ¥45,000,000/10.63663 = ¥4.23 million.

       b.   ¥45,000,000/12.29969 = ¥3.66 million.

A.14   a.   €90,000 x 14.20679 x 1.05 = €90,000 x (15.91713 − 1.0) = €1,342,542.

       b.   €90,000 x 18.53117 x 1.10 = €90,000 x (21.38428 − 1.0) = €1,834,585.

A.15   a.   £145,000/4.62288 = £31,366.

       b.   £145,000/4.11141 = £35,268.

A.16   a.   (10) $5,000 x T(1, 21, 6).

              (11) $150,000/T(2, 8, 6).

              (12) $4,000 x T(3, 6, 6).

              (13)   ¥45,000,000/T(3, 8, 8).

              (14)   €90,000 x T(3, 11, 5) x 1.05 = €90,000 x [T(3,12, 5) − 1.0].

              (15)   £145,000/T(4, 6, 8).

       b.   Asking questions about compound interest calculations on examinations presents a difficult logistical problem to teachers. They may want the students to use compound interest tables, but not wish to incur the costs of reproducing them in sufficient numbers for each student to have a copy. They may not wish to give an open book test. This device is useful for posing test questions about compound interest.

A.16 b. continued.

The device is based on the fact that teachers of accounting are not particularly interested in testing their students' ability to do arithmetic. Teachers want to be sure that students know how to use the tables and calculating devices efficiently in combination. Such a combination suggests that the humans do the thinking and the calculators do the multiplications and divisions.

A.17   (Effective interest rates.)

   a.   12 percent per period; 5 periods.

   b.   6 percent per period; 10 periods.

   c.   3 percent per period; 20 periods.

   d.   1 percent per period; 60 periods.

A.18   a. $100 x 1.21665 = $121.67.

   b. $500 x 1.34587 = $672.94.

   c. $200 x 1.26899 = $253.80.

   d. $2,500 x (1.74102 x 1.74102) = $7,577.88

          $(1.02)^{56} = (1.02)^{28} \times (1.02)^{28}$.

   e. $600 x 1.43077 = $858.46.

A.19   a. $100 x .30832 = $30.83.

   b. $250 x .53063 = $132.66.

   c. $1,000 x .78757 = $787.57.

A.20   a. $100 x 14.23683 = $1,423.68.

   b. $850 x 9.89747 = $8,412.85.

   c. $400 x 49.96758 = $19,987.03.

A.21   a. $1,000(1.00 + .94340) + $2,000(4.21236 − .94340) + $2,500(6.80169 − 4.21236) = $14,955.

   b. $1,000(1.00 + .92593) + $2,000(3.99271 − .92593) + $2,500(6.24689 − 3.99271) = $13,695.

A.21 continued.

    c. $1,000(1.00 + .90909) + $2,000(3.79079 − .90909) + $2,500(5.75902 − 3.79079) = $12,593.

A.22   a. $3,000 + ($3,000/.06) = $53,000.

    b. $3,000 + ($3,000/.08) = $40,500.

A.23   a. $3,000/(.06 − .02) = $75,000.

    b. $3,000/(.08 − .02) = $50,000.

    c. [$3,000/(.06 − .02)] x .79209 = $59,406.75.

    d. [$3,000/(.08 − .02)] x .73503 = $36,751.50.

A.24   a. $60,000 + ($60,000/.1664) = $420,577. $(1.08)^2 − 1 = .1664$.

    b. $60,000 + ($60,000/.2544) = $295,850. $(1.12)^2 − 1 = .2544$.

A.25   7.00 percent. Note that $100,000/$55,307 = 1.80809. See Table 4, 2-period row and observe 1.80809 in the 7-percent column.

A.26   12 percent = $($140,493/$100,000)^{1/3} − 1$.

A.27   a. 16 percent = $($67,280/$50,000)^{1/2} − 1$.

    b.

Year (1)	Book Value Start of Year (2)	Interest for Year = (2) X .16 (3)	Amount (Reducing) Increasing Book Value (4)	Book Value End of Year = (2) + (3) + (4) (5)
1	$ 50,000	$ 8,000		$ 58,000
2	58,000	9,280	$ (67,280)	-0-

A.28   (Berman Company; find implicit interest rate; construct amortization schedule.)

    a. 14.0 percent.

$$\text{Let } x = \frac{\$8,000}{(1+r)} + \frac{\$8,000}{(1+r)^2} + \frac{\$8,000}{(1+r)^3} + \frac{\$100,000}{(1+r)^3} = \$86,000$$

If r = 14.0 percent, then x = $18,573 + $67,497 − $86,000 = $70.

If r = 14.1 percent, then x = $18,542 + $67,320 − $86,000 = $138.

A.28 continued.

b.

Year (1)	Book Value Start of Year (2)	Interest for Year = (2) X .14 (3)	Payment End of Year (Given) (4)	Amount (Reducing) Increasing Book Value = (3) – (4) (5)	Book Value End of Year = (2) + (5) (6)
1	$ 86,000	$ 12,040	$ 8,000	$ 4,040	$ 90,040
2	90,040	12,605	8,000	4,605	94,615
3	94,645	13,250*	108,000	(94,750)	(105)
OR 3	94,645	13,355*	108,000	(94,645)	-0-

*Interest would actually be recorded at $13,355 (= $108,000 – $94,645) so that the book value of the note reduces to zero at its maturity.

A.29   a.   Terms of sale of 2/10, net/30 on a $100 gross invoice price, for example, mean that the interest rate is 2/98 for a 20-day period, because if the discount is not taken, a charge of $2 is levied for the use of $98. The $98 is used for 20 days (= 30 – 10), so the number of compounding periods in a year is 365/20 = 18.25. The expression for the exact rate of interest implied by 2/10, net 30 is $(1 + 2/98)^{(365/20)} - 1 = 1.020408^{18.25} - 1 = 44.59\%$.

b.   Table 1 can be used. Use the 2-percent column and the 18-period row to see that the rate implied by 2/10, net 30 must be at least 42.825 percent (= 1.42825 – 1).

A.30   (Present value of a perpetuity).

$30,000 + ($10,000/.01) = $1,030,000.

A.31   Present value of future proceeds = .72845($35,000) + C = $35,000; where C represents the present value of the foregone interest payments. Table 2, 16-period row, 2-percent column = .72845.

C = $35,000 – $25,495.75 = $9,504.25.

A.32   a.   Will: $24,000 + $24,000(3.31213) = $103,488.72 (Preferred).

Dower Option: $300,000/3 = $100,000.

b.   Will: $24,000 + $24,000(3.03735) = $96,896.40.

Dower Option: $300,000/3 = $100,000 (Preferred).

A.33   Present value of deposit = $3.00.

Present value of $3.00, recorded 20 periods, have discounted at .50 percent per period = $3.00 x .90506 = $2.72.

Loss of $.28 (= $3.00 − $2.72) in foregone interest vs. Loss of $1.20 in price.

Net advantage of returnables is $.92.

A.34 $1.00(1.00 + .92456 + .85480 + .79051 + .73069) = $1.00 x 4.30036 = $4.30.

$4.30 − $3.50 = $.80.

A.35 $600/12 = $50 saved per month. $2,000/$50 = 40.0.

Present value of annuity of 1 discounted at 1 percent for 50 periods = 39.19612.

The present value of the annuity is $40 when the annuity lasts between 51 and 52 weeks. Dean Foods will recoup its investment in about one year.

A.36   a. $ 3,000,000 x 7.46944 = $ 22,408,320.

b. $ 3,000,000 x 7.36578 = $ 22,097,340
        500,000 x 1.69005 =   845,025
                              $ 22,942,365

c. $ 2,000,000 x 7.36578 = $ 14,731,560
     1,000,000 x 2.40183 =   2,401,830
       500,000 x 1.69005 =   845,025
                            $ 17,978,415

d. $17,978,410 x .20   = $ 3,595,682.

A.37   (Friendly Loan Company; find implicit interest rate; truth-in lending laws reduce the type of deception suggested by this problem.)

The effective interest rate is 19.86 percent and must be found by trial and error. The time line for this problem is:

which is equivalent, at least in terms of the implied interest rate, to:

A.37 continued.

End of Year	+$3	−$1	−$1	−$1	−$1	−$1
	0	1	2	3	4	5

Scanning Table 4, 5-period column, one finds the factor 2.99061, which is approximately 3.00, in the 20-percent column, so one can easily see that the implied interest rate is about 20 percent per year.

A.38   (Black & Decker Company; derive net present value/cash flows for decision to dispose of asset.)

$40,698.   The $100,000 is gone and an economic loss of $50,000 was suffered because of the bad purchase. The issue now is do we want to swap a larger current tax loss and smaller future depreciation charges for no tax loss now and larger future depreciation charges.

The new machine will lead to depreciation charges lower by $10,000 per year than the "old" machine and, hence, income taxes larger by $4,000. The present value of the larger taxes is $4,000 X 3.60478 (Table 4, 12 percent, 5 periods). Let S denote the proceeds from selling the old machine. The new current "outlay" to acquire the new machine is $50,000 − S − .40($100,000 − S) or $10,000 − .60S, so that for the new machine to be worthwhile:

$$\$10,000 - .60S < -\$14,419$$

OR

$$.6S > \$24,419$$

OR

$$S > \$40,698.$$

A.39   (Lynch Company/Bages Company; computation of present value of cash flows; untaxed acquisition, no change in tax basis of assets.)

a. $440,000 = $390,000 + $50,000 = $700,000 − $260,000.

b. $3,745,966 = $440,000 × 8.51356; see Table 4, 20-period column, 10-percent row.

A.40   (Lynch Company/Bages Company; computation of present value of cash flows; taxable acquisition, changing tax basis of assets.)

$4,258,199. If the merger is taxable, then the value of the firm V satisfies:

(1)
$$V = 8.51356 \times [\$700,000 - .40(\$700,000 - V/20)]$$
$$V = \$5,959,492 - \$2,383,797 + .17027V, \text{ or}$$
$$.83972V = \$3,575,695, \text{ so}$$
$$V = \$4,258,199.$$

To understand (1), observe that:

V	$=$	Value of firm
$V/20$	$=$	New depreciation charge
$\$700,000 - V/20$	$=$	New taxable income
$.40(\$700,000 - V/20)$	$=$	New income tax payable, so
$\$700,000 - .40(\$700,000 - V/20)$	$=$	New aftertax cash flow to be capitalized at 10 percent for 20 years using present value factor 8.51356.

A.41   (Valuation of intangibles with perpetuity formulas.)

a. $50 million = $4 million/.08.

b.   Increase.

c. $66 2/3 million = $4 million/(.08 − .02).

d.   Increase.

e.   Decrease.

A.42   (Ragazze; analysis of benefits of acquisition of long-term assets.)

a. $270,831.

Dec. 31 Year	Cash Inflows Operating Receipts (1)	Salvage (2)	Cash Outflows Maintenance (3)	Test Runs (4)	Total (1) + (2) − (3) − (4) (5)	Present Values at 12% Factor (6)	Cash Flow (7)
0							
1				$ 20,000	$ (20,000)	0.89286	$ (17,857)
2	$ 130,000		$ 60,000		70,000	0.79719	55,804
3	130,000		60,000		70,000	0.71178	49,825
4	130,000		60,000		70,000	0.63552	44,486
5	130,000		60,000		70,000	0.56743	39,720
6	130,000		100,000		30,000	0.50663	15,199
7	130,000		100,000		30,000	0.45235	13,570
8	130,000		100,000		30,000	0.40388	12,116
9	130,000	$ 30,000			160,000	0.36061	57,968
							$ 270,831

(7) = (5) × (6).

b. $78,868 = $250,000/3.16987.

A.43 (Gulf Coast Manufacturing; choosing between investment alternatives.)

	Basic Data Repeated from Problem		Present Value Computations			
	Lexus	Mercedes-Benz	Factor	Source [B]	Lexus	Mercedes-Benz
Initial Cost at the Start of Year 1	$ 60,000	$45,000	1.00000	T[2,3,.10]	$ 60,000	$ 45,000
Initial Cost at the Start of Year 4		48,000	0.75131	T[2,3,.10]		36,063
Trade-in Value						
End of Year 3		23,000	0.75131	T[2,3,.10]		(17,280)
End of Year 6 [Note A]	16,000	24,500	0.56447	T[2,6,.10]	(9,032)	(13,830)
Estimated Annual Cash Operating Costs, Except Major Servicing	4,000	4,500	4.35526	T[4,6,.10]	17,421	19,599
Estimated Cash Cost of Major Servicing						
End of Year 4	6,500		0.68301	T[2,4,.10]	4,440	
End of Year 2 and End of Year 5		2,500	0.82645	T[2,2,.10]		2,066
			0.62092	T[2,5,.10]		1,552
Sum of Present Values of All Costs					$ 72,829	$ 73,170

Note A:
At this time Lexus is 6 years old; second Mercedes-Benz is 3 years old.

[B]T[i,j,r] means Table i (= Table 2 or Table 4) from the back of the book, row j, interest rate r.

a. Strategy L, buying one Lexus has lower present value of costs, but the difference is so small that we'd encourage the CEO to go with his whim, whatever it may be. Also, the relatively new theory of real options will likely prefer Strategy M because it gives the owner more choices at the end of the third year.

b. Depreciation plays no role, so long as we ignore income taxes. Only cash flows matter.

A.44   (Wal-Mart Stores; perpetuity growth model derivation of results in Chapter 5.)

a.   Reproduce Exhibit 5.20 for Problem A.43.
        Growth Rate for Terminal Value: 10.0%

End of Year [1]	Cash Flow End of Year [2]	Factor to Discount to End of Year 14 [3]	Origin of Factor [4]	Present Value at End of Year 14 = [2] × [3] [5]
15	$ 4,074	0.89286	Table (2, 1, 10%)	$ 3,637.5
16	4,479	0.79719	Table (2, 2, 10%)	3,570.6
17	4,927	0.71178	Table (2, 3, 10%)	3,506.9
18	5,420	0.63552	Table (2, 4, 10%)	3,444.5
19	5,962	0.56743	Table (2, 5, 10%)	3,383.0
19	327,910 Note A	0.56743	Table (2, 5, 10%)	186,066.0
	Total Present Value at the End of Year 14.................			$ 203,608.5

Note A.   ($5,962 × 1.10)/(.12 − .10) = $327,910.
        Numerator is the amount of the first collection, at the end of Year 20.
        Denominator is r − g: the discount rate minus the growth rate.
        The result of the operation is the present value at the end of Year 19 of the perpetuity with growth, whose first cash flow is at the end of Year 20 in the amount equal to Year 19's amount growing for one year at 10 percent.
        This amount is not a single cash flow, but a single present value at the end of Year 19 equivalent to a perpetuity with growth, starting at the end of Year 20.

b.   Change Growth Rate.
        Growth Rate for Terminal Value: 9.0%

End of Year [1]	Cash Flow End of Year [2]	Factor to Discount to End of Year 14 [3]	Origin of Factor [4]	Present Value at End of Year 14 = [2] × [3] [5]
15	$ 4,074	0.89286	Table (2, 1, 10%)	$ 3,637.5
16	4,479	0.79719	Table (2, 2, 10%)	3,570.6
17	4,927	0.71178	Table (2, 3, 10%)	3,506.9
18	5,420	0.63552	Table (2, 4, 10%)	3,444.5
19	5,962	0.56743	Table (2, 5, 10%)	3,383.0
19	216,619 Note A	0.56743	Table (2, 5, 10%)	122,916.3
	Total Present Value at the End of Year 14..............			$ 140,458.8

A.44 continued.

    c. Change Growth Rate.
       Growth Rate for Terminal Value: 5.0%

End of Year [1]	Cash Flow End of Year [2]	Factor to Discount to End of Year 14 [3]	Origin of Factor [4]	Present Value at End of Year 14 = [2] x [3] [5]
15	$ 4,074	0.89286	Table (2, 1, 10%)	$ 3,637.5
16	4,479	0.79719	Table (2, 2, 10%)	3,570.6
17	4,927	0.71178	Table (2, 3, 10%)	3,506.9
18	5,420	0.63552	Table (2, 4, 10%)	3,444.5
19	5,962	0.56743	Table (2, 5, 10%)	3,383.0
19	89,430 Note A	0.56743	Table (2, 5, 10%)	50,745.3
	Total Present Value at the End of Year 14..............			$ 68,287.8

    d. Comment. In models such as this, the total valuation comes largely from the terminal value. The terminal value changes more than proportionately to change in the growth rate. See that if we cut the growth rate expected for the long term in half from 10 percent to 5 percent, the terminal value drops by over 70 percent. So much of the valuation resides in the terminal value, and so much of the terminal value depends on the growth rate assumed, and the time period for that growth rate starts so far in the future that the analyst needs to be particularly cautious. The perpetuity with growth model is easy to use, but analysts will be better served to make non-uniform estimates, such as 10 percent growth for five years, then 8 percent for the next five, and growth at some macro-economic rate after that.

A.45   (Fast Growth Start-Up Company; valuation involving perpetuity growth model assumptions. (Amounts in Millions)

We find the answer with trial and error, starting with 5 years of fast growth.

Growth Rate for Early Years of Fast Growth: 25%
Growth Rate for Steady State, Terminal Value: 4%
Discount Rate: 15%
Number of Years of Fast Growth: 5

A.45 continued.

End of Year	Free Cash Flow	Discount Factors from Table 2	Present Value End of Year 0
0	$ 100	1.00000	$ 100.0
1	125	0.86957	108.7
2	156	0.75614	118.1
3	195	0.65752	128.4
4	244	0.57175	139.6
5	305	0.49718	151.7
Terminal Value 5	2,885	0.49718	1,434.5

Terminal Value
$305 x 1.04/(.15 − .04)

Total Valuation .... $ 2,181.1

Growth Rate for Early Years of Fast Growth: 25%
Growth Rate for Steady State, Terminal Value: 4%
Discount Rate: 15%
Number of Years of Fast Growth: 6

End of Year	Free Cash Flow	Discount Factors from Table 2	Present Value End of Year 0
0	$ 100	1.00000	$ 100.0
1	125	0.86957	108.7
2	156	0.75614	118.1
3	195	0.65752	128.4
4	244	0.57175	139.6
5	305	0.49718	151.7
6	381	0.43233	164.9
Terminal Value 6	3,607	0.43233	1,559.2

Terminal Value
$381 x 1.04/(.15 − .04)

Total Valuation .... $ 2,470.7

A.45 continued.

Growth Rate for Early Years of Fast Growth: 25%
Growth Rate for Steady State, Terminal Value: 4%
Discount Rate: 15%
Number of Years of Fast Growth: 7

	End of Year	Free Cash Flow	Discount Factors from Table 2	Present Value End of Year 0
	0	$ 100	1.00000	$ 100.0
	1	125	0.86957	108.7
	2	156	0.75614	118.1
	3	195	0.65752	128.4
	4	244	0.57175	139.6
	5	305	0.49718	151.7
	6	381	0.43233	164.9
	7	477	0.37594	179.3
Terminal Value	7	4,508	0.37594	1,694.8
$477 x 1.04/(.15 − .04)				
			Total Valuation...................................	$ 2,785.6

We see that assuming a bit more than 6 years of fast growth, followed by the steady state justifies a market valuation (the so-called market cap) of $2.5 billion.